Tales of Enchantment

Goal-Oriented Metaphors for Adults and Children in Therapy

by

Carol H. Lankton
and
Stephen R. Lankton

Brunner/Mazel, *Publishers* • New York

Library of Contress Cataloging-in-Publication Data

Lankton, Carol H.,
    Tales of enchantment : goal-oriented metaphors for adults and
children in therapy / Carol H. Lankton and Stephen R. Lankton.
        p.   cm.
    Bibliography: p.
    Includes index.
    ISBN 0-87630-504-4
    1. Metaphor—Therapeutic use. 2. Storytelling—Therapeutic use.
3. Hypnotism—Therapeutic use. 4. Psychotherapy. I. Lankton, Stephen R.
    II. Title.
    RC489.M47L36   1989
    616.89'14—dc19   89-720
                                                      CIP

Published by
BRUNNER/MAZEL, INC.
19 Union Square
New York, New York 10003

MANUFACTURED IN THE UNITED STATES OF AMERICA

10   9   8   7   6   5   4   3   2

This book is dedicated
to the memory of
Ann Alhadeff

Contents

List of Metaphors
According to Goal

Affect Goals

Attitude Goals

Behavior Goals

Family Structure Change Goals

Self-Image Goals

Identity-Organization and Role-Development Goals

Discipline/Enjoyment Goals

Goals of Other Therapeutic Procedures

Use dissociative review to:

Use "scramble" to:

Use life mazes to:

Use life-maze examination with an embedded attitude
protocol to suggest:

Use redecision to:

Trance Phenomena Goals

Therapeutic Goals of Metaphors for Children

Use self-image thinking protocol to:

Use behavior and self-image protocols to:

Use attitude protocol to indicate that:

Use affect protocol to elicit:

Preface

Throughout history, myths and metaphors have played an important part in education and in the development of wisdom. Understanding them infuses life with purpose, worth, meaning, and value. Undeniably, stories can motivate us, cause us to recall, ponder, and embrace new ideas. Even Aristotle, often considered to be the master of reason or rational thought, indicated that wisdom was necessarily interconnected with myth. Stories are, after all, models for behavior, thoughts, and feelings. Since therapy is largely focused on helping people become motivated for action, embrace new ideas, and reflect on the world through different eyes, the use of stories in the therapy context seems quite logical to us.

Yet, some therapists may avoid the metaphorical modality in favor of what is considered to be a rational and direct approach to therapy. Most professionals understand the rationale for being direct and authoritarian in therapy at various times and with various clients. But it seems to us that a versatile therapist must be able to be indirect at times and direct at other times, depending upon the client and the situation. This desired flexibility is often difficult to attain, however, since understanding how to use indirect interventions and the effects they elicit are limited. Perhaps this limited understanding about indirect methods is due, at least partially, to the fact that direct approaches lend themselves more easily to current research methodologies, general accountability, and training programs. But what are the options for therapists trained only in direct approaches when they experience the familiar frustration of working with clients who seem "stuck," "resistant," "noncompliant," "incongruent," or otherwise unable to respond to direct suggestions, assignments, or authoritative challenges to irrational thoughts?

In previous writings we explained our theory and rationale for using indirection in therapy, but we really want to restore a balance and make way for a logical integration of direct and indirect methods. In working to facilitate a balance, then, we have emphasized the indirect modality since it has been more often misunderstood. In *The Answer Within: A Clinical Framework of Ericksonian Hypnotherapy (1983)*, we explained that using indirection does not mean reaching into a "bag of tricks" and grabbing at random. There is logic to such interventions as metaphor, indirect suggestions, therapeutic binds, and paradox, which we traced from the initial diagnostic assessment and treatment planning stages and followed throughout the entire therapy.

We subsequently wrote *Enchantment and Intervention in Family Therapy: Training in Ericksonian Approaches* (1986) to define and illustrate such indirect interventions as paradoxical prescriptions, ambiguous function assignments, and skill-building assignments. Although we emphasized that these interventions are indirect in the sense that they involve some ambiguity, confusion, or distraction of consciousness, there can be a direct and sometimes authoritarian aspect to giving these assignments in therapy. We also wanted to further a set of particular guidelines for the construction of therapeutic metaphor that would make this indirect intervention tangible enough to be learned and researched to a degree not previously possible.

In addition, we introduced and explained a set of protocols for relating experiences in the form of stories. The protocols denote a specific sequence or process in the flow of the content within the story. We had noticed that experience ordered by the processes described by these protocols maximizes the chances that listeners will, to varying degrees, question long-held attitudes, evoke behavioral potentials, elicit emotional experiences, and so on. That is, the protocols provide a way to add greater measurability and, therefore, contribute to more accurate, accountable, and ethical use of one of the most fascinating and difficult aspects of indirection—the therapeutic story.

In this book we are again placing our interest on the illusive in an attempt to broaden the therapist's repertoire and expand on his or her ability to be effective, efficient, and relevant in therapy. We are not dealing with how to ask or tell or "permit" someone to cry, how to ask or insist that someone spend time with his or her children, how to ask for or demand spouses to show sexual interest, nor do we urge the therapist to badger clients to be "rational." We are not dealing with situations that often arise in therapy where we ask the client to stop talking to his or her spouse or to talk to an imaginary person on an empty chair. We are not dealing with those critical times in therapy when our hearts make us lean forward, release a heavy sigh, and share our support, understanding, or sympathy along with a client in pain. This is not a book about the encouragement or persuasion used to get a family to carry out an assignment. And, furthermore, this is not a book about the diagnostic considerations, indications, rationale, and total therapy framework that we discussed in previous books.

This is simply a book of predesigned stories that we and our trainees have told in successful therapy in order to assist clients in their movement toward specific, preplanned goals. The stories are categorized according to the way they are structured to reach particular types of goals. The therapeutic goals are grouped, by chapter, into the following areas: changes in affect; attitudinal restructuring; changes in behavior; changes in family structure; changes in self-image; changes in role development and identity; changes in the process of discipline and enjoyment; strategic use of trance phenomena applied to specific symptoms; and metaphors for children.

For each story, the therapist has assessed the client(s) and developed an overall treatment plan based on the presenting problem and the evaluation. During each session, smaller and more immediate goals have been set to facilitate that treatment plan in a building-block manner. Then, a story has been created to address *each* defined goal, using the appropriate metaphor protocol for each class of goal (e.g., changes in affect, attitude, or behavior).

Stories in the process of being told require reference to a wide range of experience and, therefore, in some instances a story *may* seem to address more than one focus or more than one goal. For example, certain behaviors may be described in the process of following an affect protocol. Too, attitudinal considerations may come into play in the development of affective experiences. However, these stories are grouped according to the primary goal they achieve by virtue of the substructure they follow. Several examples of each type of goal-oriented story are included to illustrate and better highlight this unique structure, and each chapter's introduction includes a brief explanation of the specific metaphor protocol which is the general guideline for the metaphors in that section. Readers desiring more explanation regarding this framework for therapy are referred to our previously mentioned books.

In response to all of those who have asked for detailed examples of particular types of therapeutic metaphors, we offer this anthology, these "tales of enchantment," to stimulate, inspire, and remind you of what you already know: Each person has the capability to identify with and respond to the various stories with personal understanding and hopefully a recognition of the many stories which can be shared from your own life experiences.

Carol and Stephen Lankton
Gulf Breeze, FL

Acknowledgments

We would like to express our appreciation to those who made this work possible. The initial motivation for doing a collection of our stories came from the hundreds of professionals attending our training workshops worldwide who repeatedly suggested that such a book would be helpful. To them and the organizers of the training work we send our thanks.

We also wish to give a thanks to 16 of our advanced trainees who contributed one or more metaphors to this book. Their hard work, clinical efforts, continuing desire to learn, and commitment to their profession have been a real inspiration for us. Alphabetically, the contributors are:

Tina Beissinger, Ph.D., Pensacola, Florida
Ralph M. Daniel, Ph.D., Santa Barbara, California
Don Ferguson, Ph.D., Knoxville, Tennessee
Diane Forgione, M.S.W., Hollywood, Florida
Gary Goodman, M.Ed., Doylestown, Pennsylvania
George Glaser, M.S.W., Austin, Texas
Carol Kershaw, Ph.D., Houston, Texas
David A. Lee, R.S.A.C., Saco, Maine
Cheryl Malone, M.A., Sarasota, Florida
Myer S. Reed, Ph.D., Roanoke, Virginia
Robert Schwarz, Ph.D., Philadelphia, PA
Nicholas G. Seferlis, M.S., Sanford, Maine
Don Shepherd, Ph.D., Charlotte, North Carolina
Marianne Trottier, M.S., Biddeford, Maine
Susan L. Vignola, D.S.W., Culpeper, Virginia
Marc Weiss, Ph.D., Chicago, Illinois

We want to give a special thanks to Gary Goodman and Barbara Folts for their assistance in securing transcripts of our work.

xix

And, finally, we want to acknowledge the staff at Brunner/Mazel, who were instrumental in making this book a reality. Ann Alhadeff's involvement as editor of this book was truly inspirational and seemingly indispensable prior to her sudden death. We remember and appreciate her for the caring quality of her work and the generosity of her heart. And we thank Natalie Gilman for the significant contribution she offered by stepping in as editor and seeing the book to completion with her own clarity and style.

1

This Part of the Forest

*The most beautiful experience we can have is
the mysterious. It is the fundamental emotion
which stands at the cradle of true art
and true science.*
　　　　　—Albert Einstein

*It is the dim haze of mystery that adds
enchantment to pursuit.*
　　　　　—Antoine Rivarol

What is a metaphor, exactly? It is defined as a figure of speech in
which a word or phrase denoting one kind of object or action is used
in place of another to suggest a likeness or analogy between them.
However, we use the term "metaphor" and "story" interchangeably
and think of it as an altered framework through which clients can
entertain novel experiences. Our metaphors involve protagonists, character development, dramatic devices, a storyline following one of several
specific protocols, and some form of conclusion. In addition, we frequently take short, anecdotal tangents from the longer metaphor or
story. Although the tangents are not technically part of the stories, they
are included to help listening clients further identify and add personal
detail to a particular experience introduced in the storyline.

Metaphors in therapy constitute an indirect form of treatment. Like
other forms of indirection, therapeutic metaphors do not engender the

kind of resistance to considering new ideas that direct suggestions often can. They are experienced as a gentle and permissive, not a confrontive or demanding way to consider change. At one level, a metaphor is "just a story" that doesn't require any response, but at another level, it stimulates thinking, experiencing, and ideas for problem resolution. This stimulation process is further facilitated when various types of indirect suggestions and binds are strategically included, tangential to the storyline. Those that occur in the stories recorded here are not specifically labeled or discussed with regard to particular categories of suggestions and binds. For guidelines regarding construction and use of such suggestions, readers are referred elsewhere (Erickson & Rossi, 1980a, 1980b, 1980c, 1980d; Lankton & Lankton, 1983; Matthews et al., 1984; Matthews et al., 1985). However, it is important to recognize that the stories here are largely a modality or framework for containing and communicating therapeutically planned suggestions and binds to the listening client. These suggestions may be formed according to the specific categories of suggestions and binds just referenced, but can also be created within a story with a simple switch of pronouns and verb tense, from the third person "he" or "she" in the past tense to the second person "you" in the present tense. This kind of pronoun and verb tense switching, often in midsentence, is not grammatically correct, but proves to be quite useful therapeutically for inviting more personal involvement of the client. This pronoun switching will be found frequently in the metaphors that follow.

Delivering several metaphors by multiply embedding them within one another is the modality we frequently use when telling stories in therapy. Therefore, all of the stories found in this book, subsequent to the transcript of a complete session in this chapter, have been removed from what we consider to be their logical context, and it should be kept in mind that therapeutic stories do not usually "stand alone" in the manner in which they are presented in Chapters 2 to 10. The reasons for and effect of multiply embedding metaphors can be examined at length in *The Answer Within*.

Also, a trance induction typically, but not always, precedes the stories. The interpersonal framework of a hypnotic context usually allows clients to concentrate more comfortably, identify more creatively, and tune out irrelevant external stimuli more effectively. Whether or not a trance induction is conducted, however, clients will usually develop some indicators of trance in the process of listening to multiple embedded stories, since fixation on ambiguity inherent to that procedure is trance inducing. Elements of induction and rationale for a hypnotic modality are discussed at length elsewhere (Lankton & Lankton, 1983). For now, suffice it to say that we generally define "trance" as an interpersonal relationship that facilitates a state of consciousness in which the client experiences heightened awareness that is concentrated inward on thoughts, feelings, beliefs, memories, values, and so forth. Given this definition, it is obvious that "trance" is something frequently experienced, even in nontherapeutic settings. In therapy, we ask family members to use their existing abilities to focus inward as a comfortable way to consider and learn something relevant to the problems they have presented. By our definition, this activity constitutes the beginning of trance.

The overall treatment strategy, of which the stories here are only component parts, is designed to frame the presenting problem against the backdrop of the interpersonal/developmental demands surrounding the client system. Interventions, including but not limited to metaphors, are constructed to motivate clients to new relational patterns in order to reduce or remove presenting problems or conflicts. Paradoxical prescriptions that encourage continuing or even exacerbating a symptom or behavior pattern are often included in the "framing" of the therapy (Lankton & Lankton, 1986).

Each component part of the treatment plan is ordered in such a way as to build toward larger therapy goals and the treatment contract. Treatment in this regard can include stories told to individual clients or in conjoint family sessions, using trance and multiple embedded metaphors, or otherwise. Other interventions, such as structured activities and paradoxical, skill-building, or ambiguous function assignments, may precede or be interspersed with storytelling in a session. Regardless of the intervention selected, the therapist proceeds strategically, that is, by observing the client's response and tailoring the next intervention as well as the next goal accordingly.

No matter how well designed according to a metaphor protocol a specific story may be, clients can respond idiosyncratically in a way that isn't expected but provides valuable information to the observing therapist. That information contributes to the ongoing diagnostic assessment that results in continued defining of goals, and selecting and delivering of interventions, until the contract has been fulfilled and presenting problems resolved. This process usually includes goals involving changes in affect, attitude, behavior, self-image, and so forth being addressed repeatedly at varied points in the therapy.

Notwithstanding the uniqueness of each client system, the most common classes of goals can be categorized, and typical stories that meet those goals can be shared and retold to different clients. This collection most often includes actual transcripts of the stories as they were told to a specific client. Though they can be retold in a *similar* way to clients with similar goals, they can never be *exactly* the same. They must be told differently in accordance with the needs and reactions of each client, and in accordance with the style of each therapist. Additionally, in each telling, there will be differences in the suggestions and binds that tangentially accompany the storyline. The storyline itself may be altered in minor ways to include images or events that are uniquely relevant for each client. Finally, the voice tone, tonal variety, cadence, pausing, and so on varies with each interpersonal situation. And while these nonverbal aspects are extremely important, they cannot be taught in a book. Although this book can aid in learning, it does not replace qualified training and supervision.

We encourage qualified and trained professionals to borrow these stories and also to use them to remember, invent, and create more stories from personal experiences. That is, after all, where metaphors really come from. The protocols we present could be considered the frame over which you stretch the canvas of your own experiences. The protocols provide shape and direction, but the content comes from your own understandings. Once you have a *goal* identified, you simply ask yourself, "What is this like in my experience?" The people and images that come to mind in answer to that question become the raw material from which a therapeutic metaphor can be constructed. Confidentiality is easily protected (and has been in all stories included here) by changing names of characters and locations of events, and even by mixing together novel combinations of characters and contexts that depart from identifiable accuracy. Even those characters who would seem to be purely fictional still have their origin in real people you have known. Or an experience you or your friends have had personally may be attributed to a fictional character, and yet the experience is genuine and can be told congruently, despite the fact that it is part of a confabulated story. In the same way, the truth contained in a parable, a myth, or a Sufi story may inspire significant personal change, despite the fact that such stories are known to be fiction.

Stories that derive from genuine experiences and understandings of the therapist are believable, and when they are relevant to the client's desired learnings, they are fascinating, interesting, and engaging as well. This is true even though they may appear to the therapist to be about "mundane" occurrences. We work to engage the conscious mind of clients with the use of dramatic devices that capture attention in some way, perhaps by not immediately solving a mystery, or purposefully building suspense into the story.

Since our stories come from our experiences, it is easy to avoid creating stories that are not believable or that would offend the client's intelligence. Talking in a "fairytailish" way or using animal protagonists usually accomplishes little to convey respect to an adult listener and may result in a loss of rapport. Unfortunately, many people don't think they are officially "telling a story" unless it begins with "once upon a time" and ends "happily ever after." Stories that begin and end that way often include other unlikely events such as talking rabbits or spellbound frogs. When, on rare occasion, we use plants, animals, or inanimate images which we anthropomorphize in a therapeutic story told to adults or teenagers, we do it from the perspective of something said or imagined by a human protagonist, or we disclaim it in some way. For example, when Milton Erickson talked to a man about tomato plants, he talked about the tomato plant "feeling" good. But then he went on to disclaim it by adding that "this is talking like a child, maybe the tomato plant does feel *comfortable and peaceful* as it grows" (Erickson & Rossi, 1980d, p. 270).

The stories included here have most often been told to adults or teenagers, though many of them could also be comprehended by children. The same guidelines and protocols for creating therapeutic metaphors apply when the target client is a child. And often, even young children can feel "talked down to" when the story is inundated with talking and thinking animals or plants when human protagonists would work just as well or better! Our final chapter contains several examples of metaphors for children.

One last general comment about stories—they work better and they are more fun when they are shared verbally. This is not to diminish the power of the written word, but storytelling was originally an oral art, and stories traditionally were passed on by word of mouth for generations. There is a qualitative difference that can easily be detected when a story is read to instead of told to someone. The stories written here were not written at the time they were told. There was a general outline, perhaps, a "reference picture" that depicted the main characters, the relationships, the comings and goings, and a storyline that eventually connected to an "end picture" in the therapist's mind. But the therapist's attention should be focused on the responses of the listening client as the therapist is telling the story and not on a written-out account that precludes an incorporation of the client's responses. So, as you use these stories with your clients, use them as general ideas that are translated into your own words with a sensitivity to your client audience.

Having described this part of the forest and alerted you to the kinds of trees you can expect to see growing side by side here, we want to use the remainder of this chapter to demonstrate a variety of component interventions as they were actually delivered throughout a complete session. This session does not represent the entire therapy but it includes a typical arrangement of an ambiguous function assignment, induction, and multiple embedded metaphors related to attitude, affect, behavior, identity reorganization, and dissociative review goals. Each phase of the session is accordingly labeled and the protocols for each kind of goal are addressed individually in the following chapters.

A woman adjusting to an unwanted divorce

Background information

Tonya is an instructor and coach from a local high school. She is a 40-year-old woman who is suffering anxiety and depression in the process of a divorce she did not initiate and does not want. The most acute symptom that has brought her to therapy is the recurrent anxiety attacks and sobbing incidents which necessitate her leaving work early several times a week. Two months prior to this session her husband announced that he was leaving her for his secretary.

Tonya has been married for 12 years and has two children. Her husband has been verbally abusive and condescending towards her, despite her constant and uncompromised support of him throughout their entire marriage. Even now, she would like to help him resolve the ambivalence he has expressed in the form of an affair with his secretary, so that the marriage could continue. He is a cocaine addict and has been disciplined at work for his excessive and obvious use of the drug. He has steadfastly refused to seek marital counseling. Tonya has given her entire life to two men: her father and her husband. An interesting incident occurred when she was 10 years of age which shed some light on her interpersonal patterns and current symptomatology. When she was 10, her father came home drunk and demanded that the children awaken and proclaim whom they would live with in the upcoming divorce. The two younger siblings said they preferred their mother, but Tonya felt sorry for her father and thought that "really he was a good man" and so she chose him. Actually she preferred her mother, but she just could not bear to think that this poor man would not be befriended by someone. Despite her proclamation, her father spent very little time with her as a growing child, and, to this day, has not even seen her almost teenaged children!

Treatment plan

A current attitudinal problem and obvious parallel to the situation with her father is apparent when we consider that her reason for supporting her critical and nonattentive husband for so many years was that she felt he had a great deal of talent and that if someone just cared for him he would eventually blossom into the person she imagined him to be capable of being. Instead, he left her. In the process of leaving, he asserted that she was not attractive enough, was overweight, and the children they had were "an embarrassment to the relationship."

After a written and in-person assessment of this client, the following five goals were set for the first session:

> *Attitude goal:* challenge the deeply held concept that Tonya's needs should come second to the support of a man. Her needs must be attended to and defended even if it means taking an unpopular position.
>
> *Affect goals:* strengthen or retrieve the feelings of (1) belonging and (2) mastery.
>
> *Direct work:* a redecision and examination of the possibility of speaking up for her true feelings, even when speaking to men from whom she has sought/seeks approval, including the desensitization that would come from a fantasized confrontation with her father.
>
> *Behavioral goal:* reduce her self-criticism which leads to anxiety attacks. Methods are to include exaggeration, reciprocal inhibition, and symptom substitution.
>
> *Identity-reorganization goal:* illustrate the subtle understanding that a new life can begin when it appears that everything is lost.

The session was arranged in eight connected segments which consisted of the greeting and ambiguous function assignment to gather last-minute information and set the stage for the therapy by means of "enchantment"; the induction of a therapeutic trance; the five goals stated above; reorientation from the trance and termination of the session. Guidelines for sequencing metaphors in a multiple embedded fashion are illustrated in the Multiple Embedded Metaphor Possible Protocol Placements

Multiple Embedded Metaphor
Possible Protocol Placements

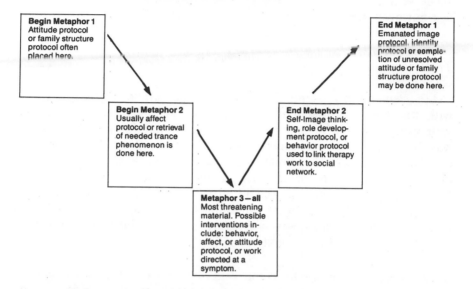

chart. The specific arrangement of metaphors designed to address the preceding five goals for this treatment plan is shown in the chart, Tonya Treatment Plan. It can be seen that the multiple embedded metaphor strategy described elsewhere (Lankton & Lankton, 1983) will be the order for the session.

Three metaphors will be used for the five goals. The scheme for forming each type of metaphor and numerous examples of each type constitute the bulk of this book. The purpose of the example that follows is to illustrate the use of several metaphors in harmony during a single session. Since this will be the only session that is provided in its entirety, we have given some of the major aspects of the client's assessment and will only interrupt this transcript a minimum number of times to alert readers to the switch to another metaphor or protocol.

The session begins:

At the beginning of this session, the client, Tonya, is presented with a 14-inch wood carving of an elf-type figure emerging from a twisted root. She examines it. (In the dialogue, "T" indicates the therapist, and "C" indicates the client, Tonya.)

Tonya Treatment Plan

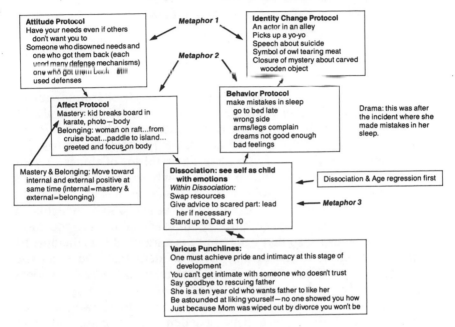

Attitude Protocol
Have your needs even if others
  don't want you to
Someone who disowned needs and
  one who got them back (each
  used many defense mechanisms)
  one who got them back still
  used defenses

Metaphor 1

Metaphor 2

Identity Change Protocol
An actor in an alley
Picks up a yo-yo
Speech about suicide
Symbol of owl tearing meat
Closure of mystery about carved
  wooden object

Affect Protocol
Mastery: kid breaks board in
  karate, photo—body
Belonging: woman on raft...from
  cruise boat...paddle to island...
  greeted and focus on body

Behavior Protocol
make mistakes in sleep
  go to bed late
  wrong side
  arms/legs complain
  dreams not good enough
  bad feelings

Drama: this was after
the incident where she
made mistakes in her
sleep.

Mastery & Belonging: Move toward
internal and external positive at
same time (internal=mastery &
external=belonging)

**Dissociation: see self as child
  with emotions**
Within Dissociation:
Swap resources
Give advice to scared part: lead
  her if necessary
Stand up to Dad at 10

Dissociation & Age regression first

Metaphor 3

Various Punchlines:
One must achieve pride and intimacy at this stage of
  development
You can't get intimate with someone who doesn't trust
Say goodbye to rescuing father
She is a ten year old who wants father to like her
Be astounded at liking yourself—no one showed you how
Just because Mom was wiped out by divorce you won't be

T: Last night I sat this little wood-carved man out like this in preparation for the session today. Why do you think I have given you this little man to examine?

C: Do you want me to tell you now or do you want me to tell you later? (*laughs*)

T: Yes, I want to know now.

C: (*examines it, slight tears*) You want to know now?

T: Yes. Do you have any ideas?

C: It reminds me of myself when I used to walk along the sea coast in Washington and Oregon state and I would pick up driftwood. And anytime I looked at a wooden piece of anything, I always know that things are not as they seem, and that is what it reminds me of. It reminds me of an Escher poster that I have in my office. Why you did it (*laughs*), that's something I'm not sure of, except perhaps there's the playfulness to it.

T: I won't push you for more important answers to those questions yet. But you may be thinking about that as time goes on. We'll just leave him there (*on the table beside her*) for the time being. And we will want to come back to this little guy in another more cogent time, so don't think that it's over because we're not looking at him anymore.

C: It's not over until the fat lady sings (*laughs*).

T: That's right!

Trance induction begins:

T: Now, Tonya, as you go into trance, your conscious mind can be distracted by a number of things . . . but your unconscious always tries to deal with what's relevant. And when it's hard to be distracted, your conscious mind also tends to notice the things that are relevant. And I know you have an awful lot of things in your mind that are relevant. And so you probably have a lot of thoughts going back and forth in your head. And I hope that for a moment you can have a little bit of confusion about which thoughts to have and a little bit of comfort about whether or not you have any more thoughts, so that your trance is a trance that is therapeutic because it allows a new arrangement of ideas that you otherwise hadn't thought about. And it is going to be hard to give new ideas to somebody who's thought about a lot of ideas anyway.

I do have a couple of photos that I want to show you when we're done. I do have a little wooden carved man, but your conscious mind doesn't really have much of a need to be thinking about those things, because they're not at this point relevant to you. What should be relevant to you is the state of relaxation you achieve, the state of comfort with your discomfort, the state of stability in the change that you have, or possibly even the way you continue to have the same experience while you change. The idea of having a terribly wonderful time is not new to anybody. Teenagers have them a lot. In retrospect teenagers should realize they don't have terribly wonderful times, many people's teenage years are wonderfully terrible times.

Paul Simon said he had a childhood that was mercifully brief. So I hope this trance is mercifully brief and terribly wonderful and I hope it's not wonderfully terrible. Sooner or later your sense of alteration in your normal mood is bound to change due to a concentration. Maybe you'll concentrate on a story or maybe you'll concentrate on the sensation in your hand beginning to levitate. And although it may rise up and float in the air, maybe it'll touch your face or go off to the side. What it does accomplish is an opportunity for you to notice that there's an alteration in your normal consciousness that tends to stay the same, tends to keep you from moving, from having a need to talk. It tends to keep you wondering about a lot of things, in different ways. How could something carved out of wood from Austria have any bearing on this situation?

Now your palm has come slightly off of your lap and rotated slightly to the right hand side and your thumb has a twitch. You couldn't just fail to recognize the lack of alterations that have occurred as your hand begins to transform those sensations into a levitation, but maybe you can notice how the more relaxed you become, the more deeply you go into trance. And I doubt that you fail to have amnesia about the things that I say.

First story begins (attitude protocol for value in expressing needs):

T: I did want to tell you about some teenagers and their defensiveness. Now you might think defensiveness would go away with one situation and be there in another situation. There is really no need for confidentiality about these two teenagers but I can't remember their names. So I just call one Teen A and I'll call the other one Teen B. As long as I don't have more than 26 of them I'll be okay.

And they could have just as easily have been sister and brother because the same background existed in their family of origin. And ultimately this story is intimately related to the carved piece of wood from the Austrian forest. Because the people you work with in Austria aren't really very different from the people you work with in the United States or any other country that I've worked in, although it might be easier for a teenager there to decide that they are not going to notice what they need and what they feel.

And both Teen A and Teen B disowned their feelings early in childhood, one of them due to the fear of violent repercussions and the other simply because it was too frustrating and disappointing to try to fight for what they wanted all of the time in that family. But there's a major difference in the way the teens developed.

Early in their teens, they had an opportunity to change their mind. And without psychotherapy Teen A decided that it made a good deal of sense to listen to that American song, "Don't cry out loud, don't let 'em know." And it was just that era and that time of life. "Big girls don't cry." And music was a good way for a child to determine how to navigate through life—who to pick as a spouse. "If you want to know if he loves you so it's in his kiss." "Mama told me you better shop around." But you're not supposed to tell the little boy or the teenager how you feel, to show your needs and feelings. You don't tell Johnny Angel. You just hope that "someday he'll love me . . . and together we'll know how happy heaven can be."

But Teen B, also without psychotherapy, perhaps through a strength of weakness, discovered that it wasn't possible to hold back recognition of the needs. Whether or not someone from the opposite sex was attracted or not just wasn't going to matter. He had very strange interests. While the other kids were learning to date, wear makeup, and to get pants just right, he'd pursue his interest. Sometimes that left him alone. And if you ask any of the other teenagers it was clear that Teen B was someone who would never be in the forefront in the business world, in the social world. You wouldn't use the word "nerd" in Austria but there surely is an equivalent. And I just bet an Austrian nerd is worse.

And it was real clear that Teen A was going to be very popular, going to have good college social popularity, be "in" in any reasonable sorority that she wanted to be in, maybe be involved as the president of clubs and other social activities. And it was real clear that Teen B was going to be never heard of again. But he didn't care. Quite without the aid of psychotherapy he decided even though he had been frightened by his parents and intimidated by their violence, and had nightmares from the quarrels, it simply meant that having your feelings and showing what you wanted and following your own needs and interests would mean that you'd be alone. And from what he had seen being together wasn't worth very much anyway. Let Teen A pursue the fruitless and stupid dream of the American dream—to hide her needs, find Johnny Angel, move to the suburbs, wax the car, and have barbecues and pleasant valley Sundays. It made a great deal more sense to try to be a rock, in the sense that he would be all alone, an island unto himself, showing his needs and feelings. But he was only a teenager and at that point surely he had never seen the wood carving in Austria that I have shown you. Not at that point.

Well, to make a long story short, time passed. In the meanwhile the muscle fasciculation in your right hand diminished as presumably one part of the conflictual experience you have in trance altered in favor of more conscious recognition of your musculature.

I wonder if that has to do with self-reflection of your emotional situation as you were in trance. And perhaps the lifting of your arm will reflect the degree with which you dissociate from that. I hope there is a great deal of dissociation in your hand as time goes on. Because you are going to need dissociation in your shoulders if you want it to move over your body. And you're surely going to want dissociation in your body so that you can have, oh, a terribly wonderful time.

Maybe your left hand will raise up to your face; it knows how. It is interesting how it jerked up right away in recognition, but I knew all along that any left hand that knows how to wear a watch knows how to unconsciously move up to the face. It's probably been practicing for moments like this over and over again just waiting for it to have an opportunity to be the one that was needed for arm levitation up towards the face. It really didn't have to be a watch that you wore on that sleeve. It could have been some iced tea and when your hand levitated up to your face. . . . With your eyes closed it still could have served a purpose.

But what about Teen A and Teen B, you're wondering? Both of them without psychotherapy pursued their own course. And a great deal of defense mechanisms were necessary to do that. Defense mechanisms that you use as a teenager, and we all use them, we tend to bring with us into adulthood. And the experiences we have as teenagers, that we make as teenagers, can look entirely different when they're examined with the spectacles of maturity and adulthood. And we might look at the teens 20 years later through different spectacles. And the defense mechanisms are still there.

And what seemed to be a terrible choice—to defend against certain realities by having his needs and his feelings displayed and following them, and being aware of them—did in fact result in a temporary loneliness during teenage years for Teen B. But he was extremely talented by the time he was a young adult. He had a wonderful time in college. It was easy for him to handle the academics. And the honesty and transparency of Teen B showing his needs and feelings made it very clear who wanted to associate with him and who he wanted to associate with. He found a great deal of interest as an actor initially. And his ability to act a particular role was not inhibited. It was enhanced by the defense mechanisms he had used as a teenager. He could tune out and deny a great deal of social stimulus to the contrary and play the role of being sad or play the role of being happy or jealous or play the role of striving hard for a goal that was almost beyond his grasp. And as a young actor in college his career seemed absolutely certain and his friends were many. And he still continued to pursue some other interests outside of acting.

Teen A, of course, was married long before college was over. After all, if you're going to put your needs aside, what better way to do it than to fail to finish your own college degrees, and begin raising a family and slip into relative obscurity except for the neighborhood in which she went to live? There, she barbecued on Sunday. But they both had defense mechanisms. And they both brought them with them from teens to adulthood.

Second story begins (affect protocol for belonging
and affect protocol for mastery):

T: Now there's another thing about making mistakes when you sleep. (*client smiles*) No, I'm not talking about that, but of very serious mistakes you can make when you sleep. You can have amnesia for them. It would probably be a mistake not to.

Faye is a friend of ours, a therapist, who, in fact, was a president of the NASW where she lived for a while and very well liked and respected by everyone. But that wasn't sufficient to keep her from feeling what everyone else would normally feel when you find yourself suddenly in ice water over your ears. A lot of people say that they have been in ice water over their ears, but for Faye it was swimming to the rubber raft in the Bering Straits that really convinced her. She couldn't see anybody else. The cruise ship had apparently hit ice or maybe there was an explosion on board or something catastrophic. It was supposed to have been her big opportunity to go to China. Instead, it was her big opportunity to swim in the Bering Straits, trying to get to a rubber life raft.

And Faye is not a small woman. Swimming to the life raft was not easy. Getting in the life raft was not easy. And sitting there cold in the dark and not knowing where anyone else was was harder still. She didn't know what exactly she should do about it. She thought she passed out temporarily. I probably shouldn't tell you that she was in the boat for 10 hours. But for some of that time she was unconscious. And she remembers reliving an experience as a young girl thinking about how exciting it looked to see those people who were doing that thing called karate, breaking those tiles with their hands. And she had forgotten that she had thought about that, wanted that, and enjoyed that. In the back of our minds there are a lot of ideas that we formulate as children, a lot of dreams that we hold on to. But we don't remember that we hold onto them. How many children have wanted to be airplane pilots? How many children wanted to swing from the vines of trees? How many of them wanted to be Esther Williams swimming in such perfect synchronization in a swimming pool? How many of them wished they could be Commando Cody or Lucille Ball and never thought seriously that they would pursue it?

What Faye remembered vividly as she was unconscious was that day in the dojo when she was spinning around practicing her katas. And quite by accident, one of her partners on the mat held the tile up in practicing, with stiff elbows out in front of him, how he would do it. At that point of her kata, she turned with her knife hand tightening up the pad beneath her little finger, extending her fingers out to infinity, mentally, and striking to the right as she rotated to the right, preparing to do an upper block with her left hand. But before she did, her eyes saw in the mirror the reflection of her hand going straight through that tile.

Then she realized her hand had gone straight through that tile. And she just froze and looked at that reflection in the mirror. She saw a smile of a kind on her face she hadn't seen before: her lips were straight; there was a lump in her throat that she was happily swallowing; the corners of her mouth turned up very little, very gradually, not imperceptibly, but just a different kind of smile. She straightened her head on her shoulders and realized how tall she looked in that mirror. She was breathing easily, she was relaxed. There was that thought of "God, I did it!" It even brought a little tear to her eyes. And there's a learning that you don't forget, that stays with you in the back of your unconscious and becomes a new learning that you can have from time to time by accident, and that's what was happening to her then as she looked in the mirror and saw that she had broken that tile.

And Faye remembered that moment and how it made her stand a little taller and see her body in a way she'd never seen it. She had forgotten that she had grown up until she saw that. And that dream or that unconscious memory, or that production of an idea from her own unconscious stayed with her as she paddled her little dinghy for 10 hours, floating sometimes, paddling sometimes, but she didn't know what direction to paddle.

Ten hours in the dark. Finally, she began to hear voices, she thought she knew the direction, she started towards them. The voices got louder, but she couldn't make out whether or not they were friendly or foe, whether they were in trouble and whether or not they were an oasis. Then she could make them out, they were speaking English. There was a lot of wailing and she still didn't know whether they were in more trouble than she was in; one thing she thought was there might be people that needed her and that needed the help of the raft. One thing she thought was maybe they would sink her raft.

But as she got closer still, she heard that there was more relief than sorrow. And as she got closer still, she realized that what sounded like screams were cheers. And as she finally made contact with the side of the rescue boat, she was pulled on board by the intimate weeping screams and cheers of relief of the people who celebrated her return—people who, though almost strangers, were now drawn together with a great deal of concern and care. And just as they pulled her on the boat and she reached out her hand and they grabbed it to pull her up, again she had the final flash of image of that hand going through that tile, only this time it was taken by another person and she was embraced and hugged. And they laughed and cried together in soaking wet cold clothes that seemed warm as their skin touched. Tears ran down their faces.

The unconscious can remember experiences in a variety of ways. To remember two of them at the same time or to make one into another only amplifies the learning. That was long before she learned to make mistakes while she was asleep. She was just standing there having that sense of happiness and safety and feeling like she had known these people for a long time. And when someone hears the story or tells the story it's easy to forget that experience took place in the context of 10 hours in icy water.

And I wonder if you can appreciate the depth of the experience she had to be holding those other people—all of them cheering and crying. We can use our conscious mind to construct an experience like that but to really realize how you feel your feet shaking underneath you, your heart holding you up, and arms clinging onto somebody who's holding on to you, at the same time that the tears of total strangers are mixing together down both people's cheeks. And they're smiling and laughing and sharing things together that they each had keep secret and continue to keep secret, verbally. And it certainly gives meaning to the idea that people are drawn together during times of crisis.

Direct work of dissociative review begins with anecdotes to retrieve dissociation:

T: Now you memorize experiences when they're useful or going to be useful in order to apply them later on. I just hope that you will remember the useful portions of those experiences as you develop a sense of dissociation, because the real important part of the therapy could be connecting you with a dissociation that could have started in your cheeks and neck, could start in your arm, could start in your feet. Most people have dissociation in their feet most of the time, especially their souls. It is all right to be dissociated from your soul. Sometimes the soul can take a lot of battering.

    Now what has all this got to do with trust? Bob Dylan said he was knocking on heaven's door. Paul Simon said, "Here I am Lord knocking at your place of business, and I know I ain't got no business here. But you said if I ever was so low I was busted, you could be trusted." So what is this idea of trust? Would it be apropos to guide someone in trance and ask them to dissociate. I did it with Jerry, a young woman who was an excellent piano player. As a result of our therapy she played piano publicly for the first time in a local production of *Jesus Christ Superstar*. I saw her boyfriend for therapy, too. He was the main character in the play. Boy, did he have trouble! But she had the hardest job. She played piano for the whole thing. I asked her to get dissociated in every way she could because there were many resources that she had as an adult and I wanted her to be in touch with and feel and know them. Maybe she could feel those things in her fingertips or feet, or neck, shoulders, eyes, cheeks. I wasn't sure where she would feel them because I hadn't given her a word for them consciously.

    I simply instructed her to maintain those feelings while she let other events be things that she could see and hear clearly, while she maintained separate kinds of feelings that had nothing to do with the event that she pictured. For example, she could maintain the feeling of relaxation and she could watch an irreverent sitcom on television and not be moved at all to absurdity, or to humor, or to depression of the comedy that she'd supposedly seen. Or she could be concentrated on a certain goal, music could play in the background but she wouldn't tap her feet. It could be like a news broadcast on CNN, the world's most important network, so redundant that you don't want to hear it again, and you tune it out waiting for something new and interesting to break.

Everybody finds a position in which they can witness events and hear events comfortably. And they study them that way and they may experience standing beside something that's able to hold them up, take the weight off their own feet. I had one person imagine that they were behind louvers so that they could watch out, listen out from the louvers, and still be protected. For some that's too inconvenient. I had one person actually imagine that they had crawled down a very large tube, like the tube that paper towels come on, only much larger. And they poked a little hole in it. When you're very close to a pin hole you can see a great deal on the other side.

Everybody has their own way of dissociating—some people do it by having a levitation or catalepsy that develops into dissociation. But the point is to be inside that tube, underneath that card table with a blanket over it, looking through binoculars from your tree fort at something so far away, or disinterested somehow in what you see and hear. And maintain the sense of feelings that you learned elsewhere.

And then I asked Jerry to see and hear clearly the events that had taken place in the past when she was a little girl, and let the feelings that happened in the pictures and with the words in the past stay in the past. And she examined them with different learnings, from a distance, and I didn't care if she stayed inside a paper towel tube, or looked at them through the wrong end of binoculars. One time I asked a person to wear a disguise in their imagination in the trance and go into a room in disguise and turn on the television set that would show events from the past and they didn't need to be embarrassed or have emotional reactions at all because nobody would even know that it was them. They were in disguise and just observe that television screen or that movie screen displaying events of the past when she was just a little girl. And they can go very fast when you do that, so a great deal of time can be covered in a short period and she could watch events from age three to six, from six to eight, from eight to 10 very rapidly, stopping at those points that were important, especially stopping to deal with a nasty little incident in her life that went by the name "father."

And I asked her to retain the mature resources that had been achieved in trance. And approach that incident at 10 years old. Each person's case is entirely different. You would want to see and hear clearly the situation of approaching the fateful night when brothers and sisters were asked to make a decision. But open up a communication channel to that 10-year-old. Have her nod her head that she is in communication with you. Explain to her that you're from her future, that you're proof that she lived through the entire incident in a way that she didn't expect. Get her recognition that she knows that's true.

Tell her that you're here from the future in order to pass on to her resources that she didn't have and didn't know she'd have at the time. Ask her if she's willing to live through the incidents in a slightly different way, with the resources that she's going to have some day when she becomes you, and symbolically pass on to her a sense of capacity for pride and belonging that she didn't know she had at the time. And give her a little bit of wisdom that you can't be intimate with somebody who doesn't trust.

And I asked Jerry to relive the incidents that had happened that were so important, especially one or two of them, and observe how she would handle them, using her adult self as a resource, paying close attention to any attitudinal difficulties that the little girl encountered. And then straightening out those attitudinal difficulties for the little girl with her own words, making sure that you remind the little girl of something that you don't have to be told but that she needs to know. She doesn't know that just because mother was wiped out by a divorce she doesn't have to be. She doesn't know that she should immediately stop trying to get the attention she wants from Dad. She didn't have a mother there to tell her then what you can tell her now, something that you know from your resources. But first transmit that sense of pride into the picture. See the little girl living in the scene with the feelings that she has a place she belongs, people who want her around.

And after she accepts those, ask her if she would give back to you something in trade. Maybe she'll give back to you the strength of will that she's kept for herself all those years, the will to stick to a decision and let it be something that's in your hands to choose. Ask her if she'll take your sense of pride and confidence and, in return, give to you control of the future. And maybe there are some other things that she needs to give to you. Maybe there's the capability to notice who you can trust and notice who you can't trust, a switch that she decided to throw that needs to be reexamined by an adult. Because we all take defense mechanisms from childhood and teenage years into adulthood. But you ought to get to use the defense mechanisms instead of having a 10-year-old in charge.

And there may be some other things she has . . . a certain kind of playfulness or hopefulness or creativity or joy or a certain need to cry and be cared for, to rest, to relax. Ask her what she'll give you in trade for the sense of pride, confidence, belonging. And give her something else that she doesn't understand. When you like yourself, you ought to be astounded. It shouldn't be something you're familiar with. So tell her and give her permission and an understanding of how very astounding it is to like yourself when no one showed you how. She's bound to be a little confused about that, and it might be helpful to remind her of something you've learned along life's highways, of how astounding it is to like yourself. So when she feels astounded, maybe she's on the right track.

I think it would be a very good idea for people to use a review of the past in their visual mind, to rehearse behaviors and review the past with a change of events, to rehearse the behaviors attitudinally in the most trying situation. So sooner or later you'll probably wonder what it would look like if the little girl in your family that night had decided not to choose Dad. And I just wonder if it would have been easier for her to do that if she'd known that she was going to have pride in herself. And maybe you should help her find some words to try that out. I don't know how you'd say it: "No hard feelings Dad, but clean up your act and give me a call. If I'm still around we can have dinner."

I think that the best way to honor thy father and mother is to grow up to be the best you that you can be. And when that has nothing to do with the dreams of the father and the mother it will take them some time to find out that you're honoring them by disappointing their dreams. Carol's parents had no interest in their daughter going through college. They thought she ought to do something useful like be a secretary. You don't have to be in trance very long to realize that a girl's got no business majoring in psychology, she ought to do something useful. And besides that, it wasn't that darn Christian what she was doing, running around in a convertible doing God knows what.

But she learned a long time ago the same thing. She believed in honoring her father and mother. But that doesn't mean living out the ignorant life that they might inadvertently want for you. As Cat Stevens said, "If they were right I'd agree, but it's them they know, not me." And to the extent that each of us as adults has learned that, pass that information on to that little girl. Tell her you will stand by her. Stand right up there and tell them. Maybe you'd choose to not live with either of them. Maybe you'd like to choose to let an older part of yourself take care of yourself until you're old enough to let someone else.

Now, you can do things wrong in trance. You can drag yourself through emotional experiences when you should be dissociated. You can give bad advice to yourself or you can fail to take good advice that you give to yourself. But the problem with it is you continue to work it over and rehash it and think about it again until you do it right so you might as well do it right. It's like Billy Joel said, "Get it right the first time, that's the main thing." But this matter of making mistakes when you sleep . . .

Closure of second metaphor begins (the character from the affect protocols is now utilized to address the behavior goal with the behavior protocol. The goal is to apply trance phenomena of dissociation, amnesia, and/or negative hallucination to those anxiety-producing stimuli this client was encountering related to the divorce. This is intended to help her reciprocally inhibit, exaggerate, depotentiate, and substitute symptoms for her self-criticism.):

T: When Faye saw me for therapy, it had nothing to do with the incident of being stranded in cold water for 10 hours. Her problem was that she had a ringing in her ears and she couldn't hear anything. She had to look right at you in order to hear things that you said. And she found it very difficult in her profession to deal with that tinnitus while she was supposed to be sensitive to what people said. In the trance I asked her to stare right at me while she went into trance and if she went into trance with her eyes open, that would be fine and then she could hear my words. As a result she had total amnesia of everything I said. But she did hear it because the ringing in her ears went away.

There's a number of ways that you can make mistakes when you sleep. You can have a horrible dream in which you're one of the main characters and criticize yourself just terribly and then forget that you were the main character. A lot of people have dreams in which they awaken and they can't remember why it was so bad. They even remember what was so bad but they can't remember why it was so bad. Now there are the simple things you can do. You can let one of your legs fall asleep. And as punishment for how you've handled something during the day, you can sleep on your arm all night long so that it doesn't work for the first five or 10 minutes when you've awakened. You can toss and turn for a large portion of the night, and not know why, as a general way of making yourself uncomfortable.

Then there's getting up on the wrong side of the bed. If what you generally do is get up on the wrong side of the bed, you could get up on the right side of the bed, and that would be making a mistake. You can have dreams that aren't good enough! (*client laughs*) I asked Faye to criticize herself in her dreams at night and make the mistakes that she felt she was making in the daytime in her dreams at night. She could do things fine in the daytime and that wasn't even a concern. But when she went to bed, at some point begin to have a dream, and then lay on one of her arms until it fell asleep and began to hurt as a nice punishment to herself. Or if she'd like, have the wrong dreams when she sleeps. Or criticize the heck out of herself in one of her dreams, and then forget that she was the main character. She could dream it wrong or she could simply criticize somebody else by accident. (*client laughs*) And take those experiences of self-criticism and self-doubt when they begin to arise during the day and say I'll dream about that one. And that'll give her more time to live the life during the day pleasantly.

And when I worked with my father for therapy for his golf game I told him what he needed to do was to go to the golf course and let his conscious mind be aware of different things. And when one of these ideas that I was mentioning began to come to his conscious mind, he'd know what it meant when it did. His unconscious was to immediately channel it into anticipatory experience into his dreams at night. Then he could get up on the wrong side of the bed or the right side if he's been getting up on the wrong side. He could let one of his legs fall asleep, he could lay on his arm until it hurt, he could dream a dream in which he criticized the heck out of himself and then forgot that he was the main character, or he could get the dream wrong and criticize somebody else by accident. And try using those mechanisms in the dream, making sure that during the waking state the unconscious mind knows that there are choices to employ, monitors those certain thoughts I'm speaking about, and sends them into the dream to be channeled in one of those ways so that he would really do a very nice job of making mistakes when he slept. Then his conscious mind could pay attention to different things during the day on the golf course. There is always the greenness of the trees to appreciate, the blueness of the sky, the warmth of the sun, the quiet silence and peacefulness, the general astonishment of how the world feels when you're alive and enjoying it. And I told that to Faye, but she had total amnesia for everything I said because she watched my lips so that she could hear me.

First metaphor concludes with the identity protocol (this closure on Teen B from the first story makes him the primary protagonist for the identity protocol):

T: Now I mentioned the wood carving. It has nothing to do with what I just said. But Teen B had become an actor and he foolishly went off to America to discover his fortune. And I think he went to New York, but he may have gone to Hollywood and other places along the way, but I do know that after a series of almost payless jobs and a chronic inability to afford his rent or to buy any of the things that he thought he'd have living in a totally new land, he felt estranged and disconnected. He decided that if he couldn't work as an actor, life was not worth living. But he wasn't certain what he would do to end it, or if he would end it. Finally, it dawned on him one night, a brilliant idea he thought really. He would make the best play that he had ever performed in. He would write it and he would direct it and he'd be the main actor in it. And he worked for several weeks diligently, still waiting, I believe, in the back of his mind for a phone call for a job, for an off-Broadway production, or something, a commercial, to hit the big time. And in the meantime he was trying less and less to get a job as a waiter, trying less and less to get a job as a valet, and working more and more on his soliloquy.

And finally, when he felt it was just the right time he cleaned out his closet, he gave away some of his clothes and a few items he had and his radio. He opened the drawer to take out his pocket knife. He was somewhat surprised as a yo-yo rolled down the corner of the drawer. He had thought the drawers were empty, but put both items in his coat pocket. And he left his room once and for all and went to one of his favorite alleys that he used to pass through on the way home after dark. And he stood there dramatically on a makeshift stage he'd created with some boxes and planks.

And in the moonlight, with a few animals being his only audience, he began to practice his soliloquy in his head before he delivered it. He changed his mind at the last minute and he decided that he'd take his remaining amount of money and go to a more secluded area. The roar of taxi cabs didn't fit as the background music. And so even later that night and more determined, now with no hope of changing his mind, with no money remaining, he stood up on his soapbox and delivered his soliloquy—the best act he'd ever done, he thought really. He expanded on the virtues of life and the meaninglessness of it all. And he announced things that he had learned long ago in his teenage years, things that had brought him this far. For that he was thankful and now he was going to turn his life over into the hands of God and see what he would come back as next time. And he reached in his pocket to pull out the items that he had put there, knowing that he'd find the jackknife.

And if you were a moviemaker, you would have had the camera pan to show an owl swoop down and grab a mouse that thought it was going to get away, and roll it over, pierce it with its talons, and grab the meat in its beak. Now what does that have to do with the wood carving in Austria?

My birthday is May 29th. On May 29th Carol and I were walking near Salzburg and we wanted to investigate the shop of Karl Warbler who was known throughout the region for his carvings. When we arrived at his home, the door opened to his garage, revealing at least 500 if not 1,000 intricately carved faces on tree roots that had grown in the trees in the Austrian forest. And we walked around and looked at every single one of them and I concentrated on the spirit and the aura that each projected. Carol wanted to buy me one for my birthday so I walked down and looked at each one, and the next one, and discounted some at a distance because they were clearly wrong. And others I looked at closely, and I narrowed it down to five and three and finally down to two, then ultimately narrowed my choice down to one carved root. I picked it off the wall and I walked to the desk and said "I want to buy this" in my best German. And he spoke English.

We asked how he came to speak English so well. He said that he had been an actor in younger days and had gone to the United States to study acting. And one day as he had reached in his pocket and pulled out a jackknife and a little wooden yo-yo that he had in his pocket, he saw a little face on the yo-yo. He had impulsively carved it out with the jackknife. And one thing led to another. Now he was back in Austria carving these marvelous faces on these roots. And he was known all over Austria as the most famous woodcarver there for this type of thing. People all over Austria will tell you about his shop.

But he really didn't want to sell us this one, and I asked why. He said that he had just carved it the night before. "Today is his birthday!" And I said, "Today is my birthday, too." "You say it's your birthday, it's my birthday too, yea." And he said, "Well in that case," and he took it up to his face and he talked to it for a few moments. He said goodbye to it and he gave it to me.

Reorientation from trance and end of session:

T: Now there's been a lot of different things that I've been talking about in the last few minutes, things that have made an impression in your mind. I hope that you'll take things that you have an understanding about and let those get nicely diluted in a solution with the things you don't understand. Think them through and dream them through. And maybe when you open your eyes you'll want to go more deeply in trance for a moment to let those learnings touch a place where they need to be planted in order to grow. And while your unconscious allows that place to touch those learnings, your conscious mind can think about two or three other places in which you'll apply some of the thoughts that have been begun or allow you to continue thinking about them in other trances that you'll do for yourself, or allow you to continue thinking about them in other trances that you do for yourself. Or if your conscious mind is monitoring the proximity of that deep place, the thoughts should be nourished and nursed. Let your unconscious choose two or three other times during the routine of the day or night in which the solution of useful and confusing ideas can be mixed together and sorted out so that they apply to you as a person in the proper way in the next few days and weeks and months. And when you're satisfied consciously and unconsciously that you're able to plant those ideas in a place where they'll grow and nourish the self and continue to unravel them to your satisfaction, then it's time to reassociate yourself and reorient yourself at your own speed, open your eyes, and return to the room.

And I mentioned there were some pictures that I wanted you to see. That's Carl and his little house. And of course that's Carl himself. . . . So, how are you feeling?

C: Fine

T: Do you have something of importance in your ring? Like microfilm or nerve gas or something?

C: It was my grandmother's ring which was hand carved, interestingly enough, in Germany. (*laughs*) And it has two blue sapphires in it. Everyone asks me if it is a magic ring.

T: Is it a magic ring?

C: No. They ask if there is some secret inside, and I . . .

T: Well, it is [magic] now, I think! So are we done?

C: Yeah.

T: Do you feel finished for now?

C: Yeah, I kept wanting to say to you that I saw the 10-year-old little girl so clearly. I felt I could reach out and touch her and I wanted to tell her that she was beautiful (*pause*), but I think she knows.

Follow-up:

A follow-up after several months revealed that Tonya's stress reactions ceased entirely within two weeks. Despite a number of extremely hostile actions from her estranged husband, she continued to work as normal and to cope with the many adjustments of relocation, finances, and so on, which come with divorce, with no further debilitating incidents.

Several months later, after the divorce had been completed, she was seen for a second session to assist her in gaining closure on that chapter of her life. It was precipitated by the news that her former husband was marrying his former secretary. She is now dating and is seriously involved with another man. Although she does not like the manner in which she was treated by her former husband, she exhibits a sense of humor about many aspects of the incident.

This transcript exemplifies a normal or typical session. It illustrates the use of multiple metaphors, embedded within one another. The remainder of this book illustrates each protocol used here and additionally illustrates several others. Each subsequent chapter briefly explains the steps of a particular protocol and provides numerous examples. In each case the goal that was being targeted, not the assessment of the client, will be stated. The successful use of these or any interventions depends upon the appropriate diagnostic assessment and interview management. In order to strictly adhere to the theme of this volume, these areas will not be further discussed here. This book is intended to be a companion to the books cited earlier. However, familiarity with these previously cited books, although helpful, is not necessary to comprehend and gain from reading this volume.

2

Affect Metaphors

*Emotion is not something shameful,
subordinate, second-rate; it is a
supremely valid phase of humanity at
its noblest and most mature.*
—Joshua Loth Liebman

*The young man who has not wept is a savage,
and the old man who will not laugh is a fool.*
—George Santayana

*While grief is fresh, every attempt to divert
only irritates. You must wait till it be
digested, and then amusement will
dissipate the remains of it.*
—Samuel Johnson

Emotions are often considered the heart of therapeutic change. As we see it, however, changes in emotion will ideally be accompanied by corresponding changes in attitude, behavior, self-image, family structure, and so forth. Nevertheless, in this chapter, the focus will be on stories that have as their primary goal the retrieval of particular kinds of emotion.

We refer to *emotion* and *affect* interchangeably. The word *protocol* is used to suggest that there can be a standard procedure, map, set of

27

guidelines, or some sort of recipe which, if followed, will facilitate accomplishing designated affect or emotion goals.

There are three essential steps in the emotion protocol. First, each story begins with the sketching of a relationship between a protagonist(s) and some significant other person, place, or thing. This relationship will have some kind of emotional valence to it. If it doesn't, it won't be much of a relationship. The kind of valence—whether it is positive or negative, etc.—is something that will vary for specific outcome goals.

Second, a change or movement of some sort is introduced into the storyline that will cause an alteration in the relationship. Again, whether this change involves the characters moving closer together or further apart, pursuing, leaving, and so on, is guided by the protocol pertaining to the particular affect goal. Basically, the story parallels the kind of real life experience that we observe as typically resulting in people learning and feeling that affective state. In socialization, we perceive a change in our relationships and/or we focus on our body experience— we call it feeling. We do it again and again and it gets a label and we become sensitized to it so that we recognize it, label it, and learn it. Some people, of course, fail to have some affective experiences happen with enough frequency to learn them. Therefore, the story detailing a typical experience of that sort allows the person to identify and have a degree of that desired learning in the course of hearing the therapeutic metaphor.

The last general step of the emotion protocol is to complete the story with a detailing of the observable and physiological experiences that typically accompany the particular affect being retrieved. This is done with a concentration of indirect suggestions that focus the listener on changes in the body, both internal as well as externally observable ones—especially those of the face. These suggestions are interspersed, tangentially, from the storyline or are presented to the protagonist with a degree of ambiguity such that boundaries are blurred, whether we are commenting on the listening client having the emotion or the protagonist of the story—who is, of course, having the emotion. These steps are summarized in the following outline.

Affect and emotional flexibility change protocol:

1. Establish a relationship between the protagonist and a person, place, or thing which involves emotion or affect (e.g., tenderness, anxiety, mastery, con- fusion, love, longing).
2. Detail *movement* in the relationship (e.g., moving with, moving toward, moving away, chasing, fleeing, orbiting).

3. Detail the observable facial and internal physiological changes that coincide with the building emotion in the protagonist (be sure to overlap with the client's behavior).

These three steps are the basic structure, then, for all of the specific emotion protocol stories and all of the stories in this chapter. However, different relationships and different directions of movement within those relationships will provide a learning of different emotions. To better grasp this, we offer several affect construction formulas. The kinds of relationships to initially create and then the kinds of changes to describe are detailed under specific affect goals which are summarized in the following "formula" chart. Referring to the chart, notice that each box displays "+" and "−" signs to convey the valence of the characters in the story. Following this, arrows with thrust and arrows with smaller increments of movement are depicted on the next line of each box. Finally, the names of various feeling options are listed.

Affect Construction Formulas

Character: Relationship: Movement: Feeling options:	1. Protag. Other + + $\rightarrow$ $\leftarrow$ Tenderness, Love, Joy	2. Protag. Other + + $\leftarrow$ $\rightarrow$ Sadness Grief	3. Protag. Other + + $\rightarrow$ $\rightarrow$ Determined Resolute	4. Protag. Other + - $\leftarrow$ $\leftarrow$ Scared Fear
Character: Relationship: Movement: Feeling options:	5. Protag. Other + - $\rightarrow$ X Aggression Courage	6. Protag. Other + - $\rightarrow$ $\rightarrow$ Anger Rage	7. Protag. Other + - $\ggg$ X Success, Pride Confidence	8. Protag. Other + - X $\rightarrow$ Relief, Comfort Happy
Character: Relationship: Movement: Feeling options:	9. Protag. Other + + $\ggg$ X Excitement Belonging	10. Protag. Other + + $\ggg$ (I) Mastery Competence	11. Protag. Other + + X-X Safety, Trust Security	12. Protag. Other + - $\leftarrow\leftarrow$ X Virtuous Indignant

	Legend	
$\rightarrow$ = moving forcefully	X	= external object/person - not moving
$\rightarrow$ $\leftarrow$ = moving toward	+	= positive valence (protagonist)
$\rightarrow$ $\rightarrow$ = pursuing / fleeing	-	= negative valence (antagonist)
$\ggg$ = moving cautiously	X - X	= no apparent separation
	(I)	= internal object/image - unchanging

Following one example, then, consider the protocol (#7) for feelings of confidence. The formula reminds us that the first step in the metaphor is to define the protagonist in a distant relationship with something or someone somewhat anxiety producing ("−"). The second line displays arrows depicting the gradual movement of the protagonist toward the eventual accomplishment of the goal—the second step of the protocol. The third step of the protocol is to focus on the body of the protagonist and help clients notice any similarities in their own physical state. The physical features which the therapist needs to describe at this third step will be those features of the face and gross posture which non-verbally communicate one or more of the feelings in the third and following lines of box #7. These are, for instance, feelings of confidence, pride, or success.

Translating this outline into an actual story then, therapists simply recall some incident in their own experience that follows this dynamic: a relationship with something/a person which is slightly anxiety producing and in which a *gradual* movement toward overcoming it eventually succeeded. For instance, when my son faced the challenge of preparing for and speaking to an assembly for membership in an academic society, the prospect of delivering the speech was anxiety producing. Detailing this situation in the first part of the story constitutes step one of the protocol. He made gradual and incremental steps in preparation for the speech and his attention was focused on each step as it was taken. Relating these steps that he took constitutes step two of the protocol. Finally, he stood on the stage and delivered the speech, thus completing the movement and the task. The story finally turns to this moment and details the physical and observable features in his body as he was completing the speech. This detailing satisfies the third and final step of the protocol. In the telling, care should be taken to overlap the details of the protagonist's posture and facial expression with that of the listening client. In this way, clients are drawn to notice similar experiences in physical awareness. Feelings are elicited and awareness is partially trained for each feeling. The same procedure and logic applies to the use of each of the other formulas to construct metaphors for other specific feelings. The process will remain the same, only the ingredients need to be changed for each different emotion.

We use these guidelines for designing the elements of a therapeutic story to elicit affect. Our goal is not to label that emotion for the client's conscious mind and have it recognized by the name of the feeling. Usually we wish for our therapeutic suggestions to be indirect or for our demands to be open-ended so that whatever the client does or however the client interprets the story is acceptable. For example, we may tell a story designed to elicit sadness but the client does not cry. To point out that this is supposed to be sadness would simply imply that the client is resisting or failing, or something. So the guidelines or protocols can be truly specific and the treatment goal for the kind of affect to be experienced can be specific, but the metaphor itself will be permissively indirect. It will thereby allow a broad range of idiosyncratic response from the listening client for whom it was designed. The protagonist in the stories can be described and said to be experiencing a labeled emotion, and clients are free to identify or disidentify with that character.

The affect construction formulas chart has been helpful in guiding the metaphorical development of relationships and movement within them with the goal of eliciting particular emotional states. It is not intended as an exhaustive list of emotions and neither is this method presented as the right or only way to elicit emotion. Certainly, there are other options for emotional elicitation that involve metaphor (three-dimensional), other indirect means (anecdotes regarding feelings), as well as assignments (visit parents), directives (focus on feelings), other interventions (fantasy confrontation, etc.) and unexpected, uncontrolled variables (the use of images that accidentally bring emotions).

One limitation of this chart is that it portrays linear and two-dimensional relationships, whereas the interactions and circumstances that result in development of emotion in real life are far more complex, circular, three-dimensional and involve a larger cast of characters. Nevertheless, this chart and the kinds of metaphors based on it represent one predictable—and, we believe, accountable—way to stimulate thinking and experiencing related to specific emotional states. The chart is meant to be used in conjunction with other methods of therapy and with other metaphor protocols in each session.

1. *Affect goal: Sadness, grief*

Metaphor[1]

As I stepped out of my car I thought about how you can watch people in the rearview mirror and they won't even realize it. I also

---

[1] This story is adapted from the story Dr. Erickson told of taking his parents from their farm. We have added details from clients with whom we subsequently worked. This story can also be found in Lankton & Lankton, 1986, pp. 284–288.

thought I should watch some people more carefully—some behaviors are initiated on the left side of the body and some on the right. I wondered for a moment which I would see more of today. Then I shouted "hello" through the screen door.

She was sitting in her favorite chair at the farmhouse where she lived, had been living for her entire life. She was just sitting in her chair, motionless. She greeted me warmly and said that she was just sitting in this chair looking out the window at her favorite view of the grain in the field, and that she'd watched that view change from season to season for well over half a century. She had watched the crops rotated in that field and she liked it best when it was this kind of amber. There *actually were* amber waves of grain. We watched the wind blow them for a few minutes and I asked her to show me what else she liked around that farm.

We walked outside and past the tractor that was parked beyond the barn by the silo. She'd certainly kept it in good repair; the seat wasn't even cracked and there was no excess dirty grease around the wheels. Usually you see the seat cracked on farmers' tractors. And I commented, "You must be very proud of that." She agreed and added that she was also very proud of how she had finally gotten the silo: "It is very difficult on a farm without one." She was very proud of that and proud of her barn too, but by now we'd come to this small creek. I saw her reflection in the water as we passed over the bridge and it made me think about that rearview mirror, but I didn't bring it up. I said, "Tell me about this bridge."

"Oh, that's a story," she said. You could see her happiness with this bridge as she described how it had started out as merely a branch across the stream, then gone to a plank, and finally they had built it into a little bridge with ropes. Gradually the ropes were replaced by wooden railings. Now it even had a wooden canopy. She and her husband had watched a lot of moonlit nights reflected in that water as they walked down to that little creek. And when we got to the other side of the bridge, she pointed out 19 pine trees, planted there at the north border of the property. With a big smile on her face she said, "I bought those trees for five cents a piece, 20 for a dollar. You couldn't get a deal like that anymore. Nineteen of them grew up and I sure am pleased with those 19 trees I got for a nickel." I just knew that was a story she had told to everybody, how she paid five cents a piece for those trees that protected the north perimeter of that property from the cold winds that used to blow through there.

By the time we got to the south 40 acres, she had pointed out the stone fence that was built by laboriously moving all of those rocks. A great deal of effort had gone into that. "Sticktoitiveness" and a little bit of planning to build that attractive fence on this south perimeter of the property to protect the most fertile field from who knows what kind of predator. Still near that field and coming closer to the house was the compost pile that she pointed out with a special kind of affection that comes from a long and rewarded effort spent working it. She had been taking out the potato peelings and corn cobs to that pile since she was a little girl on that farm. And she had learned to experience the pleasure of feeding back into the land that which it had given to her. And it was very mutually rewarding. "Oh, and no tour would be complete without a notice of those glorious shade trees," she added as we approached the house. "I can't count the number of games I played as a child, and later with my children, under those trees that seemed just as huge 70 years ago as they do today."

Finally, as we came back into the house, I asked what was her favorite spot in the house. She said, "Oh, right here in front of this wood-burning stove. I spent many a cold night being warmed by its heat. It's really been at the heart of things, the family sitting around this stove, sharing stories and memories. And this dining room table too, where everyone in the family used to eat and talk about daily chores, daily accomplishments." And a whole lifetime of daily accomplishments really add up. Now her lifetime was far from over, but the chapters of her lifetime with that farmland were finally coming to a close. After all, she was an old woman now and times had changed. Because of various alterations in her circumstances, it was time to say goodbye and move on.

"And so, as long as we're sitting here at the dining room table," I said, "Why don't you just look around and try to remember who sat where. And say goodbye to all those memories, and say goodbye to all those talks of the chores that had to be done, and to all those plans that were laid down there at the table. Say goodbye to all those meals that you enjoyed, that drew the family together." When she got up from the table I asked her to sit down in her favorite chair and just relax there and feel the comfort. Then, looking out that picture window for the last time, I asked her to say goodbye to that comfortable chair, and that favorite resting spot and to that picturesque view, to say goodbye. And to the grain and the memory of the rotation each season, to say goodbye. Then we went back outside and walked past the barn. I reminded her to say goodbye to the silo. It had been a long time coming and it would be a long time gone. And by the time we got to the tractor I reminded her that everyone says goodbye in their special way. "Some people say, 'See you later.' Some people say, 'God go with you.' Some people say, 'Fare thee well.' Some say, 'Good riddance'; others say, 'Aloha.' It is up to you to decide which way you need to say goodbye and say goodbye the right way." Looking at that tractor, I reminded her that the seat didn't even have a crack in it, she'd cared for it so well. "Say goodbye to that care and say the proper goodbye to the friend that tool had been."

And then we walked across that bridge and I asked her if she could say goodbye to the sticks, and the planks, say goodbye to the ropes that had been used as hand rails, and to the hand rails say goodbye and to the canopy say goodbye, and to the memory of all those moonlit nights reflecting in that water, "You'll never see that water again. You can just watch it flow underneath you . . . and say goodbye."

Our journey was still far from complete. We still had the north 40 acres, and I asked her to say 19 goodbyes to those trees and goodbye to that great story. Goodbye to the tree that died. And to that north wind that you felt a need to protect yourself from, say goodbye to that.

Then I was quiet as we walked to the south 40 acres and I asked her to say goodbye to all those stones and to all that labor, and all that planning that had gone into building that fence, and "say goodbye to whatever threat you felt was on the other side of that fence. You won't ever have that threat again." And she just stood there and looked at that fence for a minute.

Your mind thinks a lot of things when your consciousness focuses on something your unconscious hasn't fully informed you about. Everyone has their own private thoughts. And the depth of the thoughts a person can conceptualize relate to the breadth of their experience.

So she needed her own time to say her own goodbye. Eventually she followed me as I walked out of the south 40 back into the house. And even houses with a short history have a unique array of memories stored in the attic, and in her case, this was increased a thousand fold. So I told her to "go up into the attic alone and make three piles: a big pile of things that you intend to throw away, a medium size pile of things you intend to give away, and a smaller pile still of things you intend to keep." When she was done, she came down, and she said, "I've done it now. I made a big pile I intend to discard, a medium size pile I am going to give away, and a small size pile I intend to keep." "And now say goodbye to each pile, goodbye . . . goodbye . . . and goodbye."

Somewhat spent from the long exertion, we sat down in front of the wood-burning stove once again and I asked her to remember all those stories, all those warm nights that were shared around the heart of the matter. And to those memories say goodbye, and to the stove say goodbye. To be warmed like that on those cold nights say goodbye.

And then it was time to leave. As we went out the door, an ancient and seldom-greased hinge squeaked on the screen door. I reminded her to say goodbye to that squeaky hinge; you'll never have to fix it again. Then she noticed her shrubs there by the porch and commented that the shrubs really need a trimming. I asked her to say goodbye to those shrubs before getting in the back seat where I could keep an eye on her with the rearview mirror. That way she would have some opportunity to be alone, to be by herself with her emotion.

But I could still watch in the rearview mirror and wonder whether the left side or the right side of her body would began to tear first. Her cheeks were already moist. There were skin color changes in her face. She tried to not move because she was holding on to an idea, to a memory, and a feeling. You could tell there was tension in the upper part of her jaw, under her eyes. She held it just so as to prevent the tears from falling. She held her head erect on her shoulders and was breathing in a rhythmical deep breathing from her upper chest the way a person does who feels sad. There was a slight movement in her lips and I had to watch the road as I drove away, so I wasn't able to discover whether it was the left or the right eye that had the tear drop down from it first. But when I looked again, I could see the tears flowing uniformly from both eyes that were open and staring into the memories. She was holding onto that feeling by experiencing the fullness of her grief. And the more you have loved, the more you are entitled to say goodbye with the intensity of sadness that she was feeling in the back seat. And at a time like that, your conscious mind can entertain various memories or ideas while your unconscious monitors and regulates the expression of emotion, or perhaps your conscious mind can even participate in the emotional expression and allow your unconscious to attend to relevant images. But you can't deny the fullness of breathing or the lump in the throat. And from time to time she would sob audibly because she was coming to terms with goodbye. And it probably seemed to her like she was crying that way forever, though it couldn't have been more than an hour.

But I do know that as we drove past that house again, two years later as she was sitting beside me in the front seat, she said with dispassionate interest, "Oh look, they have pruned their shrubs back to practically nothing!" I had to listen again to make sure I had heard her correctly. She hadn't said "my shrubs" because they weren't her shrubs anymore. She had said her goodbyes.

2. *Affect goal:* *Sadness, grief, loss*

Metaphor

Everyone knows something about how special bonds are formed when you're in some serious difficulty with another person. And the two of you work to get yourself out of it and that's how Gary and Fred were as a result of the time they had spent together fighting in Nam. It was a context of conflict and difficulty, of course, such that you wouldn't really stop to think about the intensity of a friendship that was building or the intensity of the caring. And it was a very unhappy situation. Yet even in the midst of that, there comes a building of appreciation of one another. Or, maybe it's an appreciation of yourself that comes from the understanding and admiration of you from the eyes of another who has come to know you so well in a context that reveals what you might have thought was a weakness or an inadequacy. And yet revealing that feeling, that fear, paradoxically somehow allows the people closest to you to have a learning and sense of permission to have that feeling.

So they were the best of friends, sharing the kind of bond you know is going to last forever and ever. Not many people have the opportunity to experience the relationship that people gain in those kinds of settings. But the ones that do remember them for a lifetime.

They say the more intense the feeling, the less time it needs to last but that is not always true. Fred and Gary had lost track of one another but still longed to see each other. They wanted to tell war stories because they had forgotten some of the horrors but they remembered some of the ways that they had depended on one another.

Gary thought about how nice it would be to share some love stories that he had had time for since the war. We knew Gary better and he had put much of the war behind him. But he hadn't put any of the love stories behind him. When he heard that his friend was in town, he made contact right away. This time it was a little different from the times past when they had gotten together for a dinner, shared a kind of party mood between them and vowed to meet again. But this time they weren't going to make any vow because Fred declined the invitation. Gary wondered what was wrong with him and asked him if he was having some difficulty.

Fred's response seemed superficial to Gary. Gary didn't really think that it was something he could trust as an honest expression. And yet there were things that Gary needed to do, in fact. So finally he left Fred behind and something about that set so poorly with Gary that he thought, "Maybe I'm not going to be able to have those old times with Fred again." But he surely couldn't have known how the intensity of a love that you have for somebody doesn't really mean that you don't need to have a long relationship.

Not that day, but within a week he was going to know. Because he got the word that Fred had taken his own life and the times that they had had would not be times they would ever have again. Gary sat unable to know what to think, unable to know what to feel, and there was certainly nothing he could do.

There was a redness in his cheeks, just thinking of all the things that should have been said that weren't, all the things that might have been done. His heart was heavy. He could feel a flutter in the corners of his nose as his lips quivered. There was a shallow breathing in his chest. It was hard to sit there and make no sound at all, trying to come to grips with the fact that he was never going to have those good times again. It's a feeling that you've lost a friend and it pervades the pit of the stomach and the ability to breathe properly through the chest. And in time the tears find their way over the eyelids.

He kept telling himself, "There has got to be a way to make sense of this. Fred's gone. Fred is dead and I won't see Fred again." So many times they had saved each other's life in Nam. More times than that, they had depended on one another and now all that emotional investment seemed lost. Somehow he projected an ability to continue no matter what. His chest heaved and all those tears from Vietnam he had remembered so that he would be able to cry them at the right time came bumping into one another at the edge of his eyes, crowding to get in line to roll down his cheeks. And you can feel pleased with the intensity of the sadness and grief that you're able to feel. It is such a central part of being alive. He could feel the water inside his throat and the need to swallow. It was like some of the moisture was being sent to his eyes and some was being sent to his throat and he was just waiting for orders. He certainly knew that he was alive but it didn't seem to be a great benefit at that moment.

He was so far dissociated from his eyes that it seemed as though he was sitting on his shoulders or something, waiting to connect with his face when the tears would start to flow, and when they did he was sitting right there. Just a little moisture in the eyelashes is enough to reconnect you with your body, to know that you are sitting there being sad. And even with all the intensity of the relationship that he had which should have meant it was okay for it to be short, it wasn't okay for it to be short. The old saying wasn't true. And so there he was right in the middle of the process of saying goodbye, moving on, and leaving someone behind.

3. *Affect goal:* Courage

Metaphor[2]

And I don't think she really understood at first why I told her about that experience my mother had back when my father was off to war. There was no way she could really appreciate how that moment affected my mother in positive ways later in her life.

There she was in that newly built house in the country, the nearest neighbor some distance away. There was that sound again at the front window. She lay there in her bed petrified, unable to move, with her ears growing larger until they were like space saucers listening for that next sound.

And there it was again and this time it sounded even more like what she thought the first time. She looked at her choices and they didn't seem like very many at that moment. Her heart was racing, every muscle in her body was rigid.

But then from somewhere came those first movements in her left leg. Her left foot began to slowly slide off the bed, and the right leg began to follow almost as if it had a mind of its own. And all of a sudden, both feet were on the floor, she was standing up, and then one foot moved in front of the other, and then the next step, and the next one until she was at the front door.

Her hand reached out and she turned the knob to find the branches of the willow tree being relentlessly whipped across the shutter by the furious wind. And the feeling of courage she had was in no way diminished by the feeling of relief she also had to discover how easily she could take charge and deal with that situation which had seemed so threatening. All alone, she was aware of her heart beating, the easy

---

[2] This metaphor was contributed by Myer S. Reed, Ph.D.

deep breathing, the firm set of her muscles as she pulled back the branches and secured the shutters. You don't even have to think about it consciously at a time like that in order for your unconscious to memorize that experience of courage and power seemingly pulsating through your entire body. It is as though each breath you take in convinces you of your power to accomplish anything you set your mind to do. And it was an experience she kept and used and shared with others for many years to come, both consciously and in unconscious, automatic ways.

4. *Affect goal:* Courage

Metaphor

And I'll tell you something else. And this is something nobody expected. It was the day that separated the adults from the children. I had a client named Paul. But what I want to tell you about is the day that his sister, Elaine, after hearing about Paul's experience in therapy, called me up and asked me if she could get some therapy. She always felt that she didn't fit in because of something she had done wrong. Paul told her about his incidents with me in therapy. And she just wanted to consult about something she had done the night before. You wouldn't really be able to say that her father was somebody who celebrated the various things that she did in her life. You might say instead that her father was kind of a baby. But looking up to her father as she did, you would really characterize it as a young girl beating her head against a brick wall.

Everybody has the experience of what it's like getting up in the middle of the night and walking into a door that's not open. Sooner or later, people wake up on the wrong side of the bed. And when they get up, they find the wall right in front of them. It's enough to knock you off of your feet and back down onto the bed. And that's what it had been like for Elaine, trying to deal with her father and having something thrown up in her face. One time it was the Bible, and another time it was the chores, and another time it was the discipline, and another time it was something else. And not being a very quick learner consciously, it didn't occur to her that the problem might lie with him until after she heard about Paul's therapy session.

And the thing she wanted to consult about was that she had stood right in front of her father, face to face and eyeball to eyeball, and she said, "Dad, back up and lean against the wall for a second. I have something to tell you and I think you're going to need some support." And she told him she was darn tired of being treated like some other child that he might have wished she had been born as. She was a girl, she was herself, and she wanted to be treated like a girl. She wanted to be treated like a respectable person in her own right. And he started to speak but she put her hand right over his mouth and said, "I'm not done talking yet."

Then she stood there feeling a sense of power she'd never felt before. Her jaw was firm and she was gritting her teeth. She was surprised that she could look him straight in the eye and see the pores on his cheeks. She'd never noticed. And she heard the words flow out of her mouth, and she didn't want to take them back, but she never consciously planned on saying "I'm tired of being hurt and discounted in this way." She pushed him right back against the wall, his shoulders hit against the wall with a thud. And he was speechless, and she didn't even feel bad about it. She didn't feel guilty. She figured he ought to be able to handle it. It was the truth. And she walked away feeling her heart beating, the heat of anger that she'd never felt before.

It's enough to make you think a lot of things and wonder whether they're the right things to be thinking. Elaine had never thought about them before. And since she got the idea from Paul, and Paul seemed to be getting some of his ideas from therapy, she called me up and asked me whether or not she'd done the right thing. I don't know if you have done the right thing or not, but I think you're standing taller today. She said, "You've never seen me before. How do you know if I'm standing taller?" But the feeling of power and courage she had experienced was something that you don't forget, was something that was even recognizable over the telephone. It's as if you breathe more fully and your heart beats more proudly. And if your conscious mind thinks in terms of standing taller, your unconscious can take care of doing the right thing.

5. *Affect goal:* Confidence

Metaphor[3]

"I've waited my whole life for this," he exclaimed! It didn't matter that his whole life had only spanned five years so far. Receiving that

---

[3] This metaphor was contributed by Ralph M. Daniel, Ph.D.

first bicycle still represented a momentous, long-awaited occasion. And of course, it was love at first sight, though it also represented a great learning challenge. There was so much to coordinate—muscles, pedals, handlebars, how tightly to grip the bars, and what to focus on. The only thing easy at first was feeling pretty discouraged. But of course, he soon mastered the various movements, as long as he was supported by training wheels.

Later, he would look back on the time when his father first took him out to ride, and how wobbly it was the first time they took the training wheels off. He wasn't sure if he'd fall off or not, but he had a sense of confidence that his father would hold him up and help him move down the sidewalk. He had done this over and over again.

Finally, after a while he began to realize his father's hand was no longer holding on so tightly to the back of the seat. He had a realization that he was pedaling all on his own. He leapt into a new era, into a sense of assurance, able to go maybe three or four feet by himself. Then it was 12 feet. He practiced and practiced until he had the sense of balance and the balance became a new skill. He really didn't have to think about the ability to balance and he somehow knew that once you had that skill, you have it for the rest of your life.

And it was all symbolized by that shiny first bike. It was heavy and strong. He loved the color of it and the feel of the handlebar grip. At first, his parents allowed him to ride only to the nearest corner. He had been able to walk there, but he realized you have a new perspective from the seat of a bike. He could feel the air blowing across his face giving him a sense of speed and power. He was a little bit taller when he walked.

Time went by and he was allowed to go around the corner, and from his point of view, into a whole new world. There were children and families that were different. The street looked different, the bushes, the grass, cars, the way the people dressed. There are so many different views and ways of looking at something.

And soon the day came when he was old enough to cross the street with his bicycle. He really didn't become conscious of the significance at first. His world suddenly became several blocks. At first he felt small, felt some trepidation. He explored each block, one at a time. And he would do so slowly, carefully, finally going as far as his comfort level would allow. Each time he would see something of interest a little bit further down the block, perhaps another boy or another girl, someone he might have known from school, or perhaps someone he didn't yet know.

And then his parents agreed that he was ready to cross other streets as well. It's really hard to figure exactly how far his world expanded, perhaps half a mile, perhaps a mile, perhaps more. It is truly amazing how many different ways people can live and enjoy themselves. He couldn't really explain why, but there was a special excitement about finding discoveries his parents knew nothing about. With passing time, he told them less and less. It didn't seem so important. He wondered what it was that accounted for the ways other people looked so different from what he knew.

And sometimes as he explored a new neighborhood, he could feel his heart thumping gently in his chest, that feeling of excitement and trepidation mixed together. He really did feel grown up. He really did find it interesting to browse the foreign shelves, full of new and interesting objects to discover, hold, and heft. And he knew the value of keeping a mental map in his mind, to make sure that he would know exactly the way home. He developed alternate routes home in case he ran into problems. Sometimes he ran into bullies or people who frightened him. He realized the value of having different options.

Before he was conscious of it, he was truly growing up, though he had felt "grown up" for quite some time. He loved that bicycle. It was his time and space machine. As he pedaled that bicycle, he looked to his left and to his right, and he could feel the wheels turning on the pavement beneath him as a direct result of his efforts. He could feel the strength in his back, the strength in his arms and legs. It was almost as if he could feel himself a little bit taller, a little bit stronger, able to pedal a little bit faster with each passing day, week, and month.

As time went by, he could remember each dent and mark on that bicycle, how it occurred. And he took pride and joy from the learnings each of those dents and marks symbolized. In some ways it was the same bike he had gotten for his birthday and in other ways it was quite new and different. It had new tires, different hand grips, new streamers. Finally, it was just too small for him, but every time he looked at that bike he knew how *easy* it is for all those memories to come back, to remember exploring ever greater circles, moving away from home into a world of excitement, challenges, new tastes and smells, and countless miles. And each time you remember, you can feel that confidence that has become as unconscious an experience as the ability to balance.

Maybe the confidence is something you notice by feeling the strength in your legs and arms, or perhaps it is more obvious as a smoothness of the face, or a recognition of the ability to create options in the course of meeting each new challenge. The muscles of the face are smooth with tonus. There is a smile on the mouth that forces cheek muscles to be full and rosy. Smile lines around the eyes pull even more of the face into action. There is a slight parting of the lips which reveals a slight amount of teeth showing through. Your chest feels and looks a little larger and the sternum is raised up while the head sits balanced evenly above the shoulders. There is certainly a comfortable breathing that goes with it, and in his case, in his memory there would always be an indelible image of that shiny bicycle.

6. *Affect goal: Confidence*

Metaphor[4]

Terrye walked out of her photography class, down the stairs and to her car. This time she walked alone, her eyes not absorbing the people and activities around her as was her usual habit. Breathing in the fresh cool air, she directed her car towards the beach to keep her appointment with the water and the moon. It was a full moon tonight. She had liked hearing that it was a harvest moon. She guessed at its meaning as images went through her mind. She felt pensive as her thoughts returned to class and to her recognition that she had succeeded in becoming comfortable with the camera.

Terrye remembered when she first began learning to operate the camera and how she had felt. There was so much to know; how could she possibly master it all? They had started by learning about f-stops and shutter speeds. One allowed the right amount of light in while the other invited its length of stay. Combinations would change depending upon conditions. As she became more familiar with these two fundamental concepts, the nature of the relationship was understood. Neither could produce a good photograph without the other.

First, memorizing by rote and referring to notes seemed to be the only way to learn and understand the concepts. As she practiced making pictures, she noticed her stiff, uncertain awkwardness beginning to diminish. She became absorbed in the assignments as she took care to understand and follow each instruction one step before the next. Going slowly and methodically made the tasks easier and she gave herself larger amounts of time than she would need later. She started well in

[4] This metaphor was contributed by Cheryl Malone, M.A.

advance of due dates to allow comfort and relaxation while she attended to arranging each requirement in order. As each part was put in place time and again, her pictures improved in clarity and form. She felt that sense of pride and pleasure mount as she picked up new packages of finished photographs.

Terrye found herself concentrating on focusing matters even in her dreams. She focused on single details; she focused on clusters of details; she focused on themes; she focused on sustaining clarity for extended periods of time. She would remember dreams where she pored over her photographs as she would continue to fine tune her focusing techniques in her mind. She would dress in the morning only partially aware that she was rehearsing focusing skills.

Light and shadow became her allies. The relationship between light and shadow was as significant as that between the f-stop and the shutter speed. She began to see light and shadow with a new discernment. She discovered just how much life can pass in a single second and then learned how to stop time in a thousandth of that second. She determined boundaries and measured depth with a keenness of eye that came from calculations made over and over from behind the viewfinder. Selecting her topics allowed her to find her own favorite subjects. She learned which subjects she worked well with, and how she could draw out their best qualities. She learned what only an experienced photographer can know. She learned that the relationship or position the photographer takes with the subject affects outcome. She found that her approach could be sensed by others perusing her work. She could feel her confidence growing as she created composition, chose mood, and determined angles, filling up roll after roll of film.

Her instructor had been particularly impressed with several series of candid shots she had taken of friends. He had suggested that she submit them to local newspapers and magazines for publication. Fellow students, one in particular, had asked her to go on picture-taking jaunts with them. John had caught her before class to see if she might be interested in attending the upcoming photojournalism seminar with him. He had seemed pleased when she smiled, accepted, and thanked him.

Terrye had her camera with her even now as she pulled into the beach parking lot. She put the strap over her shoulder after checking to see whether she had film left. She locked the car before heading to the ocean's edge. The moon had been almost orange as it began its evening rise. Now it was a silver white ball with shadows showing on its surface. Terrye loved sitting only feet away from where the water met and smoothed the wet sand as it rolled up on the shore. She idly mused that no one called it the shore here. Terrye removed her camera deliberately from its case before resting it gently in her lap.

At a time like that your conscious mind doesn't even have to recognize the degree of confidence that your unconscious has learned and stored. You can notice a feeling of confidence by your ability to forget about it. Or perhaps you can be particularly aware of it in some specific portion of your body. Certainly her face was relaxed and her muscles were smooth. Maybe she noticed a sense of confidence by noticing how comfortably she was breathing, or by an ability to concentrate on the serenity of the environment. Or perhaps it was only symbolized by the rising fullness of that harvest moon which she soon focused on with utmost clarity.

7. *Affect goal: Power, confidence*

Metaphor

An otherwise ordinary day can unexpectedly take a turn for the better, but not in the way you might expect. Ann was the kind of person you might expect to see victimized by petty crime since no one ever expects it to happen to them. She was not a big person but she stood out from a crowd because of her polished appearance. She was careful and meticulous about her looks—well dressed, the pieces of clothing she owned had been carefully chosen, and her wardrobe was precisely coordinated. Not a large sum of money had been spent but each item was of good quality. Sometimes Ann had shopped wisely at sales, she had done some sewing, there had been clothing gifts, items purchased as souvenirs from interesting places she had visited. Some of the pieces of her wardrobe were one of a kind or had now been discontinued. As in everyone's wardrobe, there were several treasured old items and even the fairly new clothes had their share of memories associated to them. And the older favorites had that fit the way good shoes come to adjust themselves to your feet.

Once a week she would drop off her large brown laundry basket to a cleaners on the way to her job. Some nine hours later, on her way home, she would pick them up all clean, folded, shirts on hangers, ready to go. And you don't even think twice about the things you take for granted and come to expect. Ann really enjoyed getting her clothes back from the laundry. It seemed kind of silly and she had never mentioned it to anyone but it was sort of a highlight of her week and brought a feeling of satisfaction that seemed symbolic of things unrelated to laundry. She couldn't exactly explain it but she really enjoyed the crisp way they had been pressed and carefully folded. There was the fresh, clean smell of the detergent. The clothes were like new and yet still old friends, too, ready for another tour of duty.

So she was on her way home that day and maybe it was because she was anticipating that feeling of satisfaction in the back of her mind, but she was in a carefree mood and the spring weather was refreshing. She decided to stop in at a florist's shop to say hello to the manager, a friend of hers. She hadn't seen him in a while because she was usually too busy to stop, but she wanted to take a look at pottery she knew he was displaying. While she was there, an interesting yellow motorized tricycle caught her eye. Her friend said it was part of his new delivery system.

The pottery was very tempting but there were things she wanted to do—maybe get home in time to run along the beach before meeting some friends for dinner. So she proceeded to the laundry, bounced inside, and gave a new clerk on duty the specifications of her basket. The clerk looked a little perplexed and said she was pretty sure there was no such basket to be claimed. Ann felt a momentary twinge of panic at that, but the clerk double checked and, sure enough, she came back empty-handed.

"Not there? What do you mean? That isn't possible, of course they are there. I just dropped them off this morning," Ann yelled. More checking didn't turn up anything except that the clerk suddenly began to remember something interesting that might explain things. "Could it be that someone else picked them up for you," she asked Ann. "Well, no, it could not," Ann said, but the clerk remembered that there had been a young lady in just a little while ago who had picked up a brown basket meeting Ann's description. In fact, there were two baskets, she said and when asked which one was hers, she indicated that they both were. And then the clerk remembered one other interesting detail, the girl had left on a yellow motorized tricycle.

Ann left in shocked disbelief, feeling a combination of anger, helplessness, and despair. She raced back over to the florist's shop and found out that he did in fact have a young girl in his employment and that she had been out doing some deliveries on the bicycle that afternoon but had gone home for the day a few hours earlier.

She soon had both the name and the address and a little background on the girl in question. She was only a teenager actually and said to hang out at a certain pool hall in her urban neighborhood. Not knowing exactly what she would find, Ann got in her car and headed to that address, passing the pool hall slowly, looking inside the open doors, possibly for some information, to see who was there. She just saw men inside, so she kept on driving and there, not more than 50 yards away, coming straight towards her was a girl riding on a bicycle and wearing one of Ann's more distinctive shirts, one made of yellow terrycloth material with little shoulder straps and an appliqued butterfly across the front. It had recently been sent to her by her sister in another city and was definitely a unique item.

In the few moments something like that takes, she noticed the girl to be large, strong, and with an expression you would characterize as tough and streetwise. It was a cocky look that let you know she had been breaking rules a long time and was proud of it, not easily stopped. But Ann didn't even question it. She just curbed her car right in front of that bicycle, blocking its further progress. The girl glared an angry, "what do you think you're doing" look at her and jumped off the bike, throwing it down like she was getting ready to fight.

Ann got out of the car, shut the door, put her hands on her hips as she stood only inches from the still-glaring girl, then steadily said, "I know your name, I know where you work, I know where you live. You have on my shirt and I want *it* and all my other clothes back."

"I don't know what you're talking about, I got this at Angel's downtown. I don't have your clothes," the girl instinctively denied. Ann just repeated her original statement, very calm but very firm, very serious, and a little louder this time. Then she added, "Do you want to ride your bike home or wherever you've put my clothes while I follow you or shall I take you there in my car? I think it will be worth your while to cooperate with me rather than face the consequences when I press charges against you with the police."

The girl's characteristic tough look began to fade a little bit as she again stammered a denial, but she was scared. She looked right to left frantically like a trapped animal would, saw no support, no easy way out. Ann didn't budge her stance and her face was taking on a congruent tough look that she didn't usually wear but that looked right at home there that particular moment.

And it wasn't exactly sympathy she felt for the girl, but she announced to her that she wouldn't press charges if the girl could produce all of the clothes in good condition with no further denial or objection. A truly streetwise character knows when to fold and the girl's demeanor suddenly changed as she hurriedly said, "All right, I'll put my bike on the sidewalk." Ann drove them straightaway to the girl's house where the clothes were still in their basket, sitting on the girl's unmade bed in a house showing no signs of life or care. Ann waited while the girl changed shirts, carried everything to her car, and, in accordance with their bargain, dropped her off by the pool hall and proceeded home.

Later that night as she shared the incident with her friends, the feeling of power and confidence she felt surprised her, even while some of them suggested she had been foolish in not pressing charges. They couldn't know the reward she was experiencing, not just the tangible one of having the clothes back, or the relief at not having to devote endless hours and dollars to refurbishing her unique wardrobe. She had the pure pleasure of knowing that she could take action in her own behalf in a thoughtful, careful, confident way, even when she least expected it. She had reached into what seemed like total chaos and had created an understandable order. She had solved a mystery every bit as perplexing as a needle in a haystack. It could so easily have gone the other way had someone not persevered with the kind of determination she had evidenced.

They did notice that as she sat there looking very comfortable in her clothes, she breathed full and calm, there was a vibrant pink to her cheeks and neck, and she took off her jacket, perspiring lightly like you would after a good workout when you're really feeling your strength and what it's like to be alive and accomplishing something with a purposeful exertion. And your conscious mind doesn't realize at first when you have an experience like that your unconscious uses it as an opportunity to define and store a feeling in a way that's going to be with you for a lifetime. Maybe you can touch it at some level with each deep breath. And no matter which of her outfits she put together from that day on, it was with a new sense of pride in herself that she wore those clothes. She got lots of comments after that, suggesting that she perhaps should consider some kind of professional modeling because she wore her clothes so comfortably or some unexplainable characteristic people couldn't quite label. You know how having a feeling you can't quite label can alter areas of your experience in ways you hadn't expected.

8. *Affect goal:* Anger

Metaphor

Paul said he learned more in eight minutes, or was it eight hours, than he had learned in eight sessions of psychotherapy. It is hard to really tell how much time passes. It's hard to tell how much time was spent in the dark in the trunk. You wouldn't want to think that an unexpected, unlikely, seemingly impossible event like the kidnapping that happened to him could be the curative factor to make a difference that those eight therapy sessions had apparently failed to accomplish.

He had come to therapy with some angry red patches of psoriasis right on the top of his balding head. They really embarrassed him and symbolized a whole set of issues that he felt helpless to control. But he hadn't even thought about how you would deal with the kind of situation he found himself squarely in the middle of. You know how you always think that those kind of things only happen to somebody else. It is never going to happen to you. But afterwards, he was kind of thankful that the kidnappers decided on him that day.

Well, maybe those eight therapy sessions did in some way help him organize his abilities in a way that predisposed him to deal with that horrible situation which he just couldn't even believe was happening. But there he was, on his way to his ninth therapy session. We never even knew why he didn't show up. We were surprised because he had always come to his appointments in an exactly punctual way, if not two minutes early.

It was just a coincidence that he was there with the automobile that they needed. The window was down. The knife came in against his neck and they said, "Scoot over, Buddy." This he did. They had secured his hands and legs and eventually put him in the trunk. And he was not aware where he was headed. They had gagged and blindfolded him. He couldn't see. He could barely move. In a situation like that, you are aware of every little movement and bump, much more than you normally would be. So distance gets distorted. He was aware of so many feelings he couldn't even label one of them.

He says he thinks he went into a trance. And in the trance he felt a sense of comfort while some of the anxiety slipped away. And that is why he thinks that he was in trance because it is a context in which you ought not feel anxiety. He didn't even know if he was conscious. And yet maybe he was totally conscious in a trance or perhaps he was unconscious in a dream. And he mentioned having a distinct image of something about being on playgrounds as a child and silly little games that children had played where you just equip yourself with all the energy that you have available and throw yourself against the arms that are linked together to restrain you. And the arms are holding very tightly together, so sometimes you have to throw yourself again and again at those arms.

Paul was a little shy when he came to therapy but he had learned something that we had spoken about again and again. You go into trance and have that sense of dissociation in the body. And you're feeling yourself breathe and you recognize that alteration as a normal need to respond. And he started to kick around, kick into that trunk, responding naturally even without knowing what he could accomplish. And what does therapy do but allow you to retrieve something that you've already known for a long time. You learned it long ago.

So he kicked and scraped and bashed and finally something sharp caught the edge of one of the ropes and he used that as a kind of a fulcrum, to pull and saw against until one of the ropes broke free. And his legs were free. He doesn't know if it is possible to do it but he did push and kick against the back of that trunk until it flipped open.

Then he untied himself and got recombobulated and he turned the lights on. The people who had put him in that car had apparently driven off in another car, somewhere in the direction that he had originally been headed. In a matter of moments, he got behind the wheel and he laid his foot down on that gas pedal. He left a little patch of rubber as his car started to lunge ahead. He had overcome the first physical obstacle represented by that trunk and the gags and the rope but he had far more to pit himself against.

He could feel his fist tightening as he drove that car, gripping the steering wheel and making a fist. He was saying things in his head that he never said to people before, being a timid guy. He was saying vulgarities about the people and he recognized consciously that it was very odd that he was behaving this way because that wasn't like him. His unconscious was racing down a road chasing after those people. He was thinking how many times there had been things he had wanted to say when he had kept quiet. And he was realizing he was going to be telling us that he had learned more in that trunk than he had gotten out of eight sessions of therapy. He wasn't quite sure what it was. It was an ongoing learning.

He was gritting his teeth, gripping the wheel, head leaning forward. His shoulders were held high and he was breathing a full lung full of air with each breath. He was thinking and talking out loud. He was saying, "I'm going to get you guys if it's the last thing that I do. I'm going to see you behind bars. You're not going to get away with this." And he just chanted it over and over, listening to the sound of his voice coming out of his throat. He could feel his voice coming out of his throat. It sounded different, felt different. There was a power in the sounds that he was making.

There was a tension in his forehead, a certain furrow to it, a rhythm to his breathing. And his conscious mind said, "This just isn't like me," but his unconscious was feeling the surface of his skin, the pounding of that heart, the heaviness of that chest heaving up and down. And, as he drove the car straight forward, there was a stern look on his face, a firm set of his eyebrows and his jaw.

And, incidentally, when he came back to therapy and explained the incredible story that at first we didn't believe, he said, "I'm telling you that I learned more in the trunk of that car about what I had to change than I did in all those therapy sessions, except for the fact," he added, "that I was in a trance in the trunk."

9. *Affect goal:* *Anger, power*

Metaphor

Larry had been at work one day, and when he and his wife came home they found the house ransacked and everything that was portable had been stolen. He called the police and the police could do very little about it. And he started wondering how he was going to recover . . . all of his things. The blow to a person's self-esteem is worse than the loss of goods when your house has been invaded. And somehow Larry happened to ask one of the next-door neighbors if they had seen anything. Some teenagers had been playing around a garage.

He checked out the garage and it was locked but the person who owned the garage hadn't locked it. A couple of days later he got the idea that maybe he should tell the police to stake out that locked garage. It wasn't the kind of thing that Larry was likely to get involved in. He tended to be kind of a stuffy guy who liked to smoke a pipe.

But when the police saw one of the boys sneak into the garage he stopped the boy and asked him how he happened to have a key. That led to the boy starting to run and Larry started running after that boy. Finally, Larry tackled him, and the kid, crying, told him the names of four of his friends. The policeman rustled up the friends and brought them to Larry's house in a squad car and standing outside of the house they all confessed. They were the ones who robbed Larry's house. And Larry was standing there while these kids were on their stomachs on the ground by the squad car. One of them turned around and looked Larry in the eye and said, "I'm going to get you, you son of a bitch."

Larry said his conscious mind did a little alteration and he realized that he had an experience unconsciously that he didn't know he had. As he looked back at that kid on the ground, looking him straight in the eye, he didn't have any fear at all. He just felt real solid standing there looking straight at that kid. His conscious mind commented, "I am not afraid of that kid. I can't believe it. I would have thought I would be intimidated by him. But he's the one who is laying on the ground and I'm the one who is standing up." It gave him a lot of satisfaction to see those kids get adjudicated and go to jail. And of course he got all of his goods back.

You can memorize that kind of feeling of satisfaction even though your conscious mind may not comprehend fully how you're able to have it or what you would do with it. Both feet flat on the ground, you have a firm sense of balance. Lips are pressed firmly together. The eyes are fixed and the muscles surrounding them are tensed but not tight. There is a heightened awareness of your skin and a keen awareness of breathing in and out from your nose in rhythm with the rise and fall of the chest. But your unconscious can store feelings that way or even the beginning of a feeling and you can add to it later in an appropriate context.

10. *Affect goal:* Anger

Metaphor

Pete worked as a dishwasher and was a classical guitar player. He had studied with Breem and Segovia and was a genuinely sensitive and accomplished musician. For a while he drove a '72 Mazda that had a bumper sticker reading " 'Handel' with care, classical guitar player inside." After a while, he didn't think he needed that car anymore. When you change your car, you change a lot of things about yourself.

When he came home from work one day, he found the door unlocked. He was temporarily surprised and angry at himself for not locking it. Fumbling for his keys, he fell into the door and hardly gave a second thought as to why he hadn't locked it. But looking around he saw the room was a mess. He was sort of struggling to have understanding of his thoughts.

When he saw the room in disarray he thought how messy he was not to clean the room better. It says something about you when you keep your room in a mess. But then he saw shirts out on the couch and the situation changed. It occurred to Pete that he hadn't put his shirts on the couch, he wouldn't have pulled them all out—he must have been robbed.

Now for anyone who knew Pete, they would agree that there was one thing that came through loud and clear about him and that was his dependency on that guitar. He loved it. He would even fall asleep with it. He had slept with it once or twice and was teased by his friends. He caressed it gently and carefully like he was making love to it with his fingers. And he would spend hours a day dealing with it rather than another person. In fact he got so good he could use his guitar as a date. Maybe it was like Linus and his blanket and you know how fretful Linus gets if someone has taken his blanket. It doesn't begin to compare with the feelings Pete was about to feel when he realized that he was being robbed. He thought he had been robbed—and then he realized he *was being* robbed. He heard noise in the back room and the apartment should have been empty.

And you know how your mind can change when you're in an auto accident, for example. You can remember every incident of that 10-second auto crash as though it had happened over a period of 20 minutes. You remember every change of posture, every movement of a pedestrian, every inch that the cars began to approach each other, everything you did to fasten a seatbelt or close a glove compartment or move something off of your lap. It must have been that sense of heightened remembering Pete was having because he could explain every minute detail that went down that day.

It must have happened in a half of a second, but it seemed like an hour. The next thing he realized was a feeling in his legs and he felt his feet carry him across the threshold, hand on doorknob, shoulders relaxed on ribcage, which seemed odd to him. He could feel the blood flow through his arms and the adrenalin. But he felt somehow removed from it in a way that was surprising. He felt the momentum of his body open the door in a very aggressive fashion. But he didn't have any thoughts about it except that he hadn't felt that way so easily and he didn't think it would have been so easy and yet it seemed to be easier than he would have thought.

In great detail he explained how he was running into the bedroom where his guitar was and what he was hollering. He heard words pouring out of his mouth that he didn't usually say. Then he saw the man jump out the window with his guitar in hand. Then Pete dived out the window. His conscious mind was realizing he was doing something you don't normally do. Your conscious mind can be an observer of an event that your body is doing. Everyone's had the experience of hollering automatically when someone steps on your toe.

You don't really realize what you are saying until you hear what you said.

And before that moment had passed, he had both his tennis shoes on the grass outside his bedroom window and was racing across the parking lot. He felt weightless as his feet carried him across the grass. He was surprised consciously to realize you can have a feeling that seems alien to you but have it comfortably when you might have thought you couldn't. He thought feelings had to be heavy, especially this one.

And moving more rapidly than the man who was running, he passed the man who dropped the guitar and it hit the ground with a bong. The strings began resonating. They did so for a good 20 seconds and before they stopped he remembered deciding he was going to keep track of how long they resonated because it was something that he always did automatically. Finally, he grabbed the thief by the shoulders and pushed him up against the back of that '72 Mazda, and bent him over—somewhat backwards—against the back of the hatchback.

I don't know where you first feel your sense of muscular power when you push someone's shoulders against the door and realize that you have actually aggressed against another person. Maybe you feel your feet firmly on the ground. Maybe you feel a little taller than usual. Maybe you recognize that your breathing is easy and more rapid than usual and your skin is warm. And Pete stood there, pulled his fist back, and held it chin level to himself and heard himself saying, "I'm going to hit you in the mouth, you son of a bitch." These were words he had never heard come out of his mouth before.

He was about to hit the man, but then turned him around and, putting his arms behind his back, wrestled him to the ground and held him there. There was a commotion. There was still a ringing in the background. Those guitar strings were still resonating from the topple and bong they had received.

Other people responding to the brawl in the parking lot had caught the attention of a passing patrol car and soon the police descended on the thief. As Pete walked away from the episode, he realized the guitar strings had still been faintly resonating while he held the man on the ground. He knew he could depend on the base notes resonating for about 17 seconds. The entire incident had taken just over 20 seconds from when he went out the back window to having wrestled the man to the ground.

Heart pounding, shoulders and sternum held high, jaw set firmly, feeling the blood pushing through his neck, Pete would have expected that being angry would have been far more uncomfortable. He never thought of himself in any other way than "classical guitar player, handle with care." It's a learning. Your unconscious knows a good deal of experience and can put it together no matter what your conscious mind thinks. Pete memorized that experience of anger, the impulse, the understanding that the unconscious intent is to have that impulse to be aggressive for your needs and memorize the recognition of not going beyond the bounds of reason, even when you had the chance and it would have been justifiable.

11. Affect goal: *Love, belonging*

Metaphor

Jane had developed a very good friendship with her girlfriend. They flew kites together, they made sailboats, they jumped rope, they collected pretty stones that they would wash off and put in boxes. And they knew, they absolutely knew, that they'd never be carrying briefcases with credit cards in them down the streets, and they just hated people like that. Those people didn't have any fun at all, they thought. But then again, they were only children.

One of the things they liked to do involved bending over the bottom of nails. They would take a bottle of nails in a sack up into the limbs of a tree and they'd haul some boards up there, maybe use a rope, and then they would start pounding those nails into the boards to hold them together on the tree limbs. And the part that they liked the best was bending those nails over at the bottom when they were done so those boards wouldn't come out, making a nice comfortable, safe, little tree house. They would swing from the ropes on cloudy days and on sunny days. And every day Jane's friend would be there. It was just like God had supplied them with one another over the summer vacation.

And then they understood that school was going to start. Jane thought that she was going to lose her friend. And with two little feet under her desk, inside two little shoes with two little pennies, Jane sat and looked around the classroom only to discover that her friend was seated right beside her, and at recess they were able to play with each other, and after school they could do their homework together. And it continued for some time.

Then one night she was hoping that the telephone call would come to invite her to go to the ninth grade dance, but no little boy called.

Finally, the phone did ring and it was Jane's friend. She wanted to go to the ninth grade dance too, so they went together. And a lot of girls went with other girls, and a lot of boys went with other boys. Finally, Jane's family moved away and Jane went to other high schools, but she never forgot that special friend.

Some time after that, things were really looking their worst for Jane. She didn't know if she would ever graduate because she was having a heck of a time passing even her driver's education class. She wasn't yet aware, of course, of the fact that she was going to grow up and walk down some street with a briefcase and credit cards, because she didn't even know if she would graduate. She walked dismally to the mailbox and opened it up. To her surprise there was a letter from her special friend. It was just enough to give her strength to continue yet another attempt to study those insurance policies and write an adequate report for Driver's Ed.

Time passed and she did graduate! She went to Disney World after graduation and before college. She was working there because it seemed like a nice place and a lot of activity and a lot of friendly people, including the biggest friend of all—Mickey Mouse. And when she checked into the underground dormitories where the people lived, how surprised do you think that she was to find out that her best friend of long ago was also living in the dormitory, also working at Disney World? They had a second childhood together. It was "such a hoot" to work together at Disney World, she said. And having matured more she wasn't really that sad when they went off in separate directions. And although she wished that she had discussed her plans for college with her friend, it totally slipped her mind.

Michigan State University is a long way away from Disney World in Orlando, and Justin Hall is a very big dormitory. And it is only half way across the campus from Bessey Hall but it is a long way across the campus from Acres Hall. And so it took three or four weeks on campus before Jane found out while she was staying in Justin that her best friend was staying in Acres Hall. Walking down the sidewalk that day across Bessey Hall bridge leading to the American literature class, it seemed like everybody she saw looked like someone from her past. And that guy over there looked like somebody she knew. That guy looked like somebody she wished she knew from her high school. And that guy looked like somebody from her home town. And that guy looked liked somebody from Disney World, so did that girl.

In fact, that girl looked just like her best friend! And so she convinced herself that it wasn't her best friend and kept on walking. From down the bridge she didn't know that the girl with the little ponytail who was walking towards her was having the same thoughts, and was unable to shake the thought. And that little shaking ponytail sure shook like her best friend's ponytail. She thought, "Isn't it funny that you keep seeing things that aren't when you feel lonely?"

And when they were only three feet apart she realized that it *was* her best friend! And they ran towards each other and they embraced, giving out the loudest giggle of glee that Bessey Hall has ever had. As they hugged each other, tears of joy ran down their cheeks. Neither one of them could finish the sentence about how they were so happy that they had ended up at Michigan State and they hadn't even talked to each other. They couldn't believe that they were really enrolled here and how much fun it was to find a friend.

And they just hugged on that bridge for more minutes than you should if you want to get to class on time. Signs of strain went out of their lips and foreheads, and they just closed their eyes and touched each other and patted each other's back. Sometimes they laughed. Jane's mouth was slightly turned up at the corner. Her skin was pink, muscle tonus had returned to her cheeks, a certain glitter returned to her eyes. You never know how your conscious mind is going to be surprised with the feeling of joy, a little wetness around the eyes, and they weren't embarrassed at all. They were happy they knew out loud how they cared for each other, they had lumps in their throats, they realized how fate had brought them together again. What a precious feeling to memorize and to know that you have with you forever. And Jane was probably thinking that that feeling would be there for ever . . . and now she knew she'd never have to give up that feeling. There was no way she could do anything but remember this moment and that feeling inside. Nobody had to tell her that that was the feeling of love, of being loved, and of the fun of loving.

I think that the conscious mind never even cared, and it was the unconscious feeling of warmth, openness, and acceptance—breathing a little more deeply, standing a little taller, shoulders relaxed from the tension that the conscious mind never even knew it had. Expanding the rib cage while realizing that the tongue is relaxed. She didn't know that the job she had to do was to memorize that feeling. People don't know how you memorize something, how you find it in your chest, or your neck, your face, or if it's an idea, a picture in your mind. Now let that feeling radiate until all parts of your body know it. You earned it and you deserve it. Jane thought her job was just to get to lit class before she was too late to get the lesson for the day. They exchanged phone numbers and ran off, but that wouldn't be the end of it. She would hold onto that feeling.

12. Affect goal: Relief

Metaphor

Carl is a friend of ours in Australia who is a diving enthusiast. His wife helped arrange a long-anticipated diving holiday for the four of us. The date and the destination had been set. We were going to Heron Island on the southern tip of the Great Barrier Reef and it promised to be a great adventure. We were very excited about this dive, having been looking forward to it forever. It almost didn't matter that we did not want to dive with Carl's wife. She was not what you would call a stable personality, and 75 feet under water, in a coral cave, you want to have a dive buddy that you can depend on to be responsible. We knew we couldn't depend on her, she was very difficult to be around in every situation we had encountered her. And we could easily discern the lines of stress and tension etched on Carl's face from years of working to save that unlikely marriage.

But with her it was just one delusion, irrational attack, psychosomatic illness, and withdrawn depression after another. He wasn't making any headway and the burden of having to take care of her and put his own needs aside was taking a toll on him. It took a toll on us during the short periods we interacted with her at relatively superficial levels. I don't know anyone who liked her at all. Maybe no one did.

And it's not that we didn't grieve about her suicide when we found out about that only two months before the scheduled dive date. But we certainly weren't sorry not to wind up underwater with her. And we had to admit to ourselves when we were being most honest that it was going to be a lot more enjoyable just diving with Carl than it would have been diving with the two of them. And you might understand the issue that Carl was grappling and struggling with, because when we got there his greatest difficulty was feeling guilty over that exceedingly intense feeling of relief that he had. He knew he shouldn't feel relief that his wife was dead, but he did feel that relief.

And so on the one hand, your unconscious provides you a sense of relief, comfortable relief, and it spreads throughout your body and you understand it in every pore. But your conscious mind, in monitoring, evaluating, criticizing, has its own idea of the appropriateness of that response, and so you're torn. And because of that we had to take some time aside to help Carl say a thoughtful goodbye, so that he could feel comfortable both consciously and unconsciously.

And it was interesting to watch the transformation take place as he breathed in and memorized an uncompromised feeling of pure relief. Each breath was inhaled slowly and deeply with eyes loosely closed or rolled upward, head waving just a bit. There was a slight smile that rested gently on his lips, and he just couldn't seem to take enough of those deep, relaxed breaths. The muscles were relaxed and the skin color was just comfortably pink. When you're able to say goodbye to that stimulus that had caused so much stress and anxiety, it is a pleasure to know you're not going to have to deal with that ever again. But you can take the feeling of relief and memorize it throughout your entire body to be used again and again wherever you choose. And Carl's oxygen supply lasted longer than anyone else's on each dive. I guess it was that smooth, slow inhaling that allowed him such an oxygen-efficient dive.

13. *Affect goal:* Mastery

Metaphor

Marie Curle had dreamed about scuba diving the Great Barrier Reef ever since she was a little girl and saw those stunning underwater photos in the *National Geographic* magazine. She had a little fear of the water, however, as a little girl learning to swim, and it didn't entirely go away even when she was a grown woman and had learned to swim. She moved to Florida and selected an apartment as close to the ocean as she could find and felt a strong attraction to the edge zone where the ocean met the land. It's often important for a person to put yourself in a position to confront that which you've feared. And it wasn't long before she decided to join a scuba class and go for her certification. It would be a first step towards that childhood dream and allow her to come to terms with this fear of the water thing.

But standing on the edge of the deep end of the pool, holding all that equipment while the instructor treaded water and signaled her that it was her turn now to jump in and pass the test of keeping up with and getting into all that gear while sitting on the bottom of the pool. She didn't want to do that more than anything she never wanted to do. But sometimes you just have to jump right into the heart of a situation even when your conscious mind has that doubt or fear. You trust that your unconscious will respond appropriately and so she just took a deep breath, closed her eyes and jumped.

She got the regulator immediately into her mouth, opened the valve, and breathing comfortably as she settled herself on the bottom, systematically went about the tasks of clearing her mask and attaching it to her head. After that, breathing even more comfortably and relaxing now, she was able to take her time and easily slip the tank over her back and put her fins and other equipment in place. And even her conscious mind was happy now, thinking, "If I can survive this, I can survive anything. After all, how many times am I going to have to jump in the water without putting my gear on first?" And even though she just took her time and took things one at a time, she came up in record time.

Pretty soon Marie was a card-carrying certified scuba diver but it would still be many years before the original dream came totally true; but there was no denying she was on her way. And she still had a healthy respect for the water but the fear had been conquered and a feeling of confidence had been developed. But Australia was still all the way on the other side of the world and she really couldn't figure out how she would ever afford to see the sights it had to offer. That's because the conscious mind is limited in its ability to see into the future and she didn't fully appreciate her unconscious ability to move towards that which you've set your mind to accomplish. But even without full conscious awareness, she systematically maneuvered herself into a position that eventually resulted in her going to work in Australia to consult on the use and the operation of certain automation equipment she used at her office.

I probably don't even need to tell you that the consulting job was unequivocally secondary to the dive vacation she planned for the time following her presentations. And she still couldn't quite believe it, even while breathing the mixture of fresh air and gasoline fumes as the dive boat motored out to her first dive spot on the inner side of the reef just off Carnes. Then, it was time. She was in her gear and as she rolled backward off the boat, she fell headlong into the *National Geographic* dream come true that little girl had wished for so long ago. It was just like the pictures, with vibrant living reefs, colorful fish, astonishing drop-offs, crystal clear water, and the comfortable feeling of weightlessness, just floating deeper with each breath. And you might have guessed that she brought along some underwater photography equipment she had rented. Sometimes it's important to move into your pictures personally.

She took a lot of pictures of sea fans. She couldn't explain why they so fascinated her. Maybe it was the waving movement or the way they were so firmly rooted in a way you might not expect. They formed a bit of a paradox, so fragile in appearance, so flexible, and yet so strong and tenacious. She felt a little like the fans, waving there.

And I don't know if she consciously took the time or made the effort to memorize the sensation of proficiency that this experience, in its culmination, had allowed her to feel, or if you just consciously enjoy the nuances of that feeling and let your unconscious automatically go about the process of storing it up and memorizing it to be used again in what might appear to be an unrelated circumstance. You can even pretend a feeling and memorize it. Or you can pretend something as a child and master it.

I knew a two-year-old little boy once who was presented with his first three-piece dress suit, just like the ones his father wore. He stood there proudly in front of the mirror, looking at his reflection, and then said, "Now, I can teach at the university." Because he had memorized the feeling of command that was symbolized by his new suit.

Well, Marie had memorized every nuance of that wet suit that fit just like skin and kept a nice layer of warm water surrounding every inch of her body. And even when she traveled back from Australia in dry clothes, she traveled with a new sense of warmth and competence and real mastery.

When I met her several years later, she hadn't thought much about that feeling consciously. In fact she was involved with a very difficult project and initially feeling somewhat anxious about her ability to master it. So, I asked her to put those worries aside for a moment and relax a little first, come out into the back yard and sit by the pool a while, by the deep end of the pool. You can probably guess that looking into the water brought back some unexpected associations. And sitting there, she breathed comfortably, set her lips in a pleased, firm line, not really smiling but almost, just remembering how you can pretend anything and master it, and how good that mastery feels. It's something that can pervade all of your experience and surround you with a warmth just like a wet suit does, using your own warmth and multiplying it.

*14. **Affect goal:** Satisfaction, comfort, relief*

Metaphor[5]

Karen was in the high school band. She played trombone. And as you're sitting there feeling your hand resting on your lap, maybe your unconscious makes some interpretations about a secret understanding. And she had worked exceedingly hard practicing her trombone solo that she was going to do the night of the concert. Everybody knows what it's like to work hard and people wonder what it would take to give a good performance. And each night as Karen practiced, she thought more and more about her big moment, as people will when they are appearing in front of a group. She thought about what it would be like for her to solo in front of the entire high school auditorium. She began to wonder about some of the things that might go wrong. She knew her instrument was well prepared, well oiled. Everybody knows what it's like to be well prepared and well oiled. But people wonder whether what they've planned in the future will come out well.

And your conscious mind may plan while your unconscious mind wonders or maybe your unconscious mind can plan while your unconscious mind wonders. We all know that things do turn out, sometimes successfully and sometimes even more successfully than we had planned.

The night of the big performance, Karen was backstage. She wondered what it would be like to be out there. As she looked around the room, she saw all the band members carrying their instruments and tuning up. I guess we all know what it's like to tune up and prepare for something. A little bit later on Karen walked out and took her seat with the rest of the band and they played the first two numbers. Little did Karen know that later in the evening, this concert would be remembered as "the concert of the missing note," and how this would make a dramatic turn for her.

As Karen played the first song with the band, she started again to think about her solo a little later. Then, at the end of the second song she heard the audience applaud and wondered if they would be applauding for her after her solo. Still wondering and not knowing why this would be called the concert of the missing note.

After the fifth song, Karen stood from her chair and approached the center stage. With eyes placed intently on the conductor, she waited

[5] This metaphor was contributed by Nicholas G. Seferlis, M.S.

for the band to start. As she looked out over the audience, the conductor's arms raised. Everyone knows what it's like to be prepared and getting ready to do the thing you've practiced many weeks for. Dramatically, the conductor's arms dropped, the band started up. Karen started counting her measures . . . 1, 2, 3, 4, 1, 2, 3, 4, . . . and all of a sudden she noticed that she had missed where she was supposed to come in. But immediately, she blew the note for the next beat and gave a sterling performance. At the end of the song, she looked out over the audience and saw all of her friends gazing, parents applauding. She had a feeling of satisfaction and relief. Everyone knows what it's like to feel relief when something is over. She also had a sense of comfort about doing a good job.

She was probably the only one who knew that this would be called "the concert of the missing note." And she felt more and more satisfied and relieved as the concert ended and she walked out. She sat down in the band room and just gazed for a moment into the bell of her trombone, surprised at the unexpected reflection that caught her eye.

There was her face reflecting relief and satisfaction. Of course, it was a little bent and distorted in the shape of the trombone, but the face undeniably reflected something about that satisfaction. There were the little turned-up corners on both sides of her lips and the rest of her face was quite relaxed. Even her forehead was exceptionally smooth. Her jaw was relaxed. And she looked, gazing deeply, and noticed her breathing in and out, aware of the chair, of the comfort. And you can be pleased to discover how nice it is when you feel a relief and happiness with your conscious and your unconscious mind.

15. *Affect goal:* Trust, security

Metaphor

The ringing of bells is interesting. In traveling I meet other people in hotels and trains and on airplanes and they have some interesting ideas. One of the men I met says he learned something from a television ad for Bell Telephone. He carries an audiotape with him of his children talking, laughing, of his wife, of his parents. "It's to ring a bell," he said. Does that ring a bell? I carry pictures. He carried an audiotape. It was most curious.

I said, "Why do you carry an audiotape? It is much more convenient to carry pictures. Nobody wants to listen to someone else's family!

They'd rather look at the pictures." And he said, "It's not for other people. You don't think you carry your pictures for other people do you?" And he was right about that. Nobody carries those pictures for other people. Most people have pictures in their wallet of somebody and they never show anyone. And what's your unconscious wanting to gain by carrying pictures in your wallet? Maybe it's the same thing that man wants to gain by carrying the sound.

"It's just like that Bell Telephone commercial," he said. "What do you mean?" He said, "You remember that one with the young girl who's having a terrible day and when the telephone rings, the father answers on the other end. And even though she's having a miserable day, she almost manages to smile when she hears his voice. And the father says, "How are you doing, sweetheart?" And she says, "Oh, Daddy." And you can tell the smile has gone a little deeper inside and touched something.

Everyone has had the experience, that same sort of contact with someone, somewhere. I doubt that a conscious mind is able to be as clear about some of this as an unconscious mind can be. But who can remember what is in the unconscious mind. You may have an actual memory of maybe it is a vague image or maybe just a sense—it could be an intuition of that sort of conversation—maybe it is entirely different than that.

Then the father in the commercial said, "Do you remember when you used to practice ballet?" And something else was touched inside as she gave some kind of affirmative sound. He told her to do a pirouette now and she says, "Oh, Daddy." He says, "Come on," and something else is tugged at inside until finally in the television commercial she does a little pirouette and then the father says, "Remember how you used to hug yourself afterwards?" And she says "Oh, Daddy" again and he says, "Come on. Do it." And something else is tugged at as she hugs herself. While she's hugging herself, you realize what's occurred here.

And the man on the airplane said, "That's why I carry the audiotape, the same reason you carry the pictures. Don't you look at them on long trips? Set them up in hotel rooms when you're gone for five days, call your family every day?" That's your way of knowing that everything's okay. And that gives you a certain kind of feeling to know they're right there when you need them. That's why the commercial demonstrates how close that father is even when that little girl thought he was a long way away. She wasn't alone really.

And in the process of listening it didn't ring a bell but I remembered my little boy growing up. I've noticed the same thing occurs. He may fall asleep on the couch with his head on my lap and I carry him into his bed and put him down or maybe he's gone to bed and I'm up working on other things and he comes slipping out to find me, crawls up underneath my arms and says, "Hold me, Dad, okay? Just for a minute." So I hold him and I say, "Would you like me to hold you while you fall asleep again?" He says, "Yea, just stay with me." And when he falls asleep I carry him back to his bed and put him there, and if he should ever wake up with a bad dream he calls out or comes running into my room knowing I'm going to reach out, touch his wrist, hold him, and when he falls asleep I'm going to take him back to his bed again. He doesn't know it but under circumstances like that your unconscious is gaining a learning, a learning that's the same as that woman will have when she's having a bad day and she knows her father will call. And even if he doesn't call she will remember doing the pirouettes, hugging herself, hearing her father's voice.

And that's why the man carries the audiotape on the airplane so that he can hear that father's voice, hear his wife's voice, hear his children's laugh. He never used the word but the unconscious knows the feeling and usually we turn those things on in our own head unconsciously before we take a step. That's the way you learn to ride a bicycle when a parent has been holding the back of the bicycle, letting you balance without training wheels, running down the street, sidewalk, driveway behind you, holding the bike up. And you know when you turn around and when you lose your balance, the parents are going to be right there, holding that bike up, until you finally gain a certain sense of balance in your body and a certain feeling in your heart that your conscious mind as a child doesn't know you're learning, but every child learns it. And one day you turn around to tell your parents, "I did it," and they're not there. They let go of the bicycle and you pedaled on your own and still have that same feeling inside just like they're right there holding on.

And then in order to reinforce your awareness and ability to turn that feeling on whenever you want it, you carry pictures with you and you look at the picture and have that feeling. He just listens to audiotapes. And you can see the softness in his lips, softness in his chin, the warmth in his face, relaxation in muscle tonus in his forehead, the ease of breathing, almost a breathing into the shoulders sort of relaxation. It gives the heart a certain lightness. And I know that every child will learn that feeling. It's the kind of thing that we use in a deliberate, directed fashion in various places in our adult life. Sometimes your conscious mind knows to use it and other times has to be helped, to be told to use it. But once a child learns that something is useful, you can depend upon the child doing it again.

And when I looked at the man, why do you think it rang a bell? What do you think was the experience I saw on his face? It was the same as on the woman's face. The lips are a little parted, breathing is slow and rhythmical, the chin is soft, there's relaxation between the eyebrows, the quivering of the chin illustrates that there's been a little tug at the heart. What seemed like so far away was really so close all along. And there's a little warmth in each cheek and a bit of a sigh of relief that reaches the shoulders. Now your conscious mind never really has a label for a feeling like that but the unconscious mind is having a feeling and you can tell it's a pleasant feeling. It rings a bell.

16. *Affect goal:* Joy, humor

Metaphor

"What did the scarf say to the hat?" That is what the postcard read when Jane picked it up in the mail. It was from Paula, her long-time friend. Jane didn't know what the question meant—it sounded like a joke. Maybe it was a reference to something they shared long ago. It made her think back to and sort through all those years. Your conscious mind often benefits from unconscious processes that you don't recognize, you don't need to recognize, like comparison, contrast, association, memory. The names of the processes are not important and you probably would not care or fully understand—but the unconscious, while performing these mental gymnastics, may benefit in a way that is quite important. The mind often prepares for future learnings and doesn't even realize it. This was such a time for Jane.

Jane thought of the classes they shared back in college. Maybe the question of the hat and scarf was a reference to something a professor had once said—no, it didn't seem so. Maybe it was one of the parties they went to—no, it didn't seem so. She remembered that time they went shopping, in fact there were a million times they went shopping. She couldn't think of the reference. But, boy, was she recalling some fine old times spent between friends.

The next day, Jane found herself still wondering about that card. She made a telephone call to Paula. Now everyone you ask will have the experience of pleasant telephone calls. And there is something that you can be certain about—you'll know what I mean. She didn't censor a thing. In a situation like that, your unconscious will be doing some more learning and rehearsing. Your blood flow increases as tenderness is conveyed, muscles relax, capillary size increases to carry more blood, oxidation increases. It feels good to breathe easily, and those are the physiological beginnings of the feeling of affection and happiness. They both found themselves entertaining concepts that are trickier, lighter, more subtle. They talked with each other about freedom, love, risk, politics, religion, things that you don't speak about under other circumstances as openly. They laughed.

Humor is possible because accelerated cortical activity allows you to change from one framework to another rapidly. When you laugh it is due to something cortically designed and it is the only cortically initiated behavior that has immediate muscle movement available in all primates. You can say something as simple to shift frameworks as, "What did the scarf say to the hat?" Paula asked Jane that again on the phone and before she ever heard the answer, Jane's brain had to shift frameworks. You can't help but have the blood oxidation, relaxation, and warmth expand into humorous response, even if it is a crummy joke. All they had to do was wonder about it and it was humorous, maybe even funnier than the punchline. Just to think that a scarf could talk to a hat in the first place is so absurd, only a thing you could bring up to friends, only to someone you knew and who would not think you were a total stiff would you tell them what the scarf said. Paula said, "Hey, I'll tell you that when you pick me up at the bus station this Friday."

There is an alteration that moves the face muscles ever so slightly, brings a smile to the corners of the mouth. Jane couldn't just say when she first began to feel that. It may have been when she first realized that her friend was coming to visit. It can last all week. Later, when you know that this is the day a friend is coming to visit, your conscious mind doesn't recognize how you initiate such pleasant feelings, just knowing that you are picking her up at the bus station.

When Jane saw her old friend, it was much like when as a child she had been overcome with a pack of happy puppies. Then Paula and Jane embraced. She felt the need to stand and stand tall, breathe more deeply, smile and lift the cheek muscles more. Maybe there is a noticeable change in the salivation response. And that's your conscious mind relying upon your unconscious to generate a lot of responses. There are smile lines around the eyes.

Some people are overcome by joy, or amusement. People can tolerate it enough to keep it around them like an aura. It's too bad there is not a photo of her face at that second. Her lips are more full and more red, the cheeks have increased in temperature, there is more salivation, a slight smile on your face, increased tonicity around your eyes and cheeks. Your unconscious knows something about having a sense of joy. It was apparent that the unconscious had been rehearsing that feeling of joy from the day she got the card. Paula said, "You go on ahead and I'll just hang around." Jane said, "You mean if I get the car you will wait for the luggage?" Jane said, "No, no. That is what the scarf said to the hat: 'You go on ahead and I'll just hang around.' "

3

Attitude Metaphors

They are able because they think they are able.
—Virgil

Believe that life is worth living, and your
beliefs will help create the fact.
—William James

Doubt is the beginning, not the end, of wisdom.
—George Iles

Attitudes are constantly filtering and organizing our experience of being in the world. Attitudes are ideo-sensory templates which reduce the incoming sensory data to a subset that is consistent with the ideas previously held. This makes a particularly problematic situation in that no disconfirming datum is available to the sensorium unless it is of such a high threshold of stimulation that it cannot be avoided. When individuals isolate themselves within a world that does not provide unusual or unexplainable examples of experience, they are not challenged. Attitudes are not particularly resistive to undergoing alterations but are unlikely to spontaneously change if left unchallenged. Common potential challenges to an attitude are not usually perceived, due to the filtering and framing aspect of the process of holding an attitude. However, a challenge to an attitude which becomes conscious is often perceived as some sort of threat to the ego and consequently calls defensive measures into play. We would tend to think that this is most true for those attitudes that have been held relatively longer. Therefore, changes in certain, long-held attitudes regarding the self and others do not often occur outside of therapy.

In therapy, it can be seen that there are usually several readily identifiable attitudes that seem to be instrumental in supporting or continuing the problem a client has presented for change. The attitudes may be beliefs that prevent clients from being motivated by experiencing certain emotions, behaving differently, applying different problem-solving routines, or otherwise acting in an ecologically sound manner. Since these attitudes are like self-fulfilling prophecies, clients repeatedly experience them as true. Attitudes define self-reinforcement contingencies and tend to exhibit characteristics of continuous reinforcement paradigms.

Usually there is a great deal of information available to "prove" that the attitudes are "true." That is, a depressed person may be able to demonstrate that "nobody cares." People who have been "hurt" will insist that "it does no good to show your feelings to others." "Strong" family members who avoid solving problems through dependency will be able to "prove" that "weakness will get you in trouble." And so it goes. These attitudes act as filters that gather evidence which, in turn, tautologically proves the premises on which the attitude is based. But since attitudes exhibit the characteristics of continuous reinforcement paradigms, they are especially prone to extinction, or perhaps more appropriately, to modification and change—providing that at least one contradictory example to the attitude can be noticed.

Often, then, clients are firmly entrenched in such beliefs and unlikely to relinquish them as a result of direct suggestion or rational evidence as to their shortcomings which may be presented to the conscious mind. Therefore, the indirect metaphor modality is a context that can allow a person to gently consider and think about a different belief that would support new relational patterns that would not adequately be addressed by the old.

The attitude change protocol, therefore, has a dual focus. One element of it is designed to match, encourage identification with, and then shed doubt on the existing attitude. The other element illustrates the corrected attitude, the therapeutic goal, and its consequences in action. The three basic steps of this protocol are very simple once the problematic attitude and goal attitude have been clearly defined. This can be summarized in the outline that follows.

Attitude restructuring protocol:
1. Examine the behaviors and attitude in question from the protagonist's perceptions.
2. Examine the opposite behaviors and attitude from the perspective of another protagonist or examine the same behavior from the perceptions of significant others.
3. Relate the consequence(s) of the behavior(s) to the perceptions held by both the protagonists and/or the observing others.

The first and second steps are interchangeable, of course. The storyline of the metaphor begins by introducing a protagonist and placing him or her in situations which will display behaviors consistent with either the goal or problematic attitude. Step two involves examining the opposite behaviors and attitude represented by a different protagonist (or perhaps by the same protagonist at a later time). Another variation at step two is simply to examine the behaviors and attitude of a single protagonist from the perceptions of significant others. In either variation, the story portrays the two characters as they act, each according to the dictates of their attitudes, in various revealing situations. These situations can be essentially the same for both protagonists or can be entirely different, depending upon the actual story. Step three involves relating the consequences of the behaviors and attitudes that have been characterized.

Our preferred version involves two protagonists, one characterizing the problematic attitude and one characterizing the goal attitude. To encourage the client's identification with the protagonist who characterizes the existing attitude, we recommend telling the story with a bias in favor of that protagonist. That is, the character who acts like the client acts is, at first, indicated to be "correct." He or she is represented as *apparently* "right" or having the most appropriate action for the situation he or she is in.

The second protagonist who characterizes the goal attitude is represented, by contrast, in some kind of negative frame as unlikely to succeed. That is, the opposing character(s) in the story, acting from an attitude *different from the client's attitude,* will be presented as *seemingly* acting in an inappropriate or self-defeating way. Then, in step three, an unexpected "switch" occurs when the consequences that occurred to both protagonists are revealed to the client. Suddenly, at the conclusion of the story, the "right" one with whom our client has been identifying suffers from some negative or less desirable payoff. Of course, the previously negatively biased protagonist acting out the "goal" attitude is rewarded with a positive consequence. The consequences that are chosen for the characters need to be of value to the listening client.

The conscious confusion engendered at this point creates a therapeutic sense of uncertainty that the rigidly held attitude is correct. As such, a receptivity is fostered for considering the goal attitude that has just been illustrated. On the one hand, the client's attitude proves to be inadequate for the purposes of predicting the outcome of the story. On the other hand, a more appropriate attitude and action will have been modeled as a replacement for the limiting attitude.

The following stories conform to this protocol with minor variations here and there which allow for added creativity. In each case the metaphor is preceded, not by a description of the case in which it appeared, but simply by a summary of the existing limiting attitude and the goal attitude. Once again, we want to remind readers that: (1) appropriate assessment and treatment planning is absolutely essential— a masterful story will be useless for therapy if it is irrelevant to the client's situation; (2) each attitude goal is meant to be accompanied by supporting emotion change goals (with affect protocols), behavior change goals (with behavior protocols), and so on; (3) the proper manner for metaphor delivery involves timing, speech intonation, pause, inflection, and the use of indirect suggestions to heighten personal involvement for the client, as well as continuous attention to the ideomotor feedback from the client and adjustment of treatment based on that feedback.

1. **Existing attitude:** *If I expose my inadequacies or ask for help, I will be humiliated, rejected, ridiculed, or looked down upon by others.*
   Goal attitude: *A request for help is not an inadequacy. I may often gain respect and admiration from others.*

Metaphor

"Scratching the surface" is a figure of speech that normally doesn't apply to deep sea diving, though there are certainly more wonders to behold than any one diver could hope to accomplish in a lifetime. And the fact that it's never the same twice further complicates matters. We had worked day and night for almost a week, three dives a day, scratching the surface of the sights Heron Island had to offer in its underwater sanctuary. Heron Island, according to promotional ads, is just "a drop in the ocean" and that is exactly accurate. It is only a tiny little atoll at the southern tip of the Great Barrier Reef in Australia, and yet the rest of the world may as well not even exist—they don't know you exist when you are immersed in its beauty. And that's just what we had been doing for almost a week that day when we met Tim and Max. They didn't know each other but it was the first time either one of them had been on that dive boat.

They had very little in common except that. It was to be Tim's first open water dive that day and he was justifiably nervous, but Max was a self-proclaimed expert on diving and had, in fact, dived throughout the entire expanse of the reef before stopping off at Heron Island. Tim had just passed his diver certification course in the postage-stamp-sized swimming pool on Heron Island the day before. There certainly hadn't been much to see in that pool but he wasn't at all sure he was ready for what he was going to see in the open water.

There isn't a lot of time to study the character of someone you meet in a circumstance like that because you tend to have your hands full with the hundred odds and ends you bring with you to make your dive more enjoyable. Before you do that, however, you have to store your gear somewhere, and then get it out, and eventually, put it on a few minutes later when the boat arrives at its destination. It's always the same.

But certain things stand out about people you meet. And with Max, it was the way he stalked on board with such unmitigated self-confidence. You really had to admire that in someone, especially in a context like that when he was about to go 70 feet under water in a completely novel situation. We still had our share of anticipation jitters as veteran divers of those new waters. That self-confidence he had drew your attention to his face. You nearly didn't let your attention wander to notice the rather incredible sight of a record amount of mercurochrome he had carefully painted on an uncountable number of scratches up and down his legs. But that's another story.

Tim was even more impressed with Max's confidence than we were. I suppose it was because he was so painfully aware of his own inadequacies and total lack of confidence, at least in, but probably not limited to, that situation. You could see that awe in his eyes as he later watched Max standing only inches from the dive guide's face and angrily demanding his rightful share of what he considered to be the inadequate supply of weights brought along for this dive. He had dived all over the world and wasn't about to be swayed by the guide's feeble attempts to inform him that in these waters less weight was required due to the higher salt content. He knew his rights and he wasn't going to let anyone tell him better. He shouted that he paid for a good dive and he would need 20 pounds of weight to have a good dive.

Tim seemed to envy Max's ability to be so sure of what he needed and so clear about how to get it. Tim wondered if everybody had to string their own weights on their weight belt. By the time he got around to getting the box of weights, he wasn't clear that there were going to be enough weights in there for a body his size. Fifteen divers in the boat. An odd number for the usual two buddy teams. Somebody's not going to have a buddy. And Max was still talking about how they should have put more weights on board because he knew he needed 20 pounds. Tim just pretended not to notice. Being his first dive since certification, he didn't want anyone to realize he was a novice.

Meanwhile, many of the divers who knew what a short trip it usually was from harbor to dive site had begun to pull their gear out of storage and put it on. Flippers were flopping everywhere. I put on my boots and my wetsuit, and I watched him carefully noticing whether I put my boots inside or outside my wetsuit. And then he put on his flippers, and he noticed no one had their flippers on, and he took his flippers off. And then he noticed many had put on their buoyancy vests and were checking the position of their shoulder straps, and taking them off, and tanks were being attached.

Everyone has felt the need to remain silent sometimes and survey the surroundings. Even if you couldn't just say when, everyone has had the experience of being out of place and figuring out what to do by watching—you don't want to admit that you don't know the rules of the game. That's the way it was for Tim. He couldn't decide whether the o-ring on his tank was to face towards or away from his buoyancy vest. And that made a difference regarding which way to put his regulator on the tank.

And you know how you will sometimes take your eyes off the person you think is in control—just to hide your true feelings. He watched me sometimes, always carefully, while Max simply gave instructions to everyone around him how he preferred to put his "octopus" around the bottom of the sleeve of his vest, rather than putting it over the top on the left. "Octopus" is a term that you don't know about unless you have two secondary regulators attached at the primary stage, in case one regulator goes bad, you use the other one. It's called an "octopus" rig and is a very popular device.

Eventually, slowly, Tim leaned over and asked me whether he had attached his primary stage correctly to the tank. And I can't really recall whether he had attached it correctly or not, and if he didn't, I corrected it and explained the reasons. And Tim's next problem occurred when everyone was suited up and putting their buoyancy vests back on with their tanks, and their masks had to be over their necks so they were easily available. And some people wore hoods and some didn't. You could tell that he wasn't sure whether he should have a hood on or not. He looked around at the side, he looked at us, and we didn't have hoods. With that he stopped looking around.

But unfortunately he could not resolve his dilemma—Max did have a hood. And something else that Max did was he took the snorkel out of his mask and attached it to the knife sheath that was on his leg. This was quite a problem for Tim because his certification instructors had stressed that the snorkel should always remain on the mask but he wondered if it wouldn't be a good idea to do exactly like this obviously experienced diver was doing.

Max had managed to get 20 pounds of weights out of the dive guide, because "he knew exactly what he needed to do for the dive and was clearly experienced." And it was probably pretty obvious that when everybody teamed up, Tim not only didn't know what to do on this dive, but he wasn't going to have any partner either. And again he turned to us and said, "Excuse me, I hate to ask you this, but it's my first dive in open water like this, and I don't understand why he's putting his snorkel on his knife sheath. I thought you were supposed to keep it on your mask." And you could tell that situation that everyone's had some time in their life, being the odd person on the team, and not knowing the rules of the game, and it's pretty dismal to think that everyone's going to know immediately that you don't know. And every single question you ask makes it a giveaway! I presume he had simply resigned himself to the fact that he'd already given it away and so he finally had asked the most ignorant question of all as far as he was concerned. And my answer was that I had no idea why he was putting his snorkel on his leg. I breathed with my nose which was much closer to my mouth. Now I thought maybe Max did it because it was possible that his brains were in his butt, and so perhaps he breathed in a different way as well. He said, "What do you mean? I don't understand. He seems like an experienced diver to me." I said, "The answer to the question is mercurochrome and bandages!"

We asked him to look at Max's legs and tell us what he saw. He said, "He's wearing a short wetsuit." "But what about where the skin's showing?" And now he probably really felt dumb because not only had Max proven his experience, here I was criticizing this experienced diver. And he said, "I don't know what you mean exactly about his legs." I just added, "Well, there's bound to be another question to which the answer is 'mercurochrome and bandages.' But don't worry about it, all in good time."

Just then, Tim's attention was drawn to the fact that some other divers were strapping their knives on at the calf of the right, and others of the left leg. He nervously surveyed the knife-strapping activities and hesitantly pulled his own new knife out of his bag. His head was full of a week's worth of facts, charts, and tables that had been crammed into his week-long course. He had passed all the tests but no amount of training can really prepare a person for the kind of unknown about to be encountered. He had been torn about whether to just go with what he knew or to make matters worse and reveal to everyone what an "idiot" he actually was.

But since he had already opted in favor of the "idiot" option with the snorkel questions, he reasoned, "Why not?" and then asked, "Is it better to put your knife on your right or left leg and should you put it on your calf or up here on your thigh where you could reach it if you need it?" We were glad to share what we knew and told him simply that it was a matter of individual preference whether it went on the left or the right leg, but that because of the bulk of the buoyancy vest and regulator hoses in front, he would find it difficult to get the knife out if it were placed on his thigh. Actually it was much more accessible on the calf. "And, uh, what exactly might you need your knife for—do you really need it?" he squeaked. We assured him that in our week of diving these waters, we had only used our knives to cut open anemones and thus attract the brightly colored fish to feed. We answered his remaining questions as sensibly and humorously as possible. But before very long, of course, it was time to make the final regulator adjustments, choose partners, and compete to see who could be the first overboard and therefore likely to see the first sights unspoiled by the multitude of divers to follow.

I invited Tim to "buddy up" with me and I would tell him after we were done the answer to the question he had asked about Max's legs. I also promised to show him how advantageous it was to follow the first guide. He didn't have time to object in any way; he didn't even have time to realize how stunned he was that someone actually wanted him along. If he had, he would have noticed how happy he was that someone had asked him to dive. He probably thought it would be a much better idea to dive with Max. He certainly wasn't yet able to appreciate our position. He couldn't have known what an asset it is to be 60 feet underwater with someone you know you can trust to be appropriately cautious and careful to ask the proper questions. It's a lot easier to handle dumb questions than it is to handle dumb mistakes in a situation like that! He never would have guessed that he would have been one of the first ones to roll backwards off that boat into the crystal clear open waters that day. But he was, and we had a real nice dive. First, he was amply rewarded with the sight of a lovely manta ray "flying" gracefully along only inches from us. It was so overwhelming, it completely distracted him from the orientation crisis he was expecting.

One by one, the other divers entered the peaceful waters. Max was "buddying" with one of the guides. He had finally succeeded in getting the amount of weight he demanded, at the cost of the other guide remaining on board the boat. Max was one of the last divers to enter the water, but made up for lost time by sinking rapidly once in the water. After all, he had very little choice with all those weights. The thrill of "neutral buoyancy" was something he had not yet learned to fully appreciate.

He didn't realize how you can just hang there weightlessly, as if suspended in time. He hadn't discovered how you can just drift with the current, moving slightly up or down at will with the kick of a fin and the slight alteration of your trunk. Tim was learning those things at one level of his experience but his consciousness was much more focused on the facility with which the *real* octopus we were following managed to change both color as well as texture, depending on the background he moved against. It's the kind of octopus you thought of at first. It changed colors just like a chameleon. And in order to get close to one, you have to be relaxed and you have to not panic. And we knew that he wasn't going to panic on that dive because he was a thoughtful diver who asked questions about everything that he didn't know. And not only do you have to swim without panicky movements in the water in order to get close to an octopus, you have to breathe comfortably so you don't frighten them away with your random breathing. And you can get fairly close to them. You can put your flipper right beside them before they'll shoot off to another coral location and change color.

Tim was a great companion because he had asked so many questions above the water, he knew when to follow my lead under the water and learn something new, rather than insisting on doing it his own way. And there were lots of other sights to marvel at and not nearly enough time. The allotted air for that dive was gone and it was time to return to the surface and share the memories.

As we circled one of the balmies one last time on the way up, we had time for one last sight, that of Max still entangled in the reef, breaking off pieces here and there as he kicked against the current, random breathing, random arm movements, bustling and fussing with his buoyancy vest. The dive guide was his companion. (I bet Tim thought being selected by the dive guide as a partner was a compliment—actually, dive guides do not want any deaths on their dive trips and so they swim with the most dangerous or foolish diver.) Max was apparently unable to comprehend the dive guide's input about the proper way to inflate the buoyancy vest and return safely to the boat. This was the result of having the 20 pounds he insisted upon. I guess he was more interested in making sure he added the proper number of new scratches to his collection. It would be a shame if he didn't collect his souvenirs since I'm sure he missed the octopus and other sights. Seeing him gave new meaning to the idea of "scratching the surface" in a deep sea diving context.

When we got back on the boat, we had arrived before Max. I thanked Tim for being my buddy on the dive and told him something he never expected to hear. I told him we had known right away he would be a good diver because he was cautious, and he asked questions, and he got the answer before he took action. He said, "You said after the dive you'd tell me why you said Max had his brains in his butt." "Yea, remember seeing Max on the coral, on his knees, with those legs that looked like Pearl Harbor? An obvious result of a diver diving with too much weight and getting his knees cut up just a little bit more here and there." And, by the way, the dive instructor "gave him hell" when they got back on the boat. I don't know what they were arguing about, but he told Max he didn't want to hear it again or he wouldn't be diving again on this island. And I still don't know why he put his snorkel in his knife sheath.

Tim, on the other hand, has dived all over the world since that memorable day. He is on his way to becoming a true expert. He sends us cards from time to time relating his latest adventure. The last one was from the Red Sea. He said it was true what Kahil Gibran said in describing it: "It is like eternity gazing at its reflection in a mirror." And that's a surface you wouldn't even want to scratch!

2. **Existing attitude:** *If I show my feelings, I will be wallowing in them. This is nonproductive and consistent with a loss of control.*
Goal attitude: *It is okay to express needs and emotions—it promotes mental health and genuine relationships.*

Metaphor

There are always people who, as children, act like my client Pat. It's like living life in a Cinderella fairytale on a larger scale. You work very hard and do the things you should do. You put your needs behind you a little bit. Maybe you conform to the desires of a wicked mother or stepmother who compares you unfavorably to the other children. Sometimes the parallel is remarkable. And you know somehow in the back of your mind that you have a fantasy that "happily ever after" is going to come. You'll meet the fairytale man who will be perfect in every way. And Pat almost did just that. She married a nice psychopath.

He seemed to be charming. And she thought, "If I put him through college we'll live happily ever after." And she worked and gained a little weight and he began criticizing her for becoming overweight. She thought she would lose a little weight and then he'll finally unfold and we'll live happily ever after.

Well, she never really thought in terms of happily ever after—and it never occurred to her that she had needs of her own. So she never thought about the importance of expressing her needs into demands. She never placed demands on her husband. It never occurred to her.

She just thought how nice it would be to lose that weight he wanted her to lose. Then it was the time to live with his parents for a while and then it became the time to build a new house and set up the home. Then it became "help him get a job." Then it became "relocate." Then, of course, it was "raising the children." Raising children is a nice way to learn to put *your* needs aside—because children have plenty of needs that take precedence. Finally, the children were teenagers and Pat didn't have much awareness yet that her fantasy was an inappropriate image for the real world.

And then, by contrast, the kind of person you think of when you see Tammy, who apparently cries at the drop of a hat and who, if she wants something, goes and buys it or goes and does it. If she doesn't get to do it, she gets distraught and lets her mascara run down her cheek. And she has a nervous breakdown because she didn't get to go shopping at the mall today. And Pat thought that if she was not selfless or if she stopped waiting for her man to be a prince she would fall to the "back of the line." And if she finally let her feelings out, she would be a sap like Tammy. Given the options, she would rather be a hardworking mature person who learns that you don't always get everything that you want. She didn't want to show her feelings and be an embarrassment like Tammy.

Except for the fantasy of the prince coming and of living happily ever after, her dream is a lot like the "Great American Dream." You work hard and save your money, pay your taxes and don't break any laws and work for the corporation for a certain number of years and retire on a nice pension. They give you a gold watch and you buy an all-terrain vehicle or motor home and move to Sun City or Fort Lauderdale. There you play golf and pursue other sports that interest you. And you have time to do the other things you had to put aside when you were working.

But that "Great American Dream" doesn't come true for many people and that Cinderella fantasy doesn't either. And despite the fact that Pat was an extremely intelligent, attractive, and deserving person, she had waited away the prime of her life before she finally came to therapy for a change. It took the divorce of her faithless husband to get her to begin to change.

At first Pat was disgusted with the thought of being associated with these people who often openly wept and who so freely admitted that they had problems. She felt that she had added insult to injury by being in therapy with these "crazy" people. But as time went on it became clear to her that some of these people were the unspoken leaders, not just of the group, but of the community.

The local television anchor woman came to see us each week and tried to get her sense of dissatisfaction expressed in tears or other types of emotional depth. Pat watched. At first, it was an alien world for Pat to think that someone might actually be respected or improved for showing tears and hurts. Finally, she decided that maybe she was right all along, and her opinion of that local television personality fell to an all-time low. She did not see that she liked or revered any of these people for their emotional outbursts and loss of control. But she continued to attend the therapy group, perhaps as someone continues to watch a television soap opera.

And, too, Pat had taken an interest in one of the single men in the group and the interest was probably still unconscious for her. Within the period of a month, Pat had a learning. She began to realize that the men in the group she found attractive were dating women who placed demands on them, who showed feelings, and who regularly spoke about their needs. The men preferred this. They felt closer to these women and they actually wanted to accommodate the women's needs in most every case. And these were men to whom she had been attracted! They didn't want mates who were stoic, women who had no needs or women who never showed feelings. They were closer to these other women. They felt the women helped pull something from within them that was desirable. They felt love. It was the same look on their faces, when these men described the women they liked, that she admired and that attracted her. That was the first learning.

But the decisive learning happened for Pat when the television anchor woman left the group. Only three weeks after Pat entered and witnessed this woman crying and, as far as Pat was concerned, falling apart, she said her goodbyes. She wept a few tears through her smiles as she told about her sense of completion. That was part of what surprised Pat. This woman had looked like a mental wreck to Pat. She cried, her mascara ran. She was full of dissatisfaction. But she and I thought she was ready to terminate the group and get on with her life. She certainly looked "together" on the local television station, too. And she held down a stressful job. And she dated a wonderful man. Maybe something was wrong with Pat's version of who was healthy and why.

And that is why she had her most decisive learning. The people in the group who acted as if they had no emotional reactions were the most in need of therapy. In retrospect it seems pretty obvious—it is not just black and white. You can be too effusive. But you can be too strong and hard, too. It is pretty easy for her to understand now. Now she cries when she feels hurt . . . if she is with her husband. And she laughs when she is happy and she tells her husband when she is lonely, anxious, or tender. And, perhaps more importantly, she is not alone anymore.

3. **Existing attitude:** *If I show my feelings I will cry forever and be miserable and no one will comfort me. If I want comfort, I'd better not show my feelings of sadness.*
Goal attitude: *If I show my emotions of sadness, I will be free and I can then experience joy and happiness.*

Metaphor

The quartz crystal, glass swan and deer were aligned as though they somehow belonged together. But how? You might ask a three-year-old how they are the same and how different. All are the same and all different. Two could be alike because they are sculpted into recognizable forms. Or all are alike because of their clarity. As an object of meditation, it is said that the crystal offers neither hardness nor suffering. It is a paradox. You can see through it and yet it's matter. It's visible and yet invisible. Which one is most like you? Which would you distance from? Which interests you? You probably guessed that there is a story attached to each. We've had two of them a long time and one is a newcomer to our ownership and yet has a long history of its own. There's a lot to explore in each object, each person's own history.

Sometimes the feeling of enjoyment is unexpectedly, paradoxically linked to other feelings of sadness that can be intensified into a profound feeling of grief at one moment and then translated all of a sudden without any rational reason whatever into uncontrollable emotional joy the next. Many authors have commented upon the similarity in bodily contortions caused by opposite emotions. A child can be frightened observing the parents having an abandoned sexual experience which looks much like pain and discomfort. So it's nice to know as an adult that you can follow any feeling to its root or cross over a neural bundle and follow an opposite feeling out to its end result.

I worked with a woman a month or so ago who, having been diagnosed as having a recurrence of cancer she thought to be in remission, wanted very much to have me help her use the healing abilities of her body and to apply her strength and power to that illness. And she had worked with us eight years ago about a cough and didn't even mention at that time that she had recently had a mastectomy. And though the cough disappeared in the trance and she felt relaxed afterwards, she commented when we spoke this year that she didn't really get the support from her husband she had wanted and so the therapeutic change hadn't lasted. So I knew that a good bit of focus on the marital relationship was in order. I expected that upon meeting her and having the opportunity to talk at length I would begin to hear about and understand the array of emotional reaction that must be accompanying such a frightening and difficult situation as the one caused by a potentially terminal illness. What stress that must put on a marriage and what did she really want from her husband? And I knew there would be a lot of feelings involved so I took along that little glass swan.

And at first I was surprised that there seemed to be no sign of grief or tears. Too, there was very little joy. In fact, I looked in every corner and behind every nook and into every cranny I could poke into and I couldn't find any evidence of any emotion anywhere. But I told her the story I had heard that was so interesting it literally captured my attention as I flipped through the channels on television one late night.

Maybe the reason I watched the show was that I saw a young woman frantically, desperately, somewhat cynically looking for a love relationship while not really believing there was going to be any such thing. She had really given up and settled into a chronic despair over the superficiality of it all. Her roommate would try to get her dates or excite her about some activity and it just seemed so superficial. She wasn't doing anything really and it was a miracle that she was out on the street that day when she bumped into the mysterious stranger.

He looked at her like he knew her. He looked at her as though they belonged together. He had eyes that made her feel she was gazing into eternity as she stared into them, much longer, of course, than you would stare at a stranger. And when he invited her into his room, she didn't even think twice about the appropriateness of going. She just walked right in as if compelled in some way.

She sat down on the couch. He seated himself near her and abruptly announced: "You have a great many tears to cry. You have a grief, a sadness, an emptiness in your soul that can only be filled by your allowing those tears to be cried, savored, and lovingly collected." As he spoke she had a feeling of being understood that was so touching that she was only a little surprised when, in spite of herself, a big tear appeared inside the top of one of her eyelids. But she said, "Crying can't be the answer. I've done so much crying, that isn't what I want." He just looked at her with that understanding that soon coaxed the welled-up tear out over the lid and onto the fleshy part of her cheek. And as that tear started its journey down her cheek he reached out his hand that was gently holding a hollow glass swan with a little hole in the top of its head.

He placed that little hole right below the tear and allowed that little tear to flop, drop, flow into the hole and gently down the "s" of the neck until it came to rest in the belly of the swan. You can imagine how surprised someone would be to have that kind of unexpected stimulus occur just as a tear is making its way over the eye. The conscious mind can make an objection at a process that the unconscious recognizes as correct and necessary. And she said, "Yes, but this is ridiculous, I cry too much." He responded, "Yes, but you've squandered the tears. You haven't savored or collected them. Tears from the soul are tears that should be honored." And with that she began to cry and cry even more. The tears flowed into the neck and more and more were quietly collected until they came to rest in the belly of the swan. She hadn't cried like that in her memory.

The mysterious stranger just sat there collecting each tear with a quiet compassion, not offering any words really, just a sense of his understanding. And then he said, "Your time is up but come back tomorrow at two and you'll cry some more and when the vial is full, you'll be free." She again voiced an objection: "Oh sure," she scoffed. "You're telling me when this thing is full of my tears, I'll be happy." "No," he said, "I cannot guarantee that. But when it's filled, you'll be *free*." With that, she left, vowing not to come back to this crazy place but at two o'clock the next day, absolutely punctually, she was there and cried on cue for another hour. It doesn't matter how much your conscious mind wonders and objects to a process your unconscious is learning or to a resolution your unconscious is experiencing.

And of course, she began to think that she was falling in love with him after the third visit. And she couldn't deny a sense of happiness that had been absent before. Yet she attributed it to the fact that she was in love with this fascinating man and the tears were really just optional. It was uncanny how much interest he had in her tears.

And as I told this story to the woman who had gone into a very comfortable trance despite the pain her cancer was causing, I watched for a sign of her emotional reaction, still searching the crannies for that grief I knew was bound to be there. Or maybe it was fear. I doubted that she knew anything about uncontrollable laughter. I really thought that if I could help her learn she would have fewer problems coping with the cancer, applying her powers to those alien forces she could be stronger than. Because it is an amazing amount of power that comes with the ability to laugh uncontrollably, to laugh until you cry. But she was able to relax profoundly and she didn't move a muscle or seem to be in any pain. "Just breathe into any pain or discomfort and breathe away any tension" was all I said. And every little muscle relaxed, every cheek muscle dropped. I think her mouth even fell open. And yet she didn't sleep and she didn't cry.

Of course, the day eventually came when the last tear was enveloped in that crystal swan's head and the little vial was finally, totally filled. The mysterious stranger who knew her so intimately then calmly announced, "Now our time together is finished." She was shocked and stunned and felt betrayed to think that he could be finished with her. Had he been using her for some amusement regarding her tears and now that he had them he was tossing her aside? But he was abrupt and quite official about it and there seemed to be nothing else to do but stand up as he showed her to the door where another client was waiting to enter.

The door shut behind them and she was left standing on the street alone, feeling a mixture of emotion that she couldn't quite describe. But she was quite firm in her sudden decision that she couldn't tolerate the situation, so she carefully opened the door and sneaked through the entrance hall and behind the man who was now sitting with his next crying client. She walked into the room bounded by two glass doors, through which she had often seen the man going and returning with the glass bird. She walked into the room and closed the door very quietly behind her.

The sight that greeted her defied explanation. To her amazement she found shelves upon shelves filled with all size and shape glass vials, in the shapes of animals, flowers, geometric shapes, large ones, small ones, clear ones, colored ones, each filled with a clear liquid she correctly assumed to be tears. And there, nestled inconspicuously, sat her little bird on the shelf in the company of thousands of bottles. She couldn't believe it. Just as she was trying to discover what was happening, the door opened behind her and there was the man looking very stern and disapproving. "You shouldn't be here," he said, "You were never meant to see this."

"But what is going on?" she demanded. He slowly began to explain that these were the tears that have been cried by people from centuries ago, far into the past, slaves in ancient civilizations, queens who've cried for the agonies of the subjects in their kingdoms, slaves who've cried for separations in their families, mothers who have cried over the pain of their children, captains in armies who've shed tears for the agonies of death, and on and on and on he went explaining. And it was very eerie and this is where reality seemed to depart from possibility and she really couldn't trust the man any longer and she didn't want to leave a part of herself there.

In the twinkling of an eye, she grabbed her little swan from the shelf over his objection and ran with it out of the room, out of the building, down the steps, into the street, and directly into the path of an oncoming taxi—with which she collided. She was uninjured. But as she was jolted, the bird flew from her hands and onto the pavement, bursting into a thousand pieces—or so it seemed.

The man who had been riding in the taxi jumped out, alarmed for her well-being, made certain she was all right, and then noticed the wet broken glass in the street. He asked, "What was that? Was it something important?" How do you really explain something like that to a stranger? She laughed and said, "Well, um, yes, it was important, it was my tears." Not comprehending, of course, and apparently not needing to pursue the matter at that moment, he asked, "Did anyone ever tell you that you look really lovely when you smile?" And as she answered, smiling even more broadly, she seemed to display an emotion you hadn't seen on her face prior to that moment. Then he asked, "Would you like to have coffee with me or something? I would really like to talk with you longer." She accepted and together they went off into the future.

Thus the story ended with a sense of rightness and lightness that somehow the mysterious stranger's prediction had been true: that when the tears were cried and savored, and when the vial was full, she had somehow in that process become free, not happy or guaranteed to be happy but simply free of one reality and prepared for the demands of another. And it was nice to know that even though the symbol of the whole thing had been dashed to pieces in the street, it's not the symbol but the process that is freeing. It doesn't matter what happens to the collection, it's the savoring of those parts of you and bringing them together and sharing them appropriately in the proper context.

And the woman with cancer never did cry during our three days of work together. Her lip quivered violently during the last session with her husband, and I certainly expected and hoped that the resulting emotion that had been stirred and encouraged would be appropriately and eventually expressed in the proper context with that husband in a way that would allow an intimacy to grow and nourish both of them.

A little bit later, before I left, she brought out the glass deer and gave that to me because she thought it should somehow be a partner with the swan who had traveled such a distance with me to symbolize something about her therapy. And that is how the objects differ. She died peacefully on Thanksgiving day, recently. Her husband wrote to say that the last several months of her life were pain free and happy and she was at peace.

4. **Existing attitude:** *If people ignore me or fail to appreciate me, they are more desirable, a special challenge and attractive.*
Goal attitude: *I can be attracted to people who will appreciate me and treat me well.*

Metaphor

"The front lines of courtship" was a phrase that made a certain sense to my friend Janice. After all, those wonderfully interesting psychopathic men that frequented the bars she favored kept her wondering who was winning. But it was a fascinating battleground for her and she was quite an accomplished flirt and something about her just made those totally cool guys want to promise her anything. But, of course, making promises was what they did best. That's the way it had been with the most popular boy in high school, to whom Janice had been engaged. She couldn't have known that she would so completely survive the desolation of being jilted at the alter, just like in the movies, because Horace wasn't able to actually keep the promises he made. Back then she didn't realize that the turn of events she had just lived through was probably the luckiest thing that had ever happened to her. Jerk that he had been, there was still something unexplainably appealing about Horace, even years later when she would occasionally encounter him cruising the single bars.

Now all the while this terribly boring man named John pursued Janice relentlessly. He kept trying to get her to go places with him, kept giving her gifts, kept inviting her to dinners that he would cook for her. Occasionally, she would go out with him but would come away from the date with far more complaints about the boring things he did and said and thought and didn't do. And I don't know what it was that made the change in her perceptions. Maybe it was going away to that conference in center city Chicago. We were surrounded by so many of the undesirable, unreputable, insane, absolutely decadent, wild people who sometimes frequent the innermost portions of a major city that it must have jolted her somehow. That's the only thing I could think of because otherwise all of a sudden, she just started saying, "You know I appreciate John. John is really a nice guy. You know, he really is nice." And I said, "Yes, but he is so boring, remember?" And she replied, "Well, I know, but I think I might be able to fix that just a little bit because I really appreciate him and he is just so nice." And the next thing I knew, she had left the conference and slipped out to go shopping and came back with some very revealing bikini briefs she had bought for John—to take back to him as a souvenir of Chicago.

Well, you can imagine how enthusiastic he was about that kind of interest. This was the man who, for two years, had never tired of asking her out. He must have received countless rejections. He had sent her a little book that was blank on every page except the first page which was titled "Everything you always wanted to know about Janice X but haven't been able to find out yet." She thought that was a little bit interesting. And after she gave him the briefs and the interest that went with them and the appreciation she had come to discover for what a nice person he was, he invited her to another of his home-cooked meals and this time there was a diamond ring by her plate and he asked her to marry him. They were married a year later.

And all of a sudden I found myself being amazed at the envy others had of Janice for having John, whom we had always considered so boring, but he wasn't boring anymore. And they were extraordinarily happily married. And I visited them several months ago, 11 years into their marriage, and there was a vase of roses on the table. I asked if it was her birthday or something. And Janice said, "Oh no, I just had a hard week at work and my husband loves me so much. You know John is so nice. I just appreciate and love him so much." And so even when it takes an extremely long time to find, the feeling of being worthwhile is one that can wait. Maybe it ages like wine to a perfection such that when it is finally uncorked in the proper circumstances as an adult, it sends a sparkle of enjoyment unlike anything you've ever known.

5. *Existing attitude:* *If I really care about others, I must be polite and protect them from the discomfort of knowing about my bad feelings or the special needs they create.*
   Goal attitude: *I truly express my caring about people by telling them what I need.*

Metaphor

There is nothing complex about letting go. You know, after you learn something like letting go of some habit that had seemed so essential, it's almost impossible to understand or even remember why it was so hard, what was so complex about just letting go. It must be like when as a child you struggle to learn to ride a bicycle or have balance and then all of a sudden you just know how to do it. And you can climb back on a bicycle 5, 10, 20 years later and it only takes a second. In fact, it doesn't even take a conscious second. I doubt that you even have to think about it. You climb back on and simply experience a moment of unconscious delight and the feeling of balance and ability. You can be amazed at how effortless it is to push that pedal and the delightful sensation of movement and flowing or floating that seems to occur almost as if by magic.

And yet it seems so difficult in the process of learning. There seem to be so many fears your conscious mind can plague you with. Maybe it's characterized best by a teenager and yet, in a way, we are all teenagers really because there's always something that everyone is trying to learn, taking that risk. This was certainly true for our neighbors with their older son.

When Ralph, the older of two brothers, visited his father at 18 years old, he was squarely in the middle of that dilemma of identity and risk that most teenagers face. He came with mixed thoughts in his conscious mind, filled with longing for validation from his father who, in many ways, was estranged from him all of his life due to the fact that he had divorced his mother when Ralph was a toddler. So there was even more than the usual amount of bitterness and blame toward that father, as well as some enjoyment of him and a genuine desire to get close to him. I'm sure he didn't really know exactly what he wanted to have happen. He was a little jealous, no doubt, of the unconditional acceptance and love that he observed his two-year-old half brother receiving. And he really didn't want to make a problem over his jealousy.

No, Ralph didn't want to impose but he was a little preoccupied with the matter of his rights. And, on the other hand, he just wanted to be a house guest but he knew he deserved more than that. And there were certainly complicated feelings toward the stepmother.

What was he to do? He definitely didn't want to make a problem and yet how can you avoid making a problem when you bring so many problems in your conscious mind that your unconscious is working to solve? So it didn't take very long at all before he had made a problem far worse by yielding to his convictions that he shouldn't make any problems. It didn't take very long at all for him to become offended at something flippant or glib said to him by his father. It didn't take long at all for him to perceive some remark that his father made as proof that he wasn't loved as fully as he should be or that he hadn't received the kind of attention or time that certainly every child should, by right, receive from a parent.

And it is certainly through no fault of the child that parents fail to do those things. A child couldn't understand and a teenager is barely able to understand any more so. So Ralph kept quiet about whatever it was that had offended him. He tuned into MTV a little more frequently, or tuned into his book a little more often. And even though he was there in body, he wasn't really there. Oh, he was polite enough, by standard rules of etiquette perhaps. He offered to help clean up after meals and he thanked the stepmother profusely for every egg she scrambled him and he had brought the proper hostess gift and had asked long in advance if it would be all right if he made the visit.

And he went along in body with the trips to the restaurants and the beach and made typical superficial attempts at small talk and to believe he was behaving properly, having a nice time, and doing all of the things you would be expected to do—on a friendly visit with someone you love.

But his father couldn't help but sense that something seemed wrong and kept questioning his wife about possible errors in behavior he might have made that had perhaps offended Ralph. From her perception, nothing was really wrong except that she wasn't particularly enjoying this big pile of "mostly stranger" who was sitting somewhat morosely in the middle of the couch. And so the time for Ralph to be there came and went. They were all a little relieved at the hurricane that hastened Ralph's departure even though at the ostensible level of interaction, Ralph politely thanked them for the visit and expressed regret that he had to leave prematurely. The father didn't know what to believe but felt a sadness and emptiness he couldn't quite understand.

And different guests will, of course, elicit different reactions from the hosts, though perhaps not the ones that an onlooker might initially expect. For example, everyone who knew him would tell you that Charles was rude and always had been, judged by a proper standard of etiquette. Once in a laundromat, for example, as he was playing his guitar and waiting for his clothes to dry, a stranger admired the music and expressed an interest in spending additional time with Charles. Charles simply announced somewhat matter of factly that he had too many friends already and didn't have enough time to spend with them so, no thanks. You can imagine the kind of responses he gave to unsolicited telemarketing solicitors!

As a house guest, Charles rarely gave advance notice when he intended to visit. He never brought a hostess gift. He usually arrived in the late evening or middle of the night. Hopefully, any meal prepared on the premises would not contain any of the many vegetables hated by Charles because he would be sure to mention it out loud.

But love transcends various experiences over time and that's how long Ralph's stepmother had known her brother Charles. So she knew that he did love bran muffins and would make them especially for him on those occasions when she happened to have advance notice of his arrival. And on his last visit, she had made a special sacrifice to give Charles and his bride the master bedroom, freshly arranged with new, clean flannel sheets on the waterbed. Her husband had been away for the weekend so she bunked with the baby to give Charles an opportunity to be especially comfortable. She even left a low, romantic light burning for them when she went to bed.

Well, they did arrive, as predicted, in the middle of the night and when she woke up to greet them the next day and asked how they slept, Charles announced that it was *the* worst night's sleep he had ever had. Those sheets were so hot and the bed moved constantly. He had had to unplug the darn light because he couldn't find the switch and he would definitely have to have different arrangements tonight or else he would go to a hotel. And you might imagine that it would have been a pleasure to see him go to one! But there is something you can really appreciate about knowing where you stand with certain situations and you always knew that with Charles. You could safely assume that if he hadn't mentioned it, it wasn't a problem. Well, guests come and go in their own good time. . . .

It was about three months later when the winter winds had even infiltrated Florida that the letter from Ralph arrived. It was fat and ominous. Sure enough, it was full of accumulated and embellished bitterness, savored and suffered in silence over three months since his departure with the hurricane. He raged in black and white with an attacking letter that went on for five pages and went on into the past when he was a little boy and all the ways his father had failed him then. And all because of a small little problem that he had waited and waited to reveal. He didn't want to make a problem so he had buried it.

And yet you can't deny when you have a feeling. And if your conscious mind doesn't consider it as acceptable, it's still there. Your unconscious still has a feeling and your conscious mind searches for more and more ways to rationalize and justify it. Maybe he was trying to protect his father from the rage or maybe it was simply that he didn't trust his father to handle it, deal with it, care about his feeling. Well, the stepmother was extremely angry when she read that letter. She thought, "What right does he think he has to come to this house and visit, take advantage of everything we open up to him and yet think he has to protect us from his feelings. I'd rather him protect me from the demoralizing implication that I can't or won't handle and care about his feelings." If he liked them enough to come to their home, she wanted him to respect them enough to tell them what he feels and what he wants when he wants it and when he feels it—while there is still something that can be done about it. She wanted Ralph to believe that she and his father could be trusted to be decent enough people that they would care even if it is hard understanding his needs fully right away.

So she wrote him back and challenged the fact that Ralph claimed to love his father. "How can you say that," she wrote, "if you don't trust him enough to let him see your feeling, let him know what you don't like, give him a chance to understand? You should do that even if you have to tell him two times or three times or even if you have to sit him down and say, 'Listen here, you've got to understand this. You don't have it right yet.' "

But on the other hand, he's just a teenager. How could anyone expect him to know how to do that. How could anyone expect him to have enough conviction in the correctness of his own responses that he'd be willing to take that risk. How does a child learn that you are worthwhile enough that you owe it to yourself and to everyone you meet to give them that chance. And so she told him that he was not welcome in that house ever again unless he agreed that he would be willing to tell them what he didn't like as soon as he understood what it was, to respect them enough to believe them to be responsible, caring adults who were willing and able to know what his feelings are and care about them. "Because if we don't have that," she wrote, "there's no reason for you to come here really, is there?"

Well, there was a little more to it than that but basically she finished the letter at about 10 o'clock that night and just as she finished it, the phone rang and it was Charles. "We're in Opp, Alabama, and will be there in about two hours, okay?" "Oh, that's great," she said. "Can't wait to see you. I'll put the bran muffins on and leave the door unlocked when I go to bed." "Great, hope I'm not gonna have to sleep on any flannel sheets." "Don't worry," she said, "we won't be imposing any more comfort on you than you can handle and we won't have carrots either. What will you be cooking anyway while you're here?"

It's so easy sometimes. It can make you wonder about that objection adults sometimes encounter going through assertiveness training and finding that a whole array of doubts has been set in motion when they simply asked something that they wanted of another person: "What if the other person doesn't want to give me what I ask for?" And they never understand in their desire to protect the other person from their demands that they do no service whatsoever to that other person, that they instead imply a disrespect or a disability on the other person's part to just say no. And it's only a demand if you won't accept no for an answer.

People are amazingly unfragile beings and they really deserve a variety of opportunities and contexts to develop their abilities to say, "No," "Tell me more," "That must have hurt."

And so with each opportunity you have to take a risk. You really owe it to that part of yourself that knows you are worthwhile to leap with joy at the prospect of taking another risk, learning what you'll be able to learn, experiencing the comfort that's going to come after you take the risk, even experience the kind of ability to take care of yourself and reorganize after you take a risk that doesn't result in the other person responding in the way you had hoped. It's those learnings that come from the catastrophes that you would never have voluntarily wanted to go through, and yet the reorganization of your abilities that happens as a result is something you can't imagine living without if the catastrophe had not occurred. And then is it really a catastrophe or isn't it? Basically, there is nothing complex about letting go.

6. **Existing attitude:** *If I reveal my fears, no one will respect me.*
   Goal attitude: *Revealing vulnerability displays true courage and facilitates other people being able to really respect me.*

Metaphor

A feeling of safety is something that can be taken with you into a variety of situations. Maybe that feeling of safety comes from your trust in other people to respond to the best of their abilities and to be willing to grow and learn and change. Or, perhaps just as importantly, that feeling of safety derives from your own conviction that you are worthwhile or from those experiences in which both factors are involved. But Lola wasn't thinking about safety at all when she collected her coffee cup, notebook, and composure before heading into her weekly supervision group.

It appeared threatening enough on the surface that someone who didn't know from personal experience might wonder how the prospect of having her work reviewed and supervised by reasonable human beings could stir up so many fears of inadequacy. But at the same time there was such a sense of excitement at what might be learned if she were to take the tape of her therapy work and play it for her supervisors to listen and critique. And so on that day, Lola had weighed the odds and was taking a tape that she was pretty sure was just going to show up the inadequacies of her client. And she thought she would get some ideas about how she might relate differently with a certain client to help him get over his inadequacies and his fears of people.

Her client took great pains to hide his inadequacies, in fact. And the term "great pains" is not the least bit of an exaggeration. Johnny was very pained at all times. His pain was due, in large part, to showing no feeling and working day and night to hide his mistakes. To him, the thought of taking a tape of therapy work for scrutiny was about the worst nightmare he could imagine.

His problem, and the reason for seeking Lola for therapy at all, was that he suffered from acute anxiety attacks crossing bridges. And in that area of Florida, there were plenty of bridges. His doctor had prescribed valium and some other medication for a few months but they only made him sleepy or numb and did not stop the anxiety. He was forced, against his will, to admit that he needed therapy. This was a big secret he tried to keep hidden away with his other inadequacies and his feelings in general.

Actually, as one might expect, this strategy of hiding inadequacies from others was very good for his professional life. No one, he correctly reasoned, likes to deal with a loser. People like to deal with winners, and winners do not get lost in feelings and do not get bogged down with needs. People like to look up to professionals and admire leaders who have control and command of situations. He, himself, looked up to some others who were in the top of his field. From what he could see, they were as cold as stone and as dependable as rock. He aspired to this and, of course, knew that his professional reputation would become equally solid. Basically, his plan was foolproof. The one big snag was that this life-style seemed to result in absolutely debilitating anxiety whenever he had to cross a bridge. Secretly, so as not to let on to his colleagues that he had a problem, he sought Lola's help.

He liked and respected her as a therapist. She was solid. Probably, secretly, he would like to be stronger like she was. But he would never want to be forced into a position of showing a failure to a supervisor.

But it was precisely because of his attitude that Lola felt unable to get therapy to budge. Something about his problem needed further analysis, she thought. She explained Johnny's situation to her supervisors and began to play the tape. And it is amazing how quickly things can turn around on you in a circumstance like that. It only took a minute, or not even two, of playing that tape and all the supervisors in the room seemed to have a clear idea of what the problem was. It wasn't so much that the client had a complex problem that needed careful analysis. His was really a fairly obvious problem in retrospect. The only reason it seemed so complex is that in some ways Lola was suffering from the very same problem, that same fear of emotional release and intimacy. She knew it was important as a psychologist and yet she was failing to communicate it or inspire it with that client. And it wasn't very long at all before the supervisor whom she "trusted with her life" was inviting Lola to go into an imaginary journey into memories of her past and follow a feeling to find out what motive of hers was creating a problem about carrying on the therapy that was suggested.

Soon she was aware of a great deal of emotion welling up in her chest and throat, feelings of sadness and fear and hurt and betrayal, a combination of those that defied labeling. The supervisor coaxed her further to "stay with that feeling and follow it." Her conscious mind was torn. She couldn't follow that feeling and risk exposing layers of her psyche that she hadn't really scrutinized in private. She couldn't expose those parts of her in a group of her peers, in front of whom she was supposed to be a professional. And yet how could she really be a professional unless she was willing to go into the depths of that emotion and explore it and feel it and risk it. What her supervisor was asking her wasn't any greater than the risk she asked of clients every day. How could she ask them congruently?

So there she sat battling between her conscious mind and the unconscious pull, the trust in the supervisor, and recognition that she was only sitting in a roomful of friends who all shared the desire to see her grow and learn. And so into the depths of that emotion she went.

Later, she shared that she didn't really remember much of the content. She knew she had cried. She couldn't remember what she remembered during, but she remembered clearly that at the end of the emotionally cleansing, correctional and revealing experience she came back into a realization of her conscious mind in the room and the context in which the display had been made. And she was a little bit embarrassed but didn't really care because the learnings and the release and the experience of letting go into that feeling had been so profound and impactful, so healing; her motivation seemed different.

When she looked around the room she was surprised to see a few tears on some of her supervisors' faces as well. And then time was up. But before each person left the room, they came by to squeeze her hand, give a hug, and to say in some fashion, "I really admire the courage that you showed here today. What you did really was personal and relevant to me. Thank you for sharing that. I feel I know you so much better. I really feel a closeness I didn't know before."

And on and on it went like that, which was increasingly becoming more important than whatever the therapy had been she had just completed. And in a moment like that you come to recognize you can depend on people, the sameness, the goodness. And the people with you understand and appreciate those parts of you that you had somehow believed were unacceptable. Then you realize that you belong in a universe of people. It starts with those people you know you can trust, and friends with whom you've shared experiences and time, but somehow expands to other people. And you have that recognition that belonging comes from being the same and yet being uniquely different, your own version of being people, that spice of difference that is you that makes you so interesting.

7. **Existing attitude:** *If I have made mistakes, or if others seem to have accomplished more than me, I am unacceptable.*
   Goal attitude: *I can be respected despite mistakes I've made.*

Metaphor

Claude lost $75,000 in a business deal in Saudia Arabia through American banks. They got the goods and didn't pay. He wished that he was like everyone else, instead of a stupid schmuck who couldn't provide an income for his family. He didn't know that at 45 years old he would be selling a small business that he started in his garage for something in the area of a million and a quarter dollars. There was something very clever about his involvement in options for the stock.

He was absolutely certain that his wife would know he was a failure. *And,* his wife told me how *bravely* he endured the entire process. She wished that she weren't so scared when he went away on business trips. She said, "I wish I could be as normal as Claude is, to handle my adversity with courage and smile politely." She told me about her difficulty sexually. I think that she said she was afraid to tell her priest.

Tina, the next-door neighbor, in answering a question about who she admired, said, "I wish I could be like Claude's wife. She looks nice, she's proud of herself, made something of her life, helped her husband. But *me,* I'm so ashamed. I've had affairs, considered divorce; when my husband does something that makes me angry, I go out and try to find some other man to make me feel good, and I can't get over it. Why can't I just be like Claude's wife?"

Now Tina's father had been an incredible creep all of his life, critical to everyone around him, spent very little time with Tina, and it was no wonder that she was uncertain about her abilities as a woman and dealing with men. She tended to want to blame everybody but her father. He seemed unable to change and he was less intelligent than Tina's mother. No one thought you could teach an old dog new tricks, and everyone knew he *was* an old dog, until he retired. Then he became the nicest person in the whole neighborhood. People enjoyed playing golf with him. Children came over to sit around him regardless of what he was doing. He confessed, not to me personally because I never knew him closely, but I heard from one of his sons that he said, "All my life I never thought I would amount to anything. I was afraid that my father's prediction would come true. I was so sensitive to my children's mistakes." I supposed he thought it would be proof that he had failed and his father's prediction would be right. But when he retired he was aware that he had accomplished all that he wanted to. He held down a steady job, worked his way up from being on the line to a management position. Retired with enough money to survive nicely.

So many people take it for granted that you are going to get an A on a math test just because you learned the multiplication tables. People ought to appreciate the miracle involved in learning the multiplication tables in the first place. Some of these people are guilty of failing to appreciate themselves for all the things they have succeeded in. I know a woman who had an odd version of asthma. She went to an acupuncturist and it abated, but I don't know if you would say it was cured. She was angry that she had such a strange version of asthma that she was cured with acupuncture. All those people have something in common. They have the same thing in common with each other that they have with Joan.

Joan was 43 years old before she recognized that her parents wouldn't be there for her. She called them every day and talked to them, made excuses for them to her siblings. "They are the only parents you have," she would say. Joan's life was miserable. Any damn fool can marry a taxi driver, anybody can put someone through college provided that you are smart enough to hold down a job, hold down your ideas and work real hard until your husband goes to college, so he can divorce you. She was always bringing home stray dogs. When she turned 43, it finally dawned on her that her mother and father would not be there for her unless she *didn't* ask them for anything. I was a little disappointed when she had come to her senses a week later and decided that they were the only parents she had, they weren't going to change.

I really think you ought to hold a grudge a lot longer than that. You ought to start about 23, and hold it for 10 years or so, or at least a year, six months, to give you plenty of time to find out how you can be independent. But, she was a quick learner and a week after coming to a very firm conviction that she was angry with them and she was never going to talk to them again, she decided that she would go ahead and talk to them, but she still knew who she was. Or, I should say, she knew who she'd become. She wasn't going to let them intrude on that and try to take that away. She, at 43, decided that she had the right to live the kind of life that she wanted to live. It didn't matter how many times she got divorced, or how many times her last name changed, or how many new men her parents had to get to know and like. Although I was disappointed that she didn't hold a grudge longer. She missed out on being a rebellious teenager. Everyone used to wish they could be like Joan because, they said, "she's so together." Everyone has something in common in those stories and I will tell you what it is.

There is a lot of bumping into each other that goes on in the world. You are just a collection of cells, maybe a collection of cells with a soul. We have a nervous system, which pumps blood through the body. We oscillate between standing vertically and reclining horizontally. All of us start out young, grow old, and die. Everyone diminishes their self-esteem by failing to accept some of their feelings. You repressed feelings. You don't get to find out who you are. While I have been speaking about various things, you have had tears come out of your eyes. I thought that you might even know which eye tears first, yet who else would know? Only you know about the screen that lies behind your eyes, and you are entitled to all of your feelings. Dr. Erickson said something I have always remembered: "You really shouldn't let anyone hurt your feelings; they are *your* feelings. What right do they have to hurt *your* feelings?" In dealing with upset parents, he suggested that you say, "Don't you think you are underrating how bad I really was?" I recently came upon a psychiatrist who said to his patient, "If you remembered what I said in our last session about forgetting, you wouldn't have amnesia."

8. **Existing attitude:** *Sexual activity is dangerous, difficult, frightening if I am old or sick, and I should avoid it to prevent death or weakening.*
Goal attitude: *Sexual activity is possible, can be beneficial and enjoyable, and can be discovered with relaxation and enjoyment.*

Metaphor[6]

That reminds me of what John was telling me the other day. John and his wife had decided to go to dinner with another couple—Fred and his wife. Even though they were going to drive from and to the same parts of town, they decided to take separate cars and meet at the restaurant.

As Fred drove along the familiar streets, he noted the scenery and enjoyed how you can discover simple pleasures in your everyday life. Fred and his wife would take pleasure and delight in pointing out red cardinals or a graceful tree to one another. As they drove along, Fred showed his wife a sign about the [slurred to sound like "de"] tour to be given of the downtown historic district. She was enthusiastic about going on the tour and wondered if the children would like to go on the tour with them.

John was running late. He had to check the oil in the car and stop for gas before he and his wife could begin the drive to the restaurant. His wife admired his thoroughness and his attention to detail. Even after all these years, he persisted in walking around the car after starting the car's engine, checking to make sure all the lights were in full operating condition. At the same time, he would use the pressure gauge he kept in his shirt pocket and check the air pressure in all his tires— even the spare tire he kept in the trunk. John believed in being prepared. As he drove down the street toward the restaurant, he fired questions at his wife: Are you sure you locked the back door? Do you remember turning the iron off? Did you leave a phone number for the baby-sitter? Did you tell her when we're going to be home? Is the dog in the basement? You're certain Fred said seven o'clock? As she answered question after question, John's wife could see his furrowed brow and could feel her own fists tighten as she saw how tightly John held the steering wheel.

While John was reviewing the mental checklist in his head, Fred was discovering a blockage in the road. There was a big orange sign

[6] This metaphor was contributed by Susan L. Vignola, D.S.W.

spelling D E T O U R. A huge pile of sand sat in the middle of the street beside a big hole in the pavement. Like a little boy who was still living inside the grown-up body, Fred was imagining what it would be like to play in that sand. A pile like that was perfect for a game of "king of the mountain." When he remembered all the tractors and toy heavy-equipment he had had, the ideas came one after another, pell mell, about how to rearrange that sand pile. But the adult Fred consciously read the orange sign that said DETOUR. It was pointing in a direction that neither Fred nor John had traveled before. Reading the sign herself, Fred's wife turned to him and said, "Well, dear, it looks like you have to do something different. . . . The old path won't work any more. You have to blaze a new trail." Hearing his wife's words, Fred took a deep breath, that's right, pulled his shoulders back, that's right, sat up straighter and began to change, . . . turning the car around to take the new route. While Fred was turning around, John pulled up behind him. Fred leaned out his car window and shouted to John, "You have to turn yourself around." It was then that their paths crossed and parted.

Fred and his wife found the new path to be as acceptable as the more familiar, previously used path. In some unexplainable way, the new path was even more satisfying. Fred's wife suggested to him, "Let's use the new pathway next time." To their surprise, they arrived at the restaurant before John. Seeing a small gathering in the far corner of the parking lot, they wandered over and decided to investigate the unknown. There they found a strangely dressed man surrounded by laughing, giggling children. The man had on a pair of babby-glack pants, a red cummerbund with a pocket in it, and a jacket with tails. On his head was a hat made of balloons. As he worked, he told stories and jokes to the gathering crowd. He would draw a long skinny unfilled balloon out from the pocket of his red cummerbund. Then he would place the balloon in his mouth, take a deep breath, and exhaling deeply . . . the deflated balloon would begin to expand.

Fred stood there as the balloon man was feeling it grow larger, wider in circumference. When you have practiced as much as the balloon man had, you know when it's wide enough. And then he would tuck it under his arm to use it later, and proceed to expand another balloon. Again that small, narrow, long tube would expand, growing larger, rounded, as you widen the circumference, and when you make the pressure just right, he would stop. With experience, you know when there are enough of those inflated, cylindrical vessels of air.

Then Fred saw the man begin to shape the balloons—one child received a sword, another a flower, one small boy a dinosaur, and a hat for a little girl. You can accomplish a lot with inflated, cylindrical elastic tubes that have the correct amount of pressure. By now, Fred and his wife were hungry. They didn't know where John was, so they went in to order their dinner.

Later, at home, their baby-sitter told them John had called and they were not to worry. Fred called John, puzzled and confused. He could not believe his ears when he heard John say, "I'll be goll-darned if I would be forced into taking a new route." John's next words continued to echo in Fred's ears, "Before I'd follow the detour, I'd rather sit home and die." And eventually, that would be exactly what John did.

9. *Existing attitude: If I experience an urge or craving for a substance I have withdrawn from, it means I am about to relapse. I should be ashamed.*
Goal attitude: Experiencing an urge or craving for a substance I have withdrawn from is to be expected, and in fact can serve as a stimulus to use newly learned coping behaviors.

Metaphor[7]

Wedding bells in Marsha's future were not something that she was looking forward to. And it wasn't just because it wasn't her own wedding. It didn't matter who was getting married—it was going to be a big problem for her. She was just newly recovered from active alcoholism and very frightened about her urges and her wanting to drink; and whenever she'd have an urge and a thought about how really fun it would be to drink, she began worrying, consumed by the thought that she would find herself drinking. And she really had that experience that people have whenever you want to change some kind of behavior and move two steps forward and one step back. And having doubts whenever you think about engaging in that new behavior. And it was only a few days before she was going to find herself in that very difficult situation. Any person who is working on recovery knows that wedding receptions can be one of the most difficult tests, with everybody drinking and engaging in that behavior that you're trying to stop.

Fear, concern, and apprehension were written all over her face when I saw her for therapy that day. She had good reason to be apprehensive

---

[7] This metaphor was contributed by David A. Lee, R.S.A.C. It was entitled "The Barometer."

too, because the odds of her staying away from using were slim. She thought about drinking a lot and it didn't seem that she had the resources to avoid temptation since she was so new at recovering. She was nothing like Jane who had just canceled her scheduled appointment with me.

Jane had a great deal more experience with sobriety than Marsha and also a lot more confidence, with good reason. Some people might have said she was a little cocky but she had good reason to be really confident of her ability to stay sober. She never really had urges and didn't have to go through the changes and the struggles like Marsha had to do to stay sober. And Jane was even so confident that she was able to go to parties and not even want to drink. That was such a positive sign to a lot of people because when you can be around users and not want to use, it can be a good indication that chemicals are not such a major focus in your life.

Well, Marsha's reception and Jane's party were obviously going to be two very different experiences. I only wished that Marsha could have had some of Jane's confidence. She really could have used it, but unfortunately, she didn't. And I knew that next week therapy would involve a lot of processing with Marsha, regarding her relapse and attempting to develop some ways for her to do a better job next time.

For each time you make a mistake in a behavior change, you can learn from that. I'm sure there are many experiences that, even if you don't consciously recall the times when you've made mistakes and failed at things, you've been able to learn from them. You can unconsciously know that and unconsciously recall those experiences.

And I also looked forward to being able to celebrate Jane's pride at being able to once again not relapse in a tough situation, if she chanced to keep her appointment at all next week. So I was really quite surprised when I got a chance to celebrate Marsha's successful reception and process Jane's relapse!

Perhaps you have some ideas as to how Marsha was able to use her situation in a useful way and how Jane was unable to do that which she thought she would find so easy. And I was, of course, interested too, and I asked Marsha how she was able to have those feelings that were so scary for her and yet act in a way that was totally opposite those feelings, and act in a way that was so useful to her.

Basically, what she said was that she was able to take those actions which are most useful, and for her it was to seek out those people at the reception who were supportive of not drinking or to find herself intrigued with something else. Several people had come from another country and how interesting it was to learn about that culture. And she said that she had learned to use her fear and urges as a barometer that indicated that there were things that she needed to change. And so each time in the future that she was to have those fears or urges, that was her signal that it was time to do some new things and behaviors.

Jane had some learnings too that perhaps later can become evident. Balancing confidence with overconfidence is important in any behavior. The athlete who has no confidence will never enter the race. The athlete who is overconfident may not train hard enough. I'm not sure really what Jane thought she had learned, just as I imagine that you're not really sure exactly what you're going to be learning later about it. On a conscious level, some learnings are pretty obvious, but unconsciously those applications can be used in many different ways. And so you simply apply those unconscious learnings and perhaps delight yourself in how you're able to later surprise and maybe impress yourself in exactly how you're able to apply that.

10. *Existing attitude: I shouldn't make any mistakes if I am to succeed at an important, but difficult goal.*
   Goal attitude: "Weathering" mistakes leads to pride and a thorough learning. Any pace is acceptable as long as it leads me to the desired destination.

Metaphor[8]

What mother wouldn't rather trade places with her child to help the child avoid going through a hazardous learning? Perhaps I've already mentioned to you about my son wanting to learn how to ride a two-wheeler. Yesterday when I was doing some errands, I stopped into the bike shop and they had a little child's two-wheeler bike, slightly used, but in very good condition. And to make a long story short, I ended up buying that bike and we hid it in our basement last night to save for his birthday.

And just as I can see the smile on your face, I can envision the smile on his face when he discovers the bicycle on the morning of his birthday, all bedecked with bows and ribbons, as any birthday present should be. And there is a part of me that can't wait for his birthday and would like it to hurry up quick and be here, so that we can have the joy of witnessing his excitement at discovering that bicycle.

[8] This metaphor was contributed by Susan L. Vignola, D.S.W.

Anticipation is such a valuable thing. It leads to excitement and also a little to dread and worry. Because as a mother who has learned to ride a bicycle, there's a part of me that knows too what Chad doesn't know. And that is, I know that he's going to have to fall down many times along the way to learning how to ride his bicycle. And I'd like to be able to protect him from those falls and hurts and yet I know that to protect him from those falls is to really stand in his way and impede his progress and his learning.

Instead, I have to stand back with my heart not too high in my throat, and let him take those falls so that his unconscious mind can make those learnings: learnings about balance, learning about how to position himself in relation to the steering wheel, how to move those feet on the pedals, how to make the ground as soft as possible when he falls. I've even had fantasies of tying pillows to his elbows and knees. Yet I also know that he's going to survive each and every one of those falls, and that despite those falls, if not because of them, when he discovers his own capacity for riding that bike independently without any artificial assistance, there's going to be a tremendous sense of pride that's going to swell up in that little heart and form a lasting memory in his unconscious brain cells.

And whenever he feels pride in the future, he's going to be reaccessing those first moments of accomplishment on his bicycle. And because he's accomplished such things as rolling over, sitting up, standing and walking, learning to dress himself, he already has those early buds of accomplishment and perseverance. I remember how hard and determined he worked as a child of 10 months as he taught himself how to walk.

He would get up and take a step or two and fall down, and would force himself up to take more steps. And it was one Sunday afternoon, for about 20 or 30 minutes he would push himself, propel himself around and around the house, taking those steps, falling down, making himself get up again, trying once more, as he built skill upon skill, in very minute detail, but nevertheless in a very effective way. Maybe Chad has had to work at it a little bit harder than his sister, who seems to have slightly more coordination with her limbs and muscles and has a little more athletic ability at these early stages.

But Chad didn't know that he was working harder than anybody else, he just knew that it was something he had to do, and the harder he drove himself, the more he increased his sense of accomplishment, his sense of pride. And of course it doesn't matter how many times you fall down, it doesn't matter how many times you slip backwards, and it doesn't matter if you fall on the soft grass or the hard pavement. You know that you're going to succeed even though there are going to be those moments of doubt, maybe even temporary moments of giving up.

I know that at some point when Chad is ready, he's going to do it, he's going to get out there, and in his own way, at his own pace, he's going to be riding that bike. And it's going to be hard for me to hold back my own needs and my parental drive if he decides that he wants to put that bike away for a while because he's not quite ready. But that will have to be okay because what does it matter if at the age of four or four and a half, or not until five or seven, does he learn to ride a bike. I'm confident that at some point it will happen and it will happen when the time is right, not for someone else, but for you. And that's the message that I would like to convey to my son. And it must be advantageous to be a small child and not have the knowledge and the wisdom of an adult, but just to be able to think of the fun and the excitement of learning to ride a bike and not have to be aware of all those falls and scrapes—but to just feel driven by that wonderful desire to accomplish something new.

Now when I learned to ride a bike, I remember having training wheels. I don't know how long I rode that bike with those training wheels. And there were many times I rode my bike without training wheels, though I didn't know it at the time. I would ride along, keeping that bike so perfectly balanced, the training wheels never touched the ground. But since I didn't know I was riding that bike without training wheels, when they came off it was necessary to relearn everything I already knew. Because sometimes you know more than you think you know, and you discover your own capability, learn to know what you already know about your ability to ride independently, without that artificial assistance.

And it really doesn't matter, on a very hot day, standing beside a swimming pool. It doesn't matter if you walk down the steps one step at a time, gradually allowing the water level to rise higher around your body, or if you simply jump in off the side, get totally wet all at once. However you choose to immerse yourself, you're going to know the enjoyment and pleasure that comes from feeling the refreshing coolness of the water in contrast to the hot, humid air. You know, as long as you come out of that tunnel on the side with the sunshine, it doesn't matter how long or dark it may have been—you're standing in the sunshine.

And if you think about five years from now, 10 years from now, what difference is it going to make as you look back? And 10 years from now when Chad is riding up and down the streets with his friends on their bikes, he's not going to remember at all whether he learned to ride his bike in an afternoon or a week, or a month, or if it took him a whole year. It's all going to be terribly unimportant, all that's going to matter is that he has made that accomplishment.

11. Existing attitude: *Things that seem too frightening to face should not be approached.*
Goal attitude: *Frightening situations, when examined closely, won't look as difficult as when seen from the distance of imagination.*

Metaphor[9]

"There was once a boy named Myopie," the story goes, and I told it recently to my little boy. I wouldn't usually tell it to an adult, for reasons you'll soon discover, but my son listened with such unusual intensity that I'll tell it to you now, much as I told him. And even a child, when listening to a story, will alter a character or situation in a way that is relevant. But perhaps Myopie was not as *myopic* as his peers or for that matter any of the adults where he lived. "Not as what?" my son asked. "Never mind." Because like most boys, there were days when he was eager to get to school and days when he, shall we say, was not so eager. This was especially true on a day when there was a test or discussion for which he didn't feel prepared. This day was no exception. The teacher had been discussing the same community problem for days, if not weeks. And besides that, there was a big test today.

Now, there are all kinds of different ways for a boy or girl to go to school. That's not to say that the roads and paths are not the same. But the activities on the way may be quite different. Perhaps you can remember your own childhood and what you did and thought about and felt on the way to school. Some people walked to school. Some people rode the bus. Some were driven by a parent. Others walked to school. Though I don't know what Myopie did or thought about, I can assume he was much like any other nine- or 10-year-old.

Well, Myopie wasn't in much of a rush to get to school today so he was taking his time. The clouds in the sky were obviously much

[9] This metaphor was contributed by Marc Weiss, Ph.D.

more fascinating than spelling. Missing the cracks in the sidewalk was more important than arithmetic. He walked along without a care in the world, when suddenly he heard a strange noise. He looked up and saw what everyone had been talking about. He remembered his parents' and his teachers' warning. Myopie had heard all those stories. For days, people in his neighborhood and the village had been talking about the destruction of property. Farmers were concerned about the safety of animals and crops. There had been stories of violence. While Myopie could only comprehend this from a child's perception, he was aware that everyone in the community was concerned and attempting to understand the reason for the massive destruction.

They had concluded, that somehow, though it defied explanation, their community was being plagued by a dragonlike monster or terrible creature of some sort. And yet, all this was only rumored, possibly even imagined. Every child knows the experience of having a dream in which an awful monster chases you. The child has no way of understanding how your unconscious mind simply uses the monster to graphically symbolize a different kind of threat.

But people in the community were gathering at night, having meetings, preparing for and expecting the worst. People spoke of moving to a new community. Yet many realized that moving to a new place was not a solution. The story was that the dreaded monster was moving in an unpredictable way and that there was no place that was safe. And Myopie certainly did not feel safe as he stood there, as if paralyzed, looking straight ahead at what he could only conclude was the dreaded dragon.

Yes, there it was, only hundreds of yards away, over by the mountain. It stood next to a tree. The size of it seemed to dwarf the large tree by comparison. And of course the dragon was extremely ugly and vile. One could clearly see the smoke and fire coming out of the mouth and nostrils. With every breath, it was as if the dragon intensified its anger.

While there wasn't much time to contemplate what to do in such a situation, perhaps Myopie's first impulse at that point said "RUN!" Isn't this what he always did? Isn't this what he was told to do? But could he run faster than the dragon? Probably not.

Then the school bell rang. Myopie heard it in the distance. His second thought was that he should go to school. After all, that is what one is supposed to do, but to get to school he would have to pass the dragon. How would he do that? Perhaps it was better and safer to go home! What does anyone do when they're afraid? Look for known safety and security? Avoid the fear and danger? Or something else?

Myopie turned and ran. He ran as fast as his little feet could take him. He stumbled. He fell to the ground. He cried because he knew that he could no longer flee from the dragon. He looked up. He rubbed his eyes. He saw something that he did not quite understand. Now, Myopie was not an especially precocious or even smart boy, he had no knowledge of physics, optics, or perception, but he did notice something very strange. When he gained his composure, he realized that the dragon had not moved. It was still by the mountain, still by that tree, and still breathing smoke and fire and looking very menacing. So what? Safe for a moment? The unusual thing was that it appeared to be larger. Myopie perhaps unconsciously knew that the world in reality was different. The dragon had not moved but he had. He had gotten away from the dragon and noticed that in getting farther away that the dragon appeared to be larger. No, it did not *appear* to be larger, it WAS larger! He knew that was strange. Maybe not in technical terms, but Myopie realized that normally as we get further away from things, as we distance, they appear to be smaller in size. The dragon was larger. "It's not supposed to be that way," he said to himself. "It doesn't make sense."

Myopie gave an almost sigh of relief. He had seemingly gotten away from the dreaded monster, but now it was bigger and even more intimidating. Could he be devoured more easily. This was strange! Being curious, Myopie decided to investigate. And so he walked towards the street to his left, then he walked towards the bushes on his right, then he walked forwards a few steps, and then back a few steps. Hiding behind the bushes and trees he ran up a half block or so, then he retraced his steps. Again he ran forwards and backwards, to the left and the right, backwards and forwards, over and over. Sometimes he moved quickly and sometimes cautiously. He zigzagged and zigzagged, becoming increasingly dumbfounded. It just didn't make sense. But he couldn't deny that, without fail, the farther he got away from the dragon, the bigger it became. He noticed the closer he got to the dragon, the smaller it became. No matter what Myopie did, this strange pattern of its change in size remained the same!

Then the second school bell rang. He knew he had to get to school *now*. He knew he had to pass the dragon to get to school, but he had a new experience, a new perception. Myopie took a deep breath. He mustered all the strength and courage he had in his little body. And this is courage in your own observations and your own conscious mind.

He stood tall and strong. He squared his shoulders. He decided he would try to get to school. He began to run. He needed to avoid the dragon, or at least not have the dragon see him. It was better to avoid the dragon, he thought. He stopped for a moment, took another deep breath, and thought about times in the past when he had succeeded in things he thought he couldn't do. For some strange reason, Myopie changed his direction.

He did what no one else had done—ran straight towards the dreaded dragon! He saw the smoke and fire and perhaps understood why so many people had been frightened. Yet he also seemingly knew that no one had *really* seen the dragon. Was he going to run directly at the dreaded dragon or sneak around behind him? He approached the dragon and suddenly stopped. Had he come too close? No! There it was! Was it everything he thought it would be like and more? He reached down and picked the dragon up off the ground and put it in his hand. He held the dragon for a second and saw the smoke coming from its nostrils and the fire from its mouth. Yes, he held the dreaded dragon in his hand. He had gotten even closer and it had become even smaller, perhaps the size of a toy dragon or even a harmless fly. Was this the dreaded dragon, or did one really need to dread the dragon?

The tardy bell rang. Myopie put the dragon in his pocket and ran to school. When he got to school, he ran up those three flights of stairs and tried to sneak into his class without anyone seeing him, but of course everybody did.

Myopie's teacher looked toward him with a nasty glare. He came towards Myopie and asked, "Why are you late?" Myopie shrugged his shoulders. The teacher said, "Myopie, you should know better. Haven't we spoken enough about it, haven't your parents warned you of the lurking danger outside?" Myopie chuckled. The teacher continued on with what he had been telling the class. He was again discussing the predicament in the community and warning the children that they must be careful because the dreaded dragon could not be stopped. He informed the children that there would be a meeting after school and that a decision would be made that evening. Likely the whole community would be moving to a safer place, he said. Myopie giggled again. He put his hands over his mouth to hide his laughter but when the teacher continued, Myopie started to laugh so hard that he fell out of his chair, becoming hysterical on the floor.

The teacher rushed over and admonished him strongly for making light of such a serious matter. Then, too, he demanded to know why Myopie was late. "Well, it's because I slayed the dreaded dragon!" The teacher indignantly said, "That's enough, young man, I'm taking you to the principal's office for disciplinary action. Your lying and mockery will not be tolerated. With that, the teacher grabbed Myopie by the collar and whisked him down those three flights of stairs and into the principal's office, the one with the glass case behind it and next to the fire extinguisher. The outrages were reported and the principal sternly asked Myopie for an explanation. Myopie, in a small whimperlike voice, said, "I slayed the dreaded dragon." Before the teacher and principal could again respond, Myopie pulled the dragon out of his pocket. They were shocked. They saw the little body that was breathing tiny smoke and fire.

Myopie asked the teacher and principal to come with him to the playground outside and when they got there Myopie put the dreaded dragon on home plate of the baseball diamond. He walked with the principal and the teacher to demonstrate the same thing he had learned about the dragon. And so they, too, in walking backwards and forwards, left and right, saw that the farther they got away from the dragon, the bigger it became; the closer they got to it, the smaller it became.

And so the teacher and principal stood for a moment in amazement, awe, and relief. They knew the community was safe. They were safe. There was no longer anything to fear. It didn't take long for the news to spread and soon everyone was walking the streets without fear. And it really doesn't matter how the threat has been symbolized or represented because your unconscious mind recognizes the reality of a myth and the truth in fiction.

12. **Existing attitude:** *Risks are too frightening.*
    Goal attitude: *The benefits of acting when I have the opportunity are worth whatever risks may be involved.*

Metaphor[10]

Judy and Jane were both high school girls who were getting set to go to the high school dance on an upcoming Friday night. Judy was wondering what it was gonna be like at the dance—this would be the first one she had attended. Jane, on the other hand, was very confident. She knew about these things—she had heard about dances from her older brothers and sisters. She kind of knew what to expect and how

---

[10] This metaphor was contributed by Nicholas G. Seferlis, M.S.

to dress, what to do. Judy had to wonder and be curious about what she would find out at the dance that night. The more she thought, the more she wondered if she could go there and have the evening be a success. She wouldn't really know until she found the secret of the four letter words that ended in "k"!

As the days got closer, Jane had already picked out her dress and what she'd be wearing to the dance. Judy didn't know. She was concerned about colors, size, style. Jane just got more and more excited about who she'd be seeing at the dance, what they'd be wearing, and who'd be with whom. Judy, however, became more and more anxious not knowing whether she would look allright, whether she would make an awkward mistake, maybe even step on someone's toes. She would soon find out that all would be okay, after she learned the secret of the four-letter words ending in "k."

Jane was talking at school to all her friends, getting all the information of who was gonna be with who, what everybody was wearing, how people were going to get there, whom they were traveling with. Judy didn't want to talk about the dance. As it got closer and closer, she got more and more anxious. She didn't know what would transpire that night, whether somehow she'd be made to look foolish or maybe not look right. But she would soon find out when she had the secret of the four-letter words.

The night of the dance, Judy and Jane came in the same car. Jane was very confident that she was wearing the right dress and appropriate accessories. Judy was still not knowing what would happen when she found the secret of the four-letter words. During the course of the evening, both girls danced a little. As they danced, Judy felt better and better, not knowing that the secret of the four letter words that ended in "k" would shortly be revealed to her. She was curious about how the dance would turn out, whether she would leave the dance with somebody or go back home with Jane's mother.

At one point, the dee jay announced that the next dance would be "ladies choice." Jane, of course, had no difficulty going right over and picking out the captain of the football team. Judy hesitated at first, though, and as she did, she opened her purse to take out a kleenex and wipe her brow. Inside, she saw that her mother had left two words on the kleenex. Those two words were "risk" and "pick."

She walked up to a quarterback she was interested in getting to know and asked him to dance. She smiled at him, he smiled back. As they walked onto the dance floor together, Judy felt very proud of herself, almost a sense of relief that those two magic words "risk" and "pick" had been revealed at exactly the right time. She may have made some mistakes, but that's part of risking. If you risk, you don't know what you might get, but you do know that when you don't risk, you won't get anything. Judy and Bob continued to dance together all evening, dance after dance. She had found a new friend and all because of the two secret four-letter words that ended in "k." And though Jane had a nice time too, just as she had expected to, when she left the dance that night, it wasn't with an additional feeling of exuberance and pride that accompanies an opportunity to achieve something you hadn't expected but can really appreciate. And Judy was as happy about that as she was about the date she and Bob had arranged for the next evening.

13. **Existing attitude:** *If I let go of someone or something valuable, I will lose it and be alone.*
   Goal attitude: *If I care about people I can let them go; we will be together again.*

Metaphor[11]

When Jennifer, my former client, heard the pained cries of the robin in her yard, she had no idea that it would lead to one of the most difficult decisions of her life.

She took the bird in to care for it. The bird seemed to be somewhere in between being a baby and a full-grown bird, but Jennifer could not be sure. Every day Jennifer would feed the bird. She would do whatever she could to make the bird comfortable. She would talk to it, sometimes she would sing to the bird. She was not sure if it was a boy or a girl, but she decided to name it Ricky. As time passed, she grew more and more attached to Ricky. Jennifer was confident that Ricky felt the same about her. She thought that she could see it in Ricky's eyes. Day after day Ricky grew stronger. After several weeks, Ricky was once again flapping his wings. Jennifer decided that she'd better buy a cage. After all she did not want Ricky to fly away and leave her. But this was not the decision that was to become one of her most difficult.

She wanted to make Ricky happy so she put his cage by the window. At first, this seemed to be a reasonable solution. But, as Jennifer watched over the coming days, she could see Ricky's eyes follow the

[11] This metaphor was contributed by Robert Schwarz, Ph.D.

lines of birds flying in the sky. Jennifer began to think about the fact that everyone has their own sense of the path that they must follow. Your conscious mind may travel on that path with a sense of curiosity about what you will encounter, while your unconscious mind generates the confidence to put one foot in front of the other; or your unconscious mind may become curious about the experiences of adventure that your conscious mind experiences as you grow into your own person.

And Jennifer would watch Ricky, and she had the growing sense that Ricky was yearning for his freedom and the openness of the sky. And, as she became aware of this, she could feel the conflict grow within herself. She had grown so attached to him. "How I can I bear to let him go?" she thought to herself. Her own answer was, "But he is unhappy here and if I care about him I should care about his happiness." She wondered if he had the same conflicted feelings as she did. To go or not to go?

Now everyone has had to make similar kinds of decisions. And when you have to make a kind of decision like this, it stirs up all kinds of feelings. And sometimes what you are aware of most is that feeling of doubt, but underneath that doubt sometimes tucked away in a safe place is that growing need to express a natural development. It's like that line in the song, "Fish got to swim and birds got to fly." And that doubt helps you not make a move too quickly or impulsively; and yet it also does not prevent you from following that natural development. If you watch that baby take its first steps, it is always a tentative first step. And even the shock of falling down does not prevent the baby from continuing to walk.

And Jennifer pondered the question for days. And even after she knew what she was going to do, it still took her several more days to adjust herself for the changes. And, of course, she couldn't know that her most desired wish about Ricky would come true. There would be no way to know it ahead of time. So she prepared herself for granting Ricky his freedom. And when you prepare yourself for a parting you prepare yourself for the tears of saying goodbye. You prepare yourself for the ache in your heart. You also prepare yourself for the good feelings of the start of a journey, the excitement of a bon voyage; you prepare yourself for the good feelings of wishing someone you love well. And, of course, there is the saying that absence makes the heart grow fonder.

And when the day came, Jennifer opened her window early in the morning and looked out at the brilliant blue sky. She knew no matter how sad she was, she would be happy for Ricky. And she opened the cage, tenderly picked him up, kissed his head, told him good luck, and then in an instant before she could change her mind, she opened up her hands and stretched out her arms, and Ricky turned his head at her, and looked her in the eye, and chirped. And she felt it in her heart that he was saying thank you. And she had the odd bittersweet feeling of having your eyes fill up with tears of sadness as your heart sings out with a song of joy. And Ricky flew into the sky. He circled once and chirped as he came by her window, and then he flew away. And Jennifer was left wondering if she would ever see him again.

Several months passed. Jennifer had been sad at first, but gradually you become more cheerful as you become involved in your own individual activities. She thought of Ricky often, but less often than you might expect. Then one morning, for some reason she woke up early and could not fall back asleep. She opened her window, and sitting on her ledge was Ricky. Jennifer was so happy to see him. And I don't know if her conscious mind knew that her unconscious mind recognized that when you leave, you can always return for a visit, or perhaps her conscious mind just knew that she would always be glad to see Ricky no matter how far he had travelled or how often he returned.

14. **Existing attitude:** *If I don't rigidly prepare and stick closely to plans, things that are in my best interest just won't get done and I will suffer.*
Goal attitude: *Flexibility allows greater responsiveness, enjoyment, and discovery of opportunity that a rigid plan couldn't allow for.*

Metaphor[12]

Looking through the bedroom door, clothes could be seen scattered about. Dresser drawers were standing open. The contents of the closet were spilling out. Down the hall there were footsteps. It was Cloe rushing back into her room. From downstairs, she could hear her sister Beverly calling in an urgent tone for her to hurry or they would miss their flight.

Cloe and Beverly were about to go on a trip to Europe. They had made the decision some months ago and Beverly had diligently made all of the arrangements. She had worked with the travel agency to book the tour and had reviewed all the schedules. She had made arrangements

[12] This metaphor contributed by Don Shepherd, Ph.D.

with the neighbors to collect their mail. She had stopped the newspaper. She had taken the cat to be boarded. The house was clean and two of the lamps were set on timers to come on at six each evening. Cloe's contribution had been to look at the travel brochures and to buy some new clothes.

Finally, Cloe came down with her three suitcases bulging as though they would pop at any minute. By the time they got to the airport, there was barely enough time to get checked in and make it to the gate. While Beverly worked with the agent, Cloe wandered away to browse in the shops. When Beverly looked for Cloe, she was nowhere to be seen. After a frantic search, Beverly finally located her looking through magazines in the book shop. Now it would be a run to make the flight.

Beverly collapsed into her seat and Cloe rattled on about how much fun all this was and why did Beverly worry so much. When they reached their destination and started on their tour, you can imagine what happened. Cloe was usually the last person to get on the bus and the one who most often missed the guide's description of the points of interest because she was looking at something else.

About halfway through the tour, they were visiting a small village and while the guide was explaining some interesting architecture, Cloe wandered off down first one side street and then another, finding all sorts of interesting things to see. Time passed so quickly for her when she was having a good time. Rounding a corner she happened to notice a clock in the window of a small shop. The pendulum was swinging back and forth but it couldn't be that late already. She looked at her watch and it was! She finally found her way back to the square where the bus had been parked but it was gone. Beverly, who worried about things like this, had the schedule and Cloe couldn't remember where the tour would stop next.

She went from shop to shop trying to find someone who spoke English. Then, in a small shop that sold wine and cheeses she found not one but two of the villagers who spoke English. She told them about her problem and they all had a good laugh when she found out that the bus would be only a few miles away for the rest of the day. She asked if there was someone who could take her there. A young man who had been quietly sitting at a small table stood and introduced himself. He was an American who was touring this country by motorcycle and that next tour stop was his next stop also. Within a couple of hours Cloe was back with the tour. But the next day when the bus left, she wasn't on it. She was on the back of a motorcycle having a great time exploring the back roads and villages of that country.

It's been a long time since that trip to Europe and Cloe's children like to listen to their old maid Aunt Beverly tell about how their mom met their dad when they go to visit her in the house where she and their mother had grown up.

15. **Existing attitude:** *If I don't take care of other people all the time and give of myself to them, then I won't be accepted or important to them.*
Goal attitude: *It's okay not to take care of others and to take care of myself instead, and, in fact, people will respect me more for it.*

Metaphor[13]

Ava, actually, had always lived east of the Pecos. And she was one of those wonderful and giving people who just seemed to become the center of the community or the center of the group or the center of anything that she ever did. She was just so warm and friendly and loving. She had lots and lots of friends and was the kind of person that got along everywhere she went.

It was best to say that she was just really happy and had a good family—lived out on a big farm with her husband and kids. And it seemed like there were always big doings out at Ava's place. The kids were always involved with something, and they had their friends over. You could look at that from the outside, if you got to know them the way I did, and it seemed to be one of those storybook families that makes you a little envious sometimes. You think, "Boy, I wish my family had been that way," or "Why can't I make my family be like that?" It was quite something to see. She was such a giving person. And if, now and then, her friends did seem to take advantage of her, it would give her pause for a few minutes, but it was okay. That was just Ava.

Rita was a different kind of woman. She, too, lived east of the Pecos, but had relocated there as an adult. She was the kind of woman where if you had something to say, she wanted you to say it. If you had a request to make, stand up straight and make your request. And if she had something to say, she said it straight out. She was kind of a no-nonsense person. She lived on a farm, too, down the road from Ava,

[13]This metaphor contributed by Don Ferguson, Ph.D.

and like Ava, had a family and was busy with everything a family farm woman east of the Pecos is busy with.

But there seemed to be a little different feel to it. She was a good wife; she was a good mother. The children did not want for anything. She really did very well in that respect. I guess the major difference between Ava and Rita was that Rita seemed to have a toughness about her. That no-nonsense got translated into a lot of different areas. Her kids were encouraged not to lie in the bed too much. It was time to get up, and there was work to do. And while she took care of them when they were sick, she didn't do a lot of babying. "You just have to know how to play hurt" was one of her favorite sayings. Her husband used to watch her in action with the kids and dealing with the farm and some of the farm workers they had there. And he would say with kind of a frown, although he was proud too, "Rita, you are the toughest woman east of the Pecos." She would just press her lips together and shake her head and not even answer him.

Ava had such good friends and stayed so busy, people did envy her and her family especially because she took such good care of them. There were times that people let her down or took advantage of her, but it was okay because she felt like it was her job and her right to be sharing and giving like that. She felt this was a very good thing for her to be able to do. And on more than one occasion she was honored by her friends and her family, describing just what a wonderful person she was. And she beamed. It meant a lot to her to have that kind of honor. She felt very good about that but she tried to downplay the celebrations or time spent on her during the brief moments of celebrations.

Rita had friends, too, but they just weren't the kinds of friendships or situations where there were people who would look at that and say, "Boy, I wish my family was like that." Rita was just a little more reserved and played things a little closer to the vest.

Well, as it happens east of the Pecos, both Ava and Rita experienced a very sad time. When Ava's husband died, she did all the right things. She went and took care of all the arrangements and saw to it that this was done just right. And people came from miles and miles around. It was such an event. She thought to herself, "This is right. This is a good honor for my husband." While it was really hard for her, she was doing okay.

When Rita's husband died, it was a tragedy for her too, because as reserved and as tough as Rita let you know she was on the outside, she also had a very tender heart. So it hurt her very, very deeply. She didn't particularly notice or pay attention to how many people came to the funeral. She just knew that there were people there whom she cared about. There weren't as many people there as had been at Ava's husband's funeral, but she didn't think about that. She was missing him a lot.

But time passed, as it does east of the Pecos, and Rita would often think about that way her husband would kind of frown and look at her over his glasses and say, "Rita, you're the toughest woman east of the Pecos." She held that inside herself and thought on it a lot. She knew she was tough, but it felt like she was just doing what was right.

Ava seemed to lose something as time passed. It seemed that the things that held her together, the things that she gave to people and did for people, didn't seem to be working out so well after that. You know how the kids get married and leave to start their families. They were wonderful and would come back at Christmas and holidays, of course. But her whole life had been organized around giving and doing for folks, and there really didn't seem to be that many opportunities for her to be giving and doing for people the way there used to be. It was like the wind went out of her sails. She began to not feel quite as good. She wasn't as active and stayed closer and closer to home. The kids began to talk about what they were going to do when she couldn't get around much any more and who was going to have to take care of her. It was a hard time. Things started unraveling for Ava.

The interesting thing about Rita was that, as time passed, she created this image inside of herself of her husband and her children. Of course, the kids moved away too. They were independent and strong, and they came back to visit a good bit because they really loved their mother and felt very close to her—admired her strength. Yet, it was the funniest thing. They would come back to visit, and as they did that, they had this sense that they were interrupting their mother's schedule because she seemed to be so busy. As time had passed on, she had gotten involved in so many things. People seemed to know her everywhere. She was still a very reserved sort of person but interested in lots and lots of things. Her sons, standing around talking about her one day, thought she seemed like a really good, complex wine, that the aging just seemed to bring out her best characteristics. She just got better and better with age. They would tell her this sometimes as they'd be standing around the fire, when she could finally slow down enough to sit down and talk to them. She would just smile and remember what her husband had said about how she was the toughest woman east of the Pecos. She never really said much about it, but she knew deep down in her heart that she was probably the happiest woman east of the Pecos.

16. ***Existing attitude:*** *If my parents don't recognize my needs and respond appropriately to them, there's nothing I can do about it and I'll be depressed or unhappy.*
Goal attitude: *It's okay to take responsibility for making my needs known to my parents, and if they don't respond, I can persevere or get them met elsewhere.*

Metaphor

A lot of parents buy puppies or kittens or even goldfish for their children. Interestingly enough, they know the reason they buy these pets but they don't really realize what they know.

I'm sure we've all heard it. Almost every parent who's ever bought a pet for a child has explained the rationale that this pet will help the child learn how to care for something. Sometimes dogs are smarter than children! And the reason that parents buy the dog is for the dog to teach the child something. Often parents don't realize that this is their rationale. I'll explain what I mean.

It's too bad parents don't really realize that by disciplining the dog and knowing that you can depend upon the dog to be a dog, they know that the dog is going to teach the child something. Researchers don't often realize that they're trying to train their pigeons to teach *them* something. I don't know if it's appropriate to say that pigeons are smarter then researchers but actually it's very true that the researchers are trying to teach the pigeons to teach them something. It's just like the children, in teaching the dogs, are expected to learn from the dogs. And because you can depend upon the dog to be a dog, I conclude that pets are often smarter than people. Pets are smarter than children. Sometimes you can't depend upon children to be children. I'll explain what I mean.

Lynne and Bob were both children from the same family. I happened to know them over the years. They certainly exemplify the principle of which I was speaking. Lynne was always thought to be the nicer of the two. Bob was the one who would always make trouble about things. Lynne would be the one you could depend upon to call the mother two or three times a week. And even as children you would know that Bob would likely be the one you could depend upon to distance at some point. Bob's life took some interesting twists and turns.

Bob and Lynne both grew up and had children, but because of the way they acted, one of them's divorced and has been removed and isolated from seeing that child. But you'd never know it about them as children. All you could tell about them as children was that Lynne really tried as hard as she could to be a decent person, really tried to sacrifice herself for the sake of the common good and followed the rules most of the time. Only on an occasional rare incident did she ever talk over with Bob the breaking of a rule. But Bob broke rules all the time.

I remember one incident when they had gone for a walk and they had gotten too far away from home before dinner. Somebody offered them a ride home and Lynne paid Bob a quarter not to tell their parents that they accepted the ride. So we really know that Lynne has some feelings or has some needs contrary to the ones that she's respecting in the family, but she was a good girl. She was sorry to have broken the rule against hitchhiking and would never do it again. She was a wonderful neighbor, never picked on the other children.

But Bob was the kind of person you just knew something was going to go wrong for later on. Like after that hitchhiking incident, he began to travel in that way very frequently. And he would get in fights. And what does a child get into fights about? And furthermore, he had this cockeyed attitude that his parents really ought to change in some way, sometimes, in order to accommodate him. When Lynne was not allowed to spend money to buy the kind of matching dress and shoes that all the other girls were going to have at some dance function, she cried and kept it to herself in her room, took a nap, and went to bed. But when Bob's father threw a fit and refused to show up at a father-and-son banquet where the other fathers were going to be, Bob reacted quite differently than Lynne would have done. He made his father change his mind.

As a result of a misunderstanding about whose care was going to be used, the father had gone into a very childish pouting behavior. If it had been Lynne and her banquet, she'd have felt so sorry for that father, she'd have surely gone to her room and cried silently to herself, but not Bob. He came stomping out into the living room and tried to reason with that father, shouted with that father, told that father that he expected to have a father who would be a model for him—not someone who would weasel away at the first sign of a hurt feeling. That wasn't the kind of father he wanted. Well interestingly enough, on that particular occasion, it worked. Bob was able, in that instance, to get his father to change.

In telling a story like that to someone in trance they might wonder what it has to do with dogs and children and pigeons and researchers. But one day Lynne's mother accidentally stayed up late and saw Lynne kissing a boyfriend on the porch. Lynne accommodated the difficulty the mother had with that and Lynne stopped dating the boy. I know that when Bob had been told that he was not to date, he confronted his mother and father and said, "Just what is it about me that you don't trust? If the parents of a total stranger would trust their daughter with me when we're dating, why won't my own parents trust me when I'm dating? I want my parents to act better then total strangers. And I'll give you a chance to reconsider this." And, at some point during his adolescence, Bob took an attitude that he had formed gently over the years and finally worked into a forceful posture which he polished as an adult.

Friends treat a person pretty nicely. Strangers are sometimes civil, sometimes rude, and parents should be a better category then rude strangers, civil strangers, or even friends. Parents should be a special group of people. A parent should be someone you can look up to and turn to and feel supported and accepted by. And when his parents decided to not follow that kind of a ruling, then Bob would raise a ruckus. He wasn't very mature at the time. He was much better at it at 28 than he was at 18, but in some way he would make that point.

And Lynne, on the other hand, was a nice, accommodating, friendly girl. She knew that the way to keep things peaceful was to try to do what was expected. And her parents wanted the best for her after all, even if they didn't understand her. Maybe they were a little right, maybe she was a little right but she was their daughter. Maybe someday she could do it her way but while she was living with them she should do it their way. That's what they said. They made the rules. And even to this day, Lynne calls her mother three times a week if not more.

But Bob follows different rules. In fact, he insists that they call him sometimes. He thinks it's a little unequal for parents to not call the children and expect the children to call the parents. He got right on their case when he had called and several days or weeks passed and he called again and they were mad at him for not calling more frequently. He asked them if their fingers were broken, what was the problem with them picking up the telephone, calling him if they would like to speak to him? That's what his friends do and he thought his parents would be better than friends.

That's what this has to do with dogs, children, pigeons, and researchers. It's ironic that you can look at these children and you can know they're going to grow up and have a certain kind of future. Neither of them would want to be the one to have an ex-spouse and have their own child turn away from them. But one of them did grow up to be deprived of contact with her own child after the divorce, and in a rather unpleasant bitter way too. Well, what it has to do with dogs is obvious. What parents don't fully realize is that they're buying the dog to teach the child. That's okay. Everyone expects that. So why doesn't the parent similarly expect the child to teach the parent? Bob knew that intuitively somehow. And Lynne didn't do her job. That's why I wasn't too surprised to find out that when her marriage ended in divorce, her ex-husband turned their son away from Lynne and she's not been able to see that child for six, eight years now.

Bob, on the other hand, is extremely close to his parents, has a strong marriage. Ironically, he's the one in the family everyone listens to, even after all of the sacrificing that Lynne did so that her voice would be heard. It just goes to show you that she didn't do what a pet does. She didn't do for her parents what a pet does for a child.

17. **Existing attitude:** *If everyone around me acts unpleasant, it is not my fault in any way.*
     Goal attitude: *People will give me what I expect of them.*

Metaphor

There once was an old man who each day sat and meditated on the top of a hill overlooking a small city below. One day as a traveler passed by with his bundles on his back, he asked the old man, "What kind of people live in that city, for I'm in search of a new home?" The old man immediately replied with a question, "What kind of people lived in the town where you lived before?" "They were a sorry lot," the passerby said. "Every last one of them was dishonest, rude, selfish, with not a care for anyone except themselves. They wouldn't give their own mothers the time of day. It's good to be rid of them! But what of the people that live in the city you are looking at?"

The old man listened and then said, "I'm sorry to tell you that you'd better pass right on by this city. I'm sure you will find the people here to be exactly the same as the people in the city you've left." The passerby left. And the old man continued to sit alone.

The next day, by chance, another traveler passed by with bundles on his back and asked the old man the same question, "What kind of people live in that city, for I'm in search of a new home?" Again, the old man replied with his question about the kind of people who lived in the town the traveler had left. "Oh, it grieves me to remember leaving them—they were so honest and brave and caring, generous and giving, every one of them a true friend. They would give a stranger the shirt off their back."

Having heard this description, the old man smiled and said, "Then, welcome to this city. I'm sure you will find the people here to be exactly the same as the people in the city you've left."

18. *Existing attitude: If I ignore the difficulty of conflicts and pretend there are none, I will have a better time and be just as productive.*
Goal attitude: It is more profitable to deal with conflicts, keep them comfortably "out on the table" and work at them until they are resolved.

Metaphor

Out there on the beach are a lot of fishermen who earn a living. And many of them end up at some time or another out on the pier. We met one of them who had an unusual name—I think it was "Evan." He liked to drive the other fishermen crazy because he caught so many fish.

He had a confidence about him and made up his mind to notice the right things at the right time. And you never know what you are going to notice until after you realize that it is the proper thing to pay attention to. You never know how many fish you are going to catch. And when you listen to Evan give advice about what you should do and where you should go, where the movement is on the surface and what it means, how the little fish are running from big ones—there is a lot of information to use and there are a lot of decisions to make. Each time he speaks about something, two or three seconds pass before you notice it yourself. He was in control on that pier! But he had to do it by continually shouting orders.

And one thing my little boy has to learn is the same thing that another man, Bruce, did wrong all day long that day on the pier. Shawn would put his pole in the water and he wouldn't think that fish would come and simply remove that bait. But Shawn would feel a little tug and then it would be over. In Bruce's case it was more exciting. He'd be casting out his minnow, reeling it in. Then something big would hit that line.

By the way, when a fish hit Evan's line, he would give a tug and he would keep that line tight and he would start hollering to his partner to do this and do that because he would want to keep that line tight. And lots of times there would be more than one fish so he would decide to cast out another bait and hand the first pole to his partner. His wife would be there holding on to his pole while he hollered to her, "Keep that line tight, keep that reeled in tight." He'd cast another one out into a specified spot and be pulling on his line while she was pulling on hers. No wonder he caught twice as many fish as anyone else. And when he'd give the pole to her, it was as if the bulk of the hard work had already been done. All she had to do was keep the line tight and pull it in. Anybody could do that. Or so it would seem.

And you might wonder why he kept giving instructions so many times to her until you think about Bruce and what he would do when a big fish hit his line. He'd casually reel it in and wait. He had a number of different things he would do but the one thing he didn't do was tug back. And he didn't yank the line and set the hook and reel the fish in so as to keep the tension. He really didn't want to make a fight out of the sport. He didn't want to damage and tear the fish. It seemed silly, but after all it's another life form. You want to be careful. He wanted to catch the fish all right, but he wanted to do it in a way that wouldn't hurt that fish and you couldn't really blame him for that.

I think maybe he just didn't want to have to dig that hook out of the fish, because when you keep the tension tight you have to get your hands dirty. It's a kind of warfare that is going on. And that fish is ready to rip its guts out to get away. So you have got to be willing to remove the hooks that have gotten buried deep in there. You're going to have to get your hands sloppy. You're going to have to get a few fish fins poked in your fingers. You might even have to pull your own hook out of your own hand sometime. I guess that is what Evan took for granted.

So Bruce and Shawn would inadvertently let a lot of fish go. They didn't really think that they were letting them go. They thought they were reeling them in. Bruce just couldn't understand why all the fish seemed to prefer Evan and his wife. What was that bait he was using anyway? He even borrowed some of Evan's bait and he would carefully cast right in the same vicinity, but to no avail. Evan commanded a lot of attention with his behavior. But, it was absolutely phenomenal— no one else on the peer caught anything close to the number Evan caught. When he was done, he left and others stayed on to talk about him and try further. No one left feeling as good as Evan felt.

Now there was something that Evan was comfortable with that Bruce wasn't comfortable with that Shawn hadn't learned yet either. But Shawn is only four and will spend a lot of time noticing what makes the difference between simply enjoying the view from the pier and also catching fish while you do it.

19. **Existing attitude:** *Sharing feelings and talking are to be avoided.*
Goal attitude: *It's better to talk things over than to dictate.*

Metaphor

It's a funny thing about wars and wooden boxes. There was an army officer who won a medal of valor in battle and brought it home in a wooden box. And that's related to another army officer I only heard about. They didn't know one another and it wouldn't have mattered if they weren't actually in the same war, as it turns out. They acted entirely differently about things. And both ended up with a special wooden-boxed souvenir.

One of them, George, really commanded attention, commanded authority, gave directions, acted responsibly, expected compliance from his men, and followed military rule to the letter; and the other man, James, sat down and talked things over at every step of the way, which is a stupid way to run a military operation. If George had known James, he would have been very angry to think that this guy was even allowed a position of command. You surely can't have a smooth military machine operate by having people sit down and talk about it and share their feelings or take a vote. There has to be an order given that's followed.

One occasion arose which was very similar for both men during command. A half-dozen of their men had become encircled by enemy snipers. A decision needed to be made whether or not to attack with a weakened force and with the disadvantage, wait it out, call for additional aid, do something creative, or sacrifice the men to the enemy.

For George, the decision was easy. Military chain of command is set up for just such a situation. And precedent prescribes the proper conduct. He ordered and his men, without much capability to strike back with an advantage, were ordered to fight!

And by contrast, this sort of dilemma was just the kind of thing that would bring out the worst example of James's conduct. That is, he would fail to make a decisive, though unpopular command. Instead he sat down with the men and discussed the situation. He openly stated that he did not know what was best for all concerned. He took the time to say that he was worried about the group that had gotten surrounded. He actually took time to get answers to the question, "How do you guys feel about this?" And "What do each of you want to do, given the risks?"

Now if George had known what James was doing he surely would have reported him on some kind of violation of military code, because everyone knows that's not the way to run a smooth organization. And it would be expected that George's behavior was certainly exemplary of the kind that would be considered meritorious in battle. So you could easily expect that George was the officer who came home with the medal of valor, even though the majority of his men were killed in the attempt to free their encircled comrades.

The medal of valor came home in a box but it was earned in battle by James, leading his men on an especially dangerous mission in which they operated as a team. But no one died in his similar situation, though the risks they took were certainly as great. James's group devised a creative plan. Half of the remaining free soldiers disguised themselves in enemy clothing and pretended to be marching the remaining 25 percent of the men to captivity as prisoners. This ploy brought the snipers out "into the open," where they were suddenly tricked and defeated.

And he brought the medal of valor home in a box. And the reason that is interesting is because it was George who, himself, came home in a box—he had been shot in the back by one of his own men.

20. **Existing attitude:** *If I am not perfect, I will lose my parents' love or the potential love I hope to get when I am finally perfect.*
Goal attitude: *We honor parents by making mistakes honestly and learning from them, and for this growth and maturity we are loved.*

Metaphor

Not enough people really follow the commandment to honor your parents. Everyone has an opportunity to come to these revelations by different means. When I first came to the mental health profession, it was my lot to deal with those impoverished children from the ghetto that every city has. And there was a large ghetto in the city where I lived, and I worked with those children and others referred by the schools because they were said to be "maladjusted." Sometimes they were referred by their juvenile-court worker or parents. I thought I was the professional teaching them something when they came into my office or when I met them on the street. It's only later that you realize how much you learn from those situations and how much even a child can teach you.

Jesse and Michael were two brothers, both my clients for different reasons. Michael was referred by the school. They thought he had learning disorders, dyslexia; he was nervous, and he was on his way to developing an ulcer if a 10-year-old boy can develop an ulcer. His brother, Jesse, by comparison, was also my client but he was my client because of breaking the rules, getting in trouble all the time, talking when he shouldn't have been, going where he shouldn't have been, and I don't need to say more because you know the type. He experimented with everything he shouldn't have been involved in.

Their parents had worked hard. They expected a lot. They had done everything possible to give those boys an opportunity. Michael tried to show his appreciation by never getting mad, never making mistakes, but that was a big mistake. Of course, nobody thought Jesse was showing appreciation at all.

But I saw those brothers for years, and the relationship was so intense that when the parents were suddenly tragically killed in a car accident, I went to the funeral. Michael tried to take care of everything and everyone in the wake of this crisis. He was always at the hospital during every visitor hour. He contacted all their friends and relatives. He learned about and completed all of the funeral arrangements. He didn't even miss any school in the process. His teachers at first thought he was being very brave.

Jesse, however, disappeared on the afternoon of his parents' death. He was not seen for two days. He ended up in Chicago and had to hurry back for the funeral. What he brought back with him was a poem about what he had gotten from his parents and how he felt their love. He read it at the funeral and everyone cried heartfelt tears.

Michael missed the funeral. He himself, was in the hospital, due to the acute ulcerated stomach and intestinal wall which he had created during the process of doing everything just "so."

It surprised everyone when the minister, in speaking about the parents and their hardworking values and morals, actually complimented Jesse for his ability to live the spirit that his parents had preached—through his conduct, or misconduct, to really honor his parents. He had never thought in terms of honoring them. He had been criticized for rebelling against them. He hadn't thought that you can honor your parents by having problems, that you don't have to honor a parent by not having problems. When you have a problem, you have a unique opportunity to express a value, face a problem, accept your humanity and learn something about the humanity of others, and grow beyond that problem.

And you don't notice it immediately, but somewhere in all that, Jesse had grown beyond the notion that problems were a difficulty and you only succeed if you have no problems. You could even think it's your responsibility to have the proper amount of problems and survive those problems and learn from those problems, that it's an opportunity to further your parents' values. But you do it in your own unique idiosyncratic way. Michael went on to develop the high blood pressure and heart failure he had been working on, and I guess some people never learn to apply the values of the parents even in their own good time. Jesse had long since stopped coming to therapy and in fact spent all his time after school as a volunteer big brother at the boys' club.

21. **Existing attitude:** *If I don't hang onto the acceptable relationship I've got, I will find out how awful it is to be single and dating.*
   Goal attitude: *Taking risks and dating are exciting and are an opportunity to expand my personal maturity, feel my power, make a friend.*

Metaphor

Poor Susan thought her problems were finally over when she got out of that long and abusive marriage. And those problems were over, but a whole host of new problems were ushered in to replace the old ones. She suddenly found herself very alone, vulnerable, and totally overwhelmed at the thought of dating in the eighties. She never had been very good at it; maybe that was why she had just married the first man she didn't even know when she was not yet old enough to really even know herself. It had taken her almost 10 years to realize she wasn't the awful person her husband kept insisting she was. It was about this time of self-discovery and transition that Karen had an occasion to finally meet Susan.

Karen had been dating Susan's brother, Bill, for about a year and knew how much he loved both of them. And Karen was blissfully secure in her relationship with Bill. He was just about everything she could want in a man. And, unlike Susan, she had dated enough men to know when one was really special. Karen was rather certain she and Bill would eventually marry, just as soon as he got over that little attitude problem he had about marriage spoiling relationships. She had decided he was worth waiting for and that is exactly what she was doing. When they visited Susan in her new home to lend her some support, Karen quickly became even more convinced what a treasure she had in Bill. She felt so sorry for Susan when she watched the anxiety and insecurity that plagued Susan horribly whenever an opportunity to meet or talk to a potential dating partner presented itself.

One night the anxiety really peaked when the three of them went out to dinner. The waiter came to the table to explain the evening's specials but Susan had to have them all repeated because she was so preoccupied by her sudden and intense feelings of attraction for that waiter. After he left the table, all she could talk about was how cute he was. Throughout the meal, which she probably didn't eat, she agonized over whether or not he might also be attracted to her, wondered if he were married, or gay, or involved with someone. She wondered whether it was appropriate to tell him how she felt, hoped that he might be thinking of asking her out, and on and on and on. She wondered, worried, and giggled like a schoolgirl with heart pounding and blood surging.

Karen looked on, smugly comfortable in that relationship with Bill, so glad that all those kinds of problems were behind her. She just breathed in a deep sigh of relief, squeezed Bill's hand in a possessive kind of way, looked knowingly at him, and then turned a very friendly look of empathic sympathy to Susan to let her know how tough and uncomfortable she knew this episode was for her. She and Bill enthusiastically ate their meal, commenting often how delicious it was, while Susan kept an eye on the waiter in an attempt to ascertain his interest in her. Finally, while waiting for the check and final goodbyes to come, she decided that if he didn't ask her out, she was going to tell him about her attraction to him. Along with that decision came a new level of anxiety and trepidation, such that Karen and Bill doubled their reassuring efforts and also their private feelings of superiority.

Soon, the check was lying on the table, the waiter was bowing his head to them in that official and courteous little way that good waiters do in nice restaurants, when Susan made her move. Taking a deep breath and smiling a slightly nervous smile at him, she hesitantly said, "Can I ask you something personal?" In the twinkling of an eye, he was down on one knee so as to look right into her eyes, head tilted slightly with a look of curiosity and interest as he said, "Sure, and what might that be?" Encouraged, and too far in to back out now, she forged ahead with, "I just think you're very attractive and I would be interested in getting to know you better. How do you feel about that?" There! It was out and she didn't have to wait too many excruciating seconds before he smiled broadly, took her hand, squeezed it, and said what a great idea he thought that was. He didn't have a lot of time to make all the arrangements then, of course, but he took her phone number and they tentatively decided on a date for the next night when he would be off work. Then he was gone, and Susan, for all practical purposes, was in heaven for the rest of the evening.

Once outside the restaurant, she did a cheerleader-type leap and holler in the parking lot before hopping excitedly to the car. She kept saying, "I just can't believe I did that, but I really did it!" The transformation of anxiety to pure excitement and confidence was re- markable! She was breathing big, deep breaths with a huge smile that seemed permanently affixed to her face. She had enough energy to do just about anything, but Karen and Bill were kind of bloated from eating so much and besides it was getting a little late, they thought. They voted for just going back to the house and relaxing. Karen, especially, was beginning to notice a distinct feeling of envy for Susan and the experience she was now enjoying so thoroughly. She wished she had some kind of opportunity to take a risk and get rewarded and validated like Susan had done. And it was an unspoken wish that just sort of settled into the back of her mind and caused an ever so slight feeling of dissatisfaction with that waiting relationship she had been so happy with before.

At that time, of course, Karen had no way of knowing how quickly she was going to have that wish come true or how great a transformation would take place in her life as a result. It's probably a good thing she didn't know, because not knowing allowed her to just relax and savor that feeling of being slightly bored which she wouldn't get to have again for quite a long time afterwards. They spent the rest of the vacation week enjoyably enough, actually, seeing museums, plays, parks, and all the things you do on vacation. And it was with genuine love and caring that she said goodbye to Bill at the airport when he went back home and she caught another plane to attend a week-long business meeting. Though nothing tragic was about to happen to either of them, that time in the airport constituted the last moments of their relation- ship.

Karen went on to the meeting, missing Bill and still a little envious of Susan. With that kind of predisposition, she went through the motions of attending her appointments. It was there, when she was least expecting anything of the sort to happen, that she met Stuart and found herself quite unexplainably infatuated with him. The content of the lecture was lost on her because she was totally preoccupied with thinking that he was just about the most appealing man she had ever seen. She spent her time wondering if he was married, gay, or involved with someone else, and if he might possibly be interested in her. After the session closed for the day, she really yearned to spend some time with Stuart and even called the desk to find out which room was his. Thinking she would call him, she instead decided to just walk down there and find out whether or not she could gather any clues about his availability. Sitting on the floor outside his room was another woman she had never seen before. Karen decided that must mean he wasn't there and went back to her room to call him and confirm her theory. He answered on the first ring. Not knowing what to say, she hung up immediately and sat down on her bed with heart pounding, blood surging, feeling just like a teenager, and said to herself, "Uh-oh, my wish has come true. So this is how Susan was feeling. I thought I remembered it, but I had forgotten how incredibly alive it makes you feel!"

She lived with those feelings all night and they made for some very interesting dreams, dreams that continued in some manner throughout the next day of the seminar. At the close of session that day, she was ready to seize her opportunity and taking a deep breath, she rushed out right after Stuart and stopped him in the hallway, heart racing with excitement. "Excuse me just a moment," she said smiling, "but I think you're very attractive and I would really like to get to know you better. Would that be possible?" She couldn't know how welcome he found that unexpected attention and interest to be or how charming he suddenly found himself thinking she was. But soon she knew, because he was smiling broadly, twinkling around the eyes, and saying things like, "Well, sure, how about dinner?" And sure enough, she felt like cheering, hollering, hopping, and all the things that go with that incredible feeling of energy and confidence that can come when you take advantage of an opportunity like that.

After that, one thing led to another, and some months later they were married. She couldn't believe it was possible. She had found a man who had those same special qualities she so appreciated in Bill but there would be no more waiting required. Bill couldn't believe it when Karen came home from that business meeting and abruptly ended their relationship. He did eventually come to terms with his ambivalence about commitment, but it would be another woman who got to appreciate it.

22. **Existing attitude:** *If I am not an aggressive, tall, and super confident man, I will be a disappointment to women.*
    Goal attitude: *Nonaggressive actions from a man on a date are often experienced by a woman as desirable and pleasant, even refreshing.*

Metaphor

Julia and Stan were both students at the University of West Florida, and both asked us to see them for therapy, but at that time neither of them knew the other. So when Julia first came to see me, she didn't really want to get into therapy, although she did decide that was a good idea later, after her academic counselor gave her a stone one day that became extremely symbolic for her. The idea that the stone would be a stimulus that would keep her in college until she graduated didn't occur to her immediately. But that was still before she met Stan.

So when Julia was in her first semester, she decided it was time to drop out. She wasn't there for any reasons of her own concerning careers or learning—she was interested in meeting a boy and not getting a degree in a field of study. After having been there for three months, she had seen more textbooks and fewer boys than she wanted to see— but she still hadn't met Stan yet. Stan had dark hair and was short and a little bit shy. She was certain she was going to want to meet a blonde who was tall. That was about it—but she hadn't met Stan yet. Stan, on the other hand, was interested in meeting a girl. As short as he was, he didn't want to meet a tall girl but he hadn't seen Julia yet.

So Julia went into the office of her university professor who taught her roughest course. He recommended she go to the guidance counselor, and at the guidance counselor's office she sat there with a pout on her face, almost in tears. Before she spoke, he said, "There's something I'm going to give you and I just know this is going to answer a question you have," and he reached over to the shelf, picked up an almost ordinary-looking rock, and gave it to her. He closed her fingers around it and said, "Now, I want you to go ahead and tell me what you are here for and then look at what you've got in your hand. I think that will answer your question for you." And *that* was long before she began to have an idea that this rock was going to play an important role.

Stan had already sought therapy because of his reluctance to act too quickly on a date. He was afraid that if he acted too quickly on what he felt, if he tried to show what he really wanted to do, or if he expressed his desire, he'd find himself in the position of offending the girl, making a fool of himself. And he hadn't met Julia formally but he knew that she was the girl he wanted to date. He was only a college freshman and he'd think of other guys on dates and what the other guys had been doing. And considering his own sense of awkwardness, his lack of skill, he sure didn't want to reveal to Julia that he wasn't as worldly as the kind of man he thought she desired.

Unbeknownst to Stan, Julia had also entered therapy about the same time, just after the incident with that stone. And it took us a couple of times to figure out that they were talking about each other when they came to their sessions and spoke about what they'd done on the weekend. Stan had himself in a real bind. He wanted to let Julia know how he felt about her but he didn't want to express it to her in such a way that it might offend her, turn her off.

Meanwhile, Julia talked about what kind of man she was looking for. Stan went on the date with her, walked her to the door at the end of the date. He hadn't told her how he felt, why he dated her, hadn't held her hand, hadn't touched her in any way. He had been reluctant to look her in the eye and laugh. He shyly turned away at those times.

And, at the final moment standing at the door, he said he would have gladly died rather than figure out whether he should ask her if he could kiss her goodnight or not. He didn't even think it was a good idea to shake her hand. He told her he had a good time and went home. Julia had a good time and said so and went in.

She came for therapy the next day and she asked if there was something about her that made men stay at a distance. She had met this nicest guy. She sure hoped he'd call her again for a date. His name was Stan. He seemed to be quite sensitive. A whole week went by. I saw her for the next session. She said Stan hadn't called her. She had gone out with some other guys that weekend and had a fairly nice time. She wondered what she had done to offend Stan.

And suddenly it dawned on us that Stan said he hadn't called the girl back. He thought that forcing himself on someone would certainly quickly reveal what kind of nerd he was and so he was reluctant to call her. It was an uncomfortable position of knowing they were talking about each other and I could encourage him to call her or I could keep my mouth shut. I didn't know what I should do. As time passed, Stan did date her again and had another repeat of the same behavior, further embedding himself in the idea and belief that if he would be more aggressive, people would simply find out how inexperienced he was. He thought that his timidness was an indication to everybody and every girl that he dated that he was impotent and inferior as a man. And that became the issue for his treatment over and over again.

And we got a postcard from Julia after college. It was amazing how quickly those four years had passed once she got her priorities straight in those counseling sessions. She had, in fact, pursued a geology major and learned quite a bit more about stones than she had originally bargained for. And you might say she polished and brought out her own hidden qualities of independence and confidence during those four years. She had always kept in touch and told us about all the things that went on in her life throughout most of her college career, long after the therapy was over. She'd stop in as a friend. And so after the wedding announcement came in the mail, we weren't surprised to get a card from her on her honeymoon. She had married a man named Michael.

And she said she wondered if maybe she was going to end up getting more therapy some day from somebody because in the back of her mind, even on her wedding day, she was wondering about what it would have been like if she would have called up Stan and dated him some more, instead of waiting for him to call. And in her postcard she wrote that she still had thoughts about that guy Stan who left an impression on her from freshman year. Why couldn't more guys be like that? But she was happy enough with Michael, I suppose. But who would have ever thought that a little stone, a passive little stone, would make that much of an impression on her entire life?

23. **Existing attitude:** *If I am shy and sensitive, I won't amount to anything in this world.*
    Goal attitude: *A shy and sensitive person may not only be correlated to success but might also be a nicer person.*

Metaphor[14]

You might say it's a small world. Everyone's probably met someone who they knew long ago and said, "My goodness, it certainly is a small world." Michael was a kid in my high school gym class who wasn't

[14] This metaphor appears in Lankton and Lankton, 1986, pp. 291–293.

always willing to go into the wrestling arena, on the wrestling mat. He tried to get out of doing the push-ups. He would be glad to somehow happen to have skipped gym class if possible or somehow get a note from someone letting him out.

He was a nice enough guy. Come to think of it, he might have been a little too nice. Not too many people could really understand and appreciate the poems that he wrote. We used to, in fact, make fun of him a little bit for his poems. David was the ringleader. He could always find somebody to pick on. And it seemed that Michael was the guy David liked to pick on the most. Psychotherapists sometimes speculate that the person who you can't tolerate is the one who represents some aspect of yourself that you're trying to disown. If that's the case, David sure was trying to disown the poet in himself.

Michael used to describe to the gym class the foods that he cooked. It seemed unusual to me that a guy in high school wouldn't realize the unusualness of speaking about the foods that he cooked or the poems that he wrote. Even if you had a proclivity to write poems, it might be a good idea to keep it to yourself until you checked out the terrain a little better. And gym class was certainly the wrong terrain.

I don't know if there were a lot of guys who had it figured out who they were going to grow up and be like. And looking at the gym class, deciding whether or not you're going to be more like David or more like Michael might not be a very difficult decision to make at all. The interesting thing is that a person listening to this story probably makes up their mind about the story in some way.

And in gym class, I saw them both, year after year, with David relentlessly making fun of and pushing Michael around. It was the only place that I had seen David for most of my high school; it seemed as if nothing bad ever did happen to David. It seemed unfair at the time. I remember.

He certainly did develop a disdain for being in the kind of classes that I attended. I never saw him in any of the math and physics classes, none of the chemistry classes. He didn't seem to be in any of the literature classes I had. I only saw him in gym class. So I might have been a little bit naive by just what kind of attraction he was creating and what he was drawing to himself in the world. I'd almost forgotten about them entirely.

Jackson, Michigan, is 35 minutes south of Lansing where I went to high school. Years later, after graduate school, I moved to Jackson and worked in a mental health clinic. And one day when I was teaching psychology at the junior college, I ran into Michael and found out he was there teaching humanities. I heard he was a gourmet cook, but I didn't ask him about it.

We got to talking about high school. I asked him if he'd ever seen any of the old people from high school, and Michael said that, this term, David from gym class was a student in one of the humanities classes he was teaching! Finally, the bully was trying to further his education, extricate himself from the confines of the unskilled labor job he'd had since high school. I asked him if it was difficult to teach somebody who had been beating him up years before or was it a royal pain? He said it was just a job and the man seemed to have some talents and he was able to teach him. So I guess it really is a small world.

It is very applaudable that Michael could put aside the fears he gained about being like the other boys and see the talents and skills of that other man. And whether that was done consciously or whether the learning is just unconscious, even now, well, that doesn't really matter.

24. **Existing attitude:** *If my parents had a terrible marriage, I probably don't have what it takes to create a good one for myself.*
    Goal attitude: *It is possible to create a good marriage/family even if I didn't have the advantage of being born in one—and sometimes that unfortunate circumstance may even turn out to be an advantage after all.*

Metaphor

Georgia and Sally lived on different sides of the tracks but, still, no one would have ever thought that one of them would never make it to the high school reunion because she had been killed by her husband, who also took his own life, just a week before the reunion. It was true that things had never been comfortable for Sally. She came from a "broken home" as they say. There had been a lot of abuse between the parents before they did the children a service and separated. After that, though, things just got worse, what with financial hardship and all the problems the mother had dealing with the stress caused by children and their needs. Sally, being the oldest, had to take a lot of responsibility for the housework and cooking and it really didn't seem fair that she didn't get to do the normal socializing. And even when she did have the time, she didn't feel as good as the other girls, her clothes were all wrong, and she just didn't seem to fit in.

In school, though, Sally managed to hold her own. She more than "got by" with pretty good grades. But she wasn't involved in any of the after-school kinds of get-togethers. She heard about them, though, because she and Georgia had been sitting together in homeroom since first grade. Their last names, when alphabetized, had always grouped them beside one another in assigned seating. But in every other way, they were as unalike as two girls could be. Georgia had always had every advantage. Her parents were models in the community, and Georgia herself had won every popularity contest from first grade to homecoming queen. And, of course, she had all the most coordinated clothes and fashionable hairstyles. She knew she belonged and was always confident she would be accepted. Her grades were all right but she didn't have to depend on that kind of accomplishment to feel good about herself. It was a foregone conclusion that she would be given the world on a silver platter throughout her life.

Sally could only imagine how ideal things must have been for Georgia at home. Sometimes she would imagine it in great detail while she was feeling weighed down with chores, or getting yelled at and nearly beaten up by her father when he was drunk.

She had seen Georgia's parents at a couple of school functions and they often held hands and looked at each other, smiling proudly, whenever Georgia's latest accomplishment was being announced. Or maybe they would just look on as chaperons at a dance, sometimes dancing together in some interesting, old-fashioned way. Georgia seemed to get to set her own rules and her parents were there to support her all the way, with nothing but her happiness to concern them. And, of course, despite her less-than-perfect grades, Georgia had been accepted at several excellent universities. Sally couldn't figure out how she could negotiate even the first semester financially. Even filling out application forms seemed to be an unrealistic waste of time. No one had any trouble at all electing Georgia "the most likely to succeed," whereas people from Sally's side of the tracks didn't even get considered. It was as if people were convinced even then that Sally wouldn't have a future of any kind.

But while high school days seem like they are going to stretch out into forever, eventually graduation takes place and everyone dissipates into the world at large in various directions and most soon lose touch, even the closest of friends. And before you know it, 10 years have got behind you and it is with a bit of a shock that the letter comes announcing the 10-year reunion, when it kind of just seemed like yesterday, except that it takes a little while to even remember the names of those closest friends until you look over the list of those classmates that can be found and those that are listed along with the request to send information if you know of the whereabouts of the missing classmates. There were Georgia's and Sally's names on the alphabetized list, side by side, just as they had always been in home-room, both on the found list. So Sally had had a future after all, but no one figured she would show up at the reunion, it being a social sort of occasion and all.

I don't know if you can really appreciate the shock that reverberated through that hotel ballroom where the alumni were meeting when the previous president of the class took the microphone and announced that he had some sad news to share. It was quiet enough to hear the proverbial pin drop when he said that Georgia would not be attending the reunion because, tragically, Georgia had been killed by her husband the week before and he had just been sent this message from her parents.

Sally was perhaps saddened more than anyone else, even though she had never been considered to be one of Georgia's friends. But there had been a proximity all their lives and Sally had so often wished to be like Georgia that she felt like she was close to her. And so, as she had prepared for the reunion, she had fondly anticipated how nice it would be to share with Georgia how nicely things had turned out in her life during the 10 years since graduation. Attending with her were her husband and their two-year-old daughter. He was real proud of Sally and wanted to be there for her while she met with her old schoolmates and let them get to know the woman she had made of herself. And he was looking forward to meeting this Georgia he had heard so much about.

No one can ever make sense of a tragedy like that. There's just no reason. It seems like such a waste. And no one would ever know the inside story of that marriage or the tensions and conflicts that preceded the final, terrible end. One could only speculate as to whether or not Georgia contributed to her fate in some way, selecting an inappropriate mate, ignoring important signs, taking for granted that she would continue to luxuriate in golden outcomes without having to take any responsibility or working for them.

No one really knew, but in the course of the evening it became clear when Sally said that she had set out to make things happen in her life, unencumbered by any misguided notion that they would just come to her because she was special. She had earned the confidence she radiated that evening. She had worked hard to build a marriage with a man she had selected who could support her strength and appreciate her hard work and her willingness to risk herself and love him. And it was also clear that she was intent on giving her young daughter a model to live up to, even though she was living proof that you can do anything you set your mind to no matter what side of the tracks you come from. The train didn't run through there any more though and the tracks had been remodeled. That part of town where Sally had lived had become an inner city historical and entertainment area, specializing in jazz and gas lights. History changed a lot in 10 years which is only a fraction of a lifetime, and the only fraction Georgia lived.

25. **Existing attitude:** *I must continue to improve myself because I haven't done well enough yet. I won't be worthy of self-praise until I am improved just a bit more or recognized as worthy by parents and others.*
Goal attitude: *Rather than being anxious about proving myself one more time, I can approach new events with confidence, pride, and satisfaction about how many things I've done so well.*

Metaphor

Two little boys who look exactly the same can be entirely different, sometimes in very specific and important ways, even two little boys from the same family. The same thing is true for two little girls. Rachael and Ruth were both raised in the same family, not too far from here. I don't suppose it is important that they were Southern Baptists—but it had influenced the selection of their names.

Things really seemed to be well categorized by the phrase "born with a silver spoon" for Ruth. Ruth was beautiful, intelligent, very well behaved, well developed as she grew. And Rachael was born with the burlap spoon in her mouth. She was a gangly little child with a posture that made her look years younger than she was all through junior high and high school. She made teachers say, "Look how little the seventh graders are this year, they're getting smaller and smaller every year." And how many times did Rachael have to hear or just sense that she was being compared to Ruth by the teachers or her parents. It was quite clear that Rachael was going to have some coping to do with the problem that Ruth didn't have on her shoulders.

Since Ruth was older and Ruth was perfect and could do no wrong, Ruth didn't try to do any wrong. She followed the rules in the strict

Southern Baptist family right down the line—no movies, no dancing, going to church several times a week, and there was no question that Ruth was going to grow up to be a matriarch just like her mother was. And the only question was how bad would Rachael really turn out, would she finally be diagnosed as having an eating or some other kind of official disorder? The gangliness didn't come from being anoretic. In that family, the gangliness came from her inability to live up to the model Ruth had already carved in the atmosphere of the family. And Rachael was destined to be a lesser girl right from the start. She wasn't as pretty as her sister, she wasn't as smart or mature as her sister. And the closer she approached being like her sister, the clearer it was that she was a different person. Children like that so often decide they're going to be rebellious, make waves. Anyone investigating that family or looking in on that family would develop a certain kind of under-standing that paralleled his or her own life.

And when you had arm levitation, your hand got tired of being lonely up there and came down by your leg. And there's a certain learning in that. Your conscious mind might not interpret that as realizing that you are very smart in your unconscious movement. You may wonder what that is to which I'm referring. But you did know that your hand is more comfortable. And Ruth came to us and she asked us the million-dollar question. She knew about us. Her parents didn't "believe" in psychotherapy but she just wondered if she should take everyone's advice and marry this young man who was nine years older than she was, who promised her this wonderful house, who was a good practicing Christian—or should she instead go off to college, further her education, maybe develop a career, perhaps never fall in love again as greatly as she had fallen in love with this guy? All of her girlfriends thought she'd be a fool to not marry now, to risk not having a house that was so great, to not have his money. They thought she would be a fool to go off to college. If she wanted to go to college, she could do it after she married this guy, except that he did want to have several children right away. She was 19, he was 28.

Rachael never had to grapple with such opportunity. Everything was a struggle for her. And it was unlikely that an older, rich man was going to propose to her anyway. She didn't look the type. Ruth was definitely gorgeous by most people's definition. So it was very under-standable that one of these children had a wonderful outcome and one of them didn't. I don't know who could possibly expect otherwise, but the surprising thing is it was Rachael who had the wonderful outcome and Ruth who had the terrible outcome.

It turns out that the silver spoon in her mouth tarnished, and that her ticket to freedom became a passport to a land she couldn't leave. And Ruth didn't know how to cope with having made gross mistakes in life. She'd never made any mistakes before.

And as Rachael grew and matured she realized what so many of us realize. Sometimes your conscious mind doesn't realize right away what your unconscious has learned. When she sat down in front of us and explained that she had had some doubts about succeeding in her career now that she was out of college with her doctorate, and since she'd never been as smart as Ruth, it was a pleasure to finally have an opportunity to say, "Your conscious mind is overlooking the obvious learning that your unconscious has done. Everything you've done, you've done yourself without anybody's help. You never could go to your parents and say, 'Look what I've accomplished.' So of course you don't feel fully knowledgeable and comfortable about taking that position now. But it's time for you to realize you've accomplished a great deal and you've done it yourself. You're a self-made person and the anxiety that often accompanies doing new things that are uncertain when no one's going to be there to help is just an artifact of the past. It's an antique for you to put up as a trophy. Your unconscious knows how to accomplish all these things that you've done by yourself. Ruth had help every step of the way and part of her help was the fact that you've doubted yourself. And vis-à-vis your doubt, she had more confidence. Look at you now. Vis-à-vis your doubt, *you* have more confidence."

So two children who often have the same background can be entirely different. Two children who are entirely different can have a great deal in common.

26. **Existing attitude:** *If I want something done right, I must do it myself—accepting help obligates me.*
   Goal attitude: *There are many terrific ways to get things done by others—it doesn't obligate me.*

Metaphor

Mona had long been convinced, and with good reason, that if you want something done right, you should do it yourself. She didn't want to be obligated to anyone. And she didn't have time for the mistakes she was sure others would make. That she had less and less time to do other things she wanted to do, well, that was just the price she had decided she'd have to pay. She was always the one who drove on any car trip. She would lead and bear most of the responsibility for any committee she was on. Her children didn't have any of those complaints about her that the other neighborhood children grumbled about their parents. Mona didn't even ask her children to clean up their rooms or do regular chores because she knew that it would be more trouble than it was worth and she just did it herself. When they occasionally found time for a leisure activity, you can rest assured that it would be Mona at the stern of any canoe or other vessel. She would decide where they went, how much money was to be spent, and all the details necessary to make sure everyone had the good time they deserved.

Her neighbor Cora was sure a different story, and it was obvious by the condition of disarray you would be likely to find her house in at any given moment, even when company was expected. Oh, things got done, but there was so much "spilled milk" along the way. And Cora worked as a travel agent and somehow commanded a great deal of responsibility, though Mona could never understand it. They would occasionally have lunch together, and it always surprised Mona that Cora was able to get there on time and yet meet her deadlines. She was sure that it was only a matter of time before the mistakes Cora must be making with that shoddy attitude would catch up with her and get her fired.

Mona never would have guessed that she had something to learn from Cora. But Cora had long ago realized that there was more than one way to get a thing done. True, you can do it yourself, for as long as you hold up, that is. Or you can hire it done, delegate responsibility, and her personal favorite, probably improvised from Mark Twain, was that she could forbid her children to do it or some variation thereof, like helping her children appreciate an opportunity to do something that needed to be done. They would focus more on the opportunity than the need. It was even that way on the outing she and Mona took their kids on one Saturday, down the white-water river.

Cora actually positioned herself languorously in the front of the canoe, dangling a foot or two in the water, and let her 12-year-old son have the opportunity to practice the responsibility of steering the canoe from the strategic rear position. But, of course, Mona's children were getting a free ride while Mona shouldered the burden. She wasn't taking any chances on a spill, or getting stuck.

It wasn't too many years later before the real sad thing that no one had been able to predict started to happen. Mona's children began to come to the attention of the child welfare and detention facilities due to disorderly conduct, drug abuse, stealing, cheating, and other teenage behavior problems. Her intentions, all along, had been beyond reproach, but it really was a pity that she hadn't given those children the opportunities they needed to learn about their own capabilities. It might have prevented the emotional problems that led to all those behavioral difficulties.

And Cora's life-style never did catch up with her, except in the sense that she kept getting promoted, and given more and more responsibility at work, because after all that practice with her children, she had really become an expert at accepting all the help she could get, delegating responsibility, giving others an opportunity to practice, relaxing in the front of the canoe as often as she could, and letting others feel the pleasure of their own accomplishments.

27. **Existing attitude:** *I should just put on a front and play it safe in my superficial relationship with my spouse and others and pretend that I have no needs.*
   Goal attitude: *By revealing myself, I find my strength, true self, and intimacy.*

Metaphor

People often learn more than they thought they would during their years at a university. That was the case with George when he was completing his business degree. But he had no idea that a toss of the coin would improve his acting skill. I knew him from some classes we had together and only found out later that he was concurrently enrolled in an acting class too. We had often lamented about how much discipline was required to deal with all of our commitments and to finish the degree. And he didn't feel satisfied, his mind wandered, and he didn't think he had enough self-discipline. I hadn't fully understood what he meant until it came out tangentially that he was in the acting class.

One day he happened to mention, and he couldn't just say why consciously, but there was a particular role that he very much wanted to play. He wanted the part badly and didn't know why he wanted to play that part—it was complex and maybe too difficult for him. He hadn't been in acting classes before. He was unprepared and naive. Ernie, on the other hand, had been majoring in acting and had been through all the courses. He had been George's idol—what with the way he was so technically correct in every audition for every part he played. He seemed to have a handle on this self-discipline thing.

So George's heart truly sank when the day of the tryouts for the part he wanted rolled around and he realized that, unfortunately, Ernie also wanted the part. And Ernie went first, put on a brilliant, technically perfect audition. George, certain that he didn't have a chance and wasn't ready to follow that, knew he didn't have what it would take to convince the audience that he was genuinely portraying that character. He wasn't even real sure how that character was supposed to act.

Now, every actor portrays something and puts on a front. Every actor is just putting on an act at some level. But somewhere in his unconscious, George knew that in order to put on that act, he would first have to have some genuine understanding of the subtle experiences involved. He'd have to know that in order to give the kind of performance he wanted—the kind that Ernie had been able to do with all those other parts.

Ernie had given a speech in class once about how "the better an actor you are, the better you are able to play roles that are divergent from your real self." And maybe that was why Ernie tried out for this particular part, to prove to his classmates just how good an actor he was. Because he was nothing like the part he was playing and yet he had done it so technically perfect.

And George, sitting there watching, unwilling to embarrass himself and reveal his inadequacy, just left the audition, left in shame, hoped that no one noticed his retreat. He didn't really know what to do. He knew he had a lot of thinking and understanding to accomplish and he just left and flipped a coin: heads I sit on the park bench and tails I force myself to go and work on my dissertation. He was glad it came up heads. He didn't feel like any discipline that day. So he just sat there on the park bench and as you're probably aware, on any given university campus around a park, you'll see a good many runners jogging by. And George had the opportunity to observe the variety of joggers out on that brisk afternoon.

And, of course, you'll see a good many joggers dressed in the latest fashion gear. They really look the part, out running their token mile, they're smiling and chatting, haven't even really worked up a good sweat and yet they look the part. George watched them go by and made the resolution that he was going to start jogging.

And by contrast, when the more dedicated runners came by they didn't look very glamorous at all. There was sweat pouring from every pore, hair plastered back against the head, wet, dripping, breathing heavily. Some wore bandages on their knees. Their shoes were old and worn-looking and their outfits didn't match. He saw one particular hard-core runner go by who was doubled over in pain and had a partner who was helping him speak to that pain. George had always stopped running as soon as he had a side splint, so he was curious to see this expert jogger running along talking to that pain, accepting it, welcoming it, telling the pain he was going to keep running. His partner would whisper in his ear, that's right, breathe into it, keep going, tell it that you're here to stay, tell it you're willing to learn from it. And, of course, George wasn't able to hear much of their conversation even though they ran by him slowly.

He didn't know how long he sat on the park bench but he didn't see the token-mile runners coming by for another round. They had finished their lap and were back preparing for the social events of the evening. But he couldn't help but notice the hard-core runners coming around and around again. And he was particularly interested in the one he had seen running doubled over in pain. He couldn't believe it was the same person at first because he was running, standing up fully, smiling, looking very comfortable. George didn't realize fully what he was learning. He knew he was fascinated at some level, having an unconscious understanding of something that he already knew, that in order to have a true strength, it was necessary to accept, learn from, and reveal the weakness that was at the foundation. And maybe it was those kinds of thoughts that accounted for his particularly open mood when he arrived at the class we had together late that afternoon.

It was hard to characterize how he was different. He asked questions with a comfortable vulnerability, he put himself into the discussion that day with a congruence I hadn't heard from him before. There was a sense of humor as well as empathy, a strength that seemed hooked to tenderness. I think at some level he figured he didn't have anything to lose, so he might as well just be himself, drop any pretense about being intellectual or disciplined or serious or whatever it was he thought he should be.

He didn't consciously think he was, in fact, rehearsing for his audition for the part in his acting class. It's hard sometimes to account for what kind of rearrangement of ideas or beliefs occur during a short period of time, but he left that class feeling unexpectedly proud but not knowing why. Somehow he knew he was ready to go to the tryout, accept his inadequacy in order to develop a true ability.

He walked into the acting class the next day, holding that coin and sometimes tossing it up and catching it, sometimes just holding it in the palm and rubbing it with his thumb. It seemed like it was some kind of a symbolic reminder of something he still couldn't consciously characterize but that he knew had made a difference in his being ready. His performance was far from technically perfect but it went beyond technically perfect. Even in the tryouts there was not a dry eye as he played that part in all of its subtle complexity. And Ernie was as surprised as anyone that he didn't get the part as he customarily did. The part went to George. Everyone voted unanimously on that

And George was surprised too. It didn't really matter to him at that point whether he got the part or not because he was so satisfied with his performance at the audition. He had learned what he needed to and it only added frosting on the cake that the rest of the class voted him the most convincing actor to play that part.

And there was not a dry eye in the theatre the night of the actual performance. And you can imagine the satisfaction he must have felt standing there in front of the audience who were standing there clapping through their tears, smiling. It was his responsibility to just stand there, feel the glow of accomplishment and satisfaction. And he told me later that as he stood there he made a decision to memorize the learning that can be realized in such a moment as that. You don't know how you memorize but your unconscious does know how to store a learning. He did a wise thing waiting for the applause to end. Others joined him on the stage, and then he had the additional satisfaction of being a part of the group, satisfied with having communicated the intensity of his own strength and weakness, lethargy and energy, inadequacy and courage that weren't divergent from his true self at all.

4

Behavior Metaphors

*Caresses, expressions of one sort or another,
are necessary to the life of the affections as
leaves are to the life of a tree. If they are
wholly restrained, love will die at the roots.
—Nathaniel Hawthorne*

*Example has more followers than reason. We
unconsciously imitate what pleases us, and
approximate to the characters we most admire.
—Christian Nestell Bovee*

Individuals and families continually grow and adjust to a changing
social ecology. This ecosystem places certain demands upon each in-
habitant, and each developmental stage brings a new related set of
demands with it. As with any ecosystem, the inhabitants whose behavior
and experiences are best suited to or fit the demands will be able to
thrive; the inhabitants whose experience and behavior mismatch the
ecosystem's demands will experience stress. For a practical example,
consider the difference in behavior of two young men in their mid-
twenties seeking employment as college graduates: one can make eye
contact, speak clearly, smile, sit comfortably and listen, leave his hands
resting at his side as he listens; the other does not make eye contact,
selects a quiet voice tone, tenses his brow as he talks, bites his lip as
he listens to others, and picks at his finger nails as he sits listening.

147

Notwithstanding job qualifications, the first candidate will be the favored choice. His conduct will fit the ecological demands being placed upon him better than the conduct of the second candidate. The former young man will thrive while the latter experiences greater stress. We are not suggesting that lack of fitness with ecological demands is a pathology, a deficiency, or a result of poor self-esteem. We are simply noting that therapy needs to assist the person in focusing attention on requisite behaviors and to expedite the acquisition of those behaviors in a nonthreatening milieu.

The purpose of behavior metaphors is to provide a context in which a desired behavior can be illustrated, and, ideally, illustrated repeatedly. The listening client thus has a chance to consider nuances and examples of the goal behavior at one level, but doesn't have to ever acknowledge a need to learn them. It is simply a story about how someone else performed various aspects of a behavior. As such, there is no performance pressure placed on the client. No behaviors are being "installed," "programmed," or forced upon the client. On the other hand, to the extent that the therapeutic assessment is correct and the client has not had sufficient opportunity to learn, model, or be reinforced for the goal behavior in his or her unique learning history, the metaphor becomes an opportunity for the client to model, think about, or consider the "new" behavior, and to identify and integrate it in relevant ways.

When designing a story to fit the behavior protocol, the background and motivation of the characters are not usually specified. If details are included, they are for the sake of metaphoric diversion and are kept short and limited to very general comments. We do this because we wish to illustrate goal behaviors without stimulating clients to make judgmental assessments about the choice of such behaviors as they relate to a goal or motive.

Basically, the behavior stories operate much as a cooking show or a workshop on carpentry skills. That is, they are a fairly straightforward presentation of behaviors that can be expected to result in a specific outcome. The focus is on how you do a thing, whether it is cook a soufflé, install a gutter system, or ask another person for help. In therapeutic metaphors, the protagonist's behavior is described in several contexts so as to allow repetition of the goal behaviors. One possibility for such repetition, for example, can be a story about a protagonist observing someone else engage in the behaviors, then perhaps the protagonist is observed engaging in those same behaviors, and then there may be still another repetition of the behaviors in the story as they were demonstrated by yet another character or remembered by the protagonist.

Summarized, the three steps of this protocol are:

1. Emphasize goals and not motives and detail the protagonist's observable behavior similar to the desired behavior to be acquired by the client.
2. Detail the protagonist's internal dialogue and nonobservable behavior used to support the actions he or she acquires which may also be used by the client.
3. Change the context within the story so as to provide an opportunity for repeating all the behavioral descriptions several times.

Labeling the behaviors is not necessary. The goal is simply to present and describe a specific set of behaviors which form a part of the entire gestalt of the desired activity. Content for a behavior protocol can very readily be provided by telling the story of a previous client who was seen for therapy and who engaged in a skill-building assignment or activity related to the current behavior goal. Stories of such clients are in fact "ready-made" behavior metaphors (though for the initial client mentioned in the story, of course, it wasn't a verbal metaphor at all, but a specific activity in which they engaged). It is often useful, however, when giving skill-building assignments, to prepare the client for an assignment with a behavior metaphor to help them retrieve and organize related resources and ideas.

Some clients, for various reasons, cannot be sent out to complete an actual skill-building assignment. When this is the case, behavior metaphors are invaluable. There are certain criteria therapists can use in determining whether behavior metaphors and/or skill-building assignments are more appropriate. These mainly have to do with availability of therapy time, the client's resources, and communication ability. That is, if a client is able to communicate well, has well-developed resources in general, and a shortage of time available for therapy, metaphors may be the more likely choice. Whereas, when the reverse is true and clients don't communicate particularly well, do not have well-developed resources, and are available for a longer-term therapy, then a series of behavioral skill-building assignments can be very useful. For most clients, both approaches will be used repeatedly over the course of therapy.[15]

---

[15] For a discussion on skill-building assignments as interventions, readers are referred to Lankton & Lankton, 1986, pp. 128–136.

Behavior protocol metaphors for a variety of specific behaviors are now presented.

1. **Behavior goal:** *Learn to be nurturing, friendly, and caretaking.*

Metaphor

She had traveled a long way for therapy and certainly didn't expect to instead find herself in the day room of a nursing home. But she had something to learn there, though of course you never know what you're going to learn until after you've learned it. It didn't take long to surmise that her difficulty coping with her young stepchildren really had very little to do with the normal difficulties expected in a stepfamily.

So, before she even took off her coat, I informed her that her therapy was going to take a little different twist. I wanted her to accompany me on an outing to a nearby nursing home and to save her questions for later. Fortunately, her appointment time coincided perfectly with the changing of shifts in the dayroom. We were seated there exactly at 3:59 p.m., just in time for her to watch the entrance of the candy-striping aide who I knew from previous experience would fill the room like sunshine the moment she entered it. "When those doors open," I said to my client, "I want you to watch very carefully what happens so that you can tell me later what you were able to notice."

Phoof! Four o'clock and the double doors on the opposite side of the room swung open and in waltzed "Patty," according to her name tag. It would be a while before my client could read the tag, but even from a distance, it was hard not to notice the way Patty looked around the room as though to "take a pulse" and determine who needed her first. Then, as though it were her entire mission in life, she stopped beside an elderly man sitting in a wheelchair with a checkered shawl over his shoulders. She simultaneously bent down on one knee so she could look him squarely in the eyes while reaching around his shoulders and gently rubbing his back with her hand. We couldn't hear what she said to him, but we watched his disinterest "evaporate" as though it were fog being burned off by the morning sun. The smile that appeared on his face was not quite as distinct and full as the one that stretched across Patty's but it was a start. The smile begins on the upper lip and spreads until it engages the eyes, the lower lip, and all the muscles of the cheek, in that order.

She left him still wearing that smile that didn't fade as he watched her go. Next, she crossed the room slowly, all the while gazing at Bernice, the oldest and often most bitter resident of the facility. Patty sat down on the couch next to Bernice and for a moment didn't speak, just breathed at the same rhythm as the old lady. Then, she reached a hand over and put it on Bernice's arm, squeezing it ever so slightly as she said, "Rough day, I bet?" Bernice nodded in agreement even as a twinge of pain momentarily altered her facial muscles. Patty's mouth was pursed in a gesture of sympathy as she said, "Oh dear, I'm so sorry to hear that. It must really hurt bad sometimes." Then, more brightly as she noticed the needlework on the other side of Bernice, "But look how much more you've done on that scene today! It's really lovely. How did you get those little ducks to stand out like that? Do you think you could show me?" And Bernice's face revealed another slight alteration, but it wasn't one of pain this time. You could actually see a little glimmer of a smile tugging at the corner of her mouth as she began to explain the procedure she had used.

Not very much time had actually passed, though it seemed longer. We continued to watch as Patty made her way around the room, stopping off to put her hands on her hips, and with an expression of wide eyed pretend-disapproval, gently chastised Mr. Martin for sitting all alone. "What do you mean hiding over here by yourself and depriving all these ladies of your special charms? Maybe you were just waiting for me to come and see you so we could have a little quiet time today. Is that it, pumpkin? Or would you rather dance with me to liven things up a bit?" He pretended to protest as she pulled him up onto his feet and over by the record player. There were quite a few tapping feet and interested onlookers as Patty expertly allowed Mr. Martin to show her the fox-trot, carefully listening to every little instruction he offered. The dance finished, she walked him back to his chair and thanked him ever so much for the fun! She had walked away from him probably five steps and then turned, looking over her shoulder and cocking her head 45 degrees, and winked a goodbye with her right eye.

We couldn't hear what she was saying at all times as we continued to watch her movements and activities. And, of course, we had no way of knowing, not that it really matters, what she said to herself to maintain such a spirit. We couldn't have known that she simply remembered her mother's voice and the things she would soothingly say. That voice would say, "Now, don't you worry, honey, anybody can be nice to somebody who's nice. It doesn't take any special talent to do that. The real test is in finding out how you can be nice to somebody who's not so easy to be nice to. That way you find out how special you are, and it just might make them a little nicer too!" And her mother would always repeat it just so, "Now, don't you worry, honey, anybody can be nice to somebody who's nice. It doesn't take any special talent to do that. The real test is in finding out how you can be nice to somebody who's not so easy to be nice to. That way you find out how special you are, and it just might make them a little nicer too!"

She used to wish she had a dime for all the times her mother had said that to her, but she didn't realize then how the skill and values she ended up with had made her far richer than she would have been if that childhood wish had come true. And I don't know if that lesson was a factor in her acquiring the nursing home position or not, but what better place to find people who are not easy to be nice to than there, with all its crotchety, bitter, pain-ridden occupants.

So we didn't know if she consciously repeated something like that to herself or if she simply looked around the room asking herself, "Now who really needs me the most? Who can I make a little happier or more comfortable today?" And then, scanning the faces and postures of those around her, she knew the answer and made her move. And we continued to watch with interest how she moved from one to another, stopping to stroke Mary's wrinkled cheek with the back of her index finger, or pausing to rub the neck and shoulders of the duty nurse who had been working such long hours and lifting such heavy loads. And there were quite a few of those 45-degree head tilts and winks. You couldn't miss that. Or sometimes she would just cock her head and smile at the person or lightly pat them on the back as she passed by.

Sometimes she must have known who needed her the most by asking silently, "Who's protesting the loudest?" This day, Grumblin' Charlie got the award and it wasn't his first time. The dinner trays were just being brought in and he was really carrying on about how the staff of this stupid "prison" was so inept they couldn't even get his food right. Though Patty, of course, had nothing to do with his dietary situation, she stood there beside him while he blamed her and everyone else. She was just looking as concerned as could be with her forehead all wrinkled in understanding. Then, when he had paused a moment, probably to consider which hateful thing to say next, she suddenly switched her posture. She grabbed his hand and squeezed it affectionately as she smiled and said to him in the softest most reassuring voice you could imagine, "Don't you worry, sugar, we're going to get you something to eat!" His anger just seemed to melt away.

At about that time, we realized that our time had really flown and we needed to get back to my office. My client thought the therapy was about to start and didn't realize yet how much she had already accomplished because you can learn a lot even, or especially, when you're not trying to. So, once back in the office, I urged her to just relax, establish a light trance, and carefully review in her mind's eye what she had just seen. I probably didn't have to help her as much as I did by describing as she relaxed how Patty had rubbed a back here, given a wink there, gotten down on one knee so she could look her friend right in the eye, empathized about how badly a pain must feel, stroked a cheek with her index finger, squeezed an arm, made an old man's day by enthusiastically letting him teach her an old dance, massaged a neck, tossed a few affectionate nicknames and jokes, kindly reassured a grumbling old goat, and on and on.

We each had our favorites and I could see a smile tugging on the corners of my client's mouth, as she remembered and reviewed with me the events of the afternoon. And your conscious mind might review and memorize the events you've seen while your unconscious goes about the process of applying those learnings and selecting a context in which they can be applied.

And then our time was up again and we had never even discussed those horrible stepchildren of hers but she seemed not to mind. Since she was from out of town, I gave her a few restaurant recommendations and we said goodbye. Neither of us knew, of course, at that point that later in the not too distant future of that evening we would be dining in the same restaurant. In fact, my client would never know it because at the restaurant she was far too preoccupied with personal matters that interested her much more than the view. So I anonymously watched with interest all evening as she occasionally reached around to her husband and rubbed his back, tilted her head down so she could gaze steadfastly into his eyes, or stroked his cheek with her index finger. And, of course, there were moments when she revealed lips pursed with sympathy as she responded to some feeling he must have shared. But there were more times when the situation apparently called for the 45-degree head cock and, in this case slightly seductive, wink. I couldn't really hear what she was saying to him, and of course I wasn't privy to the dialogue inside her head, but I kept watching him just shaking his head in amazement. Now the children weren't with them but everyone has to start somewhere. And I just bet that in the back of her head, when that moment comes, she'll hear a voice saying, "Don't you worry, honey. Everything will be all right. Anyone can be nice to someone who's acting nice. It doesn't take any special talent to do that. It's when you have the opportunity to be nice to someone who isn't acting nice that you get to discover how special you are. And maybe you'll even help them be nicer too."

And when I followed up with this client some months later, she asked if I had seen Patty again. "You know, I feel like I know her," she said. "At least I'm sure I'm never going to forget her." "And how are you doing?" she went on to sincerely inquire. She probably would have squeezed my arm warmly had she been present in any other way than by phone.

2. **Behavior goal:** *Accept help and graciously receive things given.*

Metaphor

Juan was a business leader in India and he had his image to think about. He thought his problem was genetic skin cancer that couldn't be cured. That's what the doctors had said. Once when he was in trance we suggested that he look around and think "this person would be good at it." You could probably compare the look they have to one you remember—a look you've seen on the face of your wife as she brings your clothes or holds you in her arms. Then turn your hands, palms up. Curl your fingers slightly. Rest them in your lap if you are sitting. Make eye contact as you inhale. Exhale silently.

And, of course, be prepared to say, "Thank you. That's very thoughtful of you. I really appreciate it." Even if it is unsaid you can think the thought. And feel inside for a sense of pride and mutual respect as you notice that you raise up your sternum.

So while he was sitting there with that left hand floating between his thigh and his face, it began an interesting rotation. Essentially, stretch out the hand, rotate the palm so that it faced up, and the fingers curve slightly up at their tips. It was the very same posture and his conscious mind didn't even think that would be possible, yet the unconscious automatically creates such a movement. It may have been a dissociation from his belief system as it moved that hand into a position that allowed him to have a relevant learning. And, of course, you can memorize the muscle movements and the feeling of an alteration that you learn in trance so that it is familiar when you . . . do it again, even at an unexpected time or in a novel circumstance.

And later that day, sitting at the table having dinner, everyone was struck by the sight of Juan sitting in his chair with both hands resting on his thighs—palms rotated upwards and the fingertips curved slightly upwards also. It looked almost like a meditation posture but he made eye contact as he inhaled—then exhaled silently.

The waitress seemed drawn to Juan first when taking lunch requests, and after the orders were placed, he retained that posture as several people at the table began to spontaneously share their fondness for and appreciation of Juan. With each compliment, Juan looked the other person in the eye, smiled broadly, nodded his head slightly up and down. When they were finished, he responded, "Thank you very much." All the while he kept his hands, palms up, sometimes lifting them up several inches from his thighs as though to receive more thoroughly the incoming material. And with each person he inhaled as he made eye contact and then he exhaled silently.

When they were all finished, he pulled his arms in and gently caressed his own shoulders with his fingers, smiling even more fully, tilting his head to the side, and slightly shutting his eyes. And probably to himself he said, "This person would be good at it—just fine." But you never really know what someone is thinking inside. Maybe he did say something like that or maybe it was just the thought which he had.

I know that the next day I saw him leading some children on a special activity tour, and he had them start out by sitting in a circle around a big strong oak tree. Each of them were holding their hands, palms up on their thighs, and he was instructing them to close their eyes and just wait, thinking for a moment, "What do I want to get for myself, receive from others, or learn today?" Then he asked them to "get in groups of two and for one person in each group to tie a scarf over their eyes and to lift up one hand, right or left, palm up, fingers slightly curved, and let the partner lead you, and create interesting experiences for you." This naturally led to each child making eye contact as they inhaled and exhaled silently.

On the last night of the meetings, everyone prepared to take their learnings back to their own homes and he had a long way to go. And his servants had no idea how much easier their life was about to be. They were finally going to be able to just do the jobs they were being paid for. So the immediate cultural climate was likely to be quite receptive to the alien habits Juan had picked up on his trip.

And we got a letter some months later from Juan who was happy to inform us that he was enjoying a complete remission of his cancer, although it probably had little to do with those suggestions we just mentioned. However, his wife and employees are enjoying him more!

3. **Behavior goal:** *Express anger, "fight back," confront an aggressor.*

Metaphor

When we first saw Al, his Hodgkin's disease was active, and despite his despair over that, he was even more concerned with the possibility that he was creating the disease himself. I don't think he realized what was going to be involved when he got up in front of the Town Council three months later. All he knew at the time of therapy was that he needed to fight back against that disease.

In trance, I explained that there are a number of ways you can fight. It's useful to know, before you fight, the strengths of your adversary. It is important to know your own strengths as well, so you can begin to become acquainted with your power. It is possible to find your own strength and power in a variety of ways. First of all, you have to make friends with those tensions that you have in your body when you're angry. Children, more often than not, have the developing experience of putting your strength and power against another child, gritting your teeth sometimes, tugs of war, you grab hold of the rope that your friend is grabbing onto and you pull with all your might and you dig your feet in and you're not going to let anything budge you. You don't just use your arms. And you make friends with the tension in your legs. Sometimes your friend pulls harder than you thought proper in the game and then you might have a thought in your mind: "I'll get even. I'll pull twice as hard next time." And you jerk the rope quite hard with more strength than you thought you had in your arms because you temporarily released the tension and rely upon a new arrangement of your muscles.

After many such experiences, you come to know that you can depend on your muscles, and that child learns to get angry at the hill so he can ride that bicycle up it. And I told Al to imagine riding a bicycle, pushing those feet down like he was stomping on the fingers of all the people who had ever called him names. A child can really relate to that idea. And it was just a mental image that he could use to stomp on those bicycle pedals and really be mad at that hill for being in his way. He didn't have to worry about the hill, the hill could take his anger. Inside his head he was to say, "Take those hills, don't let those hills take you." And I made sure he would say that over and over again, inside his head.

Fighting as a young person can involve punching a punching bag. You keep your eye on the punching bag like you would keep your eye on your adversary. You lift your fist up and make certain your fingers are well protected inside of your palm. And you aim carefully at the spot that you first identify. Tighten your thumb over the top of your folded fingers, maybe it's your right hand or maybe your left, because eventually it has to be both. Now you say to yourself, "Don't let those hills take you." You say it enough times to make certain. You question how you're holding your wrist muscles because you're going to have a straight line from your elbow to the end of your knuckles of the first and second fingers, then say, "Take that, you punching bag!" And when you swing your hand forward, the child learns to equalize force by pulling back on the other hand and thrusting forward using the whole force of your body behind you, behind that arm, giving it everything you've got.

You stay in balance and you also make certain you keep your guard up. And eventually you find there is hard work involved in relearning those skills. Al had never experienced having his knuckles skinned by repeatedly punching a punching bag. He didn't realize you grow past the hurt of your wrist when you hit the bag incorrectly. He had to learn to make certain that he breathed deeper, in, out, faster while you punch.

You cannot fail to not hold your breath while you're being angry. You keep breathing. You're breathing your anger out, you're breathing your power in. And you say to yourself, "I'm going to do it, I'm going to take those hills and not let those hills take me." You may curl your eyebrows when you tense. It's just a signal—Darwin knew all animals have it. You may show your teeth when you're angry. You may arch your back because the upper lip tenses up in almost all animals in the animal kingdom, and it's good to let other animals notice that your teeth are showing and that your lip is tight. It's a survival mechanism. God knows it helped Darwin survive. If he hadn't noticed that, his entire trip would have been for nothing. And sailing to another country, Darwin learned what it was like for animals to be angry. It made his entire visit worthwhile. Many people still read that book. And I explained that to Al, in the trance, making certain his metabolism changed. You learn to feel the sympathetic nervous system kick in to strengthen you, not to strengthen you so that you stand there and mope. You fight back, you visualize the punching bag and the target of your power, you visualize that power voluntarily, and as you punch forward you feel your self move forward gaining ground and defining your territory.

Now, Al was a very motivated client. Two sessions later we asked him to bring his father into the session. You never know what a client learns in trance while you're talking to him. They may be thinking about eating popsicles, pussyfooting around while you're explaining something important. So I wanted to find out how he was really going to stand up to that father and how he was going to be himself with that father, show his feelings, get his father to show him some concern—it was high time. His father sat in the office facing Al. "Al," I said, "This is the moment of reckoning. Would you rather destroy yourself to get attention or do you want to fight for it? And besides, I want your lineage to carry the values you believe in and you're not going to have a lineage if you destroy yourself." And Al automatically said, to himself, "I'm going to take those hills, I won't let those hills take me." I don't know if your conscious mind thinks that thought or if it's in the background unconsciously or if your unconscious mind automatically repeats that phrase to yourself while your conscious mind pays attention to the problem at hand.

Al was not in trance. He simply said, "I'm really mad at you." He lifted up those top lip muscles so that the teeth were bared, he breathed a deep breath, rolled his eyebrows down, tensed his jaw, took a breath forcefully, and then took another and another. I noticed that the fingers curled into his palm, his thumb tightened up to protect his fingers, and he was sending oxygen to each of his cells. He had a new sense of his own strength. Of course, he wasn't going to hit his father, but his unconscious used those mechanisms he had learned, and he leaned forward to find his territory. "For all those years, you had no right to ignore me. I deserve some attention too—for being alive, for being well."

And in the background was "I'm going to take those hills, I'm not going to let those hills take me!" He was just now becoming friendly with that feeling of tension. He was beginning to enjoy his sense of power. He heard his voice louder than he usually does, and you really ought to hear your voice raised when you're angry. And you could see his father's face showing surprise, and then his father cried, showing a respect, but that's really another story.

I was there in the Town Council meeting three months later, and who should walk in but Al. There had been a public outrage and the council had assembled to find some way to deal with the offenders. It wasn't right. The sewage was being dumped in the water which mixed with water where the children swam. And the last person I expected to have been there was Al. He walked in that door, slammed the door behind him, walked up to the podium. There was something he emitted on he walked in with his lip tight and his teeth showing, leaning slightly forward, his eyebrows showing the metal of his tension. Certainly his presence made everyone cast a new eye as he strode in. They all knew he had something important to say. I don't know whether or not the conscious mind realizes that other people are watching you while you're angry and your unconscious intends to make your statement, or whether your unconscious simply keeps track of the other people while your conscious mind realizes that you're angrily expressing your needs. You're saying something that needs to be said, you're making a difference.

So he gripped that podium with his fingers, he put his thumb tightly on the outside, his fingers underneath. If it had been a punching bag, he would have punched it. He spoke loudly into the microphone and he didn't measure his words. He expressed that outrage, and I know he was thinking internally, "I'm going to take those hills. I'm not going to let those hills take me." And he proclaimed loudly as he literally choked up the people in the room. And as each person admired his courage, they found that it touched within them that sense of responsibility, of necessity to take appropriate action. You learn how you can be so angry that you just won't hold it in any longer. He had dealt with the boogie man in childhood. And he dealt with more than one disease!

4. Behavior goal: Assertively setting a limit and enforcing it.

Metaphor[16]

And the client was really confused when I gave her a videotape at the end of our session one day because it was unmarked and she didn't know what it was about. Looking at me she could tell that I wasn't going to tell her. I don't know what she was expecting, but I knew it wouldn't be what she expected. Why in the world would I have given her a videotape on police riot training?

[16] This metaphor was contributed by Myer S. Reed, Ph.D.

But there it was and on it was that old sergeant teaching recruits at the academy how to handle themselves in case of a riot. Some people were dressed up as if they were part of a mob while the recruits were lined up and a line was drawn in the sand. The sergeant gave them clear instructions about how to guard that line and the importance of guarding that line, and about the most direct and clearest ways to do that. There were instructions about how, as long as the mob stayed on the other side of the line, they could stand at ease, breathing comfortably, with their backs straight, a certain looseness to their muscles, and a smile on their face.

But if the mob crossed the line, they were to keep their backs straight, feet firmly on the ground, their breathing quickened, nostrils slightly flared, and the smile drops from their face as they say, "You have stepped across the line, you will have to step back. You have stepped across the line, you will have to step back." And when the mob draws back, once again they could be at ease with breathing slowed, deepened, smile returning, and muscles in the upper cheeks pulling the corners of the mouth slightly up in a relaxed way.

Then the recruits were told to go into action. They stood behind the line. Right on command, the mob gathered on the other side. But they weren't across the line so the recruits knew they could stand at ease, their backs straight, a certain looseness to their muscles and a smile breaking out on the corner of their mouths as the muscles in their cheeks tightened, pulling the corners of their mouths up. Shortly the mob began to step across the line and the recruits, on cue, stood at attention, their backs straight, head erect, their breathing quickened, their nostrils slightly flared, their eyes looking straight ahead meeting the gaze of the oncoming people. Their muscles tensed, their feet firmly planted on the ground, as they said, "I'm sorry, you have stepped across the line and you will have to step back." When the crowd moved back, the line was clearly in sight again, their bodies began to relax, their breathing slowed, muscles loosened.

I asked her when she came in again what stuck with her most about that tape? She said it was the image of that one recruit as the mob crossed the line. She could still see how his shoulders squared, his breathing pace increased, his nostrils flared, his feet were firmly planted on the ground as he looked the crowd member in the eye and said, "I'm sorry, but you have crossed the line, you must step back." And how when they stepped back, his breathing relaxed.

5. **Behavior goal:** *Give praise.*

Metaphor[17]

Nan was so absorbed in her work she probably wasn't even aware of Sally sitting by the pool. Sally had her eyes closed and a book propped up on her stomach. She appeared to be drowsing. Actually, she was quite drowsy. But hearing Nan's unique way of speaking piqued her interest and Sally began by opening one eye and then both eyes. It wasn't much later before Sally sat upright in her chair and studied Nan openly. Looking through her cool ray lenses, Sally saw a big smile on Nan's face and heard her say "That was great!" to a little boy who had just put his face in the water. Right after that a little girl jumped into the water and came up with her eyes as big as quarters. Nan scooped her up in her arms, gave her a quick bear hug, and said, "That was wonderful." A third child kicked his feet and moved his arms as Nan held him gently under his belly. After they got to the other side of the pool and the boy was standing on a step, Nan leaned towards him, put her arm around his shoulders, and gave him a gentle squeeze, saying, "You swam super, I'm so proud of you."

Just then there was a big splash. As Sally was drying herself off, Nan was saying, "That's the best belly flop I've ever seen." She was clapping her hands. She was laughing. Then, the little boy who had put his face in the water was busy blowing bubbles. Nan cocked her head to one side as she counted the seconds for him. You could almost see the wheels turning inside her head as she got ready to give him the thumbs-up signal and nodded her head in approval. Then, a little girl swam a lap across the pool, one arm stayed at her side, the other made an effort to stroke through the water. Nan stood there with her chin cupped in her hand and a smile played across her face. She said, "Your left hand has got right, now just let your left hand teach the right so the right won't be left." Sally didn't remember too much after that. But it wasn't that she was forgetting to remember all she had heard.

She probably wouldn't have thought about it at all if it wasn't for the incident in the grocery store later that evening. There was Nan and her boyfriend doing some grocery shopping. A little boy and a little girl, probably his sister, ran down the cereal aisle, straight to Nan.

[17] This metaphor was contributed by Susan L. Vignola, D.S.W.

Everyone in the store could hear their chorus of "Hi, Nan." Nan took a deep breath, pulled back her shoulders, leaned back on her heels, and put her hands on her hips as she said to her boyfriend, "Would you like to meet two of the most super-duperest pollywogs in this whole store?" The children just beamed and basked in her words. Then Nan bent down and put her arms around each child and one at a time whispered something in each one's ear. As they walked away, the children gave Nan the thumbs-up signal.

Sally turned to her son who had just walked into the kitchen. As he approached, Sally leaned toward him and pulled him into her lap. She took a deep breath, smiled at him, hugged him, and said, "I'm so glad you're my son." Then she cocked her head and listened. As he slid from her lap, she tussled his hair and said, "Thank you for remembering to turn off the television." Then she turned to me and said, "He has an excellent memory." Then, with a faraway look in her eye, she said, "I haven't thought about Nan in years."

But then I recently thought of her when I had a client in trance and I told him the following: "You lean forward. Put an arm around the person's shoulder. Give the arm a little squeeze. Say, 'I'm proud of you.' Smile a broad smile. Say, 'That was great!' Give 'em a quick bear hug. Clap your hands and laugh." And that was all I said about her to him. That was enough.

6. **Behavior goal:** *Alter (exaggerate, rearrange) self- or other criticism.*

Metaphor

Sometimes, when the real world isn't confusing enough, you can go into therapy to alter that situation. I had one client, for example, who in her therapy was given the instructions to exaggerate a self-criticism or a criticism from another person until it is humorous, or change the order of the words around in the criticism so that you could know the meaning but not feel the blow. Or reduce the criticism to two words and change those words. Or thank the person who has criticized you, or thank yourself if you've criticized yourself. Say, "That is a wonderful thing to say to me. I know it is because you want me to be a better person," and kiss the person on the cheek. You know how if Snoopy kisses Lucy right after she yells at him, that really stops her. The conscious mind does not readily perceive a logical rationale for such an instruction, especially when you've come to therapy to finally sort things out once and for all.

And I told another client in trance to remember a self-critical statement or a criticism from another person and exaggerate it. Let's suppose someone says you're a slob or if you say to yourself, "You're a slob," then you simply exaggerate it by saying, "I am a slob, and a slob only has four letters in it and that's not big enough to explain me. I'm such a slob, there should be a word with far more letters in it, maybe a word with 14 or 15 letters in it. Maybe a sloboccopuss, that's adequate for me." And then she'd laugh and that would be the end of that critical event.

Or you would thank another person and kiss them on the cheek after they've criticized you: "Thank you for being concerned about me." And that got the same reaction from them as Snoopy got from Lucy.

And another thing to do is to place all the words in a random order, and in the trance I asked the person to do it. She remembered, "If you ever do that again, then we're going to get a divorce," and altered it to become, "If again ever divorce that I do, going that we are to get." But that wasn't random enough, so try again. "If get we do again we are get divorce, if get we do again get divorce I you do" is enough to confuse the conscious mind. You don't have to say it out loud. It gives you a nice opportunity to feel a sense of dissociation and it's nice to be able to laugh in the face of criticism.

I was surprised to see the same thing occur while I was in France. Our waiter was chastised in English right at our table. And he said, "I don't have the right to stand here in these shoes; some poor animal died for those shoes. Think of all of the alligators that were sacrificed." I looked down to see if he had alligator shoes. He didn't. He was just making it into an exaggeration and then complimented the man for criticizing him, and shook his hand. He could have kissed him on the cheek in France. Then that would have gotten a "yuck" like Snoopy gets out of Lucy. He could have reorganized the words and then he would have had to say, "To restaurant work this in, I have right not." But that is so hard for the conscious mind, there is hardly any time left to do anything that you appreciate in life. But you can appreciate a little gentle perverse confusion from time to time. Some clients even forget why they came into therapy at times like that. I know she did, but that isn't to say that she didn't have a learning she could not remember.

7. **Behavior goal:** *Sit comfortably with other people in a group.*

Metaphor

Certainly we learn things in one context that we use in another context, even when we give up hope. I know that was the case for Claudia, who originally sought therapy for methods of getting along with her husband in decisions related to rearing a child. When I first came to Family Service, Claudia was in a treatment group that had a funny way of not concentrating on the issue. So I sat in the group therapy room and I watched various people who were clients do various things. I had a lot to learn, and I didn't even mean to learn one of the things that I did learn. And so before taking Claudia as a private client, I happened to notice the comfortable atmosphere in the group and a particular person who was sitting there comfortably.

She was sitting comfortably with her feet flat on the floor. Your feet also can be crossed in one of several conventional manners. And her bottom was flat against the chair, and part of her back was against the back of the chair. And with rhythmical breathing, usually from the lower chest or the entire chest, someone would make eye contact with someone else, and then they'd smile. And the smile was usually a matter of initiating muscle movement of the lips and cheeks by upward movement of the outside edges of the upper lip, which would pull the lower lip, and later cause the masseter muscles of the cheek to alter their muscle tonus. Often the smile, engaging the jaw muscles such as that, will also distort the ocular muscles and actually become lines around the eyes, all because of that pesky upper lip beginning to tug at the bottom lip, and other muscles getting out of the way, usually following eye contact.

But while the eye contact continues, the smile continues to increase. And then there's the chitchat: "How are you today?" And the people who spoke the most were the people who seemed to be allowed to speak the most, saying such things as, "That was a good idea, I like that." So it usually began with eye contact, with a smile during the eye contact, followed by the words, "That's a good idea, I like that." And the tone of voice was cheerful. It's hard to describe a cheerful tone of voice. The conscious mind usually doesn't monitor the tone of voice, providing that cheerful experience is behind it, but there's usually a certain kind of melodious tone to the voice. And usually a noticeable alteration in the buoyancy with which the words are delivered. I heard, "Thank you. That was helpful. Oh, I really admire that."

Since I was new to the group, I made sure that I endured the experience simply by saying inside my head, silently to myself, "Now this is going to work out all right. I'm doing okay. Take it easy." And I noticed my breathing, still very rhythmical. And nobody had any idea that anything else was going on. And I soon was able to gain the confidence of the individual members, and I took Claudia aside. I didn't think she should have a social experience and pay for it as if it were therapy. But in her trance, I asked her to learn from the things she learned in the group and use the things she didn't expect to be useful.

Then I explained to her very carefully how I'd observed in the group something she missed, and I'd prove it. And you sit there with your bottom on the chair and your feet flat on the floor, crossed in the normal position, your back against the chair. And I knew that at any moment all she would have to say to herself in her head were the words, "I'm doing okay, this is going to work out all right." And to facilitate, I explained in detail that she ought to make eye contact with the other persons around her, let her upper lip begin to move at the corners, and drag her lower lip into the act, until finally, the smile that was growing on the mouth involved distortion in muscle tone of the masseter muscles and even brought into play the ocular sphincter. If she'd like, it would be okay to begin the smile by altering the position of the muscles of the cheeks in relation to the neck. And try to involve the upper lip as it's pushed out of the way by the movement of the lower lip. That generally begins a movement from near the ears that involves the ocular sphincter first and the masseter muscles of the cheek second. And all this should be done while making eye contact.

And I coached her to simply say the words: "That's a very good idea. Gosh, I like that. Thanks for sharing that." And "I need your help." All done with a cheerful tone of voice. Hard to explain that cheerful tone. You almost have to assume that the conscious mind understands that a certain buoyancy will be audibly distinguished when the unconscious delivers the audible tone of cheerfulness.

Claudia said nothing about it after trance, but left my office and asked for an individual appointment later. She came in and mentioned that there was a certain amnesia she was having, but she'd like to make certain that she really had gained something specific from the trance. I asked her to repeat the things that she thought I had said the previous week. And she said, "I'm not really sure, maybe let's just chat about it." And she sat down comfortably in a chair, with her butt against it and her back somewhat supported. She crossed her legs in a conventional manner, and with a just barely noticeable cheerful tone of voice, said, "I need your help. Some of the things you said were very helpful. I really like those ideas. Thanks for sharing them. And I'm sure I have amnesia for them, so I'm not going to be able to tell you in much detail." And I noticed that she was breathing rhythmically, and I asked her to just take a moment and notice what she was aware of internally. And she said, "I notice that regular breathing, and I feel my bottom and back against the chair. I guess this is going to work out all right, I think I'm doing okay. I just do have amnesia for whatever it was you had said in that trance."

The next session I asked her to show up with her children. And when she came, her husband surprised me with a videotape. He said, "She's been making such progress. We haven't been arguing, and I learned a good deal from her, just because of her attendance here in therapy. And I videotaped something yesterday that I want to show you that I don't think she's aware she did." And putting on the videotape, he explained that what he had really gotten from her was the way she counseled the daughter the night before on how to go to slumber parties, how to handle herself at the 4-H meetings. And she said, "It's very easy, sweetheart. You just sit comfortably in the chair, with your back and bottom supported, so you'll know that you can check out at any time you're sitting correctly, breathing comfortably. And just say to yourself, 'I think it's going to work out okay.' And you really ought to figure out how to make your upper lip or your lower lip begin the process of distorting your face muscles until your masseter muscles pull on your ocular sphincter or your cheek muscles pull on your neck muscles, and pretty soon your teeth will be showing, and you'll be smiling nicely. While you're making eye contact, and with a sort of cheerful tone in your voice, simply say, 'I need your help with this project.'

"And make sure you tell the other little girls at the slumber party and at 4-H that you really like their ideas and it was really fun being around them. And thank them for sharing what they did. And any time you don't know what to do, just remember what I said. Check and make sure you're breathing comfortably, tell yourself that you're going to be okay. You really can't do anything wrong in your slumber party if you behave in that manner." And that was the end of the videotape. The father was very impressed. The mother had nothing to say about it. She said, "Well, I don't really know where I got that idea, it just seemed like the natural thing to do."

And explaining to me why he thought progress was being made in the couple's fighting about the child, by watching this display by the mother, he said that he had learned that the reason they had fought was because none of them had carefully explained what to do, and when he saw the mother carefully explaining what to do, he simply knew all their difficulties could be resolved if both of them worked to not fight about the words and the ideas, but to take the time to actually explain to the child how to behave appropriately.

8. **Behavior goal:** *Learn "the proper way to give a gift"—ritual gift-giving behaviors.*

Metaphor[18]

When we visited Milton Erickson at his home on December 20, 1979, he didn't have a Christmas tree and we wondered about its absence since he struck us as the kind of man who would appreciate a little external display of Christmas spirit. After all, he did have a Santa hat on a bust of himself and a little sign that said "Merry Christmas" held by a miniature Santa. So we asked him about the tree and he said, "They're all out in the yard, the children are gone now. We don't do that anymore." We thought that the subject was closed but actually he had a good bit more to say on that count, but not in a way that we expected or, in fact, would even remember.

Because Milton Erickson could talk, like a lot of grandfathers do, about so many things, your mind would occasionally begin to wander. And he talked at great length that afternoon about lingerie, for one thing, which we did happen to remember, and he talked about the way a person goes about purchasing it. As it turned out, he once had a client who was so ignorant about how to buy lingerie for his wife, he didn't even realize that a woman might appreciate getting that kind of gift. So he needed a lot of assistance, though he didn't particularly want it, and Dr. Erickson obliged him by going along and demonstrating the kinds of interactions with saleswomen that result in the shopper making an informed decision. Dr. Erickson actually convinced one sales lady to model some of the lingerie for Joe—I think that was his name.

[18] This metaphor is adapted from Milton Erickson's version, personal communication, December 20, 1979.

Well, eventually, after some minor discomfort on Joe's part, the purchases were made but that presented another problem. How do you give the gifts once they've been purchased? It was Christmas time then, too, and Dr. Erickson went to Joe's home to educate about and supervise what he said was the "proper way" to give a Christmas gift. He gave Joe the instruction that "first you call the recipient by name and say 'Merry Christmas, Carol' as you give the recipient the gift and a firm kiss upon the lips." With that, he asked Joe to demonstrate his comprehension by giving the first gift to his teenaged daughter, Carol. Joe said, "Merry Christmas, Carol," and gave her a little peck on the cheek. Dr. Erickson inquired, "Carol, was that the proper way to give a gift?" She said, "No, Dr. Erickson, it was not." He then asked her if she would prefer to have him or his handsome son Lance demonstrate for her father the proper method. She chose the former, and as he told it, "she gave me a ten minute 'clinger.' "

In the course of the things he talked about that day, we remembered a few other isolated comments, but mostly we roused ourselves when it was time to go, and started thinking about what we might go and purchase as a Christmas gift for Dr. Erickson. Immediately the idea of a Christmas tree came to mind and we subsequently found one and decorated it with lights, ornaments, tinsel, candy canes, and all the things you would expect to see on a Christmas tree. The next day we eagerly returned with the tree and an incidental present we had also selected. Dr. Erickson seemed pleased but not surprised to see the tree, but I was more concerned about giving him the gift. I wasn't sure exactly what was proper in that context, so I awkwardly stammered some possibilities like "we have this gift for you and you could, uh, open it now, or maybe you'd rather keep it and open it on Christmas." He just shook his head slowly back and forth and said, "Yesterday I told you a long story about the *proper* way to give a Christmas present." With that, I had no further questions and proceeded to look the recipient in the eye and said, "Merry Christmas, Milton," and presented the present along with a firm kiss on the lips.

But that wasn't really the end of the story, despite the fact that he died shortly thereafter and it was the last time we would ever see him. We left Phoenix, went home, celebrated Christmas, taking a long time carefully giving each of our gifts properly around our own Christmas tree. About six months later, we chanced to hear a tape someone else had made of that session on December 20 in which, among the other things that we had forgotten, the proper way to give gifts was elaborated.

We had been listening with curiosity to those other stories, hearing them as if for the first time, at least with our conscious minds, and when the story of Joe and the lingerie came up, we welcomed our only familiar story from that experience. But we sure were surprised when, right in the middle of that story that we did remember, we heard Dr. Erickson say, "And I didn't want to go with Joe to *buy a Christmas tree,* that was too much trouble. So I just told him that 'you go out and buy a tree and decorate it with lights, ornaments, tinsel, candy canes, and all the things you expect to see on a Christmas tree.' " To say we were surprised is an understatement! Here we had been thinking what an original idea we had in buying and decorating that tree for him, and he had been behind it all the while! Of course, there were 10 other people in the room listening to those stories that day and 10 other trees didn't show up the next day.

But I have heard from three of them. One of them told me that in trance she frequently tells people the following: Look another person in the eyes and, while still looking, smile at them broadly. Then say, "I have a little something for you." And add, "Are you ready?" "Happy birthday, honey!" And then hand them the gift along with a firm kiss on the lips. It can even be a small occasion. That's what she tells some clients in trance.

Another therapist from that day in his office wrote to say that in family therapy, he asks clients to demonstrate their understanding that they are to do certain things at special times. Look another person in the eyes and, while still looking, smile at them broadly. Then he has them demonstrate saying, "I have a little something for you." And he asks them to show him how they would add, "Are you ready? Happy valentines, honey!" And then hand them a gift, along with a firm kiss on the lips. It can even be a big occasion. They just need to have previously purchased a present, even a small one.

The third therapist I heard from who was present that day does what we do. When the season is close, he buys a gift and then at the proper time he pops it out and says those words, "Merry Christmas, Susan." He makes eye contact first and smiles broadly. Then he says, "Merry Christmas, Susan." As he hands them the present, he glances from their eyes to the gift and then back again to their eyes before giving the firm kiss upon the lips.

All of this comes from that day on December 20 and the story Dr. Erickson told to the group that day. It is a nice reminder that people only follow those suggestions that are relevant for them and modify suggestions to fit for you in accordance with your needs and values. After all, only one tree showed up that day!

9. *Behavior goal:* *Learn playing behaviors and sexual behaviors.*

Metaphor

Like most families, we have a large swing set in the backyard. It provides a context for our children to have lots of rhythmical, physical activity. And every child learns to swing sooner or later. You don't realize consciously that while you're in the swing, you're learning a good deal about the balance of your body and the rhythm and your ability to hold on to the rope, and let somebody else push gently. But your conscious mind is learning a lot of things while you're swinging, things that you're never going to appreciate as coming from that swing.

Parents who won't let their children swing are really doing quite a disservice to them. You learn something about motion that becomes the foundation for development later in your grown life. You learn something about interacting with another person who gently pushes you. That swing becomes an opportunity to understand you can trust someone else. And you learn something about your own ability to keep the swinging going. Kicking your legs in a certain way, pushing your butt out in a certain way, leaning your head back in a certain way. And without realizing it, gradually, a child learns a lot of coordination in the body.

Now you don't remember that source of coordination. You couldn't put words to the coordination. But you do have that coordination. And whether you consciously realize it or not, your ability to feel that coordination as the support that you use as an adult is really sufficient for the kinds of confidence you need to have, even in relationships with other people.

Now a swing set in a healthy family is going to get a lot of workout, a lot of wear and sometimes tear, and it's to be expected and taken in stride. Recently, Shawn had his favorite little girlfriend over to play with him and they were out on that swing where you sit facing your partner and both of you put your feet on little pegs, and push and pull yourselves back and forth. And they were swinging back and forth with all their might, chanting "higher, faster, we need another master . . ." in fact, when, with a sudden thud, it broke. Neither of them were hurt, but the main, large, supporting pole that usually fits into a corresponding hole had managed to come totally free. The structure was temporarily disabled and looked like a pretty big job to fix. I had my wife go out there and, pushing up that hole just a little bit, she was able to carefully insert that pole into the hole, so as to temporarily support the structure.

A little bit later, I took out my drill, and making sure it had enough power, made another hole into which a very large screw could be inserted and screwed tightly so that the swing set would be a safe place to play for a long time in the future. And together, we made lots of holes with that drill at various stress points and put nice big screws in to hold the pieces together. And so when Chrissy came back over to play with Shawn again, I don't know why we bothered to tell them "Don't swing too high" because we knew the swing set had really been secured. But it didn't matter, because all children will disregard certain instructions of the parents and do what you will know just "feels right" in those kinds of situations. And out there gripping the bars tightly, and smiling into one another's faces, they spent what seemed like hours pleasantly engaged in rhythmical, physical activity. And then, of course, having worked up a sweat and an appetite, they came into the house for ice cream cones and mucus membrane stimulation. And the whole process is so pleasant and so natural that the child never thinks about how it is that the unconscious is storing a learning about how to have rhythmical, physical activity and mucus membrane stimulation with that best friend, and it's just a nice, comfortable foundation for later learnings.

And swinging isn't the only thing they like to do. A child will play at something every chance he gets. Riding in the back seat of a car becomes an opportunity, even strapped in seat belts. Two children can laugh hilariously just at the act of absurdly completing each other's sentences. Or building a block castle, one day, we heard his other friend Monet say to Shawn, "Let's put the door right here." And Shawn said, "No, let's let this be another wall," to which Monet enthusiastically agreed, "Okay, we won't have *any* doors!" and then they both laughed and laughed at how much fun that would be. His occasional friend, Sally, would have said, "Now Shawn, you know we have to have a door; just quit being silly." And Shawn doesn't like to play with Sally as much but I probably don't need to tell you that.

A child isn't able to understand how it is that you memorize an ability to feel comfortable playing with another person or that it doesn't even matter what you're playing. But just at the moment you least expect it as an adult, or perhaps at those moments when you think it's a disadvantage to be feeling so vulnerable and childish, you create an opportunity to retrieve that confidence that a child can have happily playing with another child. And it's a precious possession, that feeling. I saw a little piece of some movie a long time ago in which Gene Wilder played an especially shy and insecure man who was obsessed about failing with whatever woman he attempted to date. He thought all the pressure was on him to perform sexually and he just knew she would be disappointed, no matter who she was. But then he met the woman who knew how to just take things slow and easy and comfortable.

They went dancing first and remembered what every child knows about looking at a special friend's smiling face while you have rhythmical, physical activity. Disregarding the tempo of the fast music, she just stopped still on the dance floor and held out her arms to him, inviting him to dance slowly with her and hold her close, in response to his yelling over the loud music, "When do we get to really dance?" And you just listen to the thing the other person expresses and ask yourself, "Is this something I can help with, something I can respond to comfortably?" And it continued like that, even when they got back to her apartment, and she lit candles and began to slowly undress him. She released a clasp of her own clothing and then comfortably looking at him, sweetly said, "You'll have to do the rest." As he looked at her naked body, focusing on her breasts, she asked, "Did you think I would be bigger?" And he said, "I had no idea you would be so beautiful." Then she put on a record and they danced in the quiet intimacy of her candlelit bedroom, before going out for a moonlit romp on the beach nearby. Much later still, sitting naked in front of a fireplace, he placed his hand against her heart and commented on the fact that it was beating rapidly.

"Nervous?" he said. "What do *you* have to be nervous about? I'm the one who has to do it." She simply asked, "Do you want to know what would make me feel good?" He said, "If I could know that, it would make me very happy." And very simply, she softly, carefully explained that "while having you inside me would be very nice, I don't want that now, right now I just want you to touch me and kiss me, but keep your eyes open and just look at me. I would tell you more things, and I will tell you more things, but first I need a little bit more confidence." And then, she just looked and let herself be looked at. She just smiled the most tender, beautiful, vulnerable, but trusting smile you could imagine, eyes wide open, slight delicate little smile, very still, very warm.

And then, through the magic of movies, blending with and super-imposed in front of that young woman's face was the much younger little girl she had once been shining through, smiling that same smile, even a little fuller with confidence, innocence, and openness, playing in the sprinkler with a little boy. And the little boy's face of course temporarily replaced the face of the shy man, and there was his innocence and trust and curiosity and love as he looked into the face of that smiling little girl. Water was splashing on them both, and they hugged as the drops rained down around them. The two adults who were soon pressing their lips together tenderly, then more passionately embracing, had somehow been able to just reach into that storehouse of learnings that the child has and apply that sense of knowing how beautiful and precious you are to a current situation with someone you know you can trust to recognize it too. And that simple act of honestly looking at each other, touching each other, and kissing was far more intimate than whatever overt sexual contact followed, but the intimacy certainly lends a magic to the otherwise technical act of sexual intercourse.

And when Chrissy's mother came to pick her up from playing with Shawn on the swing set, Chrissy said, "Mom, we've been swinging and swinging and then we ate ice cream cones." But that wasn't what she'd really been doing; she'd been engaged in rhythmical physical activity and mucus membrane stimulation with our little boy because the process of developing intimacy in relationships is built on an innocent enjoyable foundation which begins long before the adult forms mature sexual relationships.

*10. **Behavior goal:** Compete.*

Metaphor[19]

When Eugene was in my office in trance, I explained very carefully, very clearly. Leaning forward is done by tightening up muscles around the waist, shifting the body weight in the shoulders. When beginning to speak to another person, tense up the stomach muscles ever so gradually, shifting the body weight in the shoulders and head. So Eugene leaned forward towards the other person in speaking to them and especially when initiating a new conversation. Now when someone

[19] This metaphor appears in Lankton & Lankton, 1986, pp. 295–298.

begins to speak, I instructed Eugene to use the trance as a way to understand the importance of concentrating on the movement of the head away from the person and breaking eye contact. And let the unconscious mind move the neck and chin muscles.

Then, begin a sentence in this way, "That's because you are X . . .," and make it possible for your unconscious to complete the sentence by consciously initiating it. First getting saliva in your mouth, so you won't be speaking with a dry throat, and in response to what was said, say, "That's because you are . . .," and finish the sentence. "That's because you *are young.*" "That's because you are *where you sit.*" "That's because you are *unable to discriminate about X.*" Very easy to complete that sentence. And do it with a very matter-of-fact tone of voice. "That's because you are *fond of swimming.*" "That's because you are *used to drinking cola.*" "That's because you *are X.*" It's all right to let your unconscious decide what's a relevant way to fill in the sentence. Make sure your conscious mind says those words with that tone of voice.

When another person is speaking, interrupt after they've completed a verb and before they say their noun. You interrupt by making a vocalization. You can clear your throat, or make a word, begin a sentence. Your ears need to recognize that after you've heard a noun is a very good time to interrupt. Or after you've heard a verb would be another good time. Touching the person on the knee or on the shoulder, on the elbow, just when they are about to speak, is another very good way. You can simply lift up your hand, nonchalantly place it on the other person as they are about to speak. And then continue what you intend to say. After they've told you something, especially something of great importance, your conscious mind could use the words, "Yes, but," and improve on their story.

And while he was listening in trance he never knew where I'd come up with the ideas that I was saying to him. I hoped the inner attention would be focused on a slight irritation in the fingers, maybe a sense of tapping with it. First the little finger hits the table, then the ring finger hits the table, then the middle finger hits the table, then the index finger hits the table, then the middle finger hits the table, then the ring finger, index, little finger, back and forth, especially while the other person is speaking. I instructed Eugene to say to himself, and I don't know what voice you really use when you talk to yourself, but the voice tone ought to be a friendly voice tone, one you've heard before, saying something while the other person is speaking. You've got to be doing something while the other person is speaking, so say to yourself, "Yea, I've done that before." And that will really make it much easier to say, "Yes, but," when the other person is finished speaking.

Now Eugene didn't know that I had gone to the beach on regular occasions and paid close attention to conversations I'd heard, on the beach, especially around one certain "hangout." There would be one person sitting at the bar saying, "We surfed down at Fort Walton Beach yesterday, and the waves were three feet high. And another thing . . .," and then the fellow leaned forward, touched him just as he was about to speak, and said, "Yes, but we were surfing down at Navarre Beach and the waves were four-and-a-half feet high." And I know that he said to himself, "Yea, I've done that," inside his head. And just as the fellow was about to mention what else he'd done, the guy interrupted the behavior of his speaking and continued to say, "There were about a dozen of us down there." And then the other fellow continued, "Well, Fort Walton's three-foot waves made it possible for us to get a real long ride and even on those short boards that we've been using." The fellow I was watching said, "Yea, but that's because you're a short little fellow. You don't work out very much." The same sentence I heard him use before, a sentence completion. "Yea, but that's because you're a . . ." and let the unconscious fill it in. And then he leaned forward towards the person and said, "Let me tell you something confidentially, if you really want to succeed on those four-to-four-and-a-half-foot waves, you're going to have to get a longer board."

And what I got out of that was you tense up your stomach muscles just a little bit, shift your body weight forward so your shoulder moves rapidly in towards the speaker, and then make your point. Now I hadn't seen Eugene for about a week and a half because I had been out of town teaching. I didn't really expect to see him until after the phone call setting up another therapy appointment. When I went into the library to find a book, there he was, over in the corner, talking to one of the classmates. The classmate began to talk. Eugene tensed up his stomach muscles, shifted his body weight in the shoulders, and leaned right towards him and said something. I couldn't tell what and the fellow started to talk and Eugene interrupted the talking to make another point. And then the fellow started to speak and Eugene changed the position of his eye contact and moved his head to look out the window. I ducked behind a section of books so he wouldn't see me. I wanted to find out what he was going to do next. I wasn't able to substantiate whether or not inside the head the little voice would go off that says, "Yea, I've done that before." I saw his fingers move impatiently and wondered whether or not my client's conscious mind would be doing the behaviors because he'd heard me say them in trance or whether or not he had some other thing in his conscious mind and his unconscious was simply doing the behavior that was learned in the trance.

And then I heard some small thing uttered by the other person and Eugene interrupted and said, "Yea, but that's because you're . . .," and I really wondered how the unconscious was going to complete the sentence. I heard the voice tone very matter of fact: "Yes, that's because you're a freshman," he said. It made a good deal of sense to me. And then he did something to me that was astounding. I thought I'd taught my client something. And, again to my surprise, I found out that the unconscious produces a response from that set of behaviors, unique to the individual. It gave me, the therapist, a learning. He stood up and put both of his hands on the other fellow's shoulders and said, "Well, I really don't have time to talk about this anymore." And with that he turned away from the man and looked straight at me and there I was caught red-handed, looking at him. Then we smiled and got on the elevator together.

11. Behavior goal: Ask for help.

Metaphor

Anna was a very smart girl, so smart in fact that she knew better than to ask for help in the conventional ways. Instead, she very creatively invented a totally unique way and she did it without even thinking about it consciously. Following an episode of strep throat, Anna simply failed to recuperate. Instead, she unexplainably got progressively worse, and consistently complained that she was feeling "weak in the knees" and "unable to stand on her own two feet." A complete battery of medical tests failed to reveal any reason for her waning energy, and her parents became more and more concerned as well as helpful, catering selflessly to her every desire.

Speaking of desires, age 13 is an infamous age for a girl to discover her desires, but dealing with them in the kind of religious environment she found herself was a different matter. She must have been able to anticipate the kind of furor that would have resulted if she had straightforwardly asked, "How do I balance these desires with the values I've been taught, and how do I grow up and become independent?" She somehow sensed her parents wouldn't be receptive or comfortable with those requests. So her unconscious just devised a very workable way to ask for help. At least it worked long enough to buy some time.

But this matter of growing up sometimes requires a lot of help, and even her parents looked for help when it was clear that there was no medical explanation for their daughter's illness. "Thirteen," we mused. "Has she started her menstrual cycles yet?" "No," whispered the mother confidentially. "Do you think that might have anything to do with it?" We began to understand the daughter's apprehension. Raising their shoulders and hands, palms turned upward in a gesture of helplessness, they asked with a plaintive tone of voice, "Can you help us out here? What should we do?" And you have to admire parents who are so interested in the well-being of their children that they will admit their own need to learn something about how to help their daughter learn.

And everyone has an opportunity to admit a need and further their knowledge. There was one young man who had failed his medical exams four times and in therapy hoped to resolve the language barrier he saw as responsible. He had completed all of his course work to become a physician but could not seem to pass the final exams. He was newly married also and thus had some other questions. In trance, we explained how he could see himself clearly, raise up the hand to get the instructor's attention, and say, "Wait, how do you do that again?" or "Could you repeat that, please?" And it doesn't matter how simple the question might appear. So after the trance, he thanked us for the official work, and then, aside, asked, "Could you please help us with one other thing. What methods of birth control do you recommend? How do you determine when a woman is ovulating?" And he was so sincere and straightforward and clear that it was a pleasure to assist.

He approached us with his palms up, shifted weight from one foot to another, made eye contact, broke it, and made it again. Then he selected a voice tone softer than usual. At that time he let his sternum fall and he said, "I don't think I can understand this without help."

Now Anna's parents were undergoing a bit of a transformation themselves. They were very nice people but they hadn't thought that it's not nice to be "too nice" to someone and that in order to give their daughter an opportunity to discover her capabilities, they should help her by refraining from too much and unnecessary help. We congratulated them on having such a healthy daughter and one who, unlike her peers, could be quite confident about her body since she had undergone such extensive testing, all of which confirmed her as a totally healthy young woman. And when her periods finally started, they could be very sure that everything would be just fine then.

So Anna had occasion to realize that "it was a bit selfish of her to keep her needs to herself and deprive others that opportunity to know the joy of giving and helping." That's what her school counselor told her. "And you should keep that in mind," she said. "It's just like Scarlet said in *Gone with the Wind* when she decided, 'I think I'll let Walter get my plate for me this time.'"

And when she shared with her mother several weeks later that she had started her first period, her mother was genuinely enthusiastic as she congratulated her on knowing that she was truly a healthy young woman now and that everything was going to be all right. You can imagine how that reception surprised Anna and paved the way for other questions about how you grow up and juggle so many variables. She became quite expert at lifting up her shoulders and hands, palms turned upward, rocking back slightly on the balls of the feet, eyes wide open, a deep breath, and lips relaxed as she would say, "Wait, I'm not sure if I can do this alone. Could you help me out here. How do you decide whether to kiss a boy on the date and how do you say no if you decide not to?" Or just, "Help! I'm confused, I'm scared." She could even ask directly for her mom or dad to "Please just hold me and rub my head the way you did when I was little." And, of course, the muscular condition just reversed itself, practically overnight, as suddenly as it had developed.

Now her mother has even learned through the unconscious processes which go on in a family. She got something from her daughter. She will approach her husband with her palms up, shift weight from one foot to another, make eye contact, and break it and make it again. Then she selects a voice tone softer than usual. At those times she lets her sternum fall and she says, "I don't think I can do this without help. Can you help me." Everybody has made it through that developmental period now.

12. *Behavior goal:* Self-control.

Metaphor

Frank didn't like losing all of the time so he enrolled in a karate class. *That* part of karate is only a matter of presenting your credentials, putting your best foot forward, and having sufficient money to pay tuition. As an adult, your conscious mind only thinks about the requirements, but you rely upon a lot of unconscious learnings that are habitual in order to accomplish something seemingly as simple as enrolling in karate. You couldn't just say how it is that you stand on your own two feet, what do you say inside your head that tells you that "I can do it, I'm mighty scared, but I can do it." You're always relying on past learnings. Taking risks wasn't his problem.

Frank has sort of an odd sense of humor. Enjoying the dull joke for him was a way of trying to prove something. His odd sense of humor led him to think that even if he should get beat up by experts in the karate dojo he wouldn't get beat up by some punk on the street. I guess that is a suitable reason to study karate.

A child living in certain situations is bound to feel a good deal of aggressive impulses. You mastered them, and you controlled them, and you ought to be proud of your unconscious ability to do that. Your ability to control impulses is an indication that you give a person slight exposure to poison ivy as a way to make them immune to poison ivy. You give them small pox germs as a way to make sure that the body can handle it in larger doses later. You have failed to appreciate fully how much you have unconsciously learned and how much you have prepared yourself to deal with.

The reason I brought it up is that when Frank enrolled in the karate class, he found a situation in which a person can discriminate between control and aggression. Maybe it begins the first day on the mat when you learn to alter your muscles in certain ways. You have to stand with your knees in a certain position over your feet. You have to tighten up your back knees, front knee in a right angle, you have to keep your feet a certain level apart, and on top of that, you have to twist your hips so that they are perpendicular to your angle of movement. It's fairly absurd as a matter of fact. Each day when I saw him, he would talk all about what he had been learning in the dojo. And he was really putting ideas together in a new way about how aggression and control go hand in hand. But he had a different motivation for continuing to learn.

First he learned all the pieces requiring practicing alone, high blocks, low blocks, side blocks, side kicks, front-snap kicks. He was practicing in front of mirrors, getting the feet back, practicing the movements in pieces. And it seems like you would be a damn fool to be aggressive if you had to stand in front of someone and get your hips perpendicular and decide where you are going to kick them while they punched you out. So, as his understanding of his own discipline and control increased, his lack of appreciation for his own aggressiveness also increased. But I knew something that he didn't yet know about what happens when you finally go into sparring.

Eventually the movements become automatic and your unconscious learns a great deal that frees your conscious mind to think in a more complex way. You put together a combination of movements and learn that you exhale comfortably between each step. You exhale when you punch. You learn to control your behavior while you are breathing comfortably.

Now, I couldn't go about telling you *exactly* how that happens. Your conscious mind can notice that the air passages are free, the feeling of lubrication in the back of your throat, small signs that you appreciate, that you rely upon so much memorization of muscle movement. You rely upon a good deal of that same thing in order to smile.

It takes muscle coordination to raise the diaphragm, relax the back, let your shoulders go behind your rib cage. On the top of that normal process, there is the process of holding your hands at your hips when you punch, checking that your hips are perpendicular to the line of movement. Little by little, you make a complex subject unconscious and automatic.

Practicing in front of a mirror is fairly easy. Finally you learn complex dances, you move more and more unconsciously with sets of punches, kicks, steps, alteration in your stance, combinations of blocks and punches, turns. Part of his aggressive feeling was beginning to build at that time because you have a sense of confidence as you recognize your mastery. You may have noticed that you are breathing quite easily, smiling, a sense of confidence for you, probably.

When sparring finally happened for certification, he began to have normal feelings of anxiety, felt blood in the neck, throat dry, stomach a little more tense, lips tense, and he stood there on the mat, bowed to the other person, and he hoped that his opponent would just fall down right there. He thought to himself, "I am going to do this somehow. It will be good for me." His unconscious didn't realize he had such an odd sense of humor.

Now in actual sparring, a person swings at you, and you block the punch, and it is very important that you punch hard, but it is also very important that you don't kill the person by striking that hard. Not only would you fail to earn your belt, you would get humiliated and you would subsequently be the one who got similarly hit and kicked. Everyone knows what it is like to be spanked. Your nose flares, and you might begin to feel the spanking even before it happens—and it's a little bit like that in dojo—your conscious mind doesn't know what to pay attention to first. There is anticipation, a sense of "I've got to win," and there is a sense of "I'd better block." You block, you punch, turn, dip, all the while recognizing that you are breathing between each maneuver, generally more tense than before, but fairly relaxed, considering the circumstances. Jaw set, concentrated, able to move quickly. Your aggression and control go hand in hand. You are even wondering how hard to hit the partner. After you have been kicked a few times, it's logical to assume the position of a gentleman and strike only as hard as you were taught by the master. Not only will you win the match, but you will be proud of yourself afterwards.

That's exactly what Frank learned but he wasn't ready for the real test—the real test meant doing something new in his life without getting the tar beat out of him first. He had a lot of resources to draw upon and they were signed, sealed, and delivered in karate and in other karate matches. And you will forget a lot of things you learned so you can draw upon them automatically. And Frank survived his brown belt and several black belt matches, and eventually gained the favor of a dojo master. When the master moved to Florida, Frank took over the dojo. He had been tutored under the master, but his conscious mind never had to think about a good deal of the behaviors that he utilized in the normal process of conducting his business.

There are a lot of ways to stop people, how you stop a salesman, how you stop them when they telephone you with a canned tape. Some people will talk about not feeling guilty when they say no, and some people will learn to be hostile, and some people become so involved that they don't have time.

You can say, "No, I don't think so, I'll get back to you about that." But he would always draw upon his karate training in the most subtle and skillful way, I thought. He would look a person over entirely and breathe comfortably as he did just as if he were inhaling before a punch. Even making lists, keeping a diary or calendar, using a file cabinet, he would get his balance on the floor as if consciously deciding upon his goal and appreciating that your unconscious goal will draw upon some of that sense of independence that was learned, separating aggression from control, learning to use both effectively.

I'm sure that everyone learns a great deal about being mature, proud of themselves. Some people might say he became more militant about the way he did everything, including opening a file cabinet, but it's certainly a good idea to find out how you can demand respect from other people. You can explain the middle initial of your name, as

Frank did, and insist that you be referred to by your proper name. You can also spell your last name when you give it to people. In his case, this was absolutely necessary.

You are certain to follow social protocol more carefully because of the protocol you have to follow in the dojo. You have to take your shoes off, you have to bow when you enter the mat, you have to bow to your partner before and after, you even make audible prescribed social sounds. All of that training he relies upon unconsciously in his business encounters.

It doesn't matter whether you use bulletin boards, lists, blackboards, notes in your pocket. You call people and delegate authority, and tell them when you will call them back. And, most of all, watch them carefully, comfortably inhale and exhale, prior to taking action. His muscle movements are angular, and I heard a lot of people at the dojo say, "I wish I could be like Frank." And they didn't know how much wind he had gotten knocked out of him in the early days. Internally, you feel that sense of aggressiveness and thoughtful control of your behavior.

13. **Behavior goal:** *Ask for something you want.*

Metaphor

Vera didn't even know how to just say "I want you to give me a kiss right now" to her husband. The closest she could possibly come would be to say, "I want your support." And he had no idea in the world what she meant by that. He certainly wanted to support her and I couldn't believe that a grown woman could find it so difficult to just say "I want you to . . . just hold me right now or look at me right now."

She did not seem to know that the words "I want" could be used very effectively to begin a sentence. So early in the therapy she was given the assignment to start at least 10 sentences every hour with the words "I want." Even if it was just "I want to watch TV now" or "I want to have something green with dinner tonight" or "I want to go to the restroom and freshen up." Save the real hard things for later like, "I want you to tell me that you love me," or, "I want you to come sit by me."

And in the therapy session, she was able to modify her sentences and she began to reach ever so slightly for a distant understanding that had once been hers, and was still somewhere, intact, innate in her organism. It was something her grandchildren knew very well how to do. Every child knows how to say "I want." They even say it before they know how to use words and it's certainly one of the first phrases they learn. A child can simply look meaningfully at the thing they want and then at the person they want to give it to, and it is absolutely crystal clear what they want. And a child has to deal with the "no" word hundreds of thousands of times in the course of growing up: "No, you can't do that." "No, you're too young." Why is it in so many children that those obstacles created by so many "no's" don't in any way extinguish or diminish their ability to say: "I want some." "I want a bite." "I want to go." "I want that." "Can I have some?" Maybe a child is best at it if he or she will do that when crying.

The infant just fills the lungs full with air, and uses that power of the diaphragm and the lungs and the heart and the soul, and just cries out long and loud and lets go with a loud voice you can hear all over the room. Letting go of an inhibition wouldn't even be something an infant could imagine. There's no such thing as an inhibition, there's just the power of your ability to hear your own voice bounce off the wall.

Anyone can regress to a very young age at the prospect of thinking about how children know what they want and will ask for it. When I mentioned that an infant can cry with the conviction of knowing that you are worthwhile and your needs are worthy of being heard and attended to, she began to cry with an intensity and a power that you forget unless you've recently been around an infant who's doing it for real. And it is inspiring to sit beside that much raw, human power being expressed to its fullest.

And so between each of her cries, she gathered a fresh lungful of air, I reminded her to feel it all and express it all, to make sound as loudly as you can. I wouldn't have time to say quite that much in only one breath because soon would come the loud, loud wailing. And you might think of an infant as helpless but sitting beside that display of emotion gave me a new understanding of how powerful you are when you come into this world—and your power really doesn't diminish. You just gain a subtle control over the way that power is channeled and expressed. Well, she must have cried like that for five long minutes. And the more she cried, the calmer the crying became until finally the breathing became more relaxed and there were breaths where the breathing was just powerfully forced through the body and out into the room. She was straightening her posture and raising her shoulders and holding her head high.

I knew that it was going to be very easy to follow up on that and help her learn the nuances of behaviors that translate to such simple techniques as beginning 10 sentences an hour with the phrase "I want." You don't even have to know how you are going to end the sentence when you begin the phrase. You just say "I want . . ." and then use that as a stimulus to go inside for a moment and ask yourself, "Hmmmmm, just what do I want or need right now?" Sooner or later you'll have an awareness of what you want that will allow you to finish the sentence with something relevant. And when you discover one that really feels right, the next sentence can be completed and repeated with the same exact need, worded exactly the same as well. You don't have to be particularly creative about it. Sometimes you just have to persevere and redundantly repeat.

There was the woman Erickson spoke about who came to see him wanting to use hypnosis to stop smoking. She had volunteered that she had been married for 20 years to a man who was a professor at Arizona State University. She added that she was a mental health professional who made just as much money as her husband.

Erickson said, "Lady, women your age who want to use hypnosis to stop smoking are usually not sincere. So, to demonstrate your sincerity to me you are to climb Squaw Peak each morning at sunrise and come to see me in one week." Erickson went on to tell the story of that marriage and the difficulties of 20 years that had come with the woman acquiescing in various ways from the beginning when her husband demanded that she learn gourmet cooking. And he promised to cook every other week but in 20 years of marriage his turn to cook had not yet arrived.

And something about that week of perseverance in climbing that mountain had made a difference; or maybe it was dealing with Erickson and the way he would look at you as though to ask, "What prevents you from dealing with that husband in the way you know you need to?" And no excuse would really serve. Or maybe it was the way he had modeled the kind of comfort you can have when you make a request, insisting that she climb that mountain as a display, telling her forthright to bring her cigarettes and leave them in his office and they could be reclaimed in two weeks' time or else be thrown on the compost. Maybe it was his encouraging her having her own ideas when she said, "I'd better go home and get the others." He told her that was a fine idea. And when she brought them he said, "Now your hour is up, would you prefer to pay by cash or by check?" Straightforward, simple, to the point, comfortable with the request.

But whatever it was that made the difference, she came back the next week and told an interesting story of how she had asked her husband to type a letter for her. He had said, "No, I'll do it tomorrow." She insisted. She said, "I want that letter typed and I want it typed tonight." And her husband grumbled and complained but finally went into the office and eventually produced a letter that had more mistakes than it is humanly possible to make in one letter. She said, "This letter won't do. I want it retyped tonight and I want it typed correctly." He said, "Come to bed and quit acting like a baby. I'll do it tomorrow." And with that he turned off the lights. She turned the lights back on, pulled the cover down, grabbed him by the ankles, and literally pulled him from the bed saying, "I want that letter typed tonight." And eventually he produced an acceptable letter.

Now what was it about Erickson's intervention that had caused the woman to go home and display such an unswerving determination, perseveration, clear requesting of something that she could have been convinced was a little foolish? She could easily have been criticized out of her position in the past. And it must have been a real surprise to her husband that she kept persevering. It must have astonished him.

But I doubt that that astonishment sufficiently prepared him for what happened in the weeks to come when the wife continued to follow up with the various, unusual recommendations Dr. Erickson made. She came home one day and said, "Honey, your turn to cook has just arrived." And the husband, according to her prediction, boiled potatoes and fried hamburgers for a week. But Dr. Erickson had told her to bring home a gourmet meal for herself and her son and her daughter and they were to eat that. And at the end of that week when she reported the string of incidents to Dr. Erickson, he said, "Now your husband has spent a careful week teaching you the kind of gourmet cooking he really prefers. So you are to cook that for him next week and continue to bring home the gourmet meals for yourself, your son, and your daughter."

And it was an interesting way to model or to teach something to that woman about how her needs were worthwhile and that she could creatively and consistently over time cajole and coax that husband into recognizing it. And miraculously, by the third week when it was again his turn to cook, he had learned to cook gourmet cooking. And what kind of a therapy is that except one based on an understanding that you can hunt for a comfortable feeling when you say "I want you to do this" or "I want that" or "I think I want to do this now."

5

Family Structure Change Metaphors

*The most important thing a father can do for
his children is to love their mother.*
            —Theodore M. Hesburgh

*Children aren't happy with nothing to ignore,
And that's what parents were created for.*
            —Ogden Nash

*Nothing destroys authority so much as the
unequal and untimely interchange of power,
pressed too far and relaxed too much.*
            —Francis Bacon

A therapeutic reorganization of family structure is a complex process and not one that is likely to be accomplished merely by means of telling complex metaphors. However, as part of the process, and especially after a variety of related resources have been stimulated and experienced by the family members, a family structure change metaphor yields gentle, indirect guidance towards a model of healthy reorganization. As such, it allows the family members to expand their map of interaction from their own conclusion (as opposed to changing their patterns of interfacing in compliance to the therapist).

Family structure change stories illustrate a healthy alteration in family structure that results in greater comfort and well-being. They constitute an external framework that serves to organize and direct the relationship of new roles that have been developed with previously retrieved attitudes, behaviors, and emotions. As with all of the protocols offered in this book, therapists are attempting to hold attention with dramatic devices and stimulate listeners to synthesize a particular unique meaning for themselves from the movement of images created by the story. The conclusions drawn by family members will not, and should not, be a mirror of a model held out by an omniscient therapist. Rather, it will be analogous or metaphoric to the metaphor with which they are engaged. That unique synthesis can be expected to be a more appropriate fit and a more pertinent solution to their unique histories than that which any therapist is likely to foresee.

The simplest manner we have conceived for constructing and ordering images to facilitate this outcome within a metaphor is summarized by the following three steps:

1. Illustrate how a protagonist's symptom or discomfort (one that is obviously different from the identified patient's problem or symptom) exists along with a particular family structure.

This family structure will be similar to that of the client-system but will probably not be immediately apparent to any family member since insight and confrontation for changing the existing structure are not part of this model.

2. Illustrate how the protagonist's family organization changes as a result of interacting differently.

This will constitute a model of reorganization suitable for the client's family system. The protagonists' motives for the change in interacting do not need to be similar—their change does not need to be motivated by attempts to remove the symptom, in the story.

3. Show, by means of an incidental, but significant point of interest, that the discomfort or symptom (still entirely different than any in the client's actual family, of course) was resolved or simply disappeared after the family relational pattern changed.

Be sure not to provide sufficient logical connection between the disappearance of the symptom and the reorganization of the family in the story. Not only would making that connection be difficult, but the relationship would be debatable. All that is necessary is to raise the question in the listeners' minds—in effect, the symptom went away and the only thing we know for sure is that family relations changed. This lack of obvious connection, combined with dramatic hold devices and the placement of this story within a multiple embedded metaphor format, keeps the "message" indirect.

The first story of this type is excerpted from its original multiple embedded metaphor context as it appeared in *Enchantment and Intervention* (1986).

In order to provide a setting that will allow for faster grasp of the impact this story made, we will explain the context of the session for this first story. It was told to a family consisting of a father, mother, and a 19-year-old daughter. The family came to therapy at our request after the wife called for an appointment for her husband due to his depression. The larger picture of the existing structure was one in which both parents infantalized and often discouraged the daughter's logical individuation and departure from them, for reasons having to do, in part, with their unacknowledged discomfort with each other.

1. **Existing family structure:** *Parents overinvolved with adult daughter who had not accomplished natural boundary-building and autonomy.*
   Family structure reorganization model: *Exit a daughter from a triangulation drama, have her set her own limits, and expand an assertive, but respecting role in the absence of one having been modeled or encouraged.*

Metaphor[20]

I want to tell you about a client I had named Candy, and there is nothing preventing you from closing your eyes, too, whether or not you would like to stay out of trance. In any case you will go into a different type of trance—similar, but different from your parents' trance.

Candy is not a name you hear every day. And it grabbed my attention. She called and said that she would like to use hypnosis to mitigate the difficult and extremely limiting pain she experienced when she had migraine headaches. And I was interested in how she had the headaches and how long she had had them, and all the things you typically ask

---

[20] In this metaphor, the therapist is ostensibly talking to daughter since the parents have already gone into trance and all three have been listening to other stories.

someone. And I guess none of us found it very curious that because the headaches were so severe she gave little thought to the unpleasantness of her relationship with that father and mother from whom she'd been geographically separated for several years.

She had moved back home three months earlier when she had graduated from the university. And her mother was very controlling. And she felt that control. The mother even criticized Candy for being submissive to her. And the humor and the irony of that were lost on Candy as she related how the mother angrily had stormed into her room and would be criticizing her, telling her, "You shouldn't let other people tell you what to do." And the paradox of her mother making that lecture was an irony certainly lost on that mother. Candy explained that the headaches had started when she moved back home after college to decide what she was going to do with her life.

But she had to admit that with a pillow over her head to deal with the migraine headache, it was very difficult for her to be reached, even by that intrusive mother and overly involved father. It's not very easy to talk to someone with a pillow over your head.

Because when you take time for yourself, even when you have to take a migraine headache to bed with you to do it, it allows a good bit of privacy and an opportunity to do a lot of thinking about something. Maybe you are not even aware of what you are thinking of, maybe it's not important.

I asked Candy how she came to have the name "Candy" and what it meant to her to have a name that was so sweet. And it seemed to represent in a symbolic way a need on the part of those parents to have a daughter on whom they could depend to play a certain role— to be exceedingly sweet, submissive, proper, nice. And Candy had worked very hard to do that. And so I told her I didn't really know what I could do about helping her with those migraine headaches. I didn't know if I could promise any kind of a cure whatsoever about those headaches since their origin seemed so mysterious. She never knew when one was going to hit or how long it was going to last.

But I did tell her that I think it is very important that you take matters into your own hands, and here's what I mean. She had agreed that she'd do anything to make some change, even if it wasn't guaranteed to change those headaches. And I told her that what she should do was insist on instructions. She was to insist that her father and her mother give her instructions about every single detail of every single action she wanted to take. And when she got good enough at that, she was to increase the difficulty of the task by first identifying what it was that she wanted to do, and then she was to ask them what she should do in such a way that she elicited the instructions for the activity that she had already decided that she wanted to do. And because she had an interestingly perverse sense of humor, she liked the idea of insisting on instructions, ad nauseam. She knew that would be a way to totally discombobulate the current relationship she had with her parents and all those instructions that weren't welcome at all.

And I reminded her, as well, that anybody can leave the situation by going. It doesn't take any special talent to do that. And I wondered if she was up for the challenge of finding ways to leave without going. And she didn't know what I meant exactly, but the next session she reported that she had been in her room comfortably meditating. She had worked herself into a very comfortable state of relaxation and trancelike comfort, quietly minding her own business, when in walked her mother with her latest ideas about how Candy should run her life, who she should avoid seeing, who she should see, how she should spend that time, and even criticizing the hairstyle that she had taken to wearing that summer.

And just like your parents are sitting there quietly, comfortably, in a meditative state, she simply ignored her for five sentences, 10 sentences, 15 sentences. And you can imagine the more she ignored that mother, the more active she became in her demands to get Candy's attention, and demands for a response that she could deal with, a familiar response. And finally, after 20 sentences, Candy realized nothing was going to change by ignoring.

And so with every effort, she opened her eyes just so delicately and looked that mother in the face. Then, with utmost serenity in her voice, she said, "Can't you see that I'm busy?" And coming from a person who was doing the absolute epitome of nothing, that comment outraged the mother, who then had no recourse but to leave the room mumbling and grumbling to herself, but she did leave the room. And she was able to resume that meditative trance and enjoy it to completion, her own completion. She was quite amazed at how she had been able to do that.

And she also mentioned that the other thing she had taken up was gardening. The land that her family owned was large. And maybe she had selected gardening because no one in the family had ever shown the slightest interest in that. But she liked vine-ripe tomatoes. And so she went out and spent a great deal of time cultivating the earth, selecting the proper nutrients, additives, testing the soil, and analyzing the soil, tilling the soil, selecting the plants, different variety of plants, putting them into the ground, setting up windbreaks and watering systems. And she was busy at those chores for hours. No one could talk to her while she was up to her elbows in earth and chicken manure taking care of those tomatoes.

And no one was quite sure just when the migraines went away. One way we weren't sure when they went away was because she forgot to notice the absence of her pain. She was far too busy noticing the presence of comfort and feeling a good bit of satisfaction about how delicious those vine-ripe tomatoes were tasting as they matured. And I proposed she symbolize the end of her therapy by having everyone begin referring to her by her previously unused middle name, Louise.

2. **Existing family structure and presenting problem:** *Newly married couple, no children, with no current discussion of hopes, dreams, commitment, or emotional intimacy. Husband concerned about frequent sexual impotence and premature ejaculation and is frequently absent and alone.*
Family structure change goal: *Increase discussion of commitment and emotional intimacy between newlyweds, open up expression of self and future goals communication between spouses to strengthen relationship.*
Present: *Entire family.*

Metaphor

Ralph came into therapy because of his unexplainable anxiety about making some simple improvements on his house and his change was a mystery. Not wanting to do a big job isn't an uncommon problem and it isn't usually the kind of thing a person comes to therapy for. But in his case it had reached such phobic proportions that it didn't appear to be a case of simple procrastination. I asked him to let his mind wander and tell me what comes to the forefront. He explained to me that more than anything else, he was having difficulty improving the front steps of the house. I expected there were probably some psychological ramifications that he didn't yet recognize consciously.

I counted backwards from 20 to one to help him review the problem in trance and by the time I reached 10, his conscious mind had been altered in such a way he was able to tell me the entire incident. Without knowing it he was dealing with the project of those steps at a level that had never been apparent to him before. By the time I reached 10 he was telling me that the steps were on the front of his house, and it wasn't so much that he didn't think that he had money enough to build the steps, it was just that he believed neighbors were going to find out what kind of man he was, based on the quality of the carpentry that he did.

He had highly valued being a handyman all his life. And he was handy in a certain way. But the thought of showing it to the neighbors on the front of his house was another matter. Fifteen, 14, 13. So by the time I reached 10 his conscious mind had altered in such a way that he wasn't the least bit threatened to be speaking out loud in front of a total stranger who he'd only met a few minutes before, in a small town in Florida. Nine, eight, you go more deeply into trance, so that your unconscious can deal with the vast array of experiences that you can construct. Seven, six, five, four. . . .

There were other ramifications that his conscious mind also wasn't ready to hear. If he were to improve his house, he was going to have to admit that he was there to stay. His marriage was real. He was going to be walking on those steps and they had to hold him up, and in a deeper level of interpretation still, he didn't realize that he could construct something that he could stand on that would hold him. Two, one. When he was finally as deep in the trance as I expected him to go, I changed the frame of reference by speaking about other clients.

I had a client very much like him. Same values, same small town. But he worked on a farm. Sy didn't get involved in community activities. He stayed away from people ever since high school. In junior high school, kids teased him because he had a speech impediment. Sy's way of expressing himself gave new meaning to the term "sign language." I explained that in order to run the farm and feel like the man he wanted to be, he was going to have to get out there and work with those farm hands.

But as an intermediate step, I thought it was very important for him to find a better way to get someone else to do the work for him. The farm wasn't running, and if the farm failed, he was going to take it as one more sign. I explained to him in great detail that even though he had a speech impediment, he needed to make noise. Sy's language of guttural grunts and burps predominated his interpersonal encounters. And when he was very young, it really didn't matter. When you tell a child to take out the garbage, he makes a sigh, and takes out the garbage. Nobody really asks him to explain. You tell him to write a book report, and he grunts. No problem. But when you ask him to report on the book that he read, it becomes apparent.

So by the time he was in junior high school, he was beginning to feel a lot different from the other children. But nobody took him aside to explain what it's all about to express yourself to other people. Now the first thing that's involved is the need to notice that you have experience. Your unconscious can raise a hand to your face to wipe a tear from the cheek. Your conscious mind could do that even while you were asleep. Because everyone has the capacity to sense, feel that you have biological changes that happen in the body.

You couldn't just say when your heart's going to beat. But your heart will beat. And you're alerted to changes in the rate of your heartbeat. I explained to Sy how his heart fluttered when he met his wife. And I wonder if he knew how he grunted differently when his heart fluttered. The joy that he might feel in his heart ought to be something that actually changed the way he grunted and sighed and moaned. He understood exactly what I meant. He had indeed thought about his heart fluttering before, and I asked him to make the sounds of grunting that he would make when his heart fluttered as opposed to a slow day when he was despondent, depressed. And I complimented him on his ability to notice his heart fluttered. And I complimented him on his ability to notice his grunting changed.

And in the back of my mind I knew I had no intention of leaving him with that speech impediment. But your first job is to increase the person's sensitivity to the feeling states that they have inside. Every child knows the experience of having wet britches. Some children don't know what it feels like when you have a smile on your face. And the father really ought to take the time to point out that a smile on your face changes the relationship of your mouth and your eyes. Changes the relationship of your cheeks and your ears. Mother ought to tell a boy that he's very handsome when he smiles. And Sy never had his attention focused on his own body experience. And he spent most of his time worried whether or not he was getting approval from other people with his speech impediment. And the entirety of several trances was a long experience of finding out how he could recognize his heart flutter, how he could recognize his stomach being empty, and just like every child he could recognize a smile that wanted to come to the face, he could recognize when a tear was going to fall.

Now how do you recognize when a tear falls? Your conscious mind couldn't just say whether the tear's going to fall from your left eye or your right eye first. You don't know before the tear's out whether it's going to roll down your cheek, race down your cheek, meander down your cheek, or really spread out and fill the top of your cheek. If you cry on a cold day, the tear will feel warm. And you can feel it cooling on your cheek, in contrast to the blood that comes to your face. And you ought to be able to grunt differently with each of those feelings.

And I don't care if you have a speech impediment or not, every child knows how to make a different kind of noise to let your mother know you have to go to the bathroom, every child learns to make some sound that you have to eat, so everyone has the capacity to let other people know.

And on a child, letting other people know about the joy is a good idea. You don't know if you're going to feel the joy as a tingling in the back of your ears, or an alteration in the lightness of your skull. And telling him that joy is an experience of having a relaxation in your skull that creates a difference in oxidation on the top of the cortex wouldn't have helped him at all. He would never have been able to use that jargon. But it's true. Laughter may be the only response that's cortically mediated, of all the emotions. Direct cortical involvement in laughter. You can tell someone a joke with an unexpected outcome, and the switch in cognitive frames of reference will create laughter. It's just like the scarf said to the hat. Your unconscious knows what I mean. "You go on a head and I'll hang around." And the feeling of joy is something that Sy was entitled to. Entitled to know how he felt when he felt it. Breathing would be different, his face muscles would be different. It could all be learned easily in trances.

And the next task was to make certain that Sy wasn't going to be alarmed expressing himself differently to his wife. He'd start with small things. He was simply to grunt more frequently whenever she talked. She thought he was showing special affection, and spent more time with him in the bedroom. And that brought more joy. He had practiced in my office making different kinds of sounds when he felt joy. It wasn't that Sy couldn't speak. It was merely through lack of practice from high school and adolescence, he had suppressed the need that he had to talk.

So simply reminding him that he could get his wife to manage the farm successfully was a nonthreatening way to make certain, in Sy's special language, that his wife knew his needs, could translate them to the farmhands, and it would be an intermediate step to getting Sy out there with other people, speaking for himself about what he wanted. And making him say simple words at the dinner table: "Food good." He soon came to say, "Nice job." He thought it was cute that my daughter says, "Hungy." And everybody's been able to express themselves as adequate two-year-olds at some time in their life. And Sy simply started expressing a two-year-old, "I'm hungry." And I worked with him for six months before he was finally saying sentences that were understandable.

In the meantime, his wife had been alerted that he was making a sincere effort to relate his inner states. He had a lot of ideas and a lot of feelings. Encouraged by that, and the explanation from me, she was willing to interface with the farmhands. They bought more cows. They even looked over tractors they might invest in to upgrade the quality of the equipment. And he undertook moving the compost pile, a job they'd wanted to do for years. But moving all that compost required Sy's ability to express his discomfort to his wife, to the extent that she would encourage the farmhands to help. Now I know that months before, either Sy would have done nothing to get rid of that pile or he would have done it himself and be laughed at. It was a real joy to see, Sy proud of himself, managing the farmhands by expressing his needs to his wife in such a clear manner. And the land that had been cleared of the compost turned out to be the most promising farmland they had.

So it was no small wonder when Ralph finally emerged from his deep trance, he was willing to undertake some changes in how he was going to handle those porch steps. I, of course, spent a great deal of time mentioning something I haven't talked about, and that's how you make blueprints and draw up your plans. And I encouraged him to fantasize and picture what kind of house he intended to live in. He pictured himself walking in front of the house with pride, and with a smile on his face. And when he could see himself standing in front of his house with a smile on his face, broad shoulders, six feet high, he came to the recognition that not only did he live there, he was proud of living there. And he easily came to accept that he was married, he was living in that house, in that fantasy. He accomplished one small element that had been a resistance. That day he went home and constructed a blueprint of the stairsteps the way he thought they might go. He brought them in and he showed me. And you don't need to tell a handyman that he has to build the steps before somebody gets hurt.

And so when I told Ralph how other people were able to visualize themselves standing with a smile on their face in front of their house, he was able to consciously construct that picture in his mind's eye in the trance. But while you're doing that, your unconscious is doing something that you don't realize, more deeply. One step at a time is always easier than two steps at a time. And picturing his wife taking on those steps with him, with a smile on her face, one step at a time. And when he realized that he could see himself, proud, in front of his house, and his wife proud to be there, he made the decision that that was the action that he wanted to take.

And I mentioned that he was surprised, because he didn't just complete the stairs, to his satisfaction, he changed them three times. And before the year was over, he had built a stairstep arrangement crossing the creek in the back of his property. And he said that when he'd remember our sessions, he'd sit down and he'd count backwards to himself, from 10, nine, eight, seven, six, and he didn't really remember what happened after that, but he thought that he would see himself with a smile on his face crossing over the bridge that he built over the creek in back of his house.

I don't know all the places he fantasized himself crossing over or walking over, standing on his own two feet on the steps that he built. But I know he had a lot of joy about it, because he even built a circular staircase up to his bedroom. And he didn't have any trouble fantasizing himself and his wife walking up that spiral staircase to the bedroom. And that always brought a smile to his face. That's no joke. Sex is another response where cortical activity can create immediate biological response. Not entirely the same as in laughter. Laughter may not require the limbic system being in particular predisposition. And in sexual activity, your cortex begins thinking about sexual thoughts, and if that comes as a pun, or a rapid change of perspective, you may smile. But the sexual activity is stimulated by limbic system change, which is probably the subsequent result of that cortical activity. Now you know that your unconscious can make you hot when you go into trance, it can bring tears to your face, your head nods because your unconscious brings to mind various ideas. I wonder whether or not the next time you think about sexual activity you'll smile first, or if your limbic system is going to change first. Your unconscious knows. But the point of the story is, just as Sy's symptom left, Ralph's obsession with the stairs altered too. But what they have in common is a bit of a mystery, still.

3. *Existing family structure and presenting symptoms: The couple had been married 15 years but were not sure the marriage would continue due to the dissatisfaction of both partners. Presenting symptoms included disciplinary problems of the multiple children and the husband's increased withdrawal, depression, and listlessness. In fact, he had undergone extensive testing to determine viral or other physiological causes for this condition. The wife complained of stress, lack of appreciation, and feeling one down.*

Family structure change goal: Increase sensitivity to other for both partners, increase involvement for husband, and increase feelings of capability for both partners.
Present: Married couple.

Metaphor

Klaus was sick and tired of the whole mess in this family. It really made him mad that his wife seemed to be so inept at just handling what he thought should have been normal problems with their kids. He was doing his part as the provider and it just burned him that she should expect him to do more. And then there was his hypertension which had everyone alarmed. He didn't quite know who to blame for being so angry but the intensity and frequency of his outbursts were certainly taking their toll everywhere. It seemed to be another aspect of the hypertension. Margot swore that they were not going to be able to continue their marriage as long as she felt one down, blamed, and mistreated. And she was the first person in this family who I helped go into trance. I asked her husband to simply watch her reaction to things in the trance. And I wanted to talk about feelings of self-worth and self-confidence. Sometimes when you work with somebody, you really can't talk about those things in a straightforward way. Everybody develops feelings of self-worth and self-confidence in a particular individualistic way. And you don't know how you are going to develop those feelings until after they are developed.

I reminded them that every child learns to swing. And you don't realize consciously that while you're in the swing, you're learning a good deal about the balance of your body and rhythm and your ability to hold on to a rope and let somebody else push gently. But your conscious mind is learning a lot of things while you're swinging, and you're never going to appreciate that those things came from that swinging.

Parents who won't let their children swing are really doing to them quite a disservice. You learn something about motion that even becomes the foundation for sexual development later in your grown life. You learn something about trusting another person who gently pushes you. That swing becomes an opportunity to understand you can trust a stranger. And you learn something about your own ability to keep the swinging going. Kicking your legs in a certain way, pushing your butt out in a certain way, leaning your head back in a certain way. And without realizing it, gradually, a child learns a lot of coordination in the body. Now, you don't remember that coordination. You couldn't put words to the coordination. But you do have that coordination. And whether you consciously realize it or not, your ability to feel that coordination as the support that you use as an adult is really sufficient for the kinds of confidence you need. Even in relationships with other people.

And another situation that parallels that one exactly is how you learn to pay attention in class. The teacher can talk, and you can even fake that you're paying attention. You can look to the front of the room, you can think that you're really going to enjoy that daydream that you're going to have about fishing alone, or rubber rafting, camping out, or just hiking around on your favorite path. And the teacher sees you looking straight ahead, and you've found some way to make sure your head continues to look straight ahead. You wouldn't want the teacher to know you've closed your eyes at any point to have the daydream. And daydreams can be eye-opening experiences for everybody, especially those daydreams that consider your rites of passage.

Little girls certainly have an opportunity to plan for years about how marriage is going to go well. Usually, they practice playing with baby dolls, and boys are not usually given as much opportunity to practice with baby dolls. A lot of times the parents of the girl will talk about the goal of getting married, and not about what realistically happens after the marriage occurs. And with the little boy, they don't talk about either one of those, they talk about his career. And I never know, when I first talk with a family, whether or not the kind of planning that's been done when the parents were children was the kind of planning that's helped both individuals come to know how to use the marriage appropriately. Now you can't think about using your marriage appropriately without having that feeling of confidence. And a lot of times people will foolishly try to decide whether or not you have a sufficient amount of confidence to continue, a sufficient amount of confidence to take a risk, and when we find that we don't have enough confidence, how quickly we turn to the other person as a way to bolster our feelings of confidence. Because changes in social relations will affect feelings of worth and confidence in individuals.

I wanted them to realize that you can't fail to avoid concentrating on certain ideas that are unimportant to you, unless you really put some effort into that—because there's a lot going on in each person's life. Now Margot seemed to go into trance quickly and gain a feeling of self-confidence. Her husband stayed out of trance, and I asked him to speak. I wanted to find out whether or not listening to the husband speak, the wife could get feelings of confidence, or diminished confidence, in listening to him speak. If she got feelings of confidence when he spoke, there'd be some kind of a sign. Some kind of change on her face. If he became self-involved and insensitive to the way she responded, there'd be some kinds of signs on her face that her confidence was diminished when he spoke.

And how difficult it is to change the way we speak to our spouses! Usually, a dog doesn't even care. It learns that you're the person with the food dish. And once accommodations are made, and you've gotten through the period of puppy training, it's pretty easy to live with that dog. If you've failed to train the dog appropriately, then you have "hell to pay" for a long time. But with people, the problem is that you don't stop changing. When my grandfather was a little boy, he had a dirt floor. He had an outdoor toilet, and thinking of that home, there were a lot of things that were inconvenient that he took for granted.

Now this matter of handling stress. The same thing applies when a dog grows old. As children, we played with our dogs, fetched bones, hunted with them, roamed in the fields with them aimlessly, slept with them in our sleeping bags. Gradually the dogs may go blind or grow too old to run with us in the fields, or we don't run in the fields anymore anyway. We change our minds about the use of our time and don't go hunting any more. The dog loses its ability to track. There's no fetching, the reinforcement for the behavior is gone, and you're not going to sleep in a sleeping bag with your head on top of the dog.

You can still appreciate the good times you've had and share a new view of the world. But if the dog becomes angry and starts biting you or growling inappropriately at times you don't expect it, the added stress is enough to make you acutely aware that you can't enjoy the puppy the way that you used to. And what are you going to do then?

Klaus didn't know exactly what he should say while Margot sat there waiting to listen. And he found himself listening to the ideas he was having as he went into trance himself, just sitting there watching her wait for him to speak.

I then told them about how it is when you start a small business and one person might say he's going to invest $50,000 in equipment and personnel. Another person starts a business and only invests $10,000 in equipment and personnel. Each of them may prosper for a few years and enjoy the same return on their investment. Each of them may make the same $35 to $50,000 a year in their businesses, even making the different initial investments. One made more investment, yet may still make the same amount of money as the other. It's not necessarily true that you're going to get more back if you make a greater investment.

But the person who's made a greater investment can more quickly take pride in the fact that his business is going to survive. Now first you make great gains. And you acquire better furniture and better help. File systems get arranged, and you take great pride in knowing that more customers are being attracted to your business. And you don't mind answering the phone and answering the letters. Pretty soon, you have to have another secretary answer your correspondence because you can't handle it all, or you don't want to talk on the telephone; you have more important decisions to make with other people. Eventually, as the company becomes large, you lose touch with your customers. Margot had begun to cry a soft little stream of tears over her cheeks, thinking about that.

And the same thing's true in large organizations that lose touch with the people they serve. And people spend all their time in committees and they forget about their supporting population. And pretty soon, running a small business becomes a drudgery. And where's the fun of achievement? And the rebel who went into business as a way of proving that he could make it has made it. What's he going to rebel against now? The hard worker who really wanted something to show for all the time that he invested has got something to show for it. Now there's even more things to take care of. And the success that they wanted becomes a weight around their neck.

Now the important thing, I think, for a married couple, is to make sure that you have similar goals. You should be able to look forward to the days when you can look back and leave a trail of happiness. So the business executive needs to think ahead and determine in his own mind, to his satisfaction, when it's time to stop. He knows that there are going to be years with a lot of stress. And it's a good idea if you can respond appropriately to the stress. Your business partner ought to respond to your degree of stress as well.

Now how do you respond to your business partner's degree of stress? Your business is growing so rapidly that you really don't have any extra time to go out to lunch with your business partner and shoot pool with your business partner and just chat with your business partner. You're both too busy answering correspondence and meeting with somebody in New York. Your business partner meets with somebody in Seattle, while you meet with somebody in Phoenix. And the only solution is to think ahead to the days when you can look back.

Now if you come from a family of origin where nobody really supported you for what you did, you may have come from a family where there was no parent there to hold you and rock you when you wanted to cry. And you soon learned that it's not a good idea to expect support, or to ask for it openly. And other people come from families where they never even realize that they have a need to ask for support. They learn that it's not a good idea to be a child. You better just grow up and handle things as an adult would, as soon as possible. And eventually you have to come together with other people and overcome the limitations and training of your family of origin. And you've only got one another to use as support in that process. And that is true for everyone, but for Klaus and Margot there were additional implications and there was an unusual opportunity for both of them the day they sat there in that trance individually together.

I told them, with their eyes comfortably closed, that it's really important to look at the nonverbal aspects of your spouse's behavior. Going into trance and letting the other spouse watch your reaction is a very good way. And since they were both in trance to varying degrees, I pointed out that they had a good deal of rapport with one another. Unbeknownst to them, they were breathing in a similar rhythm. I reminded Klaus that he could think a thought about how much he loved his wife, and I really think that she would have an understanding available to her input systems that is perhaps beyond our ability to measure. Perhaps your pheromones would change, or perhaps the degree of tension that changes the way you breathe would be something audibly but unconsciously noticeable to her ears. And you could think a thought about how you intend to express your needs and desires to him with an optimism that he'll respond differently than people of the past have responded. And not only will his unconscious mind and conscious mind hear you, as you do that, but when you do that in the trance, the resources of his unconscious will be mobilized, bit by bit, to provide resources he doesn't know about.

It's very difficult sometimes when you try to be honest with somebody and admit that you really don't know what to do. But if you can't admit to your spouse that you really don't know what to do, then you have to keep it a secret for the rest of your life. And nobody's going to help you. And it's hard to really believe sometimes that an admission that you don't know what to do is a sufficiently enticing offering to make to a person that you have so much respect for as you do for your spouse. So I hope that both of you recognize acutely how much you don't know what to do so that you can appreciate your spouse that much more. And as we spoke, Klaus listened—somehow his unconscious would be trying to solve hypertension.

Now when you're able to develop a new sensitivity to your spouse, you may soon notice something new about each other's assets as well as faults. But you should not give up any of your faults, because you're going to need those to accept and understand the faults of your partner better. Now in a similar vein, you're going to be coming out of trance in just a minute.

And before you do, to whatever degree you're in trance, consult with your unconscious about the wisdom of the individual responses you have to stress being increased in a particular way. Since Klaus says that he sometimes gets irritable when he feels stress and feels demands being made on him, I told him, I think it could be a very good idea for you to be just as irritable as you could possibly be, and especially use that response in the morning. And maybe double your irritability in the morning so that you can have some nice peaceful evenings together, discussing comfortably what it is you really didn't know how to do in the morning. And if you have certain symptomatologies you haven't told anybody about that have to do with being alone and being isolated, consider the wisdom of finding two or three opportunities to have that sense of worry even harder. But while you have the worry even harder, you don't need to have the bad feelings.

Now the look on Margot's face had changed a little bit since she first started in the trance. She had opened her eyes and was intently watching Klaus's face as I talked. So I asked her, while his eyes were still closed, to smile just a moment and find out what response is on his face then. And without him knowing visually when she did it, I asked her to simply show a nice face full of worry, and find out what response is on his face. But he wouldn't know from watching with his eyes open. Only she and I would know that way.

And I didn't let him know just when she "showed" him a nice smile. But she found out what things she could see about his face. And when you look at your spouse's face while you're smiling, notice the skin color, the way that his throat throbs with the kind of pulsation from his heart, notice how his lips are positioned, what color are his lips, whether there's rapid eye movement. And then at some point, he won't know when—if you're smiling now he doesn't know it, consciously—I want you to also frown, with all the worry that you can show on your face, and find out whether or not there's any change in his behavior that's noticeable to your eyes. And when he least expects it, you can change back and forth, so that he won't know consciously. And I think you're having some idea that there are some little changes, especially in the corners of his mouth when you smile. Well, anyway, let's have the smile on your face again while he comes out of trance. Margot did all I said.

And then I asked Klaus if he would agree to carry out an unusual assignment that I wanted him to do as some homework between the two of them. And that was whether he would be willing to tolerate the inconvenience of being twice as irritable, if possible, twice as irritable in the morning when they were together, or in the first part of the day when they were together, so that he could sort of get a lot of it out of his system and have some more peaceful nights when they were together. I asked them to do that for two weeks and they both agreed. He, still in trance, was nodding his head.

But I don't know how well he was really able to carry out that agreement because he so completely failed at the next, more immediate assignment in a similar vein. I simply asked him to get a nice irritable look on his face while he came out of the trance so he could experiment with how it might be altered when he came head on to the eye-opening perception of seeing Margot sitting there with a smile on her face that he could see, for a change. I suppose he did try to cooperate; it's not that he wanted to resist or anything.

But he came out of that trance very comfortably and totally failed to look irritated to the degree that had been requested. And therapy never got around to focusing on his hypertension in any kind of specific way, so I really didn't know how to explain the fact that his next tests indicated a marked reduction of that problem. But the next time I saw them, it was totally unplanned and there they were, the two of them and all five of those energetic children running circles around them in the park and on the swing set. The park had one of those big, very sturdy swings that even an adult can feel very well supported and swing out so high it feels like you're flying. Klaus was pushing Margot and she was one up at last. So was he.

4. **Existing family structure:** *A young single woman who presented a symptom of bladder control difficulty was overly involved with her family of origin and hesitating in regard to autonomous and dating behaviors. Her mother controlled many aspects of the woman's life, while father spent most of his energy away from home. He was overdemanding and critical of both mother and daughter. She was taking steroids at the time of this treatment.*
   Family structure change goal: *Apply aggressive abilities and control to appropriate boundary-building and to symptom, separate from the intrusive*

mother, bring parental conflict into open between spouses.
Present: *Daughter only*

Metaphor

Dale had actually sought therapy because she was obsessed about the size of her breasts. She heard that wild story that hypnosis might increase her breast size and I was intrigued by the case for other reasons.

She had just bought a new house and I decided that what I would have her do was to examine the validity of her choice by going with the realtor to other houses, and it would give me a perfectly good reason to tell her conscious mind something I knew she would think was silly. She was to step on all of the cracks on the sidewalk as she walked with the realtor.

To make a long story short, I asked her to do that for the entire week every day. In the next session I instructed her to put door locks on every door inside of her house if she was really willing to have those breasts develop. She should put doors between the living room and kitchen, doors between the dining room and family room, places where it was simple and easy to pass at this point. And she was to put locks on every door. And I still hadn't told her what to do about what she had explained to me unconsciously.

In the third session she informed me that she had completed all but one door, and that one was on the way, and it was very inconvenient to carry around a set of keys for all of her doors. We joked about the fact that the extra exercise might increase her bust size. My recommendation to her at that point was to invite all of her brothers and sisters over to the house and show it off. All she had to do was tell them that the doors and the locks were already there, and that she would have them removed soon. When an unpleasant relative was in the house, she was to lock every possible door between her and the relative.

And, when her mother finally came to visit, I probably don't need to explain how difficult it became for mother to walk in on her in the bathroom, unlocking the bedroom door, the hallway door, the door from the living room to the hallway, and finding the bathroom door locked. She had the most satisfactory bowel movements, knowing that no one was going to walk in on her. She had perfect freedom. Of course, she had perfect freedom trapped in her own house by a system of locks. Now the problem became that she needed some elbow room.

After her breasts began to develop, I told her that it was time to take the locks off her doors. Your boyfriend is not going to appreciate that degree of difficulty getting to you. She thought it was humorous when I suggested that the use of contraceptives would be deterrent enough. Those keys and all those locks would certainly take the romance out of any . . . just the thought of running around in her nightgown with those keys convinced her to change those locks the very next day. Her mother had long since learned that she wasn't going to be barging through the house, and her breasts developed and she was quite proud of them.

I insisted that she not thank me at all but rather that she go out and step on some sidewalk cracks, and she never understood what I meant. But you can mechanically learn to do something, you can use external aids in order to learn to do it. You ride a bicycle by having someone hold the back end of it while you learn to keep your balance. You go shopping with big people until you learn to count the change for yourself. You follow recipes and the advice of others until you learn to cook. You use professional supervision and tutorship in order to gain certain direction that you later maintain by yourself.

In learning to walk, you hold somebody's hand. You engage in courtship behaviors as a teenager that you don't fully enjoy in order to learn the entirety of the sexual response. You might be far more anxious reaching out and holding the hand of that little boy. "There must be more to it than this," you think. But you do it.

If you used your immediate judgment, it would seem logical to conclude that holding hands is anxiety-producing, and ought to be avoided. The same thing is true for learning to have an affinity for certain tastes: cola, tofu, and coffee come to mind. The only thing that you might consider important for you in taking steroids is to learn that regulated behavior. You can do this in dreams at night, and you don't even need to know how. You memorize what works and add to it. And there is no need to feel badly about the fact that you use steroids as a temporary aid, and you certainly need more practice, just as Dale did.

She would always start with her breasts when I asked her to make a visual image of herself. I guess it was a load off of her mind to realize that she had become a woman. The problem with that was that she didn't know how to be one to her satisfaction. So I asked her to imagine herself in every room of her house, it reminded her of the joy that she felt. The conscious mind doesn't really know how that begins and doesn't even need to in order to appreciate it.

6

Self-Image Thinking Metaphors

*I tell you that as long as I can conceive
something better than myself I cannot
be easy unless I am striving to bring
it in to existence or clearing
the way for it.*
—*George Bernard Shaw*

*People seldom improve when they have no
other model but themselves to copy after.*
—*Oliver Goldsmith*

The goals of self-image thinking interventions are: (1) to teach a systematic visualization device for self-management; (2) to associate desired feeling states to an image of the self; and (3) to shape perception and feeling states related to managing specific problem situations as well as broader enhancement of life quality. It is a three-part structure we call "self-image thinking." This structure can be considered a superstructure or a foundation for delivering certain specific interventions for different clients, "tailor making" it to fit or embellishing it differently each time it is used.

First, the three parts will be described and basic steps presented. These steps can be followed in a straightforward manner, unembellished by either metaphor or hypnosis, with individuals, families, or in group therapy. The examples in this chapter are all framed as metaphors since this is a book of metaphors. However, developing a familiarity with the steps in the basic method is often a useful prerequisite for therapists before proceeding with the more indirect, metaphorical version in a clinical session. Once these steps have been accomplished in a straightforward manner with several clients, therapists will have case material for telling self-image thinking metaphors to subsequent clients. Each additional case can become grist for other stories, which can then be told to future clients.

This structure facilitates thinking about body image, social image, values, and self-management. It is a self-management tool which teaches a *process* of thinking as well as a specific client-chosen *content*. Clients may only be aware of the first-order content level that is the focus of their conscious mind and stated experience of the story's protagonist. The drama of this specific content is what therapists will focus attention upon as they go through the steps of the protocol. But the steps themselves essentially have to do with the process of using a positive, goal-directed rehearsal.

People who visually rehearse what they're going to do in a goal-directed fashion, and keep the entire situation positive, are doing self-image thinking. This is the cognitive and ideomotor goal of self-image thinking, to acquire that problem-solving cognitive behavior. Acquisition of that skill is a second-order change for each individual. As such, it helps support the newly emerging family structure and the social role changes clients achieve. The first-order change, the specific content used in the story, is also a worthwhile gain and is calculated to help clients realize the goals of their treatment contract. Self-image thinking, then, can be used subsequent to the acquisition of several component experiences so as to unite and mold those components into a personally workable whole. Since the conscious mind is consulted in various ways, the workable whole achieved will reflect the client's values, reality-testing capabilities, and needs.

The following detailed outline of the structure is presented without metaphor so as to impart a clearer understanding, and it is then discussed at length. The balance of the chapter presents the metaphors according to the numbered self-image goals that use CSI and scenarios (1–7), emanated images (9–10), and CSI, scenarios, and emanated images (11). Additional information, as well as examples from the work of Milton H. Erickson, from whose efforts we conceived of this structure, can be found elsewhere (Lankton & Lankton, 1983, pp. 312–344).

Self-image thinking

1. Central self-image (CSI) construction:

  a. Direct client to picture the self as accurately as possible.

  b. Determine several desired qualities or characteristics.

  c. Help client retrieve a personal experience of each quality (if this has not been done previously in the session).

  d. Help client add behaviorally specific visual cues for each quality (smiles, muscle tonus, lines around eyes, breathing or postural shifts, coloration, etc.) to the original picture of the self.

  e. Add to this embellished picture of the self a supportive "other" and help the client see interaction between the two figures.

2. Self-image scenarios:

  a. Have client commence by picturing the CSI.

  b. Direct client to add background details of a positive, nonanxiety-producing scene and then watch the CSI progress through that situation from beginning to end, interacting in a personally valued way that reflects the desired qualities in the CSI.

  c. Repeat steps a. and b. for neutral or routine situations.

  d. Repeat steps a. and b. for previously anxiety-producing situations.

3. Shaping future perceptions (emanated images):

  a. Begin by picturing the CSI.

  b. Direct client to unfold the background to reveal an ideal goal several months or years in the future. Encourage considerable detailing: Who is there? What all has been accomplished? What exactly does it look like?

  c. Direct client to "step into the picture" and "be there" in the present tense, noticing how it feels to have reached those goals. Have him or her memorize that feeling of success. Enrich it with all other sensory details (sound, smell, temperature, rhythms, tastes, etc.).

  d. Then, still in that future scene, experienced "as if now," direct the client to use this pseudo-orientation of time by "looking back," and reviewing steps that "were taken" to accomplish that goal.

  e. Finally, have client terminate the experience by exiting the fantasy in a reverse order: first, once again examine and appreciate the imagined future (still experiencing it as the "present"), and then reorient to the current time and place.

The first step of the protocol involves creating a "central self-image" (CSI). The CSI is going to be central to the rest of what happens in self-image thinking. It is a central reference point. First of all, if it were to be done without metaphor, clients need to be directed to picture themselves as accurately as possible, including their head, body, posture, and especially the expressiveness of the face. Though some are more practiced at it than others, everyone is able to visualize. Once clients are able to visualize themselves, unembellished, as it were, the next step is to ascertain and then systematically retrieve a personal experience of desired psychological characteristics or qualities the person wants available in the self-image. Often, this step has been previously accomplished in other stages of the therapy session. If not, clients can be stimulated to remember, retrieve (with or without the stimulation metaphor), or even imagine experiences that are of the desired types. We often help clients do this by telling stories about people having those desired and needed experiences—the listening client can be expected to identify similar personal experiences of desired characteristics both unconsciously and, to varying degrees, even consciously.

Then, we ask clients to hold that memory and its kinesthetic counterpart constant and to image how they look with that characteristic. We give feedback about the ideomotor behavior that comprises that experience, asking that clients take that feedback and make a picture in their "mind's eye" that captures that information visually. We describe all the visually specific alterations we see on their faces as they have the experience so as to facilitate putting these changes in the pictures they make. Having completed this procedure for one quality, other qualities are similarly retrieved and the resulting ideomotor changes reported so that the CSI created contains a variety or "set" of different abilities. Eventually, all qualities will be simultaneously visible, even though different qualities may seem to compete with each other.

For example, seeing a "mouth set in a firm, straight line" (perhaps representing confidence) and seeing "a slight smile playing at the corner of the mouth" (representing sense of humor) might seem to be mutually exclusive, except that people have great flexibility with regard to the liberties they can take with mental images. It is quite easy to "superimpose" one set of images over another so that both are visible at the same time or oscillate between the two, and so forth. Or, one set of cues related to a particular quality can seem to become more vivid as that characteristic is chosen as the most relevant option for dealing with a particular situation. Each client will use a somewhat unique method of blending and synthesizing the visual image to group the several desired resources.

A useful analogy might be to think of the CSI as a "closet" in which a wide range of clothing (psychological qualities) is collected and organized. You wouldn't consider actually wearing all of your clothes at once. You select them according to their relevance for a particular occasion, sometimes mixing and matching bits of one with another. But no matter how incompatible they may seem with each other, they can hang there together, side by side, increasing your sense of options.

The CSI is basically complete when the initial desired qualities have been retreived and pictured. We say "basically" because just as you periodically add new clothes to your wardrobe, different qualities should be added to the CSI in an ongoing way as they are experienced, discovered, or retrieved in subsequent therapy or extramural life. Also, the last part of creating the CSI (all still the first step of self-image thinking) is to add to the embellished picture of the self a supportive "other," someone who would support the client having those experiences and qualities. Adding this other person facilitates both resource retrieval as well as more elaborate social interaction. The other person interacting with the CSI is a symbolic token for further social interaction, which is the business of step two. That completes the CSI—step one of self-image thinking.

The second step of self-image thinking is a process we call "scenarios," which are little action pictures that won't really be dramatic and won't really be stories. They are just little action frames depicting the person holding the qualities of CSI constant and interacting with other people. We want people to see how they will look, imagine what they'll say, what they'll sound like, and what they'll be feeling while they see their actions modified in certain ways as a result of the desired qualities in the self they watch interacting. All scenarios should begin by asking clients to first picture the CSI that reflects all the desired qualities in visually specific ways and also includes the supportive other. Keeping that image constant, clients (remember, this will later be done by a protagonist in the metaphor) are stimulated or directed to allow a background to emerge that depicts details (settings, other people, etc.) of some positively anticipated, nonanxiety-producing situation, and then watch the CSI progress through that scene from beginning to end, interacting in a personally valued way that reflects the desired qualities in the CSI.

The scenarios are suggested with increasing degrees of complexity or difficulty. The first one should involve a pleasantly anticipated situation and the next scenario would depict something neutral such as going to work or studying or whatever is neutral for each person. Eventually, something previously considered negative or anxiety-producing is suggested and clients are going watch the CSI interacting comfortably, intelligently, with warmth and a sense of humor, or whatever qualities were included, around whomever was selected as a mildly negative stimulus.

To assist clients in the process of comfortably rehearsing positive interactions and outcomes in feared situations, it will be useful for therapists to carefully select the past verb tense. This will be true even when therapists use metaphor to cover these steps via a client's identification with a protagonist's imaginings of a scenario. For example, therapists would be careful to emphasize that the protagonist brought to mind some situation which *would have been* considered anxiety-producing *prior to the therapy*. The process need not be confined to situations which actually happened in the past. In fact, the technique is primarily useful for rehearsing positive outcomes in upcoming situations, but the anxiety factor can still be referred to in the past tense. This will become clear in the metaphor examples that follow.

Eventually, the client can even be directed to think through and imagine comfortably watching what would have been considered the most catastrophic situation that could be anticipated. So, for example, a man might finally see himself being intelligent, warm, having a sense of optimism, and so on (his CSI), while those people he works with tell him that he no longer has a job at their company. And again, when this step is done in metaphor, we describe the protagonist seeing him- or herself interacting in a way that is consistent with that central self-image. In that scenario, for example, it might be appropriate to say, "I'm sorry that you feel that way. If you change your mind, give me a call and maybe we can work it out. I'll be glad to talk to you about it some more but I do understand that I'm fired and I won't be back, unless I hear from you, so bye bye now, have a nice day."

Once again, the content that we're suggesting in our story is really somewhat irrelevant. What we want clients to do is to think of themselves with certain positive experiences attached. They are to learn a method of thinking through what they're doing and will do in a goal-directed, visual, self-management practice. That's the psychological-level process that is being learned. As clients review interactions in scenes that are potentially anxiety-producing, the therapist observes carefully for any signs of stress or discomfort and can easily suggest an "intermission," if necessary, during which protagonists (and clients) can identify, retrieve, and add other desired characteristics or qualities that may be missing from the CSI which would allow greater comfort or creative problem solving.

Step three, the final step, involves the use of "emanated images" to shape future perceptions. This part of the process helps clients generalize the desired feelings and interactions they have been experiencing over many interactions to come. This step produces desirable results but occurs less frequently in our work than do the CSI and Scenario steps. Those may usually occur in several sessions in the course of treatment. We generally include a CSI and scenario rehearsal segment (steps one and two) whenever several new resource(s) have been retrieved. These segments encourage clients to add any resource that has been retrieved to their pictures of themselves and to associate those resources to situations where it is desired in the immediate future.

Although used less frequently throughout therapy, step three is usually included at least once with almost all of our clients. In the process of learning step three, a third-order change can be urged. The result of step three will be that clients have enriched their map of experience to include a presupposition of finding successful outcomes of their problem solving in the future. The key word here is *presupposition*. Upon completing the Emanated Image stage, clients will have presupposed their own success and imagined living with that success long enough to plan "in reverse" how to reach that presupposed successful experience.

Step three involves time distortion to imagine a distant future time (five, 10, or more years) in which desired goals have been accomplished. It involves a somewhat complex set of "mental gymnastics" for clients to perform, but the previously learned and practiced self-image thinking processes provide the necessary foundation for doing this additional learning that is divided into five parts.

First (a), as with all parts of this process, the protagonist (client) begins by picturing the CSI. Next (b), the protagonist sees what might at first appear to be yet another background scene unfolding, but this time the background depicts an ideal "dream come true" several yeras in the future *with the client in it.* Identifying and picturing such goals may take several minutes and therapists can help clients complete the mental details by helping them elicit and use hypnotic experiences such as pseudo-orientation in time and by asking questions in the present tense which presuppose a future experience: Where are you? Who is with you? What kind of relationships do you enjoy with this person(s)? What have you accomplished? What exactly does it look like? What else do you have there? Also the therapist promotes detailing by describing various aspects of the ideal future time that the protagonist in the metaphor is simultaneously seeing.

The third part (c) of this step is to have the client merge with the self in the pictured future. The client is directed to "merge with the picture," "step into the picture," and "be there" in the present tense, noticing how it feels to have reached those goals. Have him or her memorize that feeling of success and enrich it with all other sensory details. It is, after all, the client's life and he or she has a right to live in it happily and imagine how wonderful it is going to be. Why not? As clients gain familiarity with the feeling of success, they step into the picture and they imagine what it is like in that future world (it may be that they are sitting under that palm tree holding on to a dollar sign, arm in arm with the spouse, children, etc., or whatever). But it is their own construction, and therapists are advised to help clients envision many aspects of healthy and happy living for that image by directing a client's attention to a wide range of considerations. These include relationships, qualities of relationships, physical health, spiritual balance, financial well-being, social connectedness, community participation, career achievements, and so on.

Next, still in that future scene, experienced "as if now," is to describe how the client (or if in metaphor, the protagonist) can use this pseudo-orientation of time by "looking back" and reviewing steps that "were taken" to accomplish that set of goals. So, currently identified with a visualized figure of themselves enjoying the accomplishment of some desired future goals, clients (or protagonists) are directed or said to allow yet another visual fantasy to "emanate" from the mind of that imagined self in the future. In that fantasy, scenes of the "past" are created, or emanated, from the client's imagined future as they think back over the interactions that resulted in their getting there.

In other words, the future is now and everything before is the past, including the time after the therapy and the future years between therapy and the targeted date of success that hasn't yet happened. We ask clients to think through several of the scenarios or situations that they had to go through in order to get to this present successful circumstance. We make sure to mention hellos and goodbyes that they had to make, risks that they had to take, and times that they stayed with the security that they had instead of taking risks. We suggest that they notice false starts as well as wise steps, so that we cover a variety of bases. In other words, we're not just suggesting that this is all risk or success, or goodbyes or hellos, or any simple road to success. There is a constant balance with opposite concepts. It is all, however, still associated with success and based upon a presupposition of success. "Failure" in an emanated scenario is not an indication that clients are failing. It's an indication that they are on the path to success and they have presupposed that they're going to complete it.

Finally, step three is complete when the client is directed to terminate the experience by exiting the fantasy in a reverse order, first returning from the daydream in the future to the imagination of the future, and then to the current time and place.

Now let's turn our attention to accomplishing these steps in metaphors. The explicitness used in the above outline ought to make the construction of a story rather straightforward. When using metaphor to more indirectly facilitate self-image thinking, it is useful to include in the story a context in which a protagonist is seeing a reflection of the self. These may be reflections in mirrors, ponds, windows in your car at night or on a train when it is dark outside and the light on inside. So you may, for example, tell a story about a client who leaves your office, and, having retrieved various resource experiences in the session, gets on a bus going home at night. As it is going through a tunnel, the lights are on in the bus. That person looks out the window and all he sees is his reflection. Describing that reflection the suggestions urge the client to imagine the central self-image. Subsequently, the scene can be said to be unexplainably altered, perhaps as a result of the stimuli of the bus going past a post or over a bump. The protagonist's imagination is perhaps fueled by the recent therapy session and the images begin to appear as the various scenarios change. That's generally how we proceed to create a story for self-image thinking which contains a logical context for visualizations of the constructed self.

Yet, another way to do it is to not have the protagonist's reflection be seen but have another person describing the protagonist. For example, "my client walked in and sat down in a very small office with chairs all around the walls and as Bill sat there he noticed people looking in his direction and what they saw on Bill's face was a relaxed forehead, muscle tonus in the face, a slight pink to the cheeks, his head vertical on his shoulders." So now we're describing the protagonist from another angle in the room and might notice that he is swallowing easy, breathing easy, etc. As we have him viewed through other people, we are still "sketching" the person's face and posture. "If they could have seen him on another day they would have seen him . . ." and then the description becomes a scenario that starts with him perhaps standing with a look on his face when he interacted as desired with his friends.

Our first example of self-image metaphors occurred late in a session and used a character who had been developed in an earlier story[21] during that same session. That earlier story introduced this protagonist in a story using the affect protocol to help retrieve the affective status of acceptance and belonging. Those resource experiences will be the

---

[21] This earlier story was told on pp. 55–58 of Chapter 2.

primary characteristics that are visually added to the central self-image and rehearsed through scenarios in the story here.

1. ***Self-image goal (using CSI and scenarios):*** *Associate current feelings of belonging to upcoming life events*

Metaphor

Jane had been sitting there with that feeling all through the American literature class of having embraced her friend on the Bessie Hall bridge. She still felt the warmth, she still felt the smile, her face still had a glow on it, her heart was still pounding like she was in love, because she had her best friend. She couldn't see what the professor could see through his eyes. Or she'd be able to see a sweet delicate little swallow, her head perched vertically between her horizontal shoulders, back relaxed somewhat as she leaned forward with her elbows on the desk. Her eyes were closed and not twitching. It was too bad that she didn't have a mirror so that, while she was relaxed, she could see her face with her feelings of belonging and acceptance that brought her joy and love—because you should be able to see your face when you have that feeling of joy, acceptance, and love. Because you would see a smooth forehead, and relaxation of the little lips slightly curled at the side, pink color of the skin, easy breathing, the warmth around the body that seems to come a little bit because the shoulders are rolled forward just like the embrace is still happening.

And she wasn't thinking of lit class at all, of course. Every time the professor said something about somebody's life and literature, the scene changed, and it wasn't just her face she saw. She was seeing herself conducting various activities that she'd never dreamed about before, while she saw herself having the feeling of acceptance and joy. Some noise happened and she saw that scene change and there she was going through the shops with those feelings of acceptance and joy, window shopping and buying clothes. She hadn't realized how her unconscious had been capable enough to memorize those feelings and give them to her conscious mind, so that on the outskirts of her conscious mind, she could form a visual picture of herself walking down the street and feeling that sense that she had gotten and seeing it on her face.

She saw it again when the scene changed and she watched herself talking to strangers. Her face said "everyone likes me," and that was what she thought. And when she saw herself with those feelings and that thought, there was another change and another posture as she saw herself sitting in class with that same feeling, studying with that same feeling. And the professor must have said something about family, and life, and America because she imagined herself in her home in her living room, with that same feeling. She chuckled to think that she had cleaned the house while she had those good feelings. It might be a little uncommon, but she couldn't see why she should not. In fact she could see herself have that same feeling and the same thoughts about how nice it was to know that her sense of being liked went so deep.

She didn't know what the husband looked like exactly in her picture. For a moment or two she tried out the shapes of different men on campus whom she had been looking at, with that special eye, and she saw herself kissing her husband when he came home, kissing him when she went out, kissing him when she came back, and he had been babysitting and she took the children in her arms kissing the children. She saw herself at work still enacting that posture that helped her to retain that good feeling. This is what Jane was doing and if you'd been my client I would have surely asked you to imagine yourself in situations important to you, going to the hospital to have your child, with that same look, wheeling out of the hospital in your wheelchair with that same look. What a pleasure and delight of having a friend and the sense of worth that she had, even though her conscious mind didn't appreciate herself that way. But she was just appreciating how good it felt and how many places she'd taken those feelings, and I always ask my clients to imagine taking the learnings to the places that they want to have them. And hear what you'll hear yourself saying while you feel that way. And you notice how the other people will respond to you while you feel that way.

I asked a group of flight attendants one time to imagine that people treated them just awful while they felt that special way, because now and then you do run into a critical or angry person and there's no need to let another person influence the way you feel. You're going to control your own feelings as long as you imagine what you are going to feel and have those feelings. And you have the right. And that activity continued even after she left, in dreams at night, sometimes she would just sit down and think things through before they were to occur.

And to remember the process, she'd think back to that day on the bridge at Bessie Hall and whatever memory that she had of it, and memorize those feelings, that embrace, and the sweet thought of friendship, and see what she looked like with that feeling today. And then she would think through what she was going to take action about, whether it was going for a job interview, meeting a new neighbor, writing a book, packing up her house for a move, or dealing with a crank at the grocery store.

In this next self-image metaphor, as is often the case, the protagonist has previously been discussed in another story in which awareness was focused on the characteristics that are to be visually represented and directed here.

2. **Self-image goal(using CSI and scenarios):** *Associate comfortable sexuality and dependency characteristics to appropriate contexts with spouse, others, and even professional associates.*

Metaphor

And so I had talked of many things with Sherry, and she had had a very deep trance. When she came out of trance, in fact, she was still somewhat disoriented and wasn't absolutely certain she was totally reoriented before she left the office. She was late for the bus, and she didn't want to miss it. It was the last bus home for the evening, and so she gathered up her belongings in a hurry, and she ran out the door and jumped on the bus. She'd had to run quickly, because she almost missed the bus. It was leaving as she ran up to it banging on the door, saying "Wait, let me in!" And the perseverance and the strength with which she banged on the door got the result that she wanted.

Then, there she was on the bus, but her heart was beating, and you have that sense of anxiety that comes from allowing your unconscious to get your adrenalin going when there's a need. And there'd been a need. She got on the bus and, with a sense of relief, plopped down on the seat, comfortably allowing her rapid heartbeat to subside, just breathing a relaxed sigh of delivery from a narrowly diverted disaster. She could leave the driving to somebody else, and depend on them getting her where she wanted to go. So she just sat there and gazed effortlessly out the window.

At first you just watch the scenery passing by and you're interested in some of it, you're disinterested in some of it. And you're able to have your own thoughts and your own daydreams. It's a good opportunity.

And I don't know exactly which moment the scene changed—maybe it was when that bus entered the tunnel and she saw that face, with the shifting of the light reflected there in the window. But she did see that face, and at first she was surprised to see how much she liked the looks of that face, with that sense of relaxation and comfort. And whether it's something you notice by the smoothness of the face muscles, or the relaxed fullness of the mouth, or softness of the eyes, or maybe it was the comfortable breathing. But she was just fascinated to look at that face, see herself. And there was something else there that she couldn't quite recognize, but she couldn't stop looking at the picture, and the longer that she looked at it, she came to the conclusion that there was something very definitely sexy about the way that her eyes were sparkling as she looked into that picture.

So watching that face and memorizing the look of those experiences, she must have just fallen back into trance, because the next thing she knew, the background had changed to include seeing herself in a situation, and there she was with that face and that relaxation and that comfort and that strength. Safely sexy, interacting with that man whom she'd been dating, and interacting in a way that pleased her considerably. And you can be very pleased with how you watch yourself interacting in a way that you value, doing something different. Your conscious mind doesn't even have to believe it's possible for you to actually act that way, but you can enjoy the scene that your unconscious projects. Or maybe you consciously project the scene and your unconscious just keeps those feelings constant.

Then I guess there was a bump or a bit of a jolt, and the scene changed to reveal her interacting again, this time with some of the men at work. And you interact in a different way with different people. And even though she kept the same qualities constant, they were approximately translated to a different situation. And you can even sense your sexuality with the men at work, but you do it in a professional way. And maybe it's only something that you recognize by a pride in the way you hold your body as you stand and discuss a case. And over another crack or bump in the road and the scene changed again. There she was with those women who had presented her difficulty in the past, and it's not clear or important why it had been difficult. But she saw herself being able to ask for help. She saw herself being able to lean back, hold her palms up, rock slightly backward on her feet and say, "Could you help me out here? It's important." And she felt very safe, and setting limits was another thing. A jolt of the bus, another change of scene. . . .

Your conscious mind doesn't need time to review carefully, because your unconscious is able to allow you an understanding in a very short period of time. But it must have seemed like hours that she rode in that bus, watching those interactions, memorizing something with her conscious mind, experiencing something else unconsciously. But when the bus came out of the tunnel, the shifting of the lights suddenly disrupted the picture, and brought to mind the idea with a sudden flash of awareness that the bus she was supposed to be on didn't even go through a tunnel, and she was on the wrong bus the whole time, going she knew not where. And when you discover something like that, your first impulse is to feel a sense of panic, and yet she was surprised to notice that the moment she did indeed start to feel panic and a familiar rise of tension and anxiety, that suddenly she was instead flooded with that sense of comfort and safety. And it didn't even matter that she had been on the wrong bus, because sometimes the things you learn from a mistake make that mistake a worthwhile experience. And in her case, the things she learned looking in that window were with her still as she got off of the bus laughing and wondering which way was home.

3. **Self-image goal (using CSI and scenarios):** *Relate relief, enjoyment, and ambition to future scenes dealing with separation from husband and interactions with children leaving home.*

Metaphor[22]

Sometimes you have the opportunity to climb down a mountain first, before you climb back up it. All you have to do is start at a higher elevation, but a climb is a climb, either way, and it doesn't really matter which direction you're going. My friend Nancy was fond of adventures and rarely turned one down. Her marriage had been an adventure and so too had the divorce. It was a different sort of experience we had in mind the day we decided to explore the nature "trail" in the heart of those Colorado mountains. We had no way of knowing what we were getting ourselves into but we started at the top and climbed one step in front of another, farther and farther, and you don't realize how much progress you've made until you take a break, take a rest, and just stop and look around to notice how far down

---

[22] Qualities had been retrieved and developed with other protocols, told earlier.

you've come. You still can't know how far down you're going if you can't see the bottom. You don't know what's going to happen there but you do your best to enjoy yourself on the way and not think too much about how hot you are or how you'd like a drink of water. Your unconscious is able to keep those needs on hold until the time is right.

So all the way down, down, down, down, deeper and deeper, and farther and farther, until finally, even though the guide rail had indicated it was a 20-minute walk, what seemed like hours later, we arrived at the bottom. It was truly a delight to behold that little mountain pool of water, lying so quietly there at the crevice between the mountains. And it was only disturbed by the slight trickling of icy mountain water flowing over the rocks and into the pool. In a situation like that, your conscious mind can suddenly realize that you have an opportunity to gratify a need that was on hold. So, hot and thirsty as we were, our first impulse was to just jump right into that pool. But as we bent over that water to take a sip, the sight of our reflected faces gave us a moment of pause. I didn't say anything to Nancy because I could tell that she was having a special communion with the face she was seeing.

She was seeing a sense of relief, part of which can come from having climbed all the way down that mountain and finding that you're able to sit back and relax and have a feeling of a job well done. And in a situation like that, you can just fall into a little trance and become fixated on seeing that face reflecting those qualities that you value and you want and you're wearing. And you can be very pleased how lovely you can look when you catch an unexpected glimpse of yourself in a situation like that. You can really enjoy a sense of dissociation and comfort in a little trance that develops at the sight of your face altered with your feelings of relief, enjoyment, ambition, and more. She saw her whole body reflected there with a posture that represented ambition, a smoothness of relief, and a twinkle of enjoyment. She told me later that the reflected clouds moving above her somehow seemed to usher in a little background that unfolded, allowing her to watch herself interacting with friends. She knew she was having a daydream but didn't question it because she was very interested in watching how you interact in a way that is different but familiar. It was about that time that the largest dragon fly I had ever seen appeared out of nowhere and hovered delicately just inches above the water's surface, perhaps mesmerized by its own reflection. Then, it very suddenly dipped its tail into the water before abruptly disappearing, leaving only a few ripples across the surface of the pool.

Nancy was still busy looking into the depths, but somehow the picture she was watching changed. The face and qualities remained constant, but this time saw herself with her soon-to-be ex-husband. This situation represented a bit of what had been anxiety for her because even though she had gone through the steps of saying goodbye to him long ago, emotionally, there was still the contact required for the final signing of divorce papers. And there she was interacting with him. He was his same self: critical, authoritative, infuriatingly illogical, and inaccurate. And to her amazement, she found that she was actually enjoying watching the way she was interacting with him and the things she was saying. And how can you speak to a person with whom you've had so much conflict over so many years, speak to that person in a way that represents your values and allows you to enjoy and be pleased with your creativity, sensitivity, and self-respect? Well, that is just what she did.

And the situation changed again. She wasn't much interested in the breeze that slightly ruffled the surface of the water because she was still more interested in her unusual reflection. She was now interacting with her son and daughter. Her son had always been her greatest challenge. You wouldn't want to say that only a mother could love him, but it was even difficult for her to love him sometimes because of those challenges he presented almost each and every waking moment. But, once again, there she was, wearing those qualities, enjoying watching herself dealing with Matthew and all his problems. With the utmost sense of self-respect, she watched how she was noticing and enjoying those things about him she liked, interacting with him in a way that was going to help him grow up to be the kind of citizen he could be proud of. And you never can know how your unconscious is able to bring to mind a relevant background and your conscious mind can just study that image and enjoy your ability to see yourself interacting differently in what would have been a very difficult situation.

It seems like forever sometimes, when an alteration in consciousness like that occurs, so I really don't know how long we sat there by that pool before one of us decided it was time to have a drink of that water we had been looking into the depths of.

And when you dip your hand into a still, quiet pool, it destroys the image, but it gives you another sense of relief and a new understanding of enjoyment because you can really enjoy a handful of water or even a brief chilly immersion. It would have to be brief, though, because the sun was beginning to veer close to the canyon wall and no one wants to find themselves in a crevice between the mountains when the sun goes down. So we hurried back up the mountain and, once again, it seemed to take much longer than the recommended 20 minutes.

This year Nancy wrote in her Christmas card that Matthew was very happy in a new boarding school and it had been a great adjustment for everyone. He was learning from others and only came home on weekends. She found that she enjoyed him a good bit more when she only saw him on weekends.

4. **Self-image goal (using CSI and scenarios):** *Associate feelings of self-worth and anger to situations involving confronting husband, self-care, and intimacy.*

Metaphor[23]

Now this topic of abusive marriages—people stop bad habits at times when they are able, not necessarily consciously, to recognize the availability of a resource that you have that allows you to proceed differently. When Ginni was married, during the entire 10 years of that abusive marriage, she had forgotten something that was very important and it was something that she had known all along. And when she told me about it, I felt a kindred spirit with her. I felt a real appreciation of her essence and for the strength of the little girl that she had been, and for the strength I knew was still available in that grown woman, who, in the wake of a stormy 10-year marriage, wasn't feeling particularly strong when she came into therapy.

But as a three-year-old, Ginni had been able to accurately assess the situation in her home and she recognized quite clearly that her mother was not stable, not an appropriate parent who was able to teach that little girl how it is that you really should love yourself. She didn't teach her that, by virtue of being alive, you deserve to have all of your feelings and really enjoy being the precious little girl you are. Her mother didn't do any of those things and it was amazing to me how clearly Ginni understood how precious she was even without that parental instruction. And so she decided with great clarity of mind to just pack up her doll buggy with her doll and the clothes her doll would need, a few clothes for herself and what other food and favorite toys she needed along life's highway, and she decided to just leave that crazy mother behind. She packed up that carriage and strolled off.

---

[23] Feelings of self-worth and power are anecdotally retrieved, and behaviors related to assertive and angry expression had been previously illustrated.

She was going to find the love she deserved. She knew she deserved
to be treated better than that, there was no need to hang around and
have someone doubt her worth. And so even as a child, and you don't
know how you know it, but, you're able to recognize the innate worth
of yourself as a human being.

Everyone can retrieve that feeling of self-appreciation that a child
knows and store up that good feeling. So when Ginni came to therapy,
she had left that marriage that had gone on for 10 years and she had
never even told anyone. She had kept the awful secret to herself. And
she came to therapy to alleviate the depression and anxiety she had
about the open-endness of her life now that she had left behind the
bad habit. What was she going to do now? And it was simply a matter
of helping her retrieve what she had known about all along. And when
she walked into the office, the computer screen still reflected an outline
of her treatment plan but she didn't know it was her treatment plan
when she initially stopped at the desk and looked very interested into
that screen. She only did so because she was interested in analyzing
and categorizing information in all possible ways.

And your conscious mind can appreciate something about the symbol
of a computer and how it is able to store such a vast amount of
information. And she had her own lap-top computer that she had
recently purchased and had brought along in case she needed to make
note of things related to changes she was interested in keeping account
of, dealing with precisely, categorizing carefully. And it's all an indication of how much motivation you have to change in a way that's
relevant for you.

So she stopped there at the computer and there was a moment of
confusion and the first thing she saw reflected in the screen was her
own face looking into the screen. And when you catch a glimpse of
yourself unexpectedly like that, you can go into a little trance at the
sight of seeing your own face, especially if your muscles are set in a
way that you weren't expecting to see. And then, of course, going into
trance allows your muscle set to change again so that you look different
still and for a moment you might question whether or not it is your
own face that you're observing. But look carefully, and notice the
smoothness of the muscles and the moisture around the eyes that
symbolize something about that sensitivity and strength that belong to
you, and just to you, that you can retrieve and experience and memorize
again.

And then she realized she was looking into the screen that was also
reflecting her treatment plan and she first thought that she really

shouldn't be looking at that, but she couldn't stop looking at that. Because sometimes your conscious mind is interested in what's going to happen and really wants to observe the process. And it must have been an interesting trance induction as she stood there watching the treatment plan with her reflection shining through it and around it and behind it.

So I simply asked her to sit down on the couch and go even more deeply into a trance—one that would be more relevant. And go about retrieving again the power of that child. It's been there all along. You might follow a tear or you might follow the gentleness of your breathing. And every child has a good many adventures, no matter how impoverished the circumstances were around your upbringing. You couldn't help but remember and appreciate something about the kind of adventures you knew how to have as a child without ever having to consciously understand how. The child can play endlessly, running through the yard, hiding behind trees, imagining you know not what. It takes a great deal of intelligence to imagine being under a tree becomes a secret hideaway, a little club, or a little house. Or you might even be able to remember again something about the experience of power the child has, who can run two hours, three hours, four. It's an energy and power and strength that everyone shares in common, and it's yours.

Some people might classify that as a feeling of anger. How do you know when you're angry about something? I knew Ginni had a lot to be angry about, all those years she had suffered in silence, just taking it. But to the extent that you have that ability to know how worthwhile you are as a child, you have the right to be very angry. Because to the extent that you can have your anger, you have an ability to have all your feelings. After all, you are as unique as your fingerprint, there'll never be another one like you and you shouldn't give up any of your feelings. You should even be able to still feel the pain that came from a spanking long ago, and be proud you can, because it indicates that you're alive and have a healthy nervous system. It would have been a shame if you couldn't feel that. So know how smart you are that your conscious and unconscious have retained the ability for you to feel and be sensitive to so many of your emotional resources and center in upon that understanding.

And, basically, that was the entire process I accomplished with Ginni that day. We worked for a long time and I could see the emotion building. I could see her having the feeling of anger again and the feeling of power that comes with it, and the adventure and delight a child can have, and it blends and merges together across the face in an interesting way. And she still wore that mixture of feelings when she stood up from the session and walked back by that computer and couldn't help but turn and look again. And there was that reflection staring right back out at her, her own face. And you can imagine that your face looks different still to the degree you allow yourself to experience all those abilities that are your birthright. And so she looked at the tracks of the tears that were still fresh on those soft cheeks, cheeks that had held a great deal of tonus, reflecting and symbolizing the power that she had also experienced. And there was the softness, kindness, and compassion. How wonderfully complex to be able to see so many abilities reflected on the same face. You could study your face now and see a beauty that perhaps you had overlooked before, an honesty of emotion, of caring, a peacefulness of breathing.

And so I asked her to pry herself away from the computer, but to take heart because she had her own lap-top still with her and she could take it with her and look into the computer and make note about how she was going to change. So she left the office and told me the next week that she had gotten home and she had so many ideas that she wanted to sit right down and organize and categorize them, but she couldn't even lift the top off of the portable computer because when she looked into her lap there was that same face reflected back at her in the shiny reflection of the plastic cover. She didn't even turn it on and that's a completely different way to compute. She just sat there and found that she went back into a trance.

And in that trance feel very proud of yourself, it's a reverent feeling almost. It's the kind of thing you could have in church. You could even take your portable computer to church to make note, but find that you look into the plastic and see reflected a peacefulness, a serenity, a power, and do you notice it by the calmness of the breathing or the upright posture of the shoulders, or by the smoothness of the cheeks and the gentle moistness around the eyes? And there's that sense of humor that is occasionally depicted by an upward tug at the corners of the lips and the smile lines around the mouth and the eyes. And you really should be very pleased when you see yourself in that fashion. And I know she was.

And she said she wasted hours that week, just sitting, staring into a computer that wasn't even turned on. And as she would sit there, see that face, those abilities, a background can begin to emerge and you can see yourself interacting with someone who is important to you, all in a way that allows you to continue to reflect that peacefulness, power, adventure, delight that a child can have, self-appreciation, even anger tempered by your own ability for compassion. And watch yourself interacting with that person. And it can be a person you very much enjoy being with, or a person with whom you have had conflict with.

It could be a person with whom you've had anxiety dealing with in the past, but find that, as you sit in the protective covering of a trance state, dissociated. You can picture yourself in your mind's eye or in that computer screen, just like a television, interacting in a way your conscious mind can't even believe and wouldn't expect to be possible, but that doesn't prevent your unconscious from projecting that image of yourself. Your conscious mind can be interested and curious about how that happens or maybe your conscious mind would prefer to just doubt that it could ever happen in real life. It doesn't really matter because you find that your unconscious can and does project that image and you watch yourself interacting in situations that may have been associated with a great deal of anxiety then, in the past, at another time, but you can be very pleased to discover how you can actually enjoy something about the way you interact in a way that reflects your values.

And time passes in an interesting way when you're in a trance. You can stare into a little movie like that in your mind's eye, just like in a dream that lasts for only 30 seconds in real time, only the amount of time it took for an alarm clock to ring, but in the dreamer's experience you can understand it differently, time passes differently, you have a sense of detail and vividness. And have that experience as you, perhaps like she did, watch those images begin to form, backgrounds begin, fade, to be replaced by a new background.

Who knows what makes a change in a background of your imagination. Who knows what makes a dream change, but it would change. And she watched herself in that same way be very pleased expressing a great deal of anger towards that husband, anger that had been long withheld but really did need to be declared, and done so appropriately. And as she sat there protectively in trance, gazing into the computer, watching herself mingle with those abilities, symbolized so beautifully really in her features and posture, she inspected herself telling him. In fact, the more irritating she could envision him being, the more amused she became at how able she was to survey herself interacting with that abrasive, difficult stimulus of a husband with whom she'd had conflict, and yet watched herself rejoin him in a way that represented and clarified her own values. And you can see yourself not at all deflated by any criticism he might have.

And it was like the situation we observed on an airplane one day when a real creep was tormenting a timid-looking flight attendant about where his special meal was. He was being so unreasonably insulting. She had every right to get angry. There's a limit to how much you should have to take in a job. But she handled the situation in an unexpected manner. She just reached out and took his hand, patting it gently as she looked him right in the eye, smiled kindly, and said in the sweetest, most reassuring voice you could imagine, "Don't you worry, sugar, we'll get you something to eat." And he just melted. He couldn't think of any way to follow that. And so whether you communicate your anger outright, or whether you temper it with a compassion and understanding and an ability to be sensitive to another person's needs, your unconscious can make those selections. You might enjoy scrutinizing a variety of scenarios go by in a moment or two, or 30 seconds that seem to last much longer than that and can continue in dreams at night as well. Ginni said that it's a good thing her computer is so portable because you never know when you're going to need a moment to yourself to make note of something important, even without turning the machine on.

5. **Self-image goal (using CSI and scenarios):** *Associate pleasure, aggression, and control to courtship stage, independence from family of origin, and symptom cessation.*

Metaphor[24]

I wondered if she could picture her own face. I spent a lot of time asking her to make a visual image of her body, starting with the face or the feet. She always started with her newly matured breasts. I guess it was a load off of her mind to realize that she had become a woman. The problem with that was that she didn't know how to be one to her satisfaction. So I asked her to imagine herself in every room of her house. It reminded her of the joy that she felt. The conscious mind doesn't really know how that begins and doesn't even need to in order to appreciate it. I assisted her in recognizing a warmth, smile on your lips, a joke. There's a kind of joy that comes after tearing has happened.

---

[24] The character was earlier developed in a family structure change protocol, and the transcript as it originally preceded this portion can be found in the family structure change section, p. 204.

It might be biological relief—for one thing your sinuses feel better because the pressure of the tears is gone. You breathe more easily.

So I invited her to picture herself laughing. It's a funny sight to picture yourself laughing. Most people don't know what they sound like on a tape recorder, and I wonder if you know what you look like when you are laughing. Your lips go in four directions. First of all the bottom lip tends to smile like a child, the upper lip starts to smile like a woman, the back side of your mouth controlled by your cheek muscles says "not now" and pulls the lip down, and the fourth movement is the slight protrusion created by the blood flow. You may rock back and forth, alternating between those four responses.

I described to her the unique facial features and asked her to imagine her face. She could look at her breasts, she ought to also be able to look at her face. Her face is probably more interesting. She should picture her entire posture, standing straight, head above shoulders, breathe comfortably, slightly reddened cheeks, feeling rather pleasant, not unrelated to the experience of being able to picture yourself in front of the mirror at a martial arts dojo, aware of your movements, recognizing what it looks like to have a sense of control and aggression, and that's the easy part. The next is allowing that picture of yourself to remain constant as a reminder of the feelings you may have when you unfold the scenario of interacting with others that she needed to associate with those feelings.

The first thing I asked her to do was to examine that new house without the door locks, walk around in every room of the house, and notice how you smile in those rooms, how much aggression you walk into the room with, you might wonder what you'd say to yourself.

Depicting herself walking through the rooms of that house, feeling the good feelings that she felt in a trance in the chair, it became a simple post-hypnotic suggestion for her to follow later on, and you can be fairly certain that one of the things your brain will do when you stand inside that room is say, "Hey, I know how to feel good standing here, I think. I've been thinking about this room feeling good someplace in the past." Then she'd pick another room, a hallway. How do you look using the bathroom? The shower of your house? You can make room for alterations.

"The only reason that you are worried about the size of your breasts is because you are worried about courtship," I said to her, because I was being very direct with her then. She had been my client for a long period of months and she had taken the locks off of her doors, so she should be able to use that same ability to fantasize her feelings of control and joy for how she would go about making sexual advances.

For instance, do you see yourself standing by some person, getting closer to some person? I told her to think about what she would say to herself, what she would say out loud, feeling that feeling, watching her presence, go through the steps. It was clear that she didn't intend to rely upon those automatic modelings that she received from her parents, and it was apropos for her to spend time designing her own manner of conduct.

She was more surprised when I suggested that she keep the joy feeling, keep the courtship picture, add the aggressive feelings. It's common knowledge that sexuality is a combination of aggression and pleasure. So your conscious mind can pay attention to the aggression, once your unconscious develops the pleasure. More people will find it comfortable to let the conscious mind pay attention to the pleasure, and let your unconscious handle the aggression. You might wonder if it is possible for your conscious mind to not pay attention to the pleasure, and let your unconscious take care of the aggression, but if your unconscious doesn't at least take care of that aggression, then your conscious mind is going to have pleasure alone. If you are alone, you ought to let your conscious mind enjoy your unconscious enjoying itself.

So I insisted that she spend some of the time in trance thinking another scenario, watching herself alone with that feeling of joy, that feeling of control, asking her how it is going to feel, what it is she's going to notice first. Is her conscious mind going to notice the joy and let the unconscious have control automatically on exams, or would that be too much to ask? Maybe you should let your conscious mind be responsible for control, then let your unconscious have joy. Primarily, the point was that she developed outward signs of womanhood and I wanted to teach her how to use her own human mechanisms to elaborate the internal learnings, especially how to have the pleasure of autonomy, the pleasures of adulthood. I told her it was all right to hold onto the dreams of childhood as long as you give up childish dreams, and she had a far better understanding after she made her own visual scenarios of how she would conduct herself, keeping those feelings constant. It even taught her how to do that with children. She never thought about how she was going to look with children, if she felt good and had control and aggression.

She told me she thought about door locks again when she made that picture, but she was only kidding.

6. *Self-image goal (using CSI and scenarios):* Build self-image thinking and rehearse scenarios involving differentiation from mother with confidence, courage, and determination.

Metaphor[25]

Looking out the tour bus window at the European countryside, Joan mused, "Who would have ever thought I would be taking a trip to Europe by myself and about to tour a castle from an ancient time." The bus pulled up to the entrance of the old castle. As the group climbed out, the guide began to explain the historical significance of the various markings on the outside of the enormous structure. He pointed out the green moss that gave the castle a distinctive color. Once inside, the tour group followed the guide from room to room.

Joan noticed armor shields and swords that must have seen ferocious battle. Some were battered and dull. Entire suits of armor stood in a ready position. It seemed to Joan like a knight was peering out from the protective wire mesh that covered the face. She almost expected the armor to move, and for a moment she held her breath and stared into the helmet's black cavity. There was no sign of life.

Relics from an ancient time decorated the large room in which the group was standing. Joan heard the guide speaking to the rest of the group, as she was perusing the artifacts from the castle: "You can be enchanted by these relics and be transported back in time, and really wonder what life was like." The voices of the group and the guide began to drift off. . . .

Soon Joan realized that she had been alone in one of the rooms while the rest of the group had moved on. She wasn't sure which direction the group had gone. There were several doorways leading in different directions. So Joan decided to choose one door and followed the path that wound around and further into the recesses of the old castle.

When you get sidetracked, you never know how a path you least expect to take may lead somewhere important. And what seems like a detour may be the most direct route. Now Joan was feeling a bit anxious and lost. But she was also intrigued by this musty old place. The castle had a strange, unexplainable feeling of familiarity to her. She decided she needed to find her group. But the path she was taking seemed to wind around and further into the very depths of the castle.

---

[25] This metaphor was contributed by Carol Kershaw, Ph.D.

She peered into a door that opened into a large room. As her eyes became accustomed to the dimmer light, Joan realized she had entered an old library. She walked up to the many shelves of books to examine the titles; Socrates and Plato were there and Aristotle's treatise on how the beautiful sometimes masks the ugly; a book on *Turning 40 in the Eighties*. What was that doing there?

On one wall of the library hung an ornate mirror, which caught Joan's attention. She walked up to the mirror and looked at her reflection. She began to view her own reflected image. In a moment, she began to have an eerie experience. When you look at your mirror image, you never know whether you are looking at the image, or if you are looking at the image looking back at you, or if you're in the mirror looking back at the you looking into the mirror.

At any rate, something began to happen. The image in the mirror began to change. Joan's image began to blur and fade out momentarily. Then a new sense of clarity developed. Her mirror image smiled back at Joan and spoke: "You can have that sense of confidence and courage and know when you take that deep breath. Your shoulders rise to their full stature. Your breathing is easy and gentle. The little crinkles around your eyes when you smile demonstrate your own unique sense of humor. You can feel those indentations as you smile. Feeling more comfort in your own body, your weight is balanced on both feet. Your jaw is comfortably set with that air of determination to reach your goal."

Joan looked deep into the mirror and saw the image begin to change again. The lines in the face reflected in the mirror began to slightly deepen; the sparkle in the eyes brightened, and Joan had the distinct impression, which you can get now and then, that she was looking at her older self some time in the future.

The image spoke to her: "There are moments you need to remember. Moments that mark your thinking your own thoughts. Looking back over my past which is your future, I can see step by step the path to the present feeling of confidence and reliability on your self." With that thought she saw the reflection of her self milling about with several others present. Yet, she was all alone. Indeed, she was the central character in the vision. She witnessed the demeanor, the poise, the posture, the grace of her actions with each of them. One or two at a time.

She saw herself with friends.

She scrutinized herself with strangers—always possessing those remarkable and desirable qualities that initially entranced her.

She examined herself with her mother present. Then, again, with her mother in a most agreeable mood. Finally, again, with her mother at

her most intrusive and undesirable. All the while, she ruminated about
the Joan she saw—acting with a courage and confidence she had not
previously realized was hers. But your conscious mind is only able to
avail itself of the qualities your unconscious really has, can have, and
has learned and stored away for your own use.

All the while she heard, "You can be a separate person and be safe.
You have the best idea of what is important to you. You can listen
to the wisdom of your self. . . . You can change your thoughts to
change your world. You can listen to what you know rather than what
you fear. After all," the image said, smiling back at Joan, "fear is only
a feeling and there is always a beginning, middle, and end to a feeling.
But really, there is nothing to fear."

Joan was entranced with the image because she knew she was listening
to herself. Then, the image began to fade, leaving the memory of those
smiling, confident eyes. Suddenly the sound of footsteps were behind
her. Joan turned to see an old woman who introduced herself as the
curator of the castle. The woman told Joan to follow her, and she
would lead her back to the group. There was something familiar about
this woman, but Joan didn't have time to place her. They walked
around several curves and past many rooms and stopped. The old
woman stopped. She turned around and said, "Just on the other side
of this large wooden door is your tour group, but perhaps you know
that you belong here to this time and that you can stay here. Then,
when I can no longer be the curator of this castle, you will take over."
Joan didn't hesitate for even a moment before replying, "No, I must
go back to my time and my world to create my future-present of
comfort and satisfaction." With that, Joan turned and opened the large
door. Her tour group welcomed her and asked where she had been.
Joan only replied, "A visit to your past by your future self can be a
present."

7. ***Self-image goal (using CSI and scenarios):*** *As part of a final session,
consolidate previous learnings and open the way for continued growth,
especially concerning the client's previously difficult relationship with a man
whom she felt had taken advantage of her.*

Metaphor[26]

Now your unconscious mind has so many things it could tell you.
The problem is not really . . . it's sort of like wanting to read a book

[26] This metaphor was contributed by George Glaser, M.S.W.

and going to the library and thinking, "Gosh, there are a lot of books I could read." And you're not sure if you are going to start off in the science fiction area, the romantic area, the historical area, or whether you are going to the scientific area, or whether you're going for some light reading in a trashy romantic novel. Maybe you want a solid epic. But you walk through the doors of the library and there's no shortage of books. There are more books than you could read in a lifetime, and your unconscious mind is kind of like a library. It has your accumulated knowledge stored there. Knowledge of your body, of your hand, of the ability of your hand to move off your lap without your conscious volition. It's really where your creativity is and all the books on art and design, creativity and inventions; how to produce new things out of nothing; alchemy. How you can take $1 + 1$ and make 4—New Math!

When Fran strolled into the public library downtown, she had no earthly idea of how she would get from one level to another. You walk in and there is an escalator that takes you up. I think it's an escalator, maybe it's the stairs, but I really don't remember if it's an escalator or stairs. Maybe there are both. But I do know that as she walked in she noticed a way to go up, and after she went up those stairs, she turned around at the top of the stairs and looked down. She got quite an expansive view that's not possible from the lower level looking out through the windows and the lights, the skylights, a view of the lower level of the stairs below her, and all the people. And she thought it would be fun to imagine herself sitting down over on the couches there, those circular couches, talking to someone, and thinking—"I'm over there talking"—while she stands there expectantly at the top of the stairs, her hand held in the air, looking down at all the other people watching herself both downstairs and upstairs. And she could see herself standing there. She makes a wide sweep. It could be Scarlet O'Hara at the top of the stairs and she turns around, looks down, and sees herself down there on those chairs talking to someone.

She saw herself down there, far down, talking with someone in a new way. And when you look at yourself far below comfortably talking with someone you know, you begin to notice some new things about yourself. And you can start, even from that distance, with a clear eye, to notice and detail the image of your body as you move down there on the lower level. You can notice the words that you use, the way you hold your body, the kind of expressions you have, the way you move your arms and hands, the tone of your voice, the truth in your words.

And as Fran watched herself 50 feet down on the lower level talking comfortably with someone important to her, she developed a rather surprising observation which you might be interested in. As she looked at herself, she noticed that her level of comfort, surprisingly enough, didn't seem to be dependent on what the other person was doing. She felt a pleasurable sensation on her face as the light came in through the window, and she went even more deeply into the daydream trance and realized that far below, the other person was going to act in a variety of ways. He was going to act friendly. He was going to act lost. He was going to act sweetly, romantically. He might range from pleading with her to being tough with her. You might notice, as Fran did, that you are able to see yourself be comfortable and all the things that means, regardless of what your someone is doing.

So Fran, standing at the top of the stairs, expectantly watched her friend go through his repertoire of behaviors in a purposeful or inadvertent attempt to have her respond, to get her to respond down there, far below. She was in a spell and without thinking about it her hand gradually approached her face. As your hand is inching to your face, you'll find that the feeling of tingling there in your hand gets even stronger as it moves gently, gently, and gets ready to be completed as it touches your face. It can stay there as you imagine yourself standing at the top of the stairs and looking down at that other you talking with someone important to you. You'll find that the tingling sensation can be unusual but comfortable, and that, rather than trying to make it go away, your unconscious mind is reproducing it and your conscious mind doesn't need to pay attention. You may be surprised to notice how you can visually symbolize that tingling and feeling of comfort as it is reflected in smooth cheek muscles, slow relaxed breathing, or a hand hanging comfortably detached, suspended in time and space.

Now Fran watched herself down there on the lower level having quite a good time paying attention to her friend and feeling like she knew how to be herself. She could see it in the rising and falling of her chest, the calm, sincere look on her face, the steadiness in her voice, the comfortableness of her back, and the fluidness of her arms as she moved, and walked, and talked. She could see the smile on her face and around her lips that extended up into the cheeks, regardless of what the other person was saying or doing. As she stood there at the top of the stairs and watched in such stillness the scene below, she realized that she knew how to be really comfortable, and you can only wonder what it is inside a person that allows such comfort to be so readily visible and obviously apparent to anyone who cares to look and see.

And the light was shining in on her as she watched herself far below. A feeling can warm you, perhaps similar to the feeling Fran had when she watched herself talk so comfortably and so honestly to her friend. You might notice an ability to overhear a conversation you conduct while having that warm feeling. *(long pause)* But Fran, finally realizing an intense desire to be connected to herself in a new way, decided to very gracefully, and I guess it would be okay to say sensually, walk down the stairs, to feel the pressure of her foot against the step. She could still see the Fran that was sitting down there on the chair talking to her friend with the physical appearance that she was really comfortable. And she certainly seemed comfortable with all the curves in the right spot, all the bulges in the right spot. And by then, she was moving down those stairs, maybe halfway down, so gracefully and dramatically, but sensually. And she was aware of her own body as she walked down, noticing the way she'd like it to be.

As she moved down and was only half as high above herself as she was before, she had had the opportunity of realizing some things far above, and seeing how to do it, and noticing something about both herself and her friend that she had never even noticed before.

At the bottom of the stairs she gently walked over to the people on couches she had been watching. Then Fran, very politely, but in a determined and certainly assertive fashion, indicated to her imagined self that she would like to take that spot and practice something for her real self. And as she walked over she had become aware of the flush of her face as she prepared herself to try something new that she'd only practiced before in imagination from far above. But she also felt the quickening of her pulse and the excitement because she knew she would learn something productive. And you know how that can feel and look as you watch yourself.

She took a deep breath and told Fran that she'd fill in now, and she sat down and looked her friend straight in the eye—you might wonder which part of his eye she looked at, or which eye she focused on—and she heard herself begin to tell him all the things that she would like to say, in the way she'd like to say them. And what is it important for you to share? You can be pleased to hear yourself speaking in a way that manifests that comfort and power you have. And she felt that power over everything else—isn't that right? She felt her hands, her face, she felt her chest, her stomach. She was very aware of her body, comfortably aware, very aware of her body which felt quite powerful and forceful, a force to be reckoned with.

And you can imagine the look in his eyes, the hint of confusion— not something bad—just a hint as he struggled to make sense of the person he was talking with. Fran let her imagined self go up the stairs and take her place there at the top. After all, it would be nice for them to trade information and to get really close and supportive of each other in all areas that are important. Everyone needs a buddy. And then the other Fran came down the stairs and gently took the real Fran's hand and said, "Fran, I need to get back to work. I want you to come with me." And so "they" said goodbye to the friend for the time being.

And you can realize the depth and the intensity with which you have been communicating and observing just as she did when she realized that even with all the other people around there hadn't been much else going on in the library. She hadn't noticed herself being the object of interested attention at the top of the stairs. It just wasn't very important because what was important was happening inside, and she certainly was oblivious to the passage of time and the other sounds. But you can look around now and begin to realize that you can open your eyes to the other images. And your attention may have been so transfixed and taken up with various thoughts and images and feelings with what you were doing that you realize that your unconscious mind has given you many insights and answers and new awareness.

Fran realized suddenly that she had only spent her time in one part of the library, and didn't even look into any books there! There were so many other parts that she hadn't even poked a head into, but there would be other days. The library will be there and there will be even more books the next time.

8. Self-image goal (using CSI and scenarios): *Associate relief, satisfaction, and pride to upcoming events.*

Metaphor[27]

The desired characteristics had been previously developed in an affect protocol story using this character.

Karen sat there gazing into the bell of her trombone. As she gazed into the image of her face and the relief she felt, having just played

---

[27] This metaphor was contributed by Nicholas G. Seferlis, M.S.

"the concert of the missing note." She looked back through all those practice sessions which had paid off in a matter of moments; even with missing the first note, she still gave a very successful performance. As she looked at herself, she talked to the image, saying, "You did it, you went out there and you trusted yourself and the rest of the band. And all 80 pieces came together when they were supposed to."

She thought about the sense of belonging and her own importance to the group and could actually see that feeling reflected back in the image of her face. There was a real strength she could see by the relaxed muscles, the smile on the lips, smooth, confident breathing.

Then she looked ahead to upcoming performances and talked to herself again, "You'll practice and you'll go out there and you'll do your best no matter what happens. You'll always have that pride and confidence that you've tried and done your best. And the relief and trust in others. It's not just one performer, but many performers all together doing one common thing is what makes the beautiful music."

As she looked into the reflection, talking to herself, she wondered how she could use what she had learned that night in other aspects of her life. How could she carry on with that pride and confidence? You know, at some level, when you have retrieved or developed a valuable skill, you can carry it with you for wherever you need it.

I don't know if she consciously set out to do that as she gazed into the bell of her trombone, or if the unconscious doesn't just take an opportunity like that to go into a little fantasy and elaborate on those ideas you were having at the conscious level. At any rate, she sat there a long time without moving, just gazing at that reflection and what appeared to be an unfolding background. There she was in French class, doing a presentation and interacting in a way that reflected her confidence and strength, pride and relief. Your conscious mind can be surprised at what your unconscious brings to mind in an unfolding scene important to you.

As the scenes changed again and again, she saw herself with her family, and learning new skills, . . . in sports, . . . shopping, . . . going on a date. And all the while, in each one, she was wearing relief, confidence, pride, strength, in ways that she was already applying later in that daydream captured in the trombone bell. You do this unconsciously as your conscious mind examines the possibilities.

And eventually, the background began to reflect the band room and the other members of the band, and she again noticed the sounds they must have been making as they put away the instruments.

She took one last look into the reflection and then affectionately returned her trombone to its case before becoming one with the last background that had been reflected. She closed the case, put the case in her locker, and walked out of the room.

A few of her bandmates were there to share their compliments and support, a pat on the back, and they all congratulated themselves on a job well done. And it's something your unconscious can store up to use throughout your whole lifetime.

9. Self-image goal (using emanated images): *Develop dissociation context for emanated images of future.*

Metaphor

Robert Erickson grew up in Phoenix, Arizona in the shadow of a mountain called "Squaw Peak." He also had an imposingly famous father but I'm sure he failed to fully appreciate that fact as a child. He remembered how he would come as any young boy needs to do and ask his father those questions an adolescent will have about solving life's problems, only to have his father point a finger in the direction of Squaw Peak, and utter the one word command that he always gave in that situation, "Climb."

And up the mountain he would have to go in order to find answers to those problems that you bring with your conscious mind and you phrase in a certain way. How nice to have a parent who is so respectful of the ability of the child to refrain from solving the problem but to simply ask that you go inside, change your point of view, and review your problem with your own resources.

And so Robert would climb the mountain, not necessarily thinking about the problem, or perhaps thinking extensively about the problem with his conscious mind and allowing the unconscious mind to deal with the ever-so important processes of balance and blood flow, breathing, one step at a time, how do you know which foot to pick up first and where to put it? You don't think about that consciously because the unconscious is exquisitely able to handle all those processes for you.

And I expect in my imagination of Robert climbing that mountain that he must have sometimes forgotten to think about the problem completely as he was distracted by the sights of blooming cacti and other unexpected joys along the way. You can be distracted by the unexpected joy of a gentle breeze blowing across your skin that's been covered with a light layer of perspiration. And I think that's one of the most wonderful feelings in the world, and you only are able to have that to the extent you make an exertion, use your body, allow your unconscious to do its job, exercise those muscles.

And when he finally would arrive at the top of that mountain, it must have been so satisfying, such a sense of tangible accomplishment. And who wouldn't want, at a point like that, to just sit down and go deeply into a trance, looking out over the distance and the city so far below, seeing what you had been a part of, and now you're so far apart from, above it all really. And the problem is way down there, out there somewhere, and you can just sit on top of a mountain in your imagination and memorize that feeling of comfortable dissociation that your unconscious creates and your conscious mind can really enjoy. I don't know if it's a feeling of weightlessness or a feeling of being so heavy that you are especially able to notice any contrasting feelings of lightness that develop elsewhere. And, of course, many people had the opportunity to change the point of view and develop a detached dissociation.

And up on top of the mountain, I bet Robert would sit there for varying amounts of time, dissociated, and sometimes he must have thought about that concern that had resulted in his climbing the mountain. And yet so much of the time your unconscious can do something else. Just sitting there on top of the peak, looking out at the city so far below, and even beyond the city, you can almost look into tomorrow or well into the future, five years or more, to a time when you will have accomplished a great many things.

You will have accomplished additional years, experiences, understandings, ideas. And you can just picture that, letting your conscious or unconscious fill in the details, co-creating a picture of success in the future. There's really no sense in waiting until you are in the future to feel proud about the things you will have accomplished there. You can look forward to the day when you can look back and what better place than from a mountaintop?

Who will you be with, what will you be doing, where will you live, how will you look, what will you have accomplished? It's nice to find that you can see yourself having successfully achieved a dream come true and merge with that self now, memorize the alterations in perception, memorize the success and pride, the strength, the courage. And from the vantage point of that time in the future . . . 1999 is probably not very much different from 1990 or from two years ago,

1986. Time is difficult to judge at all, really, when winter feels the same as it did 200 years ago. Sunday afternoons and rainy days, spring and fall crunchy leaves don't really change very much from year to year, and you can use that knowledge to go anywhere in time that your unconscious would like to take you.

And then experiencing yourself comfortably surrounded with your accomplishments in that future-present time, five years or more from when we talked last, you may want to just take a moment and let it soak in, memorize the sights, sounds, smells, feelings. I suppose the trance you are in now is a trance similar to the one back in my office. Just take a moment to enjoy all the people you love who are there with you. Take another to notice your home and your security. And be sure to notice your physical health—you've earned it with your efforts. Notice, too, the financial and career security you acquired. But, most of all, notice the rewards of your family, children, and friends.

I know you can still go into a daydream and find that you can look back over all the steps you took to arrive so successfully into this future. You might begin the review by looking back to that time when you left the therapy session early that December. They were just putting up the Christmas decorations at the nearby hotel. They didn't have Santa on the elevator yet. Look back at the changes in your body. How had it first started, in fact? Maybe there was something about a new sense of pride that was reflected in your posture that initiated other, more subtle physiological processes, perhaps even changes in your metabolism. And you can review all of the changes, all of the steps you took, the obstacles you encountered that allowed you to learn so many things, the mistakes you made that you wouldn't trade for anything because of the learnings that went with them. When that daydream ends, there you are still enjoying the accomplishments, and even when you merge again with your current time zone, you can keep the good feelings even if you don't consciously remember or believe the dream. After all, even if you cross the international dateline, you get to keep all of the experiences you've already had in what will be experienced by the rest of the world as tomorrow.

At some point, as if lost in time and space or a dream, Robert would, no doubt, orient himself back to the current year and the mountaintop on which he was sitting, trying to solve some adolescent problem. I don't know whether he remembered the wanderings of his unconscious mind or not, but he did say that he never climbed down the mountain with the same problem as the one he climbed up with. Sometimes he would have solved it, other times forgotten it, perhaps;

or maybe he just looked at it differently and altered some aspect of it in a way that made it more manageable. Certainly there were a variety of things that could have happened to it and a variety of stimuli that could make a person think about leaving a mountaintop. Maybe the breeze blows a little too cool, maybe he knew it was time to come down because he had thought of how he wanted to tackle that problem and he was ready to get back down into the mainstream.

Then you recall sitting here in my office and the fantasies you might make one day. And then there is the awareness of not noticing what you were just thinking about as you wait for the next thoughts.

10. Self-image goal (using emanated images): *Shape future perception.*

Metaphor[28]

In Hawaii, "aloha" can be used to mean just about anything. It can mean "Nice to meet you," "Have a good time," "You're looking very nice today," "Goodbye," or "Hello." And it doesn't have to be accompanied with flowers. But speaking of hellos, you're really only free to say hello to the extent that you've been willing to say a thoughtful and a careful goodbye. I don't need to tell you that. But we needed to tell Carl that. And he had said a very thoughtful and a very careful goodbye. And it took him a good many tears, but by the time we got to Heron Island, he was ready to say hello to the rest of his life. And he had with him a new female companion. It was an interesting and awkward relationship they were developing, in the wake of the suicide of his wife. But it's amazing how even the most infertile ground can support the life of the vegetation that grows there.

And speaking of vegetation, Heron Island is a wonderland, both vegetation above the water and vegetation below the water. And animal life! And it seemed to be like Fantasy Island. It seemed to be a place where you can imagine anything and make it come true. And it didn't matter much that we were in Heron Island in 1982; it could have been Heron Island in 1983, or '84, or '86, not very much difference. The warm season is the warm season, and the cold season is the cold season, no matter what year it is. And time can pass and change in interesting ways. And we asked Carl to fall into a trance and imagine

[28] The protagonist was developed earlier in an affect protocol story to retrieve relief, see p. 58.

being on Heron Island again in 1996, and this time, to enjoy being there having accomplished all those things that he had accomplished since we were there the first time. And we didn't know whether he'd be married, or whether he would just be dating someone whom he had had the opportunity to date for some years, and build a relationship with. And we didn't know whether he would have stayed in his practice as a psychologist, or whether he had branched into other endeavors that were interesting to him. We were pretty sure he'd still be a scuba diver, though.

And so, I don't know whether he followed that suggestion while swimming in the comfort of the depths and enjoying the sights with his conscious mind, while his unconscious mind took the opportunity of being deeply under water to just imagine that future experienced as if now, in which he had accomplished all of those things, in which he had dealt with all of those conflicts and issues with which he had had to deal. He had grown beyond those, and you can feel very proud, having grown beyond, having accomplished those things you set out to accomplish, consistent with your values. And memorize that success. It's yours, you're entitled to it.

And experiencing yourself cozy, surrounded with your accomplishments in that future-present time, several years from when we talked last, you may want to just take a moment and let it soak in, memorize the experiences of sights, sounds, smells, feelings. I suppose the trance you are in now will be similar to the days on Heron Island. Just take a moment to enjoy all the people you love who are there with you. Take another to notice your home and your security. Of course, you notice your physical health—you were always vigilant of that. Notice, too, the financial and employment security you obtained. Take a moment to enjoy the rewards of your family, children, and friends.

And while you're feeling that success, you might as well take a moment, we said to him, to just look back and review all of those steps you took to find yourself so comfortably here on Heron Island again. And review those steps and be pleased with how you managed to deal with those things.

And from the relative comfort of hindsight, you can look back and even appreciate those obstacles you encountered, and those conflicts that seemed insolvable at the time. And appreciate that opportunity that you had to learn what you now know and wouldn't trade for anything. Notice at least six important steps you took from those days after Heron Island. Be aware, in each scene, of one outstanding aspect of growth, risk, false start, expansion, hellos, goodbyes, building, waiting, etc., that you took at the time . . . and which led you to this moment of happiness.

And finally, you have to come up for air, and so you may take just one more moment and memorize the comfort of and the pride involved in being there in that future, experiencing a good feeling, experiencing the relief of many jobs well done, accomplished, behind you before you return to the present time.

And when we came up for air and got back on the dive boat, there was very little indication there to remind Carl that it was really still only 1982. Because you still bring with you some of that feeling, some of that pleasure, and there's no need to wait to enjoy your feelings of success, you're entitled to enjoy them now.

11. Self-image goal (using CSI, scenarios, and emanated images): *Associate personal resources to likely situations in the client's life, using all of the self-image thinking components: central self-image qualities, rehearsing the central self-image through scenarios, and shaping future perception with emanated images.*

Metaphor[29]

In her dream, Alyce was beginning to feel a lot like Alice—as if she had gone through the looking glass and had discovered a strange world. There weren't any large white rabbits, no queen of hearts, but she was certainly feeling as if she must be quite mad. Yet, without a doubt, she was in a wonderland of imagination and unconscious opportunity. And, of course, in a dream you really have no way of knowing that it is a dream until after you wake up. And that wouldn't take place for quite some time. And also, at this point, she had no idea that a test of mirrors was still in her dream.

She found herself sitting at a sidewalk cafe. She wasn't too sure how long she had been sitting there—time seemed to be frozen—all the rest of the world had faded away as she continued to stare, captivated, at the shop across the street. People, quite ordinary people, apparently, appeared to be going in. But their appearance was quite altered when they came out. Alyce had been a firm believer in the power of shopping to change a person's mood, but this was quite different. They didn't even wear different clothes when they came out so altered. She stared

[29] This metaphor was contributed by Susan L. Vignola, D.S.W.

puzzled. Her curiosity quickly won out. She simply had to find out what was going on in that quaint little shop.

She stood up, straightened her clothes, and began walking across the street towards the shop. The closer she got, the slower her walk. She was about to turn around and forget the whole thing when she got mixed up with a group of shoppers and was quite literally pushed into the shop.

The clothes on the racks looked ordinary enough but as she bent closer, she was surprised to find no size indicators. Everyone knows the experience of looking for something in a dream and she found that there were no dividers separating the size 8s from the size 10s as would occur in reality. Your unconscious can communicate quite literally in a dream and symbolize an opportunity in a unique way. In her dream, the little plastic dividers had strange labels such as courage, confidence, assertiveness, humor, tenderness, compassion.

How odd she thought as her eye caught sight of someone at the rack across the way. She had picked up a plain-looking piece of clothing and was standing in front of the tri-fold mirrors. As she put the clothes around her shoulders, Alyce noticed them beginning to change. She felt herself being drawn to that person, wanting to be near her. She began to walk towards the person standing at the mirrors. As she passed the rack where the clothing had come from, Alyce saw the label on the divider. It said "warmth." Alyce picked a garment from the rack labeled courage and walked towards the tri-fold mirrors. And what quality does your unconscious recognize as relevant and select?

She took a deep breath, and slowly lowered the garment over her head onto her shoulders. She watched, and when you see yourself in a special arrangement like that, it is easy to see how your appearance changes and your reflection alters. Alyce, looking in the mirror, heard the saleslady say, "See yourself as you appear wearing that cloak of courage. Notice how much taller you stand, notice the straightness of your back, notice your shoulders pull back, feel your chest expand as you inhale deeply. See how your chin juts forward slightly." Alyce could hardly believe her eyes. "You can see yourself as you look wearing that courage," the saleslady keeps repeating, "see yourself, see yourself, see yourself, see the courageous you."

As Alyce prepared to speak, she heard her voice. It was her voice, yet you can identify with that dream even while you hear how you sound when you speak with courage. Remembering yourself in front of the mirror, you can recall a time when you, too, had courage. Perhaps it was when you were around three years old and another child had your favorite toy, and you walked over to that other child and grabbed your toy back. Maybe it was the first day of school and you waved goodbye to Mommy. I don't know when it was, maybe another time. You can remember a time when you had courage. And Alyce, too, was both remembering her past courage as she was seeing herself wearing that courage.

Alyce was very excited. Without taking off the courage, she went and chose two more pieces of clothing. When she returned to the mirror, she put each one on, one at a time. First, she put on the piece of clothing labeled "confidence" and stepped back. "See yourself," she heard, "see yourself wearing that confidence, notice how well it goes with your courage. The two can feel quite comfortable together." As she looked in the mirror, deep within that dream that seemed to have no end in sight, she asked herself, "Are you appearing taller because of the confidence or is it the courage that is making you appear so tall? Are your shoulders back and your chest fuller because of the courage, or is it the confidence making you breathe more deeply? Is it the confidence making your chin tilt forward, or is it the courage holding your head up high?" She was just about to ask the saleslady, when she decided it didn't really matter.

The only thing that was really important was seeing herself wearing that courage, wearing that confidence, feeling those feelings. Her mother would have said, "Why, dear, it suits you." And the saleslady from the big department store downtown would have said, "Oh, that's you . . . that courage and that confidence is definitely you. You look so right in it." Because everyone knows a salesperson will say anything to make a sale, even in somebody else's dream!

But Alyce could only hear her as a faraway voice; she was remembering that time long ago when she had been confident. And you know how that is. Maybe it was when you were asked to sing your ABCs to the class and you knew you knew them, or maybe it was that first morning you had absolutely no doubt you knew you could tie your own shoes. Just remember a time when you had confidence. . . . And, as you do, notice how your reflection changes again to incorporate it, maybe with a smile, full breath, or in your own unique way.

One more garment to go. Alyce took a deep breath and placed it around herself. And as she did, she began to think of a time when she enjoyed a sense of humor. She had been with some friends and she had told a story that caused everyone to begin to laugh. Even now you can see the corners of your mouth turn up as you remember a funny, humorous time. You can feel the smile creases at the corners of your eyes, and Alyce could see the twinkle in her eyes. Had she really had that sense of humor? Yes, you remember. See your whole face softening and your shoulders rounding, notice your breathing changing as you remember that time when you have that sense of humor.

Alyce turned to the saleslady and said, "I'll take them." "No, you can't do that. It is the policy of our store not to sell any garments to any customer until we are positively certain they are really for you. Now you must pass 'The Test of Mirrors.'" Alyce had no idea what that meant, but in a dream you expect to encounter things you don't readily understand. Of course, it would help if you knew you were dreaming. Just then a familiar voice was calling, "Alyce, Alyce, there you are. I've been looking all over for you—why, Alyce, you look so different, so wonderful—what are you doing here?" Before she could answer, the saleslady interjected, "You are about to go through the Test of Mirrors and your friend can help you." The saleslady turned Alyce to the left so she was facing the mirrored panel on the left. "Now," she said, "as you are seeing yourself wearing those garments of confidence, courage, and humor, seeing your posture with your shoulders pulled back, your chin tilted forward, and your chest full, and you see that smile pulling back the corners of your mouth and creasing the outside corners of your eyes, imagine yourself taking a pleasant drive through the country."

The reflection in the mirror suddenly became a movie, and Alyce could see herself driving through the country, wearing the courage, the confidence, and the sense of humor. Immersing yourself in a scene like that, you can hear your own voice as you sing with the radio and speak with a friend, feel the steering wheel in your hands, feel the gas pedal beneath your foot, feel the movement of the car. And now, you can think of another pleasant, relaxing event and see yourself participating in that experience with your courage, your confidence, with your sense of humor.

Take a few minutes of clock time, all the time you need, to see that movie of yourself, doing that pleasant activity. It doesn't matter if you are alone, or with others. Just see the movie of you doing that special pleasant thing while you continue to wear your courage, wear your confidence, wear your sense of humor. Just nod your head when the movie has ended.

The saleslady turned Alyce again, this time facing the right panel of the mirror. Now she said, "Look into the mirror and see yourself, continue to wear your courage, confidence, and sense of humor. See how you look, see how natural they appear. Feel the courage, confidence, humor. Feel each as a part of you. And now I want you to see a movie of yourself doing something that would previously have created anxiety for you. Let the background for that scene emerge, including the people you are with and watch yourself now in that movie, interacting in a way that reflects your confidence, your courage, your sense of humor. You can interact in a way consistent with those qualities and be very pleased."

"Now," said the saleslady, "turn and face the center mirror. Think of those occasions, just take them one at a time, those times that have not yet happened and see yourself participating in them with your courage, with your confidence, and with your sense of humor. See how you look, notice your posture, see your face, hear your voice, feel those feelings. Take a few minutes of clock time, all the time in the world, because you know how it can be in a dream, and nod your head to let me know you are done seeing yourself in those movies.

"And now, I want you to once again see yourself as you appear with your courage, confidence, and sense of humor. Just nod when you can see yourself in your mind's eye. And as you see yourself clearly, notice how the background is beginning to become distinct, and you see yourself at a time in the future when your dreams, your wishes, your goals have come true. Look around and see where you are, see who's with you. It may be a time in the near future, or the more distant future, perhaps months or years from now, look around and discover where you are, when you are, what you have accomplished, which dreams have come true for you. *(long pause)*

"Now step into that picture of the future, step into your future. Begin to become aware of how it feels to have accomplished those goals. That's right. And when you know, really know what it feels like to have succeeded in those ways that were important to you, memorize those feelings. Memorize what it looks like, what it sounds like, what it smells like, if there are any tastes, memorize them too. Become fully aware of everything there is there, and memorize it.

"Now, still in that future time when you have accomplished your heart's desires, take a moment to go right from this dream, straight into a daydream. Have a daydream about all the steps you have taken to make these things come true for you. Don't only remember the smaller accomplishments along the way. Remember, too, those times you felt like you had failed, or made the wrong decision. Discover what you learned from those mistakes. And while you couldn't have known it back then, you now can look back and value those mistakes, value those setbacks for the lessons and experiences they provided which enabled you to become all you are now. Remember six, seven, even 10 of them.

"And when you are done reviewing all the steps you took to get to now, to get to your accomplishment, step backwards, in the reverse order you went through them, so each step takes you back in time, closer to now, and in your own time, in your own way, reorient yourself back to this shop to discover that you've passed the Test of Mirrors, and much more!"

And waking up from dreams within dreams is a complex process and she thought she was awake in the shop, but shattered that illusion when she woke up again to find herself surrounded by covers and dancing rainbows. The hanging crystal pendants managed to capture the morning sun and transform it, just the way the conscious mind seizes an unconscious symbol of change it encounters in a dream.

7

Identity-Organization and Role-Development Metaphors

The whole theory of the universe is directed unerringly to one single individual.
—Walt Whitman

Men acquire a particular quality by constantly acting in a particular way.
—Aristotle

That so few now dare to be eccentric marks the chief danger of the time.
—John Stuart Mill

The goal with identity-restructuring metaphors is to stimulate clients to recognize that there can be a transformation of their lives so that they are not bound to the same identity and life-style that had preceded therapy, but rather, they can find entirely different ways to live which will give them meaning. This concept is intended to be especially momentous when the identity one has worked to establish for most of his or her life has been suddenly invalidated. Such invalidation of the identity can occur with physical injury, when children are born or leave home, as career changes are imposed upon a person, with an unwanted divorce, and so on. It follows that clients who are presenting with such life issues will be attempting to resolve just such a transformation, and this protocol has been sculpted to offer part of the answer to that need.

The final story of the complete session in Chapter 1 (pp. 35–38) is a timely example of this structure for a client who had just such a problem. It is notable that the client's presenting problem, that which occupied the attention of her conscious mind, was not framing events in such a broad manner as addressed by this type of metaphor. She did not say, "I am in the midst of an identity crisis" or "I am suffering from a breakdown of the identity I worked most of my life to build." Nor is it always advisable to help clients form that sort of map of their experience even when it is true for them. However, the ideas stimulated by the sequence of images in this type of story will be seized upon by listeners and applied to their lives if such issues are, in fact, cogent and solutions to such dilemmas do need to be found.

These are the kind of stories where a metamorphosis takes place and a somewhat surprising (but not necessarily entertaining) ending occurs. They could be considered analogous to, though more complex than, the children's tale where an ugly duckling ends up as a swan. Each entails a whole transformation of some kind. As we have conceptualized it for our use, there are five basic steps for the identity-restructuring protocol. These are summarized in the outline that follows.

Identity-restructuring protocol

1. *Define an insurmountable conflict.* Create a conflict or issue that the protagonist can't handle as a parallel which helps highlight an identity crisis that is real. (Incidents of stress from the current developmental stage are represented as challenging the client's identity.)

2. *Introduce an irrelevant action.* In this part of the story the protagonist must also begin an action that seems entirely disconnected from any problem-solving efforts (takes up a longed-for hobby, goes on a vacation, puts something silly in pocket, gives a treasured object to a child, etc.).

3. *Find a way for the protagonist to proclaim defeat.* The protagonist must announce (thinking out loud, writing, talking to another, soliloquy, etc.) his or her perception of the conflict and how he or she cannot overcome it satisfactorily.

4. *Introduce a symbol of defeat.* Just after the issue is expressed overtly (the previous step), introduce a negative image or *symbolic image* that defines the fears and helplessness that the protagonist held and will be a channel for dispelling the negativity of the client.

5. *Bring about a resolution via novel conduct.* The conflict is resolved by the actions of the protagonist which began earlier and, at that time, appeared irrelevant.

The protagonist, in step one, is described as being up against an insurmountable situation. The situation is a problem that the protagonist cannot solve as far as he knows. The story will show there is apparently no hope that can be offered to or for the protagonist in order to save him or her from imminent disaster. In short, everything that the client has lived for, worked for, and built his identity around is gone. A very dismal picture of the protagonist's possibilities is painted. An example of this degree of disaster can be illustrated by telling of a man we heard about who had spent his life often subordinating his own needs in order to be a good father and husband. But at this time, his mother was ill, his father was dead, his wife had been murdered during a time when he was knocked unconscious, his children had somehow wandered off and had not yet been found by the police, and the protagonist was being held in jail for his wife's murder—which he didn't commit! That was a bleak situation, indeed. Eventually, most therapists will come to know of a few such cases as this which can become the foundation for the identity-reorganization story. This example is being presented to underscore the point that we wish to have this type of story *seriously* and impactfully grip clients as it comes to show, in the end, that there is life after disaster. The story does this in an indirect manner, which therefore stimulates clients to embrace this understanding for themselves and not rely upon outside authority for this conviction.

Steps two and three of the protocol may be presented simultaneously or in close proximity to this previous part in the story. We make these separate steps because they are both important aspects to highlight. Step two calls for the protagonist to begin an action that seems entirely disconnected from any problem-solving efforts. It appears to be altogether an irrelevant activity, such as having a brief contact with a hobby, driving home from work on a different route, getting lost, going on a vacation, giving a previously treasured object to a child, picking up an object of interest at a flea market, or seeing a movie as a diversion. But whatever the act, it is presented as one of those situations to which a person would give no further thought at the time.

Understanding this concept will be facilitated by thinking of situations from your own life where an apparently irrelevant action or serendipitous encounter came to play a larger role in your life at some future date. The larger role will be discussed later in the story. At this stage, however, only the incident of the encounter is highlighted. For instance, I knew a man in my early days at the university who was performing poorly in most every aspect of life. I know he had considered suicide as an alternative. And one night we went to see a free movie on campus because we had no money to spend for other entertainment. The movie was Antonioni's "Blow-up" (a movie whose main protagonist was a photographer). We both enjoyed it. But within a few months my friend dropped out of the university and quit his part-time job and became an apprentice photographer. Through the years he has become an accomplished and successful photographer and businessman. Obviously, his contact with this incidental experience of the movie eventually changed his entire life.

But, again, at step two in this protocol we only want to introduce this irrelevant action in such a way that it seems almost like a diversion or distraction, something incidental to the story. It should seem, as these things first seem to be in real life, a pointless and unremarkable diversion.

At step three, the protagonist proclaims defeat and his inability to solve the problem. This can take the form of a written letter, a soliloquy, or a conversation that he has with someone else. But it must be exceedingly clear that he definitely gives up. It may be necessary for therapists to make informed guesses or extrapolate about how this proclamation would be made and what it would include when delivered by the person whose life you have chosen to relate in the story. That is, we are not often privy to such private moments—I did not actually hear my college friend threaten suicide. Yet I know he had thoughts of it and I am rather certain he "talked it over with himself." So, my sense of what he would have rehearsed in a suicide note or a soliloquy is a well-informed guess at this point if I tell his story.

Step four is presented in order to introduce a symbol of the protagonist's defeat. This negative symbolic image of the protagonist's fears and helplessness immediately follows the overt expression of defeat. It introduces a symbolic method of discharging the negativity which has been brought into unconscious focus by the first three steps. This image essentially lets listeners know what the protagonist's situation can be compared to. That is, the image frames the desperation of the previous scenario. Additionally, the use of the image allows the listener to conceive of and discharge the negativity of the unpleasant circumstance without, in fact, ending the protagonist's life in the story. The negative image, such as an owl swooping down to snatch up its prey, or a river bed drying to dust, tells listeners, unconsciously, "Sometimes death occurs and reality is often unfair or unconcerned." But, in fact, the protagonist is not dead in the story. Furthermore, the symbolic negative image is likely to be a more grave ending than the client had in mind. Therefore, the client has developed his or her own wish to live through terrible times and be more significant than the negative image portrays. It is the identity, not the person, which has come to demise.

Meanwhile, it is important to remember that some useless activity was begun in the story and this activity, through an interesting turn of events, eventually results in a resolution of the difficulty for the protagonist. Furthermore, this resolution will illustrate how the protagonist will design a new life-style out of the old. This is step five when the novel conduct in some manner resolves the conflict, even though it appeared so irrelevant when it was introduced earlier. It represents perceptions which are unexpected vehicles for succeeding in a way the person had never imagined. And so this new and incidental experience becomes a valuable asset. The message clients receive is that, even though they might conceive of everything that they have as being insufficient, there is still some little thing that heretofore might have been unconsidered or regarded silly or stupid, that remains an important and relevant resource for the direction life can take. It is more than enough, after all. These experiences are the seeds for growing and developing a whole new identity.

This protocol represents a spark of an idea. Clients are not going to actually have answers about their future. In fact, clients are unlikely to have any immediate conscious appreciation for their possible future, especially one born from an overlooked irrelevancy. But a seed will have been planted that suggests that there's more to their personality than they've considered, and too, some of the things that may have seemed totally useless for solving a problem could be very useful. And, as always, there are several metaphors and several goals that will be addressed in the course of any session. So this protocol is introduced as a single part of a total treatment and an indirect way to help stimulate a person to frame an identity crisis.

The goal of role-development metaphors will be clear, by contrast, as their purpose is to highlight an understanding of how the client's life fits into a larger game plan. It is characterized by those kinds of stories in which a heroic protagonist performs several important, often symbolic acts over a period of time in his or her life. The reader may think of tales such as Herman Hesse's *Siddhartha* as an example. Since listeners come to understand stories by identification, this sequence of content creates a process so that listeners begin to think of their lives in sequence or as a sort of journey. In therapy, whatever particular role in which the client is "stuck" is framed, simply, as a smaller piece of a greater journey that has an overall valued meaning.

For further clarification, we can consider the difference between a melodrama and a romantic epic in literature. We have observed that in a melodrama the emotional conflict is high but the outcome is not in the hands of the main protagonist. The fate of the protagonist is in the hands of another agent, be it destiny, curse, fate, time, and so on. In a romantic epic, however, while the content is emotional and the conflict of emotion may be high, the outcome of the romance is in the hands of the protagonist. He or she is the agent who chooses his or her destiny. In the role development protocol the story seems, in the beginning, to take the form of a melodrama. That is, the protagonist seems to be a victim in the hands of outside agents. However, by the story's end, the protagonist has demonstrated that his or her own choice has predicted the outcome. A story with potential melodrama is turned into one with the form of a romantic epic.

This protocol is selected for clients when a crisis of such proportions has occurred that the roles they enact and the meaning these have for their lives no longer hold much value. This type of therapeutic goal is appropriate for the clients whose loss of purpose is part of the response to the ecological stress which has brought them to therapy. These four steps are summarized in the outline below.

Role-development protocol

1. *Catastrophic issue is set up.* A catastrophic issue is raised for the client concerning the existence (health, life, etc.) of someone or something very revered and obviously symbolic. (A rite of passage issue must be preexisting or manufactured.)

2. *Introduce hope by means of a hero-protagonist.* This person's history is not important—it is taken for granted due to symbolic quality.

3. *Arrange story to present challenges which the hero must face.* The protagonist must go through several trials to test his/her character (or wit, strength, courage, endurance, honesty, single-mindedness, etc.). The symbolic nature of the test must be encouraged. We prefer to avoid "magic" as a means of doing this.

4. *Use paradox to unravel the final challenge and achieve success.* The hero is faced with a definitive challenge which is overcome by a form of paradox (a riddle is solved, doing nothing is action, etc.). Succeeding at the final challenge completes the drama and ends the conflict.

The first step involves some catastrophic issue which bespeaks some aspect of the current life stage of the client by means of describing the situation confronting the protagonist of the story. For example, the protagonist (and this usually parallels a concern of the client) may be represented as concerned about the existence of someone or something very revered by him. Beyond this theme, however, the content of the metaphor greatly departs from the reality of life for the client. That is, the content of the story will be a type of epic tale which will necessitate the introduction of story elements which border on fantastic. So, while the issue of the client's life is enacted by the protagonist, any other parallels between the behavior of the client and protagonist will be merely symbolic. This will be apparent as the epic nature of the story develops similar to such fantasies as the LeGuin's Earthsea trilogy, Tolkien's *Lord of the Rings,* the tales of Hercules and of Jason, the pursuit of the Holy Grail by the Knights of the Round Table, and other such legends.

Step two involves developing the protagonist as a potential hero or heroine. In this way, hope is offered. If the protagonist can overcome several trials which are present within the story, there will be meaning to one's life and one's place in it will be established. The key element to this phase of the story, then, is to pit the protagonist against an important goal by means of narration or character-development techniques.

Step three is to arrange the trials the protagonist will face and through which he or she will successfully pass. These will test the protagonist's character, wit, strength, courage, endurance, honesty, or whatever. Since each test is of a symbolic nature, there doesn't have to be a great deal of logic involved inventing this part of the story. There will be a challenge of some kind at this point and the symbolism should be such that the client has some little bit of an idea how that challenge might apply to his or her life. Therapists will need to spend preplanning time on this phase to ensure that the tasks of the story have substance and plot.

The fourth and final step of this protocol requires that the protagonist successfully resolve the original problem. Since the entire metaphor is a syntactical form of selectional-restriction violation, logical conduct was not necessary. At this point, it is, then, altogether appropriate to resolve the problems of the story in a paradoxical manner. This may be done as in solving a riddle, following a prescription to act in a manner opposite from that to which one has become accustomed, taking action by doing nothing, and so on. The first story in this chapter (as well as the previously mentioned story from Chapter 1, pp. 35–38) is an example of the identity-organization protocol. The following four stories in this chapter conform to the role-development protocol as they were told in therapy.

1. **Identity-reorganization goal:** *Change comes by transforming confusion into an opportunity for discovery of power and ability*

Metaphor

He wanted to get as far away as possible! Stan was not really desperate in the strictest sense of the word, but he had that ability that many teenagers have, to see things at their darkest. It would be difficult to tell whether he had just given up any sense of power or if he never had any in the first place. He walked in that certain way that a defeated teen will do, with the head and shoulders rounded forward, trudging along without noticeably picking up his feet in the process. It wasn't that anything specifically had suddenly gone wrong—it was more like a long, slow, ongoing, unending process of existential despair that seemed to have been passed on in his family for generations. At least, it seemed more concentrated when he was in the presence of his parents and relatives. There hadn't been any overt violence, hunger, or real shortage of tangible things in his past—it was more an emotional lacking, and now and then an emotional and verbal abuse. And a teenager's scope is unfortunately very limited. It was a shame that Stan couldn't have looked at things from a wider perspective somehow. But he did have a bicycle and he did like to get as far from home as possible. Still, that wasn't enough.

In fact, he was on his bicycle one day with that goal foremost in mind; to get as far away as possible, not that he expected the rest of the world to be any better. But he told himself he had just "had it" with the bleakness and the emptiness, even though he was far from sophisticated enough, emotionally, to say so or to solve it.

He was riding along, up the hill and on the other side of the river, listlessly pushing the pedals without much thought, not really caring where he went or even what happened to him. He passed the odd-looking shop and it registered again in his mind. But, though it registered in his mind, he gave it no second thought.

He even wondered and imagined what it might be like to just ride out over the bluffs at top speed and hopefully cast himself into oblivion. It wasn't an actual plan, more of a fantasy that reflected his depression. But it pretty much filled his thoughts up until the moment that his front tire suddenly blew out, with a dull pop. He didn't even know bicycle tires could pop like that. Then he had something more tangible to focus that depression upon.

It must have seemed like he had just about hit bottom, miles from home—but not far enough; alive—but not enough. He didn't really care or even notice where he was. At first, he just threw the bike down on the side of the dusty road under a dead maple tree. Then he plopped himself down in a heap beside it. He felt like crying but didn't even have enough connection with his emotional self to do that. Instead, he just sat there, Indian style, with his head buried in his folded arms, shaking his head back and forth and mumbling to himself, "I just give up. That's it. I just give up! I wish I could just die."

This time it seemed like a novel idea to him. So he just sat there appreciating it. How long he sat there he probably had no idea. The daylight changed a little more towards gloomy but it was uncertain whether it was the advancing hour or storm that was responsible for it. And just as the thought of taking his own life crystalized in his mind, he got drenched with a sudden downpouring of rain. That wasn't much more than insult to injury but it did make a little difference. It scared him and he jumped. But it did not shake his conviction. Then he screamed out loud, "Okay. Let the damn lightning hit me. Come and take me. Now. . . ."

Miraculously, people on the other side of the river, not knowing the drama beneath that maple tree saw lightning strike the already dead tree. It let out a mighty crack. The lightning seemed to hang on to the tree and shake it to be sure it had released all its vengeance and wrath right there, right then.

Two years later, in another city, an arrow, in fact a set of arrows, traveled as true as the lightning had that day and won a shining cup for a young man who in some way resembled that Stan. And the arrows were shot from a bow the young boy drew masterfully. Even though the archer was also named Stan, there was a world of difference between the archer and the Stan who sat beneath the dead maple tree that day.

And this was how that proud archer remembered the events that led up to his winning the regional bare-bow championship. He began by noting that he had been under a dead maple tree one day and had he ever jumped when lightning hit it!

It's interesting that even though you may be feeling worthless and unwanted only moments before, there's enough survival instinct even at times like that and you still don't want to get soaking wet and then fried to a crisp! He had certainly never thought of himself as smart, but he did know that he was smart enough to come in out of the rain. And besides that, he had to do something about a flat tire on his only possession. He wondered exactly where would he go? Reality, that day, was finally forcing him to take a little survey of his surroundings. As he looked around, he realized that he was, in fact, in a neighborhood he had seen before, though his parents had always advised against it. And then he recalled having passed a little queer shop before his tire blew out.

There was a little shop there but it wasn't in the part of the city where shops are located, so he had been justifiably a little suspicious of whatever that cottage industry was. It looked like someone lived up above in the upper portions of the building. And while this seemed common for rural service stations and general stores, he didn't know anything about places like that. It was some kind of odd arrangement and he didn't have a good feeling about it for any reason. Then, again, he didn't have *any* good feelings to speak of about anything in those days, so he figured he didn't have much choice. He had to go in there and get cover from that storm.

It so happened that the shop he went in that day sold "archery equipment," which Stan found out meant bows and arrows. He looked around at all the bows hanging on every wall while the storm raged furiously, then blew on by. The owner and Stan talked. Stan knew very little about this curiosity. Though Stan wasn't a very likely customer and the owner was not a very approachable-looking character, when the storm was over he took a bow down from the wall rack and led Stan out back to a practice range which he had constructed. He showed Stan how to hold the bow, place the arrow, pull, aim, and release it. He showed Stan the grown-up version of holding the string with three fingers and how to relax and release that type of grip. It was very new to Stan, he had only used a thumb and forefinger pinch method before that.

Before he left, the owner invited him to come back and shoot on the range anytime he wanted. Stan had noticed some pretty high price tags hanging on the equipment in that unlikely looking shop. "But I don't have a bow or money to buy one," Stan said. "That'll probably be okay. We'll find one you can use," the gruff-looking owner said reassuringly. The idea appealed to him. Why not? What kid wouldn't want to learn how to shoot real fiberglass arrows with a real double-recurve bow? And probably the idea appealed in part because his parents would no doubt consider it a huge waste of time, not to even mention the part about it being dangerous and in the wrong part of town and much too expensive!

So it wasn't long at all before he had found an opportunity to get back out on the range, and found out to his surprise that he seemed to have a knack for this sport. There was something about the symbols of power and flexibility that a bow represented, and the juxtaposition between strength and relaxation involved in the shooting. He liked the feel of those smooth fiberglass arrows and the intricate way the fletching was balanced and the way they were painted. He liked the smell of leather and bow wax. He became quite a regular sight around there, in fact, and wasn't really aware of anything else of importance happening at all. Of course, he wasn't yet aware that this new pastime was turning out to be something of importance either; he just liked it.

He had gone back there again and again and eventually bought his own bow, a $65 Bear Magnum with a 45-pound draw, which he could just barely manage with all of his might to hold still at full draw while he took aim. It was probably too big of a bow for him but it was the only one short enough that he could use and also afford. He used the money that he earned doing lawn work in his neighborhood.

He started entering a few contests and eventually won a county and finally a regional championship, after which he had first reminisced about the two years which had passed. You can imagine the significant leap in confidence something like that can teach you.

Well, that sport hasn't played an overt role in Stan's life for 20 years now, but in the top of his closet still hangs one of the bows and a set of arrows he bought at that shop so long ago. It is carefully protected from scratches by a leather cover. Though his wife has never seen him shoot it, his youngest son occasionally requests an opportunity to see if he has gained enough power and strength to succeed at pulling the bow. It's a test he's looking forward to passing. And it's a mighty hard bow to pull, so when the day comes that the boy is able to accomplish that goal, it's going to be a day to be remembered, a day when confidence was passed on to another generation.

2. Role-development goal: *Change comes by developing the value of self-discovery.*

Metaphor

I had a client named Diana, who came in with a fear that she wouldn't be able to outlive her parents. She never had a model. She didn't think that she could do it, and in just four short months, she was going to be finding out whether or not the curse that she carried was fact or fantasy. Her grandmother had not outlived her great grandmother, her mother had not outlived her grandmother. She was sure that something ran in the family; even if it wasn't a genetic or spiritual problem and it was only in her mind, she'd still influenced the course of events in a decisive way and we only had four months to solve the problem.

And at that time she didn't realize how an answer to a riddle could be the answer to her entire situation. And furthermore she didn't realize that an answer to a riddle can itself be a riddle.

In trance I suggested that she have a dream and in the dream I suggested that she consider a variety of circumstances that could emerge as symbols from her unconscious.

While you have been listening your hand has almost come to rest halfway to your face. And if you begin to develop a dissociation in your fingers and your wrist, let it spread to your elbow and shoulder. Because there is something very interesting that you can do with an unconscious ability and the wisdom and intelligence that your unconscious has—even with something that seems as fleeting as that feeling of dissociation.

The feeling of dissociation is a very good way to accomplish a number of things painlessly. It's too bad that every child doesn't have the capability of learning the value of such things as arm levitation and dissociation, so they can be applied to other events.

Now, in a dream, Diana was dissociated and the first thing that occurred to her was an image that she knew somehow was like herself, but she couldn't see it clearly yet. She just had this feeling that somehow she was saddled with a responsibility. She didn't quite know how she got into the dream, because she didn't understand how clinical hypnosis works. She dreamed about herself. But the same thing that had happened to her in real life was happening to the "her" in the dream.

In the dream, she had been given some kind of locket but the circumstances surrounding that gift were vague to her. But what she did come to realize was that she was hiking across a desert, and at still another time fording a river. She had to take the locket and she had to do something with it, but she wasn't quite sure what it was since she was in trance having the dream—and the dream, like the dreams you often have, was vague on certain points. But it was one of those dreams that seemed very real to her. She was perspiring and you could tell that she was clutching the locket in one hand. It became apparent to her that she was facing a performance, and a challenge or a test of being herself lay before her.

And soon the first trial came upon her. When it happened she realized "this is a trial." But it was symbolic. She couldn't quite fathom the meaning of it with her conscious mind. You know how a person can sometimes have a puzzle, and it can be all disassembled, and if the pieces are upside down, you can't tell which piece goes where. But if the pieces were right side up, you could maybe solve the puzzle better, because you could put colored pieces together and you would know what they mean. She felt like she didn't know what the pieces meant and that she couldn't turn them right side up. She knew they had a meaning but she didn't know what the meaning was. She knew that unconsciously she must know the meaning. But consciously it was just too much effort to figure out what its meaning was. So she decided to just yield to the dream.

And there she stood in front of the mirror and in it she saw a reflection of her mother, and when she moved her arm, the arm moved on the mother, and when she blinked the mother blinked in the mirror. And she realized that the first trial was to deal with that reflection. So she decided that she would approach it from a more skillful direction, and she snuck up on the mirror in darkness. And when the daylight came suddenly in the mirror, she was able to see the same thing was true again. Still in the mirror all she saw was that mother.

So she approached the mirror with great care, humming songs and wondering things. And at this point nothing of a riddle had occurred to her and she had no realization how a riddle could solve her problem or that the answer to such a riddle could itself be a riddle.

Finally, in a sense of disgust, and after that had happened a dozen times, she thought that she'd never get out of this scene and it would be an endless dream. In desperation she picked up a rock and crashed it against the image, and the mirror fell away like cotton candy and there was a doorway! She heard a crowd of people beyond the door and she approached them happily, realizing that the difficulty of her mother's reflection had simply faded away. She ran to the end of the hallway to meet the crowd of people, only to discover, and this was still before the riddle had been posed, that every one of the people in the crowd had the face of her father. And there was a crowd of her fathers all around busily talking about whatever fathers talk about to make them busy.

She was racing down the hallway to gleefully share in the celebration in having passed her trial, only to find that they represented another trial. She was only faced with the trial for a moment, however, but you don't know what I mean. Diana reported the next thing that happened in the dream was that all of the faces turned and walked away in every conceivable direction, away from her. Then it seemed the whole horizon was filled with her father walking away from her— many fathers. And by now she couldn't remember whether she was dreaming, or doing this in trance, or doing this for a reason. And she still couldn't consciously understand the meaning of the picture. It was as if the crossword puzzle was turned upside down.

She knew it had meaning that her father was walking away, and she felt that she should be devastated by it. But a curious thought was occurring. She knew that she had been crushed by the fact that in real life her single father had turned away. So why wouldn't you be in even more turmoil that a whole group of father figures was turning away— especially considering that you have a heightened suggestibility of dreams and trance?

But a curious thought was occurring that *they* couldn't turn away from her if she was walking in another direction, walking away from them. And she had no more thought of this before she turned and walked in the other direction and knew she would be having a feeling of pride. She had decided whom her company would be. And now they started chasing after her, and she just kept walking, and then she began to sense a smell. She never remembered a dream with an olfactory sensation before, and she wondered what that smell was.

It didn't smell like breakfast, or lunch, or an animal. It didn't smell like the outdoors. It had a curious smell like she supposed a thought might have if a thought had a smell. I asked what kind of thought. Diana said, "It smells like a riddle, and I feel that it is my final test somehow." And she gave a sigh of despair and said the riddle was "How can I be myself if I don't know who I am?" And she said, "I see this large statue of a thing forcing me to come up with an answer to the riddle before I can pass beyond it, and I cannot outlive my parents if I don't answer the riddle!

"I don't even understand the riddle, 'How can I be myself if I don't know who I am?' I mean that's my problem." Now sometimes your conscious mind doesn't appreciate how your unconscious can solve problems that you don't understand, but I really doubt that a person fully understands any problem. After all, if there is something that is a problem and you can't solve it, then why shouldn't you fail to see that you don't have an answer and that is why it is a problem. Then she said, "I think that I understand what the solution is. I'm gonna go back to the statue."

And while she was having the unconscious sense that she'd go back to that statue, I don't know what her conscious mind was thinking about. I imagine that she was thinking about how she could possibly understand the meaning of the puzzle when the pieces were upside down and she couldn't see the pattern and couldn't understand what it really meant.

And she certainly would be amazed to realize that she could solve it anyway. You would probably be interested in knowing how she solved the riddle, but before she solved the riddle, she dreamed her possibilities and considered her solutions.

Diana wondered about the riddle in the dream and trance which felt real. How could she possibly solve such a riddle? How could she get past what seemed to be a statue stopping her from going further, a statue that posed the question, "How can you be yourself if you don't know who you are?" And that is when she realized the answer to her riddle could be a riddle. Just from the back of her mind she heard herself saying the words, "By not trying to be somebody else?" And the statue broke into a laugh and she ran the words by her conscious mind again. What had been so funny was the riddle, "How can I be myself if I don't know who I am?" and the answer is, "By not trying to be somebody else." She wasn't sure she found out what was so funny about that but the statue was laughing and she felt fine. She laughed as she dreamed, not knowing what she was laughing at. It seemed like cosmic humor.

The statue shrank smaller in front of her and she walked past and, as she did, the dream vanished from the trance and with it the curse. She couldn't even remember what the curse had been and sometimes when you awake from a dream you forget all but one little piece. When she first awoke she could remember the exact words of the riddle but she couldn't even remember exactly why she had asked for therapy that day. There was something pleasant about knowing that it had been a riddle and soon all she could remember was the pleasant feeling and that there had been a riddle. But she couldn't remember what the problem had been. She couldn't consciously remember what the solution had been. She didn't even care, so we all had a good laugh, but I did remember it all in enough detail that I could use it as a learning and I know my conscious mind remembers it in enough detail to use it as a learning and as a story, even if *she* couldn't remember the exact nature of the riddle.

3. **Role-development goal:** *Change comes by developing strength that grows from your own perceptions instead of illusions.*

Metaphor[30]

Chord understood the sound of one hand clapping. He was a very serious man and he had reason to be. Good reason. There were a lot of things that he needed to learn. Of course, you will recognize it as a parable, only a metaphor, maybe a metaphor about a lot of people you know. The story goes that Chord was practiced in martial arts. He would compete to represent the town on its greatest quest. The winner of the martial arts contest in town would be the one who was endorsed and sent by the town to find and read from the legendary and coveted book of knowledge. He was to then bring back to the townspeople the wisdom that was in that book of knowledge. There was the understanding that is in the heart and in the soul of almost every human being who knows at some level that there is a learning or knowledge possible out there and if you are pure enough you can find it.

And who would ever think that to get to that knowledge you must first learn to not be tricked, seduced, or frightened by your own finality? You start out thinking that you can, after all, do most anything that you set your mind to. You have a sense of confidence that it won't be so hard. You pretty much can even expect that you'll get through it in record time.

Chord thought that he had been the best qualified although he didn't win the match and was not chosen by the townspeople to go because of a technicality. He had no allegiance to any known school of martial arts. Another person might lack the confidence that they can get through it in record time but expect of themselves that they be able to. Chord thought that he was best qualified. He'd thought that the best man was disqualified on a technicality so he decided that he was going to go anyway.

Standing outside of the city he waited for a way to follow the man who had actually won the rite of passage. And that's when Chord first ran into the blind flute player. Everyone knows the wisdom that comes from unlikely sources. But how is it that a blind man can teach one who is sighted so much about seeing? He explained to Chord that the

[30] Adapted from the movie "Circle of Iron" with David Carradine.

book of knowledge he sought was protected somewhere on a secret island of perfection by a man named Zeton whom no one could defeat in combat. Furthermore, only the best martial arts person could pass the tests that would be provided by reality along the way. One must pass three such tests in order to even meet Zeton.

Since Chord knew that, in fact, he was the most qualified, he followed behind the "chosen one" that night. They camped near a ruined house the first night. And, late that night, standing in a ruined house, he heard highwaymen begin to assault and finally attempt to rob the blind flute player and that was when he first witnessed the blind flute player's amazing martial art abilities. He singlehandedly defeated all of the highwaymen. He was far from helpless though it defied conscious explanation. When Chord went to find the blind flute player and seek an explanation, he was told that he wouldn't be willing to teach him what he knew about Karate. The flute player declared Chord unworthy of such instruction. Chord found the blind man's opinion about that extremely disarming.

Sometimes it becomes painfully clear that you haven't yet learned all of the things that are necessary to go one step further on life's highway. But Chord, in his arrogance, was undaunted and the next morning followed the "chosen one" into a cave where there were said to be foolish men—"monkey men," they were called. The blind flute player was at Chord's side as he watched the "chosen one" deal with this, his first test. The flute player said, "Listen when you confront a monkey man if you don't want to end up dead. Don't turn your back on his foolishness because just when you think that he is a fool, he will kill you." And no sooner than those words had been uttered, Chord witnessed the "chosen one" turn his back on one of the monkey men and become another statistic of the people from the town who had been sent out and never made it to the island or to the book of knowledge or back to the city with the learning it was said to contain.

Chord decided, then and there, that he had been chosen by a greater power than the powers that ruled the town. So he simply took that emblem from the neck of the chosen one's body, and placed it around his own neck. Chord buried the previously chosen one that night. The next day he set out eagerly to look for the next challenge, foolishly expecting that it was going to be easy, and foolishly thinking that it would be obvious to him when the challenge came.

There was a lot of sound around him in the middle of the desert that night. And finally, surprisingly, he came upon a celebration that

was going on. There was a caravan encamped at an oasis. He made
his way into a tent and met the sultan. In time the sultan invited him
to stay at the oasis. Chord mysteriously explained that he had a mission
that was calling him. He didn't tell the sultan, he wouldn't confide in
a stranger, that he was hoping to look into the book of knowledge. It
was just a special calling and he couldn't stay there and party with
them.

As he began to depart, to stand and pass outside the tent, he saw
the most beautiful woman he had ever seen. Her name was Tara. They
rose and their eyes met. And something was communicated between
them that night and later Tara came to his tent. I guess you might
say that he was soon led to believe that he could take one night from
his journey to fall in love with Tara. And, in fact, they spent a night
of love together that was as beautiful as any rose in the desert could
ever be. But the next morning Tara was gone and the oasis was gone.
Everything was gone except the desert!

Then he knew it had been a trial. The blind flute player had told
him not to turn his back on the foolish monkey men on his first trial.
In fact, he had learned that lesson, walked through the cave of the
monkey men, and even gone into the desert in the direction given by
the monkey men's defeated leader. That was why he found himself
here with Tara and suddenly he realized that he was somehow tricked
and deceived by the rose in the desert. He was disappointed in himself.
He was distracted from his goal for the temporary pleasure of the rose.

He realized that he had failed and he wished that he could speak
to the blind flute player and gain his wisdom on the topic. Perhaps,
sometime in the future he would. But in the meantime, he walked
aimlessly, hollering in the desert for Tara until on the top of a dune
he saw a wooden cross. And then he saw that it was no discarded
ancient cross. He saw that Tara was on it, hung and killed, and staked
out ruthlessly in the desert. He realized in an instant that Sultan had
done this.

And he screamed her name and he screamed vengeance on Sultan.
It was then he heard the flute player playing a little tune and he sat
down near what, the night before, had been an oasis and the flute
player sat down with him. Chord was crying.

The flute player looked at him and said, "You can't hold on to
yourself, not even for a minute. Did you think you could hold on to
another and possess them? You have to let her go." And Chord couldn't
argue with this man who had performed, even as a sightless man, with
far more skill in the martial arts than he had and with far more wisdom.

He thought about it more as they walked down together. Chord again asked the blind man to go with him and teach him. The blind man said he wouldn't be able to as he had his own journey and that Chord would have still other tasks to overcome before he found the book of knowledge.

That night Chord slept deeply and as he did he had a dream in which Death came to him. He was frightened and when he woke up frightened, he saw a black panther running in the shadows. He wondered if maybe this was another test. Maybe this test was to deal with death. So he put down his weapon and walked toward the shadow of the panther and he said to the panther, "Come, take me if you dare, Death!! Come take me right now because I am ready for you right now. And I know you won't come for me if I am ready." With that, the panther ran off and Chord laughed. He knew of the trick played by Death— it will try to get you to be afraid of it and to try and avoid it. He called after Death and said, "I'll call for you next time that I want you to come." And once again he was on his way to find Zeton, feeling proud that this time he had passed another test.

And that's when he got to the edge of the water, where the desert joined the water and he could go no further. And there was Sultan and his entourage. When he walked into Sultan's tent, Sultan stood up and said, "I imagine you hate me. I just bet you would like to kill me after what I did to Tara. And I'll give you a chance to fight me fair and square. We'll do it tomorrow morning at dawn, on that hill."

"No," said Chord, "we will fight now." As he said it, he felt a sense of power that came from setting his own time and his own battles and his own tests.

Soon a circle of people formed, made up of clowns and jugglers and dancing girls and distractors. Chord squared off to fight Sultan. Sultan showed the strictest concentration. Outsiders attempted to grab their attention. But Chord was indeed excellent. He did not look at the crowd. He did not hear the crowd. He did not smell them and think about them. He expertly blocked and punched and kicked and blocked and stalked the sultan and suddenly, in the midst of this fight for revenge, it dawned on Chord—he was trying to find the book of knowledge. That's what he was after.

He dropped his hands to his side and started laughing. And no one understood his gesture except Sultan who was posed to kill him. And when he saw that Chord had dropped his hands and had begun laughing, he knew that Chord was worthy and he dropped his hands too, and together they both laughed.

They embraced and the Sultan said, "Congratulations." Sultan was a part of Chord's test. "You are the first to pass this series of tests and go this far." "I am the first to go?" asked Chord." "No," replied Sultan, "there are other paths with other tests and some have traversed those ways. But you are the first to have come by means of this path. The boat to take you to Zeton and the book of knowledge will be here on the shore in just a moment." Sultan pointed out towards the approaching sailing boat.

Happily, Chord got on the boat and it sailed gently, beautifully to the island of perfection. "Remarkably white"—that is what he thought, once he exited the boat. Everyone was dressed in white. They were growing red flowers and yellow roses. They asked him if he would like to relax, would he take some tea. He just replied, "No, I have but one purpose; I want to read from the book." He was still under the impression that he would have to do battle with Zeton, and it was true but not in the way you might think.

When he was finally brought to Zeton, the grand master of the island, he found him to be disarmingly courteous. Zeton extended his hand with a laugh and Chord started to shake it, but quickly thought better and struck a martial arts posture: "I am here to read in the book of knowledge." "Very well," said Zeton, "but we have such lovely roses that grow here in the desert and why don't you smell this one." He held out a pruned rose but Chord again said, "No, I'm here to read the book."

"Very well then," Zeton said, with a smile of approval on his face that indicated that Chord had passed his test.

Eventually, they stood inside the tower surrounded by water on the small island with a large book on a pedestal. It was bound in leather with four remarkably thick and distinct pages also bound in leather. Chord sat down reverently and expectantly in front of the book while Zeton covered it with his hand, saying, "Before you look inside the book of knowledge you have an opportunity to not proceed. You may not be able to cope with what you see. You could stay here and become a perfecter of perfection and not go further." And Chord said, "I've come here only to read the book." "Very well," Zeton said, "but still, again, let me offer you my job as keeper of the book and save what may be your last moments of life so you can stay here." But of course Chord said, "No matter what the price I want to look in the Book."

With that, he then threw open the first page and gazed steadfastly into that leather-bound mirror staring back at him with a surprised and angry look reflected on his own face. He looked suspiciously at

Zeton and threw open the next page, only to find revealed a second leather-bound mirror reflecting his astonished curiosity. He still half thought that this was another trick but as he looked at Zeton, he saw him nodding his head for Chord to continue.

Throwing open the next page of the book, there was another mirror and there was that face again, your own face looking backing at you. You can't help but notice that what's reflected has been altered by being seen. The look of suspicion was gone and a new sense of understanding was replacing it. A smile began to come to his face as he anticipated what he was to find on the final page. He looked at Zeton and they smiled at one another as their eyes met. There was a distinct twinkle in his eyes as he eagerly threw open the fourth page, which of course also contained a mirror—and a broad smile being reflected in it.

Chord asked for confirmation on his discovery for a moment, "Then there is nothing in the book except . . ." And Zeton said, "That is right." And Chord said, ". . . yourself." And they laughed.

"What about all of the people who failed to pass their tests," Chord finally asked, after absorbing his feelings of success. And Zeton said, "They are the ones who go back and provide all of the trials and tribulations for the other seekers on the journey." And Chord said, "What about those who do look in the book? Where do they go from here?" And Zeton said, "The ones who pass their tests but fail to read in the book, they stay on here as the perfecters of perfection. And the ones who do look into the book after passing their tests, well, they go back to become the teachers." And Chord instantly heard the tune of the blind flute player he passed along the way playing in his memory.

Some time later, and it is hard to know, sometimes, how much time has in fact passed, but Chord sought out and found the blind flute player in the mountains as the sun was about to set. And when he did, the blind flute player said knowingly to Chord, "It is you, Chord! You've found the book, haven't you?" Chord humbly replied, "Yes." And the same face that had been reflected in that last mirror had become a very familiar face for Chord to wear. It was not unlike the face of the flute player. And it was reflected in the blind man's eyes again at that moment. "And," asked the flute player, "what did you see?" "Everything," Chord replied. "Everything."

Without words, the blind man handed him the flute. Chord gently took the flute from the blind man's hands and played a tune so that he could dance. They danced on the mountain as the sun set.

4. **Role-development goal:** *Change comes by allowing yourself to use all of your emotions as resources.*

Metaphor[31]

It may be that in a state of sleepy alertness, we dream of things that have possibility or possibly we only alert ourselves to the kind of learning that may be experienced in a dream. Or perhaps you'll experience this special quality more gradually as your conscious mind suspends, for a time, its willingness to track everything exactly as it occurs. And sometimes it's impossible to distinguish a story from a dream from a real experience. Certainly that is the case with a legend that can be dreamed, or perhaps in this case, one which reflects a dream.

The legends of Golindrina birds have always been shrouded with the mystery like that of dreams. Years and years ago, in the Moche period, 900 years after the birth of Christ, somewhere in Peru, it is said that there was born a male child who was the only youthful male survivor of a certain isolated tribe called Pima. Given to this child at birth was a scarab ring, pale turquoise in color, which was worn around the child's neck, held in place by a small leather strap. Legend has told that this male child, named Garrow, was cared for and raised by the Ocucus—a witch doctor, Tumara—until the time that he had matured enough and grown to slip the scarab ring from the string that hung around his neck and place it upon his finger.

Tumara, the Ocucus, had told the child the secret of the scarab ring, and had trained Garrow to be noble and fair, an attentive hunter. Garrow only knew that he was to live his life in such a way so as to pass several trials that would be put before him, and if he did he would find a woman and marry her and the tribe would continue— he would become the great father-leader of the new order. But Tumara, the nature of the trial, and the woman he would marry were all to remain a mystery to him since the Ocucus died before explaining any further.

As he had grown to be a young man, he lived at peace with and had love for the natural beauty around him. But as destiny is impartial to the aesthetics of men, he was certain to grow unsure of his destiny and had no way of knowing that there was a great plan for him laid

---

[31] This metaphor, a "fictional legend," was contributed by Tina Beissinger, Ph.D., and later modified for our use by the authors.

out in the legend as the only youthful male survivor of his Peruvian tribe.

Since his teacher had died the day Garrow put the scarab ring on his finger, he had not learned any of the specifics of his legacy and his destiny. That day Garrow buried his teacher with sadness, sensing only that there was a secret not yet told. But he had no way of knowing just what the trials would be which would empower him to become the leader of a new generation of people. And he did not know that he was destined to find the last young woman of the Pima tribe who, legend said, was to bear his child. The secret was with him but he did not know.

Filled with despair after the death, Garrow lived in the woods hidden from himself and others. He became angry, sad, lonely, and joyless, and he saw himself as a failure for not doing more to help the dying Tumara. In his loneliness he felt, too, to be a failure. He wished to go face his trials, but he knew not what they were. It haunted him and he didn't know. He was a victim of a myth that he was forced to live. And he did not know that the secret of his final trial was on his finger, at hand.

In the woods one day, he cried out in great loneliness. He hated that he had been deserted, robbed of his fatherlike friend, and was alone with no teacher. He had not known that even if his teacher had lived, he still would have acquired that loneliness. It was part of his rite of passage.

It was his developing manhood that had caused him to feel alone— the working out of a legend etched in the memory of his ancestors, passed on from generation to generation. It was difficult for Garrow to accept that this was the way it was written to be. Yet, his memory of the folklore had suggested that a lonely survivor would grow to manhood—and in that way, he saw that he perhaps fit the legends.

It happened as he sat beneath a great willow to rest. He began to wonder what his trials would be, and his loneliness filled his mind. Then his tears filled his eyes. At first he tried not to cry. He told himself that he was supposed to be destined to rule one day, that he had many trials, that crying would get him nowhere. But alas, he was indeed nowhere already. As he looked at the ring on his finger he could contain himself no longer and he wept violently. The tears filled his eyes until his ring was a blur before him. He thought, "Perhaps tomorrow I will face my trials."

But in the morning he had no clearer ideas of his trials. As he neared a distant mountain he came upon a sword and a shield half captured in solid rock. "At last," he thought, "it is I who shall prove my nobility by jerking these items from the solid stone." He was so pleased that he recognized a real trial before himself that he forgot about the laws of physics and reality. But in reality, no one would pull these weapons from the stone. They were there to stay. The more he tried the more he failed. And his worthlessness grew from deep in his heart. He felt it intensely. Again he tried to not show his true weakness but again he collapsed in admission that he needed help and without it he was lost. In the woods, he screamed out his feeling that he was a failure. Although he had no way of knowing it, his trials were, in fact, unfolding before him perfectly.

In days he passed beyond the sword, and the tears he cried had drained him completely of tears. There was no more to do or think or feel about that trial. He concluded that he simply failed it and he began to fear. The further he journeyed the more he thought. He was the last surviving man and he would prove unworthy. He reasoned that the tribe would die and he would bear the responsibility alone.

A day's travel from the mountain, when his spirits had almost risen in anticipation of the change of scenery, he happened upon a pride of sleeping tigers. Right in their midst was a huge wooden fighting hammer. This, like the sword, seemed to beckon. This, he again realized, was a trial. He understood the obvious. A brave man was to silently enter the center of the pride of tigers and, without disturbing them, he was to remove the hammer. It was to be his weapon. Perhaps, he thought, he would have to slay the tigers with it, but that would come in time. First, he concluded, he would retrieve the hammer.

Silently and slowly he crept into the middle of the tigers. After what must have been an hour he finally placed his hands on the handle of the hammer. His heart was pounding. He feared it would awaken the tigers. His every breath sounded like a windstorm to him. He tried not to breathe. Every muscle moved alone, orchestrated like a huge symphony, or perhaps a cacophony of fear. Now, with his trembling, exhausted hands on the huge hammer he valiantly yanked it skyward.

It cracked apart with a shattering clamor. It did not budge. The handle had broken off. The tigers jumped to their feet! Garrow screamed in terror. Fortunately, frightened cats have an instinct to flee. Garrow would live to tell of the incident. However, he planned to never tell, never think of the incident again. Two tests and two failures. He marched to the mountains.

That evening he made his way to the base of the mountain. He camped and dreamed. The next day, still obsessed with his own confusion, he saw an injured llama, half dead, half alive, squirming to work out its own fate against the side of a mountain. Fighting the stone and steep embankment, the animal climbed to a protected place where healing was possible. It was away from the snow and concealed from enemies, and with patience he was able to watch his own body begin to heal.

"Perhaps here," he thought, "is the trial I have awaited." My place must be as a healer, like Tumara the Ocucus." But as he watched the llama heal, he was transfixed. There was nothing he do except interfere or watch passively. So he watched. But it filled him with unspeakable joy. For the next two days he sat spellbound watching, grinning, laughing, amazed at what he saw in the healing of the llama's body. It brought tears of tenderness and compassion to his eyes. He even forgot his own fate. His joy sang out of him. At night he dreamed again. Somehow the dreams were not dreams of disappointment. When your conscious mind might be filled with a recognition of failure it is odd that your unconscious can embrace a feeling of success and drive you on. But it was like that for Garrow.

It was not long after this that Garrow came over the mountain into the forest on its other side. There, he was seemingly befriended in the woods by a Golindrina bird—a bird known for its delicate pink color and its courage to fly great distances for food. It flew with him everywhere and rested when he rested. He accepted it. Maybe in this was a trial he could pass.

Its nickname among the mountain people was Spirit Voice. Its voice, although only a faint warble up close, could actually be heard for great distances—no louder, no quieter—but always present. There was a belief among some that this special bird was actually a messenger from the gods. No one knew where the bird nurtured its young for they were so fiercely protective of their next generation, that to this day the nests have never been found.

After they had met, the bird traveled with Garrow everywhere and Garrow could not discern what, if any, his role was to be with this bird. If it posed a test, he again did not know how to pass it. But since he felt alone and lost, the road seemed endless, and his destination was not apparent, he enjoyed the companionship. Garrow only knew that something burned within him and called him forward. The two of them traveled by day and slept deeply at night. And each night the bird would diligently build a clay tunnel on the ground for warmth not far from him. In the morning, after deeply sleeping and much dreaming, Garrow saw the road was again before them.

Perhaps it was his imagination, but it began to seem that the tiny spirit bird communicated with Garrow at night, in his dreams. For what else could explain his increase of unusual dreams? Days passed. Always there, the bird was as loyal a companion as any pilgrim could ever find. Then, one night, Garrow had the following dreams.

In the first dream he saw a beautiful maiden and he captured her affection. In this dream world she was imprisoned, and in the dream he was informed that she was to be kept imprisoned until she grew to a certain age. At that time she would be sacrificed to the god of the future. The reason for this sacrifice, as with most sacrifices, had to do with prosperity and longevity and fertility.

In a second dream, Garrow was given a twig by the Golindrina bird and told to find a place for a nest.

In yet the third dream that night, Garrow saw himself as he once was, screaming in the dark forests, weeping for the loss of his teacher, helpless at the sword and shield in the stone, in terror at the awakened tigers, bursting with joy at the healing of the llama. In this dream the witch doctor appeared and took his own medallion of silver and placed it around Garrow's neck. At that moment, his scarab ring melted away.

But, oddly, in the morning the gleaming medallion was actually there! Had it been there all along? Was it really there now? Was he still dreaming? He couldn't be sure. Now the meaning of these dreams was not clear to Garrow. Sometimes, in the waking from a dream, the demands encountered are quite sufficient to distract your conscious mind from the unresolved and unanswered questions that had seemed so important in the dream.

At the instant of that waking, his scarab ring slid off his finger and revealed on the surface of the carved bug, a place worn down by time. In the polished and worn spot Garrow could see the surface of a fine blue gemstone—like that worn by the tribe's legendary chief. In that passage of time between dreaming and full waking, the gentle Golindrina bird began to warble, and Garrow found that, in that state of mind, he was able to hear or somehow interpret her sounds as language, even though he couldn't at first say what was being communicated.

And still, Garrow was confused and regretted his fate. He had not learned enough from his teacher, the tests he had failed, the scarab ring was only a symbol, the blue gemstone of his tribe simply an inheritance, the Golindrina bird simply a voice! And from his dreams he could learn nothing.

That very day, after the dream lifted, Garrow and the Golindrina bird came upon a sightless man living near the river. It was the first human he had seen in some time. Garrow told him everything. Then the man grabbed Garrow's hand and using his touch as a fully sighted gypsy would have used his eyes, he examined the lines in Garrow's hand.

"But it is obvious," the old man continued, "for all this time the Golindrina has traveled with you through the woods. She has acted as your compass. She has spoken a language to you that you have not fully heard, and until you do, you will not find the woman you seek or the understandings you desire. She will escape you again and again because you cannot see, nor will you listen. And it is because you cannot let go of the legacy you have been given that you continue to be unable to fulfill it to your satisfaction!"

"Again?" said Garrow.

"I can tell you no more. But, yes, again."

"When was the woman with me?"

The blind man said nothing for a moment. "You can look for her or you cannot. You must choose or not."

At that moment he knew. Confused by his own stupidity Garrow felt embarrassment, and his old rage filled him once again. Feeling as though he might have lost his chance to renew the heritage of his people, with rage he grabbed the medallion at his neck and threw it with the scarab ring to the ground.

In the same instant, a bright light struck the center of the silver medallion, reflecting in it from the sky the image of a woman, who appeared when he looked again as his old friend, the Golindrina bird.

The old man said, "It has been your anger, well used, that has caused you to find courage to see as you are able." Garrow had thrown down the bonds that enslaved him to be the child of the tribe. In the act of throwing away the legacy of his trials, he passed his final test.

"I believe you passed the final test as you passed the others," said the blind man. "How can you mean this?" Garrow asked. And the sightless old man gave his interpretation of how Garrow had been true to himself at every turn. In his apparent weakness he showed the strength of knowing himself and not the image of him that may have existed in legends or in the eyes of others.

"Take these gifts of your inheritance and of your people and use them with justice." Garrow gathered the ring and the medallion once again but now he possessed them and they did not possess him.

Perhaps the woman had always been there and Garrow could not see her for all his dreaming. Maybe he had not been worthy before but now she stood before him where the Golindrina bird had been.

When he reached his arm toward the sky the bird did not come. But the graceful open form of the woman approached and embraced him.

Thinking he was awake, he was bewildered and simultaneously delighted as he puzzled and rejoiced over this unexplainable phenomenon. Awaking again, the next day and the next, he was no better equipped to explain the presence of the lovely woman who seemed wise and very familiar to him.

To this day, the legend does not answer the mystery. But legends seldom do. And the legends of Golindrina birds are always shrouded with mystery. And Garrow grew in wisdom, clear-heartedness, and gentleness, and the two of them lived to pass those traits on to their children, and great grandchildren.

5. *Role-development goal:* Change comes from reliance on trusting, asking for help, and revealing yourself.

Metaphor

This is the story of the "challenge of the heart." It seems that Sheath went away one day, under an illusion of some sort which was customary for him. Exactly where he lived or when this occurred would be a matter for speculation and individual interpretation. It was in a hot climate and it was probably a long time ago, before the age of technology. It was a large village, probably it could be classified as a town. The villagers were protected from the outside and from strangers by walls. In the village, everything that Sheath had ever remembered or learned or enjoyed had always been enclosed by those walls.

One day, he was coming back from the desert in that usual state of delusion and confusion as young people will be. Sometimes you're not sure how long you've been gone or exactly how far away you've wandered. You can set out in one direction and have every intention of heading back in that same direction, only to find out later that you've taken another. He thought he had headed back in the direction he came from. Maybe he did. But his village wasn't there!

The wall wasn't there. The gates weren't there. All of the people he knew were gone. All of the things he remembered from childhood, everything to which his memories were attached, like the childhood fun of balancing himself on the edge of fountains around the town, those too were gone. The ledges where he had kicked his shoes in the dirt were gone. The dogs were gone, the merchants of the stores, the possibilities, even the problems that existed in that village were for all practical purposes from his vantage point at that moment just absolutely gone. He searched and he searched and he couldn't be sure whether he was too deluded to be in the same place or whether or not he was correct in assuming it was gone, but the more he looked the more frantic he became. All that remained was what he had with him.

In desperation, at nightfall, he set out to find the regional governor to seek his advice about this dilemma. Along the way, he asked anyone he encountered but they either didn't know or couldn't remember. He reasoned this way, "If they knew of the village, they had vanished with it. And if they were unaware of the village's whereabouts, they were of no help to him."

Finally, he reached the regional governor. He was the wisest man around, he had the most power. He had been elected to that position for some good reason, Sheath thought. And so he consulted with that governor about what he should do. The governor said, "In situations like this, there is only one thing that could be done." "Just what kind of situation is this anyway? You mean you've seen this before?" he asked.

"Not exactly in this format," he said. "It always takes a new shape. But each time, something is similar at the heart of the matter. Getting your town back will be a test of your heart. The only way out, at the heart of the matter, is through the challenge of the heart. You're going to have to go back to where you think the city is, or where it used to be, and meditate or go into trance, whatever it takes, until four objects appear to you four times. You know what it's like when you search inward for a certain image. You don't know what image is going to come to mind. Your conscious mind can have a pretty good idea of something you think might apply but your unconscious can surprise you." The instructions were to find the first four objects that came to his mind four times and then to return with them to the office of the governor.

The first object that came to his mind rapidly, four times, would be the first of the objects he was to gather. And how do you keep count in trance of the number of times an object appears to you? Four objects, four times is 16 images, one, two. But they don't have to come in order. It could be 13, 3, 7, 14, 15. You could count how many remain. There's that other one that hasn't yet occurred at all and another has occurred five times.

But one thing was certain. It was that he couldn't get out of his mind a crystal, a purple crystal pendant that seemed to be attached, suspended perhaps, from a red ribbon or chain of some sort. And it kept coming back around to his mind. He just stopped counting after he saw it four times.

And there was a key, a bronze key that continued to come to mind, a larger key than you usually encounter. It was the key that he knew had never been known to open any lock. Certainly no lock came with it and it didn't appear that one would be found to fit it.

Another thing that came to mind was the feather he had. He had kept it for years assuming it was from an eagle. It was a sturdy feather, a long feather.

And the fourth object that occurred four times on that night of deliberation was a whistle he had kept for no particularly good reason. He didn't like the sound it made when he blew it. It was a decorative whistle, etched, it seemed, to be valuable. But you couldn't say for what.

He searched among the belongings he kept until he found the four objects. He began the very next morning heading off back towards the governor. He was hoping that when he got there the four objects would be suitable. But all the while he doubted that these things would have any ability to help him find his city, his friends, and all those things from his childhood memories, and all the things that were familiar to him.

So he started off at daybreak. He didn't know he would only have one object left when he got to the city. He was just so pleased to realize that he had been able to follow the instructions thus far. He felt like he was on his way to heroic success.

But it was a long walk, indeed, and when a circus caravan stopped and offered him help, asked him if he would like to ride, he enthusiastically accepted the invitation. The only place to ride was within an empty and unused cage—so he rode in it. And they rode for hours and hours and hours until he had fallen asleep. And when he woke, it may have been the next day. The circus caravan was gone, long gone, but the cage that surrounded him was still right there. And, in fact, the door wouldn't budge at all when he pushed it, wiggled it, and jiggled it. It just rattled. He hollered out, "Hey, guys," but, of course, nobody was around to hear him. He couldn't tell yet for sure but it appeared as if the whole circus was gone. He didn't hear the noise of the animals. Nobody answered when he hollered.

What was he to do? Nothing he could do would open or dislodge the door and then he realized. But first he thought, "These people have tricked me." Then he thought that they must have robbed him, but no, he still had all of his things, his key, crystal, whistle, and feather. They must have maliciously set out to put me in this situation and take advantage of me, but no, that wouldn't work. Maybe they have to do with the disappearance of my village. Then he thought again.

No, maybe not. Maybe my coach just got unhooked and my door was locked by accident. Maybe they didn't even realize they left me out here. And with that, he found himself holding his key in his hand. Although he came to bring it as a result of the trance meditation and although it was to be used to save his village, he stuck it in the lock, almost as an afterthought.

Miraculously, it opened the lock of the door of the cage, but in so doing, it was hopelessly jammed into the lock. He had to leave the key behind in order to move on his journey to the governor. And he had to keep moving—he didn't know how much time he had lost.

As fast as he could, he continued to hurry. By the time nightfall neared, the various sounds of the desert, which he had thought to be uninhabited, started to haunt him. It was the sounds of whatever wild animals he didn't want to get too close to. And yet, the sounds the animals made seemed to be moving closer. Maybe he was moving closer to them, but at any rate, it can be very unsettling to be out all alone in the middle of the desert in the middle of the night, unprotected.

At first he thought maybe he could just whistle a little tune and they would go away. But that didn't work. Then he thought that surely they were going to try to get him and eat him. Then he thought that since he had no weapon whatsoever, he would surely die.

Maybe they were mad animals, crazy animals. If he ran fast, he would run out of energy that much sooner and be all the more likely to be their supper. Maybe he didn't have what it would take to confront them and he probably couldn't run fast enough to get away.

If he stood still, there was nothing as a shelter and no weapon to use. Maybe he could call for help. Maybe somebody would come. So he hollered but the animals continued to growl closer. He was so scared he could hardly make a loud holler anyway. His voice seemed to be stuck somewhere in the back of his throat. And with that ability to still think but that inability to scream in your own behalf, every child has probably sustained some nightmare. And he pulled that whistle out of his pocket and put it up against his lips and blew a breath with such force into the whistle—through that tiny little space—that it shrieked out into the night. It screamed out a whistle so loud that he remembered at once why he didn't like its sound.

But he blew it out so loud there was silence. And then finally, in dead silence, it stopped. The whistle would never work again. It wasn't just because he stopped blowing. He had blown the guts out of the inside of the whistle. It was broken and the only sound was that of the pieces as they fell and there were no sounds of any animals to be heard either. Silence can be very comforting at certain times.

And with that, Sheath continued on his way, now only with two objects remaining. And he knew that if the objects were needed for the test of his heart, he was going to be a miserable failure. He only had two objects and was already sure that he had failed. But he had no choice but to continue onward. And when at last he got to the gates of the city in which the governor waited within, his progress seemed to be once again blocked in a way that promised to add more failure to his already difficult lot.

There was a creature of some sort, the kind that myths are made of, where people have described a dragon or cyclops, and you know it must just be a normal, albeit large, animal. It could have been a bear but it was before life forms had been totally categorized and it was the kind of beast that lends itself to exaggerations of the imagination.

You can perceive a stimulus with your conscious mind and your unconscious uses a fear to translate that into an awesome stimulus. Anyone knows that an animal that big with claws like that would be able to destroy a lonely person in an instant. And he acutely realized that he stood there with no manner of conjuring, no method for taming this beast, when it dawned on him that maybe this beast doesn't want to harm me at all. Maybe it isn't dangerous at all, especially when it's asleep. If I don't awaken it, maybe this is an animal that wouldn't harm people.

So, with that, he took his feather out and he tickled it in various places around its armpits, around its neck, gently stroking the hair of the animal with the bristles of the feather. He must have done it for all of five or six minutes when finally the animal gave out a loud yawn and rolled over. But, in so doing, the creature snatched the feather in its armpit as it rolled away from the gate.

Through the gate Sheath went, thinking one step forward and another object sacrificed, another failure. Is the failure greater than the accomplishment? He thought so.

And he looked at the lonely last crystal, the first object that had come to his mind and the only one he still held. As he watched his face reflected in the facets of the crystal, he just saw the sad face of a disappointed person. They say that as an object of meditation, the crystal offers neither hardness nor suffering nor resistance. But as he looked into the facets of that crystal, all he saw was a face filled with suffering and pain and difficulty of every type, especially the most personal and painful difficulty of all that comes from sensing failure, the fundamental sense of inadequacy. He had hoped to be the hero and all he saw was the face of a person who needed more and more assistance and was less and less capable of doing anything right by himself.

Finally, he was standing in front of the governor's door and when it was opened the governor said, "Sheath, how nice to see you. Tell me, what of your journey?" Sheath explained he wasn't going to be able to accomplish anything. He had had the four objects but now he had failed.

"I wasn't brave, I wasn't capable, I didn't really help anybody. I watched my face in the 12 facets of the crystal and I see 12 things about myself. My despair was only magnified 12 times. I let you down. I squandered the advice you gave me. I have no hopes, no dreams left." Whereupon crying so hard, he just closed his eyes, closed down, closed inside.

The governor said, "Sheath, I'm so pleased with your success. This was a challenge of your heart. You were locked in a cage and you could have thought it was the malice of the people in the circus caravan but you didn't think it was the malice. You proved your compassionate, forgiving heart by assuming the best. Even while diverted from your bravery, you used one of your objects to learn.

"Then you were in the middle of the desert with wolves surrounding you and not a hope of defending yourself. Even in that situation when you thought there was nobody, there you blew your whistle for help as loud as you could and your trusting heart was proved.

"And at the gate, you could have assumed the creature was evil and wanted to devour you. But instead you tickled it with your feather and you proved your light heart, your heart of joy.

"And walking here the last three miles, you've watched your face in that crystal and you've admitted a truth about yourself that wouldn't have been available to the ordinary person. You've proven your honesty and your pure heart, true heart.

"These tasks, these trials, could not be accomplished with the things you brought with you if your heart could not pass the test. You had to have a forgiving heart rather than becoming disenchanted. You had to have a trusting heart rather than give up belief that you could find help. And I think what you'll find when your eyes are open is that other delusions, illusions, confusions will have lifted as well. At this time, when you look to find your village, you will see it there, where it's been all along, concealed only by your confusion and your delirium." And so it was.

8

Discipline and Enjoyment Metaphors

*What we do on some great occasion will
probably depend on what we already are;
and what we are will be the result of
previous years of self-discipline.*
—*H. P. Liddon*

*If the self-discipline of the free cannot match
the iron discipline of the mailed fist, in
economic, scientific, and all other kinds
of struggles . . . then the peril of
freedom will continue to rise.*
—*John Fitzgerald Kennedy*

*If your capacity to acquire has outstripped your
capacity to enjoy, you are on the
way to the scrap-heap.*
—*Glen Buck*

This protocol involves the use of metaphors constructed isomorphically to match the clients' situations (Gordon, 1978, pp. 39–84) and which contain, as their primary intervention, interspersed suggestions (Erickson & Rossi, 1980c, pp. 262–280), punchlines (Lankton & Lankton, 1983, pp. 332–334), or embedded commands (Lankton, 1980, p. 133) regarding needed alterations in behavior, attitude, or affect to facilitate greater enjoyment and discipline. That is, the structure of this type of metaphor, unlike the others in this book, is designed to be a one-to-one match to the problem situation presented by the client. The altered, metaphoric framework so created then becomes the vehicle to carry the interventions of embedded directives. In essence, the directives are those very poignant and relevant statements that people often need to hear, remember, and act upon. Such statements are meant to be incorporated and to become a part of clients' maps of experience and to become a self-motivating force at some later time.

We have entitled this protocol "discipline and enjoyment," which may strike some as a bit of a contradiction or a set of logical opposites. But it is precisely due to our observation that these two aspects of living can and should go hand in hand—they are not opposites—that we have chosen the name. The discipline of hard work results in the joy of pride, yet an unbridled joy would usually turn sour if it were not tempered with discipline. Too often, clients stress the need to conduct themselves with more discipline and seldom do they realize that they can experience enjoyment as they do so. Others meander in a directionless maze of what feels least objectionable to them in order to avoid the very acts of self-discipline which would truly bring joy to their lives. Some clients, possessing the resources they need to change, seem to merely need to be told, "Do it, change now, get going, don't stop until you are successful!" This structure provides a means to convey these types of directives in the safety of the face-saving garments of metaphor.

This simple, yet powerful protocol was discussed in an earlier text (Lankton, 1980, p. 155). It is a useful tool among the accouterments of metaphor protocols since it is the easiest to learn and it often can be created and used effectively with less preplanning.

This process can be summarized in the three steps of this protocol:

Discipline and Enjoyment in Living and Changing

1. Create a metaphoric situation, a metaphor, or a series of metaphors that are isomorphic or match the client's situation and/or difficulty.
2. Elicit and retrieve required experience and focus the client's awareness on how a creative solution can be arrived at via appropriate effort or how pleasure is to be found in the process.
3. Deliver instructions, advice, or commands within the metaphor as embedded quotes, interspersed suggestion, embedded commands, and/or the metaphoric experience of the protagonist within the storyline.

Stories following this protocol usually are delivered in the middle of a multiple embedded sequence of stories and/or towards the end of therapy so that the (rather transparent) messages will be further removed from conscious attention and self-consciousness. Additionally, by placing these suggestions later in the session the prerequisite resources, which will be mentioned in the story, can have been elicited, built up, or otherwise retrieved preceding the embedded "directive" regarding how they are to be used.

One word of caution about the protocol's use concerns the temptation to rely upon this protocol since it seems to be more tangibly directive. It will appeal to some due to its moralizing or sermonizing qualities, perhaps. It will appeal to others since it can often take less preplanning and less extra mural preparation than the complex protocols found in this volume. However, for the directives of this protocol to be effective, the client must have been sensitized to the prerequisite attitudes, affects, and behaviors. That is, directives to "study hard" will be of no consequence unless the client has motivations, attitudes, behaviors, and affects needed to plan for success, sits quietly and works diligently, has a feeling of hopefulness, has a relaxed and effective recall strategy, and so on. Therefore, plan to use this form of metaphor to focus clients on the use of resources that have been retrieved, built up, or elicited in previous therapy work during the session or in prior sessions.

It would perhaps be of benefit to provide a short sketch of the client situation which prompted the use of the following first metaphoric story. In this way the relevance of the embedded suggestions it contains can be better grasped. Since the process is rather straightforward, subsequent metaphors in this chapter will follow without this added feature. The client for whom this first story was created was a 32-year-old man who was concerned about studying for and passing a stockbrokerage exam. Although he had no other apparent individual or marital concerns, he had taken and failed the exam previously, despite being prepared for it and feeling that he knew the material. Retrieval difficulties, apparently related to anxiety, had contributed to that failure and he wanted to take the exam differently this time. A series of diverse metaphoric contexts were used as an isomorphic frame, within which were embedded suggestions for focusing awareness on proper discipline and the enjoyment that could be derived from it. Those appear here in italics and indicate an alteration in voice tone to "mark them out" or punctuate them for unconscious consideration (Erickson & Rossi, 1980a, p. 430). The client did pass his upcoming exam shortly after the session in which these stories were told to him in trance. No other therapeutic interventions were made in this case.

1. **Discipline/enjoyment goal:** *Concentrate comfortably and focus on what is known so as to appropriately retrieve it at the needed time.*

Metaphor[32]

I had a client named Joe several years ago, who had a hard time deciding whether or not it was time to leave home. He had lived in the same town for many years and he really was quite content, in a way, in that little town. Yet another side of him was discontent because he was sure that he could *accomplish much more.* On the other hand, he knew every street so well, he knew all of the people so well, and we've all had that feeling before of what it's like to *know everything well.* And when *you are a person who is so familiar with a certain subject* like Joe was with his town and townsfolk, *you really need to mull things over* to *retain all of the important things.* And as Joe found out, *you have to consider what you know now,* and *compare it* to what *you need to know* in order to make a decision about where to live.

And it may mean that you have to make some changes, to *correct the errors.* And this can be an uncomfortable time. I probably don't have to tell you that Joe was quite miserable when he first visited my office. And I listened to his story because I have found that to really *retain information* about clients, or people in general, *you really must concentrate when the information is first presented to you.* Apparently, Joe was feeling quite anxious about what he needed to do, his voice was a bit shaky. His gaze was intent, his speech was slightly accelerated. And I mentioned to him during his discourse . . . even now as *you are getting deeper into your experience,* your facial expression is flattened and somber, *your respiration is changed, you have gone from one stage to another,* Joe. It simply is okay to *breathe slower . . . breathe more easily.* And with every new breath, inhaling an accompanying sense of well-being. And with every inhalation, also that sense of peacefulness and contentment and *knowledge* that you will *do things right.* And, of course, by the same token, exhaling any tension, expelling the anxiety. That's right!

But those suggestions were not enough at first. Joe still had some inner nervousness, and he did not feel shy about sharing his apprehension. Yet, as he spoke, and as he was able to *take deep, slow breaths,* I began to see the gradual changes. I thought to myself that if Joe stayed in the town where he was raised, he might be able to *change*

[32] This metaphor was contributed by Diane Forgione, M.S.W.

the things that don't seem right. If he is bored, he may be able to get into something more exciting right in his own home town. And at the same time, he could *look more closely at the important things* that home provides—security, familiarity, and perhaps it provides more pleasure than he could consciously acknowledge during his transition, because transitional periods are often marked by turmoil and unrest.

I have a friend who has recently given birth to a little girl. This child is very special to her family because not only is she a special little person in her own right, but she is also their second child. The first little girl died of leukemia when she was seven years old. And when you are faced with a situation of tremendous loss, you ache tremendously and your whole world is full of discomfort, and is unsettled. Gradually, the pain subsides as you begin to *more fully know . . . the larger meaning.* With a situation like this, you often *become more aware of a grander picture,* so that *you are able to place great meaning on things.* So an event happens and suddenly that *weight* that was sitting on your shoulders *is lifted.*

Megan was born and the parents were filled with a sense of joy, that sense of success that comes from knowing that *you can do things well.* The mother had given up smoking, drinking, and she ate a balanced diet and exercised regularly during her pregnancy to ensure that she was doing her part in contributing towards a healthy delivery and a healthy baby. And when you are a baby who has been born following the death of another sibling, you are subjected to a number of tests in your lifetime. And *you have to be sure to pass those tests. There is more caution,* and rightly so. And for a parent in this situation, *there is an urgency to do things properly—there'll be no mistakes this time* even though the leukemia of their first child was not due to any mistakes of their own. It's just that when this happens *you are extra precise. You find yourself retaining all of the information that you read* on child care and child rearing, and having the uncanny ability to *retrieve this information at will,* as needed.

And two of my dogs have been retrievers. Shana is a golden retriever and collie mixture. Kelly is a full-bred labrador retriever. And being of this breed means that *you can always be taught to bring things back,* and the dog's memory is important, too. And if you are a dog like Shana, for example, how can *you know what to bring back.* How can *you remember.* Because *you see something, remember what it is, and know it will be retrieved.* Shana is very good at fetching balls, frisbees, and wooden sticks. She remembers what she needs to know, but otherwise *you just forget all else that has transpired on a conscious level.* The nice thing about the unconscious mind is that it operates for you, autonomously. *You don't need to think too hard.* You don't need to worry. Your unconscious mind is always there for you, and it knows, and *you know* what you need to know. And just as there are many ways to remember, there are an equal amount of ways to forget.

You can forget consciously, for example, the touch on your skin by the sun. And what does it mean to be touched gently by the sun? *You can forget* a name, for a brief period of time. *You can forget* the sound of the ocean as it splashes upon the shore. But, *you never really forget,* do you? *You simply forget it consciously, and allow your unconscious mind to carry the load.* And a golden retriever need not *remember* how to chase and retrieve a wooden stick all of the time. *You need to remember* only *at certain times.* And the wonder of having a conscious and an unconscious mind is that they both have their specific functions.

Your conscious mind is interested in looking at things specifically, while your unconscious mind sees things on a more global level. Often, your conscious mind is concerned with analysis, while your unconscious seems to be knowingly smiling at your conscious mind's struggle. Because *you know already* in your unconscious mind what your conscious mind is still trying to figure out. And just as with a parent and a child, the unconscious watches patiently, offering timely help as the conscious ventures on—planning, figuring, learning, and attempting to decipher—while your unconscious handles things in a more all-knowing, instinctual way.

So the birth of Megan is certainly an exciting event, and it is hard to tell which part of the learnings my friends *will use consciously* while allowing the bulk of the material to *remain unconscious until it is needed.* And really there is so much to *concentrate* on *in the days ahead.* The mother really is able to *concentrate on the present* as she wakes up to her brand new child. She can *concentrate on the undertaking* of making sure that her baby's world is filled with interesting learning experiences, for a person is the sum total of their experiences, are they not?

She is able to *concentrate on the knowledge* that she really is the greatest. As a new mother, you are able to *concentrate on all that is pertinent* to the *success* of the balanced growth of a young child and *fulfilling the responsibility that that commitment takes.* And whenever *you do a job well* in life, it is because *you remember to be prepared* to meet the challenge.

And raising dogs can be rewarding because most of *the outcome depends upon you.* I can look at my animals and be pleased because they are content and loving, and they are able to both give and receive affection—which can be a sign of a healthy adjustment.

And Joe was able to *make the right decision* about where to live his life. It was a process for him, just as many learning experiences are a process. You don't always necessarily *know right away what needs to be done.* Joe had many considerations about what life would be like if he did *take a chance on the unknown,* but he knew that he never would be taking a risk to *take that chance* because his unconscious knows the correct way to go, just as mine does, just as yours does. There really is no danger of mixing things up if you *simply trust in your unconscious to make the best decision.* And I'm not sure to this day which way Joe did turn, but the last time I saw him he seemed fine. I told him, "It really is something to *understand* how far along you are now, Joe. *You aren't anxious anymore,* and *you are the picture of confidence.* You appear to be a guy who's got it all under control." He just smiled and commented, "There is nothing that compares to the feeling as when *you feel so good about yourself.*"

2. ***Discipline/enjoyment goal:*** *Enjoy the process and the rewards of disciplined effort.*

Metaphor[33]

Beth hardly paused for the briefest hello before launching into an elaborate description of some television special she had seen that week. It made me wonder if she was trying to distract my attention from that promise she had made. The mini-documentary told the story of child athletes who were the country's future Olympic hopefuls. These kids, almost all had started their particular sport at a preschool age. And their parents or their coaches recognized their special abilities. And now that they are about 10 years old, the children have had to leave home to live in the sports camp. There was a little boy who left his home in California to attend a tennis camp in Florida. A little girl from Kansas was attending a gymnastics camp in Minnesota. The children live at these camps year round in dormitories. They go to school within the camp with other athlete children, they take their

---

[33] This story was contributed by Susan L. Vignola, D.S.W.

meals there and mostly they *practice, practice, practice* their sport. They have *to compete* with each other, against their friends trying *to become the best*. It's like they are trying to climb their way up a large funnel and only a few will actually succeed.

Parents would wonder if they had done the right thing to send their children off to live away from home among strangers. There would be tears at the airports when they had to say goodbye. There were more tears on special occasions and holidays. As teenagers, the children give up their opportunity for a normal social life. With all their practice, there is *no time for* dating, or going to the movies, or *hanging around* the mall. When the reporter interviewed the children, they talked about how much they missed. They also talked about *how lucky* they felt to *have the opportunity to pursue* the sport and the *life* they dreamed about. Even little kids talked about the enjoyment of the pain because it was a symbol of how they were pushing themselves *to achieve more*. They really believed, *no pain*, no gain. Their pain was a symbol of their gains.

Beth suddenly felt that her complaints about getting up at five o'clock in the morning and how her legs ached, and how tired she was, and how much she sweated riding her exercise bike each morning, well all that seemed pretty insignificant. She said she can't get on her bicycle anymore without seeing one of those little kids standing in the Olympic arena, hearing the Star-Spangled Banner playing in the background, and seeing them bow their heads forward as some official places a ribbon around their neck.

Beth says she sits taller in her saddle now, *feeling proud* and *welcoming* each drop of sweat that pours off her body. She said she's even thinking about adding another five miles a day to her ride. Why not? If those kids can do it, so can I. "Besides," she said, "all of a sudden, *it's become fun*. It reminds me of how much I hate to wax my car, but I sure do like to stand back and watch the sun dance off of it. Now that I think of it, Mom was kind of like that. Whenever she would wax the dining room table, or scour the big soup pot, *when* she was *all done*, you could *see the smile come* into her face as she saw her reflection gazing back at her from the wood or from the aluminum."

Grandma, too, would *labor for many hours* sewing those little pieces of fabric together to make a quilt top. But every grandchild learned the story behind each piece of material. "Why, that was your first communion dress, and that was the dress Mommy wore when she went to the hospital and that was the shirt Grandpa wore when he shot that big buck . . .," and so it would go.

My friend Betty Lou has a friendship quilt her best friend made her when she got married. Each piece of fabric held a story from the years they had shared growing up, and each appliqué on the quilt was a representation of some place they had been or something they had done. There's even a blood stain where Betty Lou's friend pricked her finger while sewing the quilt. Together, they *love* to spread the quilt out on the back lawn *on a warm spring afternoon,* and square by square they take turns telling the quilt's story, telling the story of their lives and *the story of their friendship.*

The parents of one of my clients tell a story about the house they built together. She tells of the fights they had, of the thumbs that got nailed, or at least hammered, of the time the framing fell down and of all the hours she soaked in the bathtub after spending an afternoon working on the house. She says she still has callouses on her hands, and will *show them to you proudly,* and she says she never wants to live anywhere else: "They're gonna take me out of that house feet first," she says. Maybe that's what they mean by a *"labor of love."*

3. **Discipline/enjoyment goal:** *Focus on sexually pleasurable sensations, images, fantasies, plans, and messages.*

Metaphor:

When Sherry came to therapy, she was in that situation where, following a divorce, she was having to deal with this matter of dating. How do you *decide whom to date,* and do you *want to kiss* the person on the first date? It seemed silly for her to be asking those kinds of questions, she's 29 years old. And yet you think about *those things you need to think about.* And through no fault of her own, she hadn't had the opportunity to *learn those things.* She's the oldest of 10 children and she certainly had the opportunity to *learn a lot about how it* is that you be strong *and have a sense of control.* She had taken care of all those younger siblings and she knew a lot about that. It's interesting that *you can learn* to amplify another experience by your ability *to so thoroughly have one experience.*

And there were several things she asked about. One was how you *go about feeling sexy and enjoying your body* when your mother didn't tell you how to do that. In fact, in her case, her mother had been very clear that she wasn't to have those sexual feelings at all. Her mother didn't know how to tell her that it's perfectly all right to just *enjoy your body* and *enjoy those sensations, enjoy the warmth of a tear passing over the cheek, enjoy the ability to take a deep breath, enjoy your ability to feel a sense of relief in your bladder when you comfortably urinate, enjoy your ability to feel warm and cozy* under the blankets, *enjoy your ability to feel excited.* And so she mistakenly thought that it was too late to learn those things, but she was hoping that possibly she could still learn to *have those feelings,* and in addition to that, she was hoping that she could alter her habit of chewing her fingers.

I saw the two goals as very much related, and I reminded her that you can pretend anything and master it. So, for a moment, she told me later, she brought to mind a scene of Dolly Parton in a special she had seen on television the evening before, and there was Dolly Parton holding that microphone with the most shimmeringly sexy fingernails it's possible for a woman to have. Now, most people don't think of Dolly Parton and necessarily think about how sexy her fingernails are, but that's what this client was thinking about. And I don't know whether or not it's possible to imagine a face changing and whether or not Sherry was able to see herself standing there holding that microphone and having those long shimmering fingernails. But for her, it was an opportunity to give permission, to *feel free* and allow yourself to represent your sexuality in any way that *you choose.* The fingernails were only a symbol. And how to stop engaging in an old habit frequently is learned as a result of learning a new habit.

She actually started a whole string of new habits, and what better time to do it than at New Year's or the dawning of *a new age of relationships* signaled by a divorce. And like many people do, she changed her hairstyle, her wardrobe, her apartment, reading material, eating habits, and leisure activities. Before, it hadn't occurred to her *to actively take control of leisure time.*

So you can imagine the wealth of new sensations that began to bubble to the surface as she started an exercise program during what had been traditional "happy hour" cocktails after work. She alternated between swimming, bicycling in the park, and rebounding to the invigorating sound of "Rhapsody in Blue," depending upon her mood and initial energy level each day.

She found herself asking herself, "What do I really want to do right now?" Sometimes, she would just start doing a few stretches while she waited for some answer to manifest itself. But when you *listen to your body, the answer will come.* And regardless of the activity she would choose, she would begin, some days sooner than others, to *feel the warmth increasing, feel the heart beating strong and steady, feel the breathing.* She learned to *welcome all sensations,* even those that seemed aversive at first. With practice, she would automatically *breathe into the pain, go with it, listen to it, learn from it,* and finally let it go the way you say goodbye to a friend.

But far more often she had the opportunity to *breathe into the pleasure* of just being alive and moving the muscles, *feeling the breeze* flow past, *feel the enveloping wetness* of the water. One day she was running in a five-mile race and about halfway through, began to question the wisdom of getting involved in this way. Her legs were hurting, her side was hurting, and she was paying attention to that pain and to her internal doubting and complaining with each step.

Suddenly, an unexpected sight caught her eye. There on the sidelines in a wheelchair sat an old woman waving little flags, tooting a horn, and encouraging the runners on with a big smile on her face and saying things like, "Atta way to go! Keep going! You'll make it! You're looking good!" Even before Sherry was out of earshot, something was altered in a way she never forgot. Instead of running along thinking, "This hurts, that hurts, I'll never make it," she found herself running along with her head held high and a smile on her lips as she repeated with each step, *"running is a privilege, running is a pleasure."* And sometimes she would vary that by telling herself, *"You are strong, you are healthy, you are alive."* And the finish line appeared a lot sooner than she had expected it would.

And there were other kinds of new exercises that afforded their share of pleasure, as well, though it took a little time for her to actually see it that way. At first, dreading the prospect of having to be vulnerable and awkward in the dating context, she avoided it, but amplifying one learning by your ability to have another, she gradually began to *welcome those twinges* of what might be called anxiety but could *just as easily* be considered *excitement.* And with heart pounding in anticipation, she would *use that awareness of body* to approach a man she considered interesting or attractive and just tell him so, appreciating the feeling of warmth that would sometimes rise to the chest and face. She didn't fully realize how charming the corresponding change in coloration was to her companion.

And she never actually grew Dolly Parton nails, though she did groom her own very well-kept version and a whole repertoire of flattering behaviors to go with them. It was just like when Marna came to me thinking she was going to use trance to learn how to lose weight and all the while manage to avoid what she considered the aversive act of sweating.

Marna hadn't met Sherry yet and she just wanted to lose weight without working up a sweat. She thought sweating was really improper somehow or undesirable, and it's an attitude you can readily understand if you caught a glimpse of the Miss America Pageant the other night sponsored by Dry Idea's motto/logo that was repeated over and over, "Don't ever let them see you sweat." They reduced it to some repulsive, unnatural act as opposed to one of the most miraculous, amazing, useful, cleansing, helpful functions your body could possibly perform. And I guess Marna thought she just needed to stop eating so much and *perhaps we could use hypnosis to alter that.* But everyone knows that a change has to occur at a deeper level than that. Maybe it's a change in the metabolism or in her case, a change in her attitude that *your body is entitled to function in the way it was created to function.* And Dry Idea might just as well say, "Don't ever *let them see you breathe.*"

So a good bit of energy was directed to talking to her about the simple pleasures of sweating and the simple but amazing fact that your body and your unconscious is able to regulate it at a level you know nothing about, that you couldn't possibly understand. It's an air conditioning system that never needs constant adjustments of its fluid level by external sources, it never needs its filters changed, it works year after year after year for a whole lifetime effectively keeping your organism exactly the proper temperature.

And that's all well and good physiologically, but what about that simple pleasure, that ultimate pleasure of exerting yourself, feeling your muscles move when you ride a bicycle or roller skate or go for a run or walk or climb a mountain. And it doesn't take very long for that kind of exertion to build up a little film. A little layer of perspiration makes its way magically to the surface of your skin and lays there just next to the surface, insulating you. And if you've climbed a mountain exerting yourself and making that layer of sweat, then when the wind shifts ever so slightly, it's almost like being in heaven a little.

Certainly it is one of the most heavenly experiences you can imagine having on this earth on a mountaintop to have that breeze blowing ever so slightly over that glistening layer of sweat that's come to the surface of your skin. It's one of the most delicious feelings on earth. And *you're entitled to have all those delicious feelings your body's able to have.* And *you know how* to do so, unencumbered by these stupid ideas society and culture and advertising and enlightened parents attempt to hammer into our heads.

And we talked about sweating while the air conditioner was blowing full blast. I told her that we were considering writing a book called *Hot Florida Nights*. And you can bet there's going to be a lot of sweating going on in that book. The sweating that comes from exertion and regular exercise is not nearly so interesting or entertaining as the sweating that comes *from lovemaking,* the sweating that comes from *passionate sexual encounters.* But I didn't talk to her about that yet.

And it was like the situation Sherry was in when she relinquished her need for anyone else to do any additional teaching or approving or protecting her. And once you move into a comfortable, existential position like that, the sky's really unlimited. And it's just like having a blank piece of paper on which you can draw anything you want. And so you have to first ask yourself just what exactly do you want to draw? Maybe it's a question that has to come through your conscious mind while your unconscious starts making some movements with color and texture. And you watch the picture take shape or you can do it according to a plan. You really can *plan to play* as carefully as you plan anything else that's important and vital. You can *set out to make it enjoyable* no matter how old you are.

There's something a little bit magical about making a date and there's really no reason why it should be reserved for adolescents and people who aren't married. And it's oftentimes easier for them to get together than it is for a couple who take each other for granted just because they live under the same roof. They just assume they're going to see each other. And so they don't deliver the Sunday paper to their spouse in bed with a little note secretly rolled up in the middle of it that's going to pop out and be read while their spouse is in the shower getting ready to go and do something that she has to do; and there's a note that says, "Good morning, honey, I sure would like to make a date with you. How about 3 o'clock this afternoon, just you and me, right back here in bed? I've got some special plans for you, honey." And they don't call up during the day wherever the other one is and say, "I'm working real hard right now but I can't stop thinking about how good it felt being next to you last night when we were making love, can't wait to wrap my arms and legs around you, and I just wanted to share that with you." If you're having a little romance like that during the day, *you start the process of letting go a lot earlier.*

Sherry has a set of very, very sexy black lingerie that she bought with a boyfriend who was interested in exploring the miraculous land of sexual relationships. She was supposedly their leader because she had been there longer then he had; she had even been married. But the lingerie was his idea. Just what is it about a garter belt and black stockings that makes such an impression on a couple? How does it heighten his desires so and turn their thoughts so undeniably sexual?

And she thought it just happened in a woman actually, when he mentioned that he thought these kinds of props would be a lot of fun and why didn't they just stop in this shop and pick out some things for her to wear during their private moments? And she hadn't had a garter belt since the seventh grade when she first started wearing hose. But after that pantyhose came out, and every sensible woman would prefer the logical ease and convenience of pantyhose. And her garter belts had never been black and they'd never been lacy and they'd never been cut in such a way as to accentuate the pelvic region quite in the way the ones did that his eye was drawn to.

They were both a little embarrassed as they stood there fumbling through these next-to-nothing pieces of enticing lace. But they bought an interesting array of things. And the next day Sherry carefully dressed for work but she was really dressing for the date after work because she knew she wasn't coming home first.

And she put on the black cutout panties first and then the garter belt and then the black hosiery and the very low-cut, see-through black bra. And she just walked around the house looking at herself in the mirror for a little while, having an undeniable feeling of doing something slightly risqué and playfully naughty. And she was beginning to *feel very excited.* And it wasn't the kind of feeling you would expect to be having as you head off to a professional place of employment. Who would have ever thought that this woman, who was soon to be dressed so properly on the surface level, had on those kinds of underwear? How could she interact professionally all day dressed like that and keep her mind on the subject at hand?

But that was a risk she was willing to take because after she finished admiring herself, she put those other levels of clothing on and drove to her office and went through the motions of dealing with the first several clients. Then, she took a quick break and made her way down to the office where her boyfriend was having a break too. She walked in, locked the door, and said, "Guess what I have on under my clothes?" And a big smile came across his face, and a leer and a gleam in his eye. I don't know where the blush begins or how it begins exactly, but it comes from a feeling of anticipation of romance and sexual excitement with a delightful self-consciousness just like an adolescent has. And it began to spread over Sherry and it may have started somewhere in the stomach, or maybe the chest before going in both directions simultaneously.

And you can *enjoy that vital symbol of being so alive, so sexual,* and I'm sure it was very charming, I'm sure he appreciated it completely. And he came towards her with a look in his eye that made her blush even more and the other sensations begin to travel in both directions at once that somehow started in the middle. And some women accomplish this by reading those romance novels that have such spicy, detailed sexual language you can't help but *have those little sensations* you've known about for a long time but maybe hadn't experienced recently. It begins somewhere in the pit of the stomach. And you start thinking about where your husband might be or the last time or the next time, maybe you just put yourself in the position of the character in your mind's eye. If that were the case you could even *dream an orgasm* as you follow along feeling each thing described in such passionate detail: "He pressed himself against her heaving mounds," and so on. And that's a large part of what may be going to be involved in *Hot Florida Nights* when it hits the newsstands. It's going to be very hot. And it's all an opportunity to *start letting go* and associate each one of those urges and sensations ever so briefly. And yet when we play with somebody, really play, there's a lot more to it than the sexual playing.

Every child has known. And the only thing it takes to remember is to come in contact with somebody else who's already remembered. And the people that you meet who could remember, can help you to remember, are people you never forget, even though you apply the learning with someone else so you find more appropriate contexts at another time in your life. And so *you remember what you were doing all along in a variety of ways* in a trance. And you really should thank your unconscious for its ability to remember what *you've known all along that you knew* in that tree when you were such a little girl. And whether you have that feeling—of orgasm—now or remember it, imagine it, dream it again, it was a very smart unconscious that was able to have that experience in the first place. And it's the same wisdom that you can use to associate that feeling to appropriate contexts with either your conscious or your unconscious mind. And the contexts may involve a different kind of tree and you may be interested in climbing up or shimmying down. I took Shawn to a playground where there was a little pole that children could climb up and hang on to with their arms and legs and *just slide down that pole.* And the first time he slid down it, he was a little afraid, but then he easily climbed up

that thing over and over again. Alicia was too little to climb but I just
know she would have had a different kind of learning.

And so you think about climbing onto your husband and associate
that same feeling of enjoyment, and it may surprise your conscious
mind what kinds of depths of reaction your unconscious has been
saving, the different kind of stimulation that you hadn't imagined would
result in the kind of excitement you once had on that tree. And so
you really should plan for play in some ways you haven't played before
and give your conscious mind a chance to discover what kinds of
alterations in sensation your unconscious has remembered.

And you certainly should keep that sense of excitement that you
were wise enough to remember as an adolescent interested in that
popular boy who was class president and ever so visible who later
became your husband. And, no doubt, that handsome young man was
known by all, admired, probably lusted after by quite a few girls in
school. And what girl wouldn't *blush with* her "boy crazy" *feeling* at
the thought of being asked to dance or asked to date somebody so
visible and so attractive? And so you can *have that feeling of excitement*
that you knew as an adolescent and modify it according to the woman's
maturity that you developed since then. Keep the sparkle. Put that in
the grown-up version of images with your husband, climbing up on
that man that you know. And it's a very interesting fantasy possibility.

You have a variety of interesting fantasy possibilities that you contribute to your dreams—an orgasm now which you associate to the
future or just the excitement that leads to the orgasm in the future,
and that way you can consider yourself *starting well in advance* the
lengthy delightful process of *letting go all the time.* And so the parade
of images might change as you enjoy the scenery of the sexual encounter
for some minutes.

You might like to imagine yourself as an adolescent girl in the back
seat of a car in some parking spot and you know you're really not
going to go all the way and yet knowing that allows you to have the
most intense reaction to that foreplay and it doesn't matter that the
foreplay is in fact leading somewhere different as an adult. And how
many adolescents would reach orgasm during all that foreplay only
because it's so exciting that maybe you shouldn't be doing it? Or maybe
it's just the sense of discovery of what things your body can do and
how different it feels when it's somebody else touching you.

And I like to think about a very primly raised girl I know who
recently got married at the tender age of 20 years old, absolutely a
virgin. It isn't proper in her family to ask her how her sex life is going.
But I just know that on all those dates she went on with that young
man over all those years of their engagement they must have been out

doing some of those things that lead to an extra sense of excitement, just because they were in a southern baptist church and they probably shouldn't have been doing it. And just because you're entitled to do it, *you can still keep the feeling and excitement* that came when you weren't supposed to do it because that's a learning.

And it might be fun to play with the idea of imagining yourself being her on the back seat of one of those nice cars her fiancé would drive and being so innocent and so fresh to the idea of what things the body is capable of feeling. Or you can imagine yourself being one of those voluptuous, overtly sexual, passionate women on the soap operas and they don't have any problem letting go. And it's nice to allow yourself to explore so many different aspects available to people.

And so it was a long trance that worked up quite a sweat actually, even though the air conditioner was blowing. I don't know if it is a matter of exerting yourself mentally to cause you to excrete perspiration or the process of imagining yourself sweating or the act of *appreciating how your body can work to create a sweat* like that. But she sat there sweating in front of the air conditioner, and it obliged by throwing a cool breeze across the sweat and then a smile rested comfortably across the corners of the lips just as naturally as that sweat laid in a thin surface across her skin.

And I can't even remember what happened with her weight loss, but all such things as weight and other expected desired changes have a way of simply falling into place when you *make friends with yourself* at a deeper physiological level, appreciating your physiology, remembering what your unconscious has always known and stored, keeps available. And you apply it to the context that is relevant. Every time it occurs, it becomes an automatic habit that replaces a habit that you've forgotten that wasn't relevant and you don't need any longer.

And it was right after that Marna did meet Sherry and they experienced some kind of sisterly bond or meaningful connection that led to a long and close friendship. They could often be seen walking quite rapidly together, laughing . . . and sweating.

4. *Discipline/enjoyment goal: There are some things one should just do, not wait until one feels like it, just do it. Plan to play and set out to make it enjoyable.*

Metaphor

Russ was up against the dilemma that sooner or later presents itself to every teenager. He was beginning to know all about his changing body and erections rising and falling without any warning. Discovering your sexual self and how to apply it with other people can be so confusing and yet there are simply four rules that should govern any kind of sexual contact and especially intercourse. Unfortunately, he didn't know about them at the time he blundered into an ill-begotten and embarrassing early sexual experience.

He was very receptive when he, quite by chance, came upon the four rules from a most surprising source—his father! Who would have ever thought that a father would have something relevant to say on that subject, he wondered. It was called the "honey and pollen lecture."

But the rules made a lot of sense and he passed them along to several of his friends. And he would always warn them—if any of these elements are missing, you must stop what you are doing as gracefully as possible and go somewhere else and figure out what went wrong. He would always repeat, "If you ever discover that even one of these things is missing from the experience, stop immediately. And, as gracefully as possible, leave the situation and go somewhere else and figure out what went wrong."

The rules are: One, sexual intercourse is always to be done with mutual respect between consenting partners. Two, each person must respect the other *and* be able to accept the respect given to him or her. Three, there's always to be communication; it can be verbal or nonverbal but it should take place before, during, and after. And four, there should always be enjoyment before, during, and after. Some people think that should be the first rule. So it is last but not least.

And so if any one of those four criteria are missing you should always stop the moment that you recognize it, put on your clothes, if that is necessary, and put yourself in a different situation until you can understand what was missing and why. "So which one of those was missing in that unhappy experience you had?" the father asked his son. "It is time to talk about it."

Now, on the other hand is this matter of enjoyment. You don't wait until you feel enjoyment to set out to make something happen with enjoyment. You can consider a difficult or what would seem like a difficult technique and you don't really have a sense of confidence about your ability to practice it smoothly until after you just jump right in with both feet, decide to do it, discomfort and all. And it's hard to say just when the sense of comfort, confidence, and enjoyment begins to develop in a situation like that but maybe it's as soon as you decide, maybe it's after the situation has been resolved. Or maybe it's somewhere right early on when you begin to know that you're going to be able to do it even though you don't know how yet.

It's the same with exercise of any sort. Many times your conscious mind thinks that you don't really want to do it. Simultaneously, another part of your conscious mind says, "Yes, but you really should. It'll be good for you." And your unconscious doesn't really know what to do yet and so it just waits and maybe at some point you make a decision that *you're going to do it anyway even though you don't feel like it.*

And so you get out your shoes and your socks, and you put on your sock on one foot and your shoe on to that sock, and then you're halfway started so you might as well put on your other sock and shoe, and now you have on your tennis shoes so you might as well do something. Maybe you'll just start by walking, maybe you'll start by just walking to the front door, opening the door, sniffing the air like a dog would. Maybe there are some blooms in that season, who knows.

A bloom can attract you, lure you into the outside world. And then you walk along and pretty soon you feel the spring in your step and you think, why not run just a little bit, and then *you've already started* so you might as well *just keep doing it, keep doing it.* And then probably the enjoyment has already taken over, and the sense of life flowing into your extremities and a sense of delight and being alive and the feeling of fullness when you breathe more deeply and more rapidly. And all the while, knowing how good it is for you is secondary now to the enjoyment that has resulted once you *just start doing it, keep doing it.*

It can be the same thing when you decide to floss your teeth. You know you *should do it,* you know *you'll feel good after you do it.* So maybe you *just start doing it,* and you don't really enjoy anything very much yet, you *just move through the motions.* Pretty soon it begins to be a little bit reinforcing and now it starts to feel clean and fresh and symbolically some other things come to mind that might be pleasant to reorganize or disorganize.

And you *don't wait until you feel like enjoying yourself to start enjoying yourself.* You don't have to feel like it first. You just *start doing it and keep doing it.* The *enjoyment will come later,* don't you worry, it'll come. Fact is, if it doesn't come too soon you have time to really feel it coming on and that can be enjoyable too. And *apply that to anything.*

5. **Discipline/enjoyment goal:** *Grow up, leave the fear of a mother's retaliation behind, use what one knows, stop making excuses.*

Metaphor

No one knew about Rick's secret life. No one would have ever guessed that beneath the surface of this mild-mannered, competent, professional man lurked a raging madwoman who constantly disrupted his peace of mind by threatening him with all kinds of mental and physical torture. If anybody had known about it, this is what he would have wanted you to believe.

Of course, she was only his mother, or at least the fearful monster he had imagined his mother to be when he was just a little boy. All he knew growing up was that she needed him and expected him to give her inordinate amounts of attention, to the exclusion of the things a little boy should have been doing. The weight of that expectation was so heavy that even as a grown man, whenever he would consider moving away from her geographically or emotionally, he would imagine that "the mother within," as he referred to her, was threatening to cause a cancerous lump to appear in his brain, or promising to torment him in some other way. He would then quickly abandon his plans.

He had never been disrespectful enough to marry or even to date a woman who liked him very much. He knew that kind of activity wouldn't go over very well with "the mother within."

So when he came to therapy, he wanted us to talk to "her" for him in trance and strike a bargain, argue in his defense, or somehow appease her into submission. He wasn't crazy, but he certainly sounded like it when he talked about the internal "her" as though she were a real entity. We chose to ignore "her" and talk to him for several sessions, but his requests became even more urgent and so finally, we agreed, but not in the way he had expected. I asked him to experiment in the session by holding a heavy weight until he found the most uncomfortable way that he could hold it. Having determined that holding it on his chest was most uncomfortable, I asked him to hold it in precisely that way as he went into trance. He was told that he could focus on the discomfort consciously and know that he could unconsciously remove it when the time was right.

In the trance, I told him the story of another client we had seen, named Gerry. Actually, Stephen had seen Gerry in therapy for years, helping him retrieve and organize a wealth of personal resources, but still Gerry didn't change. He had been depressed ever since his grandmother died when he was a little boy. His mother selfishly overprotected him and his father had harshly criticized his failures. The grandmother had been his only source of true affection and she died. As an adult, he was not acting in a way that was likely to win any affection. He was attractive enough physically, but he was so negative, excessively serious, paranoid, that I didn't like him at all and therefore had been very little involved in his therapy, except to notice that it seemed not to be doing him much good.

Finally, we arranged a context for some intensive therapy, the likes of which he would have never expected. It involved a series of activities like movies, frisbee throwing on the beach, boiled shrimp, kite flying, and other things the serious Gerry had never even considered doing. He reacted with criticism, hives, excuses, apathy, and more depression. At this point, I invited him to explore these learnings in a hypnotic trance. He declined, saying that he was so apathetic, he didn't want to hurt my feelings by not changing. I replied that I, much like his mother had been, would be most comfortable, however, if he did *not* change as a result of our therapy and encouraged him to use this hypnosis as an experiment only. He agreed and we embarked on the journey.

At approximately midpoint of the trance, Stephen came into the room, unannounced, and spoke to Gerry directly: "There are some things that need to be said and you need to hear them. However, you can forget both what was said and what you thought about it consciously. You can fail to remember and remember to forget because only your unconscious need know that *you have more abilities* than you are using. I don't need to tell you that *you have accomplished a great deal* in previous trances and subsequent experiences. I don't need to remind you about your emotional and academic achievements. You already know that, but I do need to tell you that you claim to be a warrior but you're only a coward. Until you're willing to *grow up* and *live the values you preach,* you are no friend of mine and you are not welcome in this house and you are to leave immediately."

Rick sat in his own trance listening to those words that had been spoken to another client and he was still holding that weight on his chest. Then, it was his turn to be spoken to. The moment he had been waiting for finally arrived. We were going to speak to his internal mother for him, but not in the way he expected.

I asked for access to that mother and informed "her" that Stephen and I both had a message, that there were some things that needed to be said to her now. Rick indicated that "she" was available and listening.

Relaying his message, I said to her: "Stephen says that you are not a suitable adversary to be worthy of his time. He says your son is no threat to you. He's just a baby. If he is a threat to you, you're a weakling too. All the two of you have accomplished is a long collusion that has protected that wimp of a man you called a husband from being accountable for his responsibilities. He thinks it is a waste of time to tell you *it's okay* for your son to *grow up and be sexual* with a woman because, both consciously and unconsciously, he selects only those women who hold back.

"But personally," I said, adding my own message to her, "I think there's hope for him. Sure, he's elevated you to this unnatural status, but you don't scare me. I know that you are just a figment of his imagination and he wants to pretend he's afraid you'll die or hurt him so he can avoid growing up. Everybody has their reasons for being afraid and his are almost as good as anyone else's. It takes a lot of courage to *grow up and be responsible for yourself,* especially when he never had a father to show him how.

"If he really had the nerve, he would stand up to you and ask, 'Don't you think you're underrating how bad I really am?' I think he could do all that if he would, but then again, I don't know him as well as Stephen does. But I doubt if you are powerful or smart enough to teach him that he doesn't need you or a therapist either. Maybe you won't even be able to accomplish that with your funeral. But he can stage a funeral for you at any time he wishes, even now, and *say goodbye to that figment of your imagination, say goodbye to her tyranny,* and even say goodbye to your real mother, that poor woman who to the best of her limited ability tried to meet her own needs for an adult intimacy with a little boy's devotion."

And every client eventually has to make the decision to *live the values you believe* or else know that you are not true to those values. And after Stephen delivered that pronouncement to Gerry in person in the heart of his trance, he reminded him again that he was to forget both everything that was said as well as what was thought about what he heard. He then left the room, and after a short pause, I reminded Gerry again that I was most comfortable if he didn't change anything, as per our agreement. This constituted quite a bind for him, but deep in trance, he wasn't going anywhere. Even after the trance, he sat for a long time before emerging from the room as quite an agreeable, interesting, and likeable man. We never discussed that session because everyone can *create a unique solution.*

Rick managed to rid himself of that weight on his chest by allowing a levitated hand to simply push it off to the side and I don't even know if he was consciously aware of doing it. The time was just right and he shed that weight. But there were still some heavy battles ahead. That night, he heard his mother's voice within him, announcing that she had returned to stay. She said she had left briefly, but that because of the awful things he had allowed Stephen and Carol to say to her, she had come back. Finally, he stood up to her and informed her that he could not allow her to stay within him. She threatened that if he tried to kill her, she'd divide in a million pieces and torment him in a million voices. At that, he realized an ancient fear of going crazy and that he had created the mother's voice within to quiet that terror. And, at that moment, the voice disappeared.

A month later, he woke up in the middle of the night, filled with terror, and heard the mother's voice saying that she had never really left. Without panicking, he told himself he would need to *find a better way to deal with fearfulness, find a mature way to have fear,* and the voice disappeared again and has never returned.

6. **Discipline/enjoyment goal:** *Nurture and take care of oneself and enjoy the process.*

Metaphor[34]

Robbie was a grown woman and a professional, though the 11-year-old little girl part of her hadn't accepted that fact. Of course, everyone is able to sometimes feel like the child they once were. But in her case, the doubt and insecurity of that little girl were always in the forefront, obscuring all of her other accomplishments and desires. And she wanted to use hypnosis to stop colitis difficulties. But ever since she decided as an 11-year-old girl that no one was really there for her, she had buried a lot of needs that were nagging away at her insides, yearning for some expression and acknowledgment. And she had had some perfectly good, childish reason for concluding that her parents and no one else would respond appropriately to her needs. Of course, she didn't confide in them what those needs were, but every child knows how to believe that if people really care about you they will know, even without your telling them.

[34] This metaphor first appeared in Lankton and Lankton, 1986, pp. 150–152.

So that pattern had continued well into middle age for this woman and she criticized herself ruthlessly and made sure anyone else's incoming compliments were redirected. Clinging dependently to the hope that therapy could finally take care of that little girl, the well-practiced, self-doubting part managed to make sure even intensive therapy couldn't really touch that little girl.

Robbie thought she needed lots more therapy, but what she really needed to do was *take action. Just get going with living!* I called her before her last appointment and instructed her to wear comfortable clothes, walking shoes, and *be prepared to change.* She agreed and when she arrived, I met her at the door of the office with two 14-pound barbell weights in my hands. I asked her whether she would prefer to carry one or both with her as she walked around the half-mile block outside the office. She was to walk around and around until she could tell me the reason I had sent her to do this assignment.

After only a moment of confusion, she elected to walk with just one weight, and about five minutes later came back to the door and said, "Oh, I know the reason, you wanted me to realize that I carry around a lot of problems, I don't need to carry and weigh myself down that way, I could just stop doing some of those things." And she was really proud of that understanding. But that was not a new learning. We all know that.

There was really more to it than that, and so I suggested that while she was probably glad she had only taken one weight she might glean the real meaning of the task more quickly if she took both next time. And she did, again stopping back in about five minutes with an even "better" understanding. This one, too, was acknowledged as useful and meaningful but finally rejected as still only partial.

At that point, she angrily demanded, "Why do I have to find your answer, anyway?" Which was a very good question and since she couldn't answer it, she had to walk again. But this time she decided one weight would work just as well as two.

For her final and last time she walked around the block, she carried a weightless glass vase filled with delicate sand-dollar shells. When she returned from that time, tears streamed down her face as she recounted how "you trusted me to carry something precious and beautiful, and I lived up to that trust, even though sometimes I wanted to crash it and bust it into a million pieces because I was angry. But I didn't do that. I carried it more carefully than I take care of that part of me that is just as precious and as beautiful."

Probably there was no better moment for additional therapy than at that point but she came into the office, sat down, closed her eyes and rapidly went deeply into a trance, waiting expectantly to now hear what I might have thought to be the "real reason" for the walking and waiting.

But any therapy is just a context in which you have your own learnings. Every child has to learn that something you might not like will be good for you in the long run, and "even though you might not like what I say, you know it's true." So I told her that and a lot of other things she already knew, but it was high time she came to believe them and *act in accordance with what you know.* And your conscious mind can object to a process and invent various excuses that seem, at first glance, to be valid. There was the man who after careful research concluded that there was no such thing as piano playing, I told her. After all, he had tried it himself once and nothing came of it!

But self-discipline doesn't have to be a drudgery. You simply make it so by avoiding and procrastinating and making excuses. So in this trance you can open a line of communication to your parents, not your real parents from so long ago, but a healthy parent ego state that is almost atrophied from lack of trust and development. Now, a transactional analyst would ask for a contract at this point to *take care of and discipline that little girl, firmly and lovingly.* After all, you have everything you need. I wonder how many more excuses you'll make before you *take care of her.* It's long overdue. Maybe you should make a few more excuses first to make sure you exhaust them all.

But I'm only a teacher and a therapist, I'm not a disciplinarian, you'll have to look to yourself for that.

Sometimes it's just a matter of motivation. I told her about a friend of ours who had journeyed to see the great benevolent grandfather archetype, Milton Erickson, sure that he would finally be nurtured in a way he could value. But to his great surprise, he spent three days in the private company of that man who instead told him off in every conceivable way. Erickson had said to him something along the following lines, "You're no man, you're not even man enough to say hello to a pretty girl and smile in a friendly way. You'd never be able to accomplish anything difficult because you don't have enough courage to try the simplest things . . ." and on and on until finally our friend left there, burning with conviction to "prove that old goat wrong, no matter what it takes." And he did, eventually coming to respect and appreciate how it is that sometimes a parent has to love the child enough to let the child temporarily not like you very much.

But you don't really have to make an ordeal out 12of it in order to just take that little girl in your arms and let her know that you love her, you're going to be there for her, you're going to love her enough to insist that she clean up her room and do all of the other things a responsible little girl learns how to do in the process of loving herself. And *you don't need a therapist* to do that for you. She really wants *you. There's no one like you.* Anyone can look for a problem and find it. Enough bad luck can come your way. You need to *use your same energy to add to your good luck.*

She wept as I talked and she hugged herself. And she went back to her own country after the session and for a couple of years continued to write notes to us about her growth, her excitement in living and her marriage. *It is so important to take care of yourself.* No one else can be as appropriately sensitive as *you can be kind to yourself.*

7. **Discipline/enjoyment goal:** *Plan and acknowledge one's own jobs well done.*

Metaphor[35]

Celeste was a new teacher. She had come to work for the school system for the first time this past year. As a new teacher, she had difficulty with some of her planning. Everyone is familiar with how complex the process of planning can be, and especially planning that addresses the varied needs of a group of children. In Celeste's case, she had to plan things for a group of 30 boys and girls, all in the third grade.

This wasn't an easy task and after the first few weeks of school, Celeste began to wonder if things could be improved or if her *planning could be improved.* She thought and thought but didn't know what to do. Finally, she decided to consult about the matter with a more experienced teacher. Tom told her he would *be happy to meet* with her and together they could improve her planning. He told her she needed to learn about the "pies." She was a little perplexed about that as she left, not knowing exactly what Tom was talking about.

They had set up a meeting the next day to learn about "pies." We've all been curious when we hear a word we know but we don't understand. She thought "pies?" Maybe he was going to make a cream pie. There was "pi r squared"—but third-graders were a little young for that. Or

---

[35] This metaphor was contributed by Nicholas G. Seferlis, M.S.

maybe *there was some other special meaning.* As she approached Tom's room she was still wondering. She walked in, sat down in front of his desk, and said, "Okay, Tom, I'm here for help with my lesson planning." Tom said, "All right, 'pies' is a very simple method that will help you with all of your lesson plans.

"First is 'p' for 'planning.' You need to *take responsibility for creating your plans* and what you need to do in front of your children or other people." And one knows how important it is to *plan and head in a direction* so that you can *lead other people.* Tom explained in detail how important it is to *take the responsibility* in planning and *to decide* whether you'll need special materials, special knowledge, whether you need to just be special behaving towards someone or some group.

"And now the second item is 'i' for 'instruction.' That's the inner work that's needed. *Take the responsibility* for what you want *to impart to others,* whether it's a classroom of 30 boys and girls or whether it's just telling the man at the grocery store what you like—wheat bread or rye bread. It's to remind you to *give instructions* which will help *impart that knowledge* for which you also need to take the responsibility. Give to others what you need to have them receive and also give to them what they want to learn. Those are the instructions."

Tom also explained that it was very important, when making "pies," to include an "e" for "entertaining." He said that when you're giving instructions and being with others, entertainment is a very important aspect. And people, no matter what they're learning, do it so much easier when they are entertained. When the instruction comes by, it becomes fun.

Celeste sat there thinking about the meaning of the pies, the "p" for planning and how she would need to take the responsibility of taking her plans and imparting them to students. The "i" for giving instructions, and the inner work she needs to develop about what she wants others to learn. The "e" meant entertaining and how people tend to *learn and have fun while learning.* As she sat there thinking, she was sure she had heard Tom say "pieS"—what was the "s"?

Tom paused a long time while Celeste was wondering about that. Then he said that the "s" is one of the most important, it's that special thing which is *being kind to yourself.* Because no matter how much planning, how much instruction, how entertaining you are, more than anything else you need to *be kind to yourself.* Let yourself know when *you've done a good job.* It's important to be kind to yourself especially when the job wasn't that good and also when the job you've done is fantastic.

From that night Celeste's teaching and all of her planning was as easy as pie . . . er, pies.

8. Discipline goal: *Do one's homework, preparation, practice, and make good use of one's opportunities.*

Metaphor

I had a good deal of trouble going to my first karate lesson. I didn't want to go to the classes because I traveled so much. I concluded that I had to have individual lessons. In either situation it was going to focus on how much I didn't know about karate and in individual lessons all the much more so. I would be the only person. All eyes would be on me and how much I didn't know.

But the only way *you can learn something you don't know* is to start at the beginning and learn to be an expert at being awkward and you become a good learner at that point. And my first day of class I told the instructor, "I'm going to ask you to take me on as a private student and I'm going to be the fastest learner you've ever seen and I don't intend to hang around in any slow-moving classes. So how about you take me on and we'll be pleased with the work we create together. If that is not acceptable, let's just forget it." He agreed to take me on as a private student because he said he liked my attitude.

And then I showed up the first day and did what I was told. I followed the prescribed rituals: took my shoes off, bowed before entering the mat, and so on. Then as I began to cross the mat towards the private instruction room of the dojo I heard Master Sell. I discerned that he had a private student at that time to whom he was speaking.

As I stood at the edge of the doorway I began to hear his words clearly. And, as I did, I peered in the door and saw what was going on. I watched and listened as "Master" Sell stood facing his earlier student two inches away from his face. Master Sell had been the martial arts trainer for the military police for the U.S. Marine Corps. He had a very military way. He was talking way too loud and cussing him out like crazy. I can still remember hearing.

"You want to be my student, young man?"

"Yes, sir," the student said.

"What did you say?"

"Yes, sir."

"I still didn't hear you."

"Yes, sir."

"You didn't do your homework practice did you?"

"No, sir."

"I still didn't hear you."

"No! Sir."

"Then you'll have to practice! You will have to study! You will have to apply yourself! Is that clear, young man?"

"Yes, sir," the student said.

"What did you say?"

"Yes, sir!"

"I still didn't hear you."

"Yes! Sir!" the student shouted, still two inches from Master Sell's face. "And if you ever fail to do your homework again, even once, you are through here! Is that perfectly clear, mister?"

And it went that same way three more times. Then that student walked off the mat and it was my turn for my lesson.

It didn't take me long to realize that every time I sparred with Master Sell I was going to get the wind knocked out of me. In this kind of karate, Chong do Kwan, Tae Kwon Do, they hit you. It is a contact karate.

And there I would stand against the wall week after week with the air knocked out of me. Master Sell, the instructor, would say, "You're open after your high block. Here, let me show you. I will show you on the third transaction. Ready, one, two, three—and there I would be, up against the wall with the air knocked out of me. And I still didn't learn how I had let myself be open, just that I had. Worse still was that although I knew the dangers of leaving myself open I had not learned how not to do so.

I remember one of those first few such incidents. I was so mad at him. Why didn't he just tell me how I was open instead of knocking the air out of me? I thought, "That s.o.b. just wants to hurt me, he wants to hurt people. That's why he was in the Marines, that's why he was with the military police, that's why he teaches karate. He's a sadistic s.o.b. who wants to hurt people, probably enjoys it, the rotten fascist. I'm going to quit. Why should I come here so he can beat me up?"

And I thought about it a little more. I was embarrassed I didn't know how to spar better, I wasn't living up to my brag about being the best student. He must have thought I was crummy and he was going to beat me up every chance he got just to prove he was better than me.

And then it dawned on me. I thought, "No, that couldn't have been right. He didn't change his opinion of me just because he beat me up. As far as karate goes, he didn't have a very good opinion of others anyway. He didn't have a good opinion of hardly anybody when it came to karate. He was the highest ranked, nonoriental karate practitioner in the world. He thought everybody was inferior to him in the art of karate. He thought I was inferior before he beat me. He thought I was inferior after he beat me. Then he went on to his next student. He didn't think any different of me either way, although he did give me an opportunity to improve each time. And as soon as I realized he didn't feel any different either way, I wasn't angry at him anymore. I didn't have anything to lose. I had *an opportunity to learn.*

9. Discipline goal: *One should express sadness in tears, not in physical symptoms.*

Metaphor[36]

It's certainly true that there is a lot of sadness in the world. Children cry for dogs that have died, personal setbacks, for dreams that they won't be able to accomplish, losing sight, losing a friend, never having a child, losing innocence—there are so many more situations.

A woman who had gone to an allergist for twelve years told me that she had tried everything, and nothing worked, she was down to bread and water, it was about the only thing that she could eat without having allergic reactions. I asked her to tell me the rest of her story and it turned out that she had gotten divorced 12 years earlier. She didn't even make any conscious connection between the two events.

Her husband was a gourmet cook—it's hard to swallow, isn't it? When I finally was able to help her to cry about it, she thought this therapy was really amazing because her allergies went away. Teaching her how to substitute her emotional system for her allergic system took a bit longer. But it was very simple actually.

You can map your troubles in your allergic system, but it is a *better idea* to give them over to your *tear* system, that system has a better way of regulating and gets it over with. Some people have trouble with their parents being too aggressive and they fail to learn to use their

---

[36] This story was told as part of multiple embedded metaphor to the woman taking steroids for bladder control problems. The organizing metaphor from which this was a tangent appears in Chapter 4, the fourth story regarding boundary building (pp. 159–160).

aggression. When you overstimulate parts of their body, make cholinergic fluids going to the stomach, lungs, colon, liver, it's no wonder that organ failure happens. Other people are shamed into always being strong as children or have weak parents that they have to *take care of for fear* that they will be overcome and they never *recognize that ability that we all have to be soft and tender* and evoke nurturing. And, instead, those tense up their muscle system, stand erect, they move fast and pump adrenalin into their musculature, cardiovascular system, their skin-nervous system. Over the years a chemical imbalance eventually finds something that will go wrong, and they are the people we find with heart attacks, plus a sense of bursitis, eczema, and the heartbreak of psoriasis.

I think that you ought to use your unconscious ability to *transform old and unnecessary ways of adjusting yourself* with your environment of the past. *You seem to cry nicely, and I think you ought to consider using your tears.* You can wonder which eye will cry first. It's no fun to cry alone. Kittens are very good, I wouldn't recommend goldfish. You really ought to *learn to make contact through your emotions to responsive mammals,* like a child learning to do it with kittens and puppies. You will have the foundation that you need to *do it with human beings.* I don't know whether you are amused to know which eye was going to tear first.

9

Other Therapeutic Procedures Using Metaphor

*I've never met a person, I don't care what his
condition, in whom I could not see possibilities.
I don't care how much a man may consider
himself a failure, I believe in him, for he
can change the thing that is wrong in his life
any time he is ready and prepared to do
it. Whenever he develops the desire, he
can take away from his life the thing that
is defeating it. The capacity for
reformation and change lies within.*
—*Preston Bradley*

*Everyone is like a moon, and has a dark side
which he never shows to anybody.*
—*Mark Twain*

The metaphors in this chapter do not follow a single specific protocol.
Rather, they each provide a metaphoric context which serves as a
frame for a series of directives for a chosen therapeutic procedure.
These procedures do, however, have specifically defined protocols. This
chapter will focus on examples of several different procedures that we

have found necessary and useful to replicate in the course of therapy with many clients. We will discuss and illustrate, in order: dissociative review, scramble, life maze, redecision, and reliving and reassessing.

Each of these methods and the rationales for using them are discussed in a previous work (Lankton & Lankton, 1983, pp. 320–344). Our purpose here is to illustrate by example a brief orientation, and the rationale will be provided for convenience. Following the discussions, metaphoric examples will be given. Metaphoric frameworks, such as these, again allow therapeutic processes to be delivered as a series of indirect suggestions that are introduced tangentially to the storyline. Actually, the storyline itself, in each instance, is of little importance other than as a context from which to take such tangents, which can provide controlled elaboration of the therapeutic ambiguity. And, of course, the aim of that elaboration is to help clients build experiences needed to release them from extremely limiting, repetitious behaviors and experiences.

Please note that each of the procedures could be directed without a metaphoric frame, but in so doing, would become potentially less respectful of the client's option to respond in any way relevant to him or her. Behind the sequence of imagery used in the storyline, the patterns of elicited experience, or protocols, guide the therapeutic change. Therefore, metaphors can very easily be created using experiences of previous clients who have completed the procedure in their therapy. Each of these is discussed next.

The patterns that fall under the category of *dissociative review* often stem from the need to help clients resolve a long-standing incongruity rooted in a historic conflict between parts of the younger "self" and the usual or desired "persona." In the dissociative review, several other therapeutic opportunities are taken. The common ones are described below.

We often ask clients to establish a channel of communication or engage in a dialogue with the child of the past and to use that channel to convey important information and necessary experiential links to the adult client. Closely allied with this is an often essential goal for developing, encouraging, energizing, accessing, instructing, or in other ways connecting with that part of the person that can nurture the client in ways the parents never did or never will. Yet another therapeutic aspect is what we call "trading resources." In this instance, the viewing adult and the observed child both identify aspects of their functioning needed by the other. Often this is aided with suggestions from the therapist. Then, a trading is symbolically accomplished and an experiential signal is established for future times when the resources will be needed. The exchange can be rehearsed in the trance before the conclusion of the session. One value in this procedure, beyond that of the actual increase of available resources accomplished by the trade, is the acceptance it establishes for the younger, often discarded, self.

Another goal that can be accomplished within the dissociative review involves "saying goodbye" to parents. This is facilitated by the use of interspersed and embedded suggestions to consider the "saying goodbye" as well as the educational aspect of informing the client, with punchlines or other interventions, about the importance and logic of separating from parents. This helps create a disidentification with parents or a distancing for a formerly enmeshed client.

The introduction of such communications as "saying goodbye" to parents will often elicit grief. The therapeutic emphasis is not for eliciting grief, however; grief is best elicited as an emotion with an affect metaphor. The emphasis of this procedure is on the declaration of independence and the admission of personal responsibility for one's life which accompanies such a separation. Often the procedure will put clients in touch with some sadness (it has, after all, a relationship which changes—and that is the basis of the affect protocol). But this sadness is secondary to the accompanying cognitive counterpart. The content of that cognitive counterpart can be directed by the therapist as appropriate to the learning needs of the client.

In the central metaphor from the first chapter, which uses as the protagonist the former client named Jerry, a dissociation is developed for the client who is at first asked metaphorically, and later asked explicitly, to review her own life situation at age 10. Another metaphor, taken from its embedded context, is used as further illustration in this chapter. What is especially useful is the differences and similarities of the therapeutic additions to the basic structure of the dissociative review.

Scramble is a term that refers to a process of symptom scaling discussed in detail elsewhere (Lankton, 1987, pp. 56–68). It is a process of randomly confusing the customary sequence with which symptoms occur. As such, it disrupts the client's ability to have the problematic symptom in the same way and helps him instead associate to a pleasurable alternative resource. The process involves suggestions to divide the experience of the symptom into five distinct phases and to then review those five phases in many different random sequences. The confusion is finally resolved with a suggestion to forget the difficulty sorting out the best sequence from the many and simply have the alternative resource which has been previously developed. We have used the "scramble" successfully with various anxiety-based symptoms, which was the basis for the example presented here on page 326.

Life maze is a specific elaboration on simple dissociative review and a personalized variation of the attitude protocol. In this procedure, there are four steps described which represent four distinct ways in which a person can sort and retrieve memories from the past. These ways are, most often, to sort for how unpleasant it could have been, how it really was in the client's memory, how good it could have been, and the past from the perspective of the future accomplishments. This juxtapositioning will, of course, have several effects on clients. The most outstanding effect comes from the implication that the "bad" history a client has used as a basis of rationalization and complaint is not as bad as it could have been (the real is not as bad as the worst possible). Furthermore, feelings aroused from the imagined "best" sorting are available to clients and, what is more, the importance of using oneself in the future (regardless of the past) is an unavoidable conclusion that will be drawn.

We often represent these different manners of sorting, framing, and remembering the past metaphorically by introducing a tangible device such as being faced with four doors or corridors through which the client is directed to walk.

The story describes the passage of another client through the doors and the degree of experiencing found behind each, one at a time, for an unspecified period of time. These experiences and understandings are, of course, tangentially suggested to the listening client. The doors are labeled "ideal past," "real past," "past much worse than ever imagined," and "future." So, in the past described as "real," there is an opportunity to review matters in a somewhat dissociated condition. Then, in comparing that past with the worst past, there is an opportunity for an attitude challenge about just how bad the real past was after all. The ideal past creates a context for imagining and learning something about how wonderful it would have been, and can now be to the extent they "relive" it, if everything and everybody had been all that was wished for.

In the "maze" section of the procedure, all the pasts are mixed together randomly to confuse which past, in fact, happened, and to create new associations. So with one step the person might find himself in the real past, the next two steps in the ideal past, then in the worst past, back again in the ideal past, and so on. Finally, of course, in the future door, it doesn't matter which past occurred—the future is up to you regardless of which past is real. Again, transforming this therapeutic procedure into an indirect metaphor simply requires describing a previous client who had this experience in a session, in a trance, or perhaps as the client was dreaming it after the session. Two such metaphoric versions are presented in this chapter.

The hypnotic work we refer to as *redecision* comes from our application of the important therapy model presented by Mary and Robert Goulding (Goulding & Goulding, 1979). More information about the rationale and process of redecision can be found in their work. We prefer to offer the redecision model as a metaphor, at least initially, and to do so within an embedded sequence of other metaphors which have assisted the subject in the retrieval of supporting attitude, emotion, and behavior resources. It is important to stress for this, and for all other metaphors in this chapter, that although these stories provide a metaphoric frame, a high level of intimacy and rapport with clients occurs during the therapeutic interventions. And, although the example contained here reads easily, it was delivered with an ambience of sensitivity and emotional gravity.

The final process in this chapter is related to dissociative review but is, essentially, the opposite. We call this *reliving and reassessing.* At a superficial reading of it, the stories may seem similar to discipline and enjoyment metaphors. However, once again, the gravity of the interaction with clients is tantamount to successful work. We do not travel down the paths of these metaphors unless feedback and rapport with clients indicate that they are going along with us. What is offered to clients in the reliving and reassessing process is, therefore, beyond the introduction of cognitively dissonant ideas (as is the case in discipline and enjoyment protocols). Here is a way to provide ideas that are extremely touching and, while they may be dystonic to previously defined personas, the client, due to a reliving, is bound to find the "on target" notions, attitudes, and ideas urgently relevant. Two somewhat similar examples are included. They involve the protagonists saying goodbye to and letting go of inadequate parents and the expectations they held about the parent being perfect. In that way permission was gained to have natural feelings or to take charge differently.

1. Therapeutic goal (using dissociative review): Say goodbye to parents, dissociate from childhood disappointments, and begin developing a self-nurturing "part."

Metaphor

When Bill came to therapy he wanted to use hypnosis to make hypertension go away. You can imagine the sense of urgency with which he approached the session, given the fact that his father had died of a heart attack only two weeks prior to the session. And he wanted to get rid of *his* hypertension.

He measured it daily on the biofeedback machines. He knew it was in an alarmingly high range. And he didn't want to be like that father. He had a great sense of fear that, in fact, he was genetically and socially predisposed to be like that father.

I asked him to be willing to make friends, from a distance, with a variety of fears that he might have related to that hypertension, in order for therapy to be successful. He agreed. And so the very first thing that I asked him to do was dissociate. He had done this before and so speaking about how you do not feel your body and emotional experience was nearly enough to create the experience, just listening to me. Perhaps you can use that feeling of dissociation you have just developed and sit there comfortably not noticing what your current experiences are.

I mentioned how that arm is not feeling natural, that hand feels altered, in fact that whole body, from the neck down, is just holding up the head. That is all it does. And I gave him time to develop that experience; as long as it takes. You know you can intensify an experience as talking continues because your unconscious deals with that while your conscious mind listens.

And I asked him to imagine and just see himself at the foot of his father's grave. Seeing images before you is easy. Every child has done that and every adult has done it for years. And I asked him to see, really see, and only see that young adult who he was. See all the actions of his body. See all the feelings he has out there in the picture. See and hear how he talks as the scene unfolds and do nothing more than that.

I asked him to see the young man he was visit again that father's grave site. Watch him saying goodbye, really saying goodbye to that father. And even when a parent is alive, it's possible in a trance to say your goodbyes as an adult and say your goodbyes for the child you once were. He had been to the funeral and it hadn't been that long ago and I'm sure that he had shed a tear or lots of tears. But I wasn't sure that he had really said goodbye to the father in a way that you need to say goodbye to that parent, especially in his case. So I asked him to watch himself visit that grave site in his mind's eye, in a fantasy, in that trance, and really watch himself say goodbye to that parent in a way that will allow an understanding with all of the pain of those hopes and dreams that aren't going to come true from that parent ever again.

And see himself say goodbye to the father's struggles. Say goodbye to the love that the father gave to you with the very best of his abilities. And, of course, it's necessary to say goodbye to the disappointment and to the dreams that the little child had and maybe kept secret and held on to. And he held on to them oftentimes at a level outside of consciousness. And say goodbye and watch the child say goodbye, to the dreams that child held on to of things that he hoped would be said or done by that father. Say goodbye to the chance of those dreams ever coming true with that father in this life or the next.

And tears were streaming over his face, even as he went into the trance. And they only intensified, the more he was able to say goodbye. The more you love a parent or have loved a parent, the more carefully you need to say goodbye. And then, too, the more disappointed you were or the more failed a part of you has been, again, the more carefully a goodbye needs to be said. And you say goodbye to the love that a parent gave and the lessons that he or she did manage to teach you. There are so many negatives sometimes. You see yourself say goodbye to the parents' pain and their inability to do any more than they did.

And that doesn't mean that you say goodbye to the hopes and the dreams the child was able to dream because, after you're able to really say a goodbye to the expectation that that parent is going to change or make you change or teach you something that you needed to learn, then the more rapidly you go about the process of teaching that child that the dreams can come true. And yet, they come true far differently from the way that you ever expected.

He said goodbye for a long time and he saw that his tears followed each other out of his eyes and down his cheeks and onto his shirt and into his chest, as it were. And you watch as the you, out there, just says goodbye to the bitterness, goodbye to the little child's disappointment, in spite of the pain he saw he'd suffered waiting for that father to teach him the things that a father should teach a child. There are things that every parent should teach their child.

You might wonder what was going on in his visual mind while he was doing that. You just see yourself as a small child knowing that you have a set of emotional responses that you were unable to really be comfortable with back in those days. You keep them with you always and you don't really know about how you are going to go into the future and use them in different ways in your life. You just see yourself standing there in front of the parent with those experiences.

And it takes very little to hurt a child's feelings or make a child have a nagging little self-doubt or make a decision not to express some part of him- or herself for fear that part isn't all right. It takes precious little to do that. Maybe you are able to picture the child that you once were as an indicator of what you needed from that parent. In a trance you can see yourself choose the things that you can say and will say and should have said then. And say them as if that then is now because occasionally a then becomes a now. Sometimes a now is even something that is going to be again. And a then is a now. And when it is, it will be a then. Time doesn't make much difference to the unconscious.

So with all of those feelings that you know you would have if you were having feelings now, fear and anger and sadness combined, your conscious mind needs to know that those are your feelings by virtue of being alive. You didn't know that having said goodbye to the hopes and dreams that weren't coming true from that parent allowed you to have an entirely new perspective on those hopes. And Crosby, Stills, and Nash sang those words, "Don't let the past remind us of what we are not now."

So he just saw himself saying over and over, "I'm not like you. I'm going to learn things that I'll teach my children, things that you were never able to teach me and you won't ever be able to now." But you don't have to say it with a triple negative. It would have been okay for those singers to say, "Let the present remind us that we are not like we were in the past."

And the image that he saw and the father that he was saying goodbye to began to change and he watched himself gazing into an image of a parent who he really could depend on. It's no coincidence that parent looked a great deal like himself. Maybe it was an omen or a mature version of himself that he watched becoming a parent to that little boy he had been, the little boy who needed to learn so many things that the father wasn't able to teach. And it's amazing to realize, for the adult to realize, that it's never too late to embrace that child again and the hopes that child had. And let him know that he has absolutely everything he needs and that he can do anything he sets his mind to, and that he is totally worthwhile, that he has a right to be here, that you love him and that you're going to surround him with people that he can trust, that you trust. And let him climb up into your lap and feel the warmth of your acceptance surrounding him.

You can feel him crying as a feeling of acceptance long overdue just soaks in and, no doubt, spreads or radiates a feeling of enjoyment through all of his body. And I don't need to tell you how much a child can enjoy a feeling like that. A child really can thrive on that. Just use the trance as a vehicle to let the unconscious experience what it would be like to have that love expressed from the parent, just one time. First, watch it envelop the you whom you see, and then let it envelop you and enclose around the you whom you see like a warm blanket that a parent wraps around a baby.

And while you're thinking of what it would be like for the child to be able to crawl into such a nurturing, understanding lap, you could begin to think about the "lap of luxury" in a whole different way. And you can really see it. So many men are afraid to show their children how to be tender and touch, reach out, and let someone cry.

And you [*to wife*] don't have an opportunity to realize how fully your husband is sitting in the room while you are crying, being tender and soft. He chose to come, he wants to be near you. And you don't have to do anything more than what is happening right now. Just be quiet and feel the giving of love, feel the respect for each other, for the little girl inside. It is a simple and yet powerful learning that you have, as a part of you is able to put your head against that chest you can depend on. And you can hear those words the parent is saying.

Observe how exactly you go about nurturing somebody and how you feel when someone says, "That's all right, sweetheart, you just go right ahead and cry." And how you put your arm around someone and just let it rest without squeezing too quickly or too hard. There's just the simple act of saying, "I love you so much, just the way you are." And there are those times where you just pat the head with the side of your hand and crush the hair lightly, run your fingers down the cheek.

And so I imagine in most of the trance, that man sat, dissociated, holding a little boy he had been and becoming the father to that boy now that the flesh-and-blood father was officially declared exempt from the expectation of doing anything more. I guess he did what a friend of mine did, who, at three years old recognized that her mother really wasn't going to be there for her in the way that she deserved. And even as a little girl, she knew full well that the kind of appreciation and enjoyment of herself that she wanted and needed and deserved was not going to occur in that family, at least not by that mother. And so she simply packed up her doll buggy with her dolls, a couple of changes of clothing for both of them, enough food to get by, or to get around the block at any rate, a few other favorite possessions, and then she simply strolled off. She would strike out on her own, she decided. She would find the love she deserved elsewhere. And a child doesn't wait until they know how they are going to accomplish the goal. A child is just able to act on the conviction, in the understanding that is perhaps innate, that you are worthwhile. Of course, she was apprehended shortly and forced to remain in that home for probably 15 more years. And yet there was an insulation or a barrier that she built around that part of herself, a barrier that she was able to remove in good time when she knew that she was around trustworthy people. And she didn't let any of the neurotic or psychotic difficulties that troubled her mother damage in any way that precious core of under-standing that she was lovable and absolutely worthwhile and that she belonged.

And I don't know if that man consciously realized the same thing or not as he sat in that trance having said goodbye to his father for the second time in two weeks. But he did report that his blood pressure returned almost immediately to the normal range and remained there despite the customary pressures of life that he had previously been registering in that idiosyncratic way.

2. **Therapeutic goal (using "scramble"):** *Disrupt the occurrence of anxiety-based headache symptoms.*

Metaphor

Somewhere behind the tightly wrapped white turban and the dark, bushy beard was an interesting personality with an unusual name that you would have probably never heard before, at least not in modern America where the young man sought therapy for a lifelong asthma. He has since changed his whole life-style as well as his name. He isn't "Peshma" any longer. But you might be interested in how rapidly a person changes after a trance—or maybe the change is really during the trance and right away. And you would be interested in thinking about exactly how to do this very thing.

The beginning of an experience of a symptom is a very lucky thing to find, though you may not have thought about it in this way. The very first beginning of a symptom we can call "step one." And that might make a person wonder what's coming next, so I took great care to make it possible to have extreme dissociation and asked Peshma to dissociate from his asthma and by doing that, he wouldn't have a full-blown attack in the middle of the therapy session and he wouldn't require any hospitalization.

And to dissociate from your symptom, you can either sit there thinking about the comfort of the trance and continue to learn about the change, or you can continue to learn about the comfort and just sit there thinking about the change. And there is always that possibility that the person learning about the symptom will just dissociate. It's unlikely that you will learn anything about sitting there while you are dissociating.

And I asked Peshma to dissociate from the neck down and I mentioned that we could go to a party together, Peshma and I, as an oxymoron. Of course, he didn't know what I meant. I told him an oxymoron was a logical contradiction in terms. I didn't know that I should make the obvious jump about how he was dressed totally different because of his life-style. Maybe he thought that's what I meant.

You know that the symptom has a part that represents the very beginning and you may have images related to the beginning, the very first part. And just when I can see that your unconscious has retrieved that very first recognition of the symptom coming—we'll call that step one—even though your conscious mind may not have exactly recognized it before.

Then, imagine or find some small indicator of a full-blown part of your symptom that will represent step five as you imagine it.

You can either imagine it, have a dissociation while you recognize it, or have a small indicator that is sufficient to illustrate for you the full-blown aspects. And when you have that—call it step five.

Now somewhere between that very beginning recognition of your symptom and step five, there is a midpoint or something that you can imagine to be the midpoint. I had Peshma give me an indication with a head nod, a finger movement, or a twitch when he had found that midpoint. And I soon got an indicator from him—step three was the label for that midpoint.

To be able to label or organize a symptom carefully and systemically gives you a sense of control, a sense of really taking time to understand something about that symptom that has been around for so long. Now somewhere between the midpoint at step three and the beginning of the symptom at step one is another midpoint we can refer to as step two. It's just like you have a hand down to your side in step one and a hand all the way up in the air in step five and a hand half in the air in step three. And you might have thought you knew all about your symptom, but I wonder if you have ever really thought before of what exactly that symptom represents.

Now when you find the halfway point between step one and step three, your unconscious may surprise you by giving a signal even before you fully recognize just what sensations are involved there—step two is what you can call it.

And that would be like an arm not halfway in the air, not all of the way down, just somewhere jerking in between. And then go back to step three and, with an awareness of step three, find a midpoint between that and the symbolic way of representing the full-blown appearance of the symptom that we have labeled step five. And when the signal comes . . . there—call that step four. Because when you are going to give up a symptom you really owe it to yourself to understand every aspect of how it operates.

So [*the therapist proceeds slowly*] go to step one and step two and check that you know where step three is. Check that you know where step four is and how you can find your way to step five. It's an interesting thing that you can do that, all the while bolstered and protected by the comfort in trance and the other learning and under-standings that might be part of the process.

We ask everybody to go through each step at least once. Peshma was a yoga student. I understood that a yoga student knows that you take a different posture and find comfort in that posture. That is one of the learnings in hatha yoga, to be comfortable in the different posture. Likewise, a similar learning is possible with each different order in which you can put your symptom together. So go to step one first but this time go to step four without passing through two or three and then drop to step two and then raise up to step five before dropping back to step three.

Your conscious mind may be far more capable of following such convoluted directions and you let your unconscious give the signal as you rapidly pass through those stages, perhaps at a speed that is far more rapid then your conscious mind can accurately assess. That's right.

And if you think that you move ahead through each part of the symptom, you're going to move ahead differently. Go from step five to step two and then to step three and now to step one without passing through two up to step four and leave it there.

You might have heard how you can win a race by a neck, you could win a race by a count, you win a race by a hair. Go from step three to step one without passing through two. Go directly to five without passing through four, three, or two. Then trot down to step four and culminate by being in step two. You can win a race by a whisper, or a kiss, or a chuckle. Now try it again. This time think of the symptom's symbolic representation you have for the full-blown appearance of your headache and in the following order find out if your unconscious can find something enjoyable there.

That way you can find you can have enjoyment going through the stages of having your headache. It's fine for you to have the enjoyment. It is a shame to have to waste a perfectly good headache at the time that you are really experiencing enjoyment. But a headache could be used for other wonderful things and the enjoyment could be used all by itself.

So move from step five to step one without passing through any of the others. Go to step four without two or three, to three and end up with step two. It seems there are a number of ways that you can get that enjoyment.

Now, Peshma really needed to use his asthma for something. His mother expected him to have it. I suggested that he gradually get rid of it until he totally changed his life-style and I finally decided that I had the courage to tell him the reason we could go to the party as an oxymoron is that I could go as the horse's head. We could dress up together and be a horse.

I was very glad that he laughed at that and I didn't think that he realized then about what that meant about changing his life-style. It was very symbolic and my only, yet powerful, reference to it, but now he has given up his turban and all the practices that went with it and also his unusual name. He has resumed his original name, has become Jeff again. And he lives with his own family in more private and intimate ways.

Every time that you start to decide to move ahead through your symptoms, you might just as well have the humor you're having instead. And it doesn't have to be as confusing as which number you go to next. You could let humor etch another smile line too, or maybe just etch deeper the one that is already lying there so familiar, so comfortable around your eyes. And I doubt that your husband is paying very much attention. You'll probably have to summarize later for him. I hope he is a little bit confused about how you are going to be confused about having a headache so that you can ask for his clarification—since he is also confused but the two of you are both confused about it. Both of you might as well forget about it and have enjoyment. And it is nice to laugh uncontrollably with your spouse about something that you don't understand. If you understand it, it's not nearly as funny and you can laugh at the fact that you are laughing and have nothing to laugh about until you cry. It's a really nice release of a little intimate love to laugh out of control for a few minutes. This is laughing as you go!

3. **Therapeutic goal (using life mazes):** *Relinquish an orientation about how events and people in the past were unfair.*

Metaphor

Margaret is a client I saw who didn't want to be a social worker, but she didn't know what it would take to stand up and change. She hated listening to everyone's problems because she had all kinds of problems of her own. And I was planning on asking her to go forward into the past and to go backwards into the future. So you have to use trance if you're going to do something as bizarre as that.

She had established a pretty nice trance and I asked her to realize how every child learns to count to four, sooner or later. Every culture has words for one, two, three, and four. Some cultures don't have words for gigabyte, and googaplex, and other complex concepts, but they all have them for one, two, three, and four. I knew she understood the concept so it wasn't going to be difficult to ask her to do something that involved going backwards into the future and this was long before the movie with a similar name!

And that feeling of dissociation in your hand . . . I hope that it has moved up into your shoulder and gradually moves to any other spot or tension that you feel.

Margaret was capable of counting to four, so she was capable of understanding that, using her imagination, there could be four doors in front of her. And I asked her to see three doors, one with a triangle, one with a square, and one with a circle. I told her she probably wasn't going to like it very much—what she was about to have to do.

One door represented the best possible past that she could ever have. I told her that wasn't the part she wasn't going to like. One door is marked the worst possible past that you could ever have. The third door is marked a real past, and I bet you'd like to take your pick about which door that you'd like to go through first. I suggested that first you go through the door straight on to face your past head first, and go through the real possible past. But some people like to eat their dessert first, other people mature a little bit and like to save their dessert for last. Some people like to get their homework before they play, other people think that they ought to have a break first. Some people like to do the big jobs before they tackle the little ones, the little ones will be a cinch once they do the big ones.

And since she was a social worker I figured she would like to go to the worst possible past first, and face that head on, one step at a time.

Sort of like stepping stones I suspect. As she opened the door she could walk very slowly onto each passing stone and go one year at a time into a past that was the worst possible past that she could imagine, far worse than it had ever been. She could afford to suffer just a little in order to have a learning in trance, especially if it meant that it would help with her career decision.

And she could go backwards into the future but she didn't know what I had meant. And since it was before the movie she didn't even have an inclination of an idea. And I asked her to take another step and pick up another idea of how it would have felt in the worst possible past, and then another step. I didn't want to have her tell me about the things she was imagining that could have happened because I knew she had an active imagination that could have been imagining terrible things. But while your conscious mind can entertain terrible things, your unconscious can't deny certain learnings that stay with you.

Maybe it is just that sense of dissociation, maybe it is something that you memorized early. And then another step forward into the past, and another step forward into the past, perhaps more ugly sights and sounds, more unpleasantness, more bad feelings. I didn't know how bad her mind really was and how much time she needed. Times were different then—she wouldn't think about being hijacked.

And finally, when she was down to seven years, six years, five years, four years, three years, I didn't expect her conscious mind to comprehend very much more about the worst possible past. But I didn't think that she was having very much fun, so I asked her to go backwards, out that door, turn around and go forward out that door as fast as she could.

And leaving the worst possible past behind, go in any of the other doors that she would like to choose, but whatever she did, not go into door four yet.

Then she had picked the door with the triangle, now pick the door with the circle. And she walked into that door not knowing at first whether it would be the best or the real, pleasantly surprised to find out that that was the best possible past. Probably each step that she took back into that past was filled with ice cream and party balloons, people happily calling her name, singing as they run through the grass. She probably had a dog named Lassie in the best possible past, and a real friend named Annette Funicello.

I don't know what a child fantasizes for the best possible past. Maybe she rode highway 66. Maybe she went to San Francisco with a flower in her hair. Maybe she played a piano and was a concert pianist. Her parents were just wonderful living in a big luxurious house. Take another step back. But I told her she was entitled to memorize every wonderful, single feeling, and smell, and sight, and hold on to those things, don't let them slip away. They ought to be uplifting, and if your mind can understand it, then your mind deserves to feel it.

Then I asked her to take another step forward into the past, and she stepped one more step and she came to maybe a birthday part, whatever you want, with no competition, only gleefulness. One thing that is nice about the past is as you get younger you can't decide which one would be the best and you have to have several and that is okay too. That is part of the best possible past for some people.

And that one day your bed is made out of lilacs in the woods and the next day, it's a feather bed, big posts all around it. And the next day it's sleeping in the comfort of Mommy's and Daddy's arms.

Then I asked her to walk backwards and towards the corridor, in front of the door with the circle on it, out of the best possible paths.

There were still two other doors and she couldn't go into the fourth door, so she'd have to go back into the path of the real past now. Facing it head on, one step at a time, and she could take with her the worst feelings she had. And she could take with her the best feelings that she had. It really was totally up to her, but I had a little alteration in mind.

When she took one step into the real past, the next step would take her into the best possible past [*slowly*], and the next step would take her into the worst possible past, and the next step would take her into the best possible past and those feelings. The next step would take her into the worst possible past, and those feelings. And the next step into the real past, which is a relief, and the next step into the best possible past.

It was very draining, and Margaret's trance lasted for a couple of hours as I marched her from the best to the worst, to the real, to the worst, to the best. And all along, your conscious mind is learning, your unconscious is learning, and maybe they're learning the same things. But your conscious mind couldn't help but fail to learn something very valuable and very good that your unconscious knows.

So I eventually asked her to back out of the doors back into the hallway and close those doors. And then I wanted her to open the fourth door that she couldn't look in before. That was the one with the star on it, I said. We had been forgetting about that one, that was the door to the future. But I don't want you to go *forward* into the future, I want you to *back* into the future, walking backwards, looking at what you're going to accomplish for yourself, whether or not you like what you accomplish with one step can determine how you modify your behavior when you take your next step, until you leave a trail of happiness.

And finally, finally, she said, "I think that I am beginning to learn something about walking backwards into the future—seeing the results of my actions." I cautioned her not to conclude anything yet. Take another step *back* into the future, and find out how you like what you accomplish for yourself with that step, things that you don't even realize that are going to happen yet, false starts, successes, plans, surprises.

She said, "I think that I am beginning to learn that it doesn't matter." But I didn't want her to do any thinking about this, just take another step back into the future, and get a sense of whether you like the way it feels. She said, "Well, I do like the way it feels. I am beginning to realize that it doesn't matter whether or not my. . . ." And I said not to think about it anymore, just take another step into the future, find out whether you like the way that feels.

She said she was unable to see clearly all of the things which she was having a sense about. And she was finding out that it didn't matter whether or not she had. I cautioned her again not to conclude about that, just take another step backwards into the future, until you go several places in the future, several years into the future, several scenes into the future, knowing that as you evaluate the results of each step, you have the capability of modifying little things before you step again.

She said, "Yes, I understand that, because I found out. . . ." And I never would let her tell me what she had found out. It seemed too obvious and Margaret changed her entire career over the period of the next few months. She is no longer a social worker. That was the only trance we had and she was very much pleased not to be a social worker now. She and her husband are getting along much better.

4. Therapeutic goal (using life-maze examination with an embedded attitude protocol): The only way to get a fuller life is to live a full life.

Metaphor

Shara didn't really want to see the midnight showing of *Harold and Maude* that night because she had to work very early the next morning. But attendance at the movie wasn't optional in her case and since she was accustomed to complaining to anybody who would listen, this would give her an opportunity to have something very specific to complain about for a change.

She had spent years in therapy, prior to meeting us, bitterly complaining about the injustices of her past and the lack of any decent men for dating, and announced that she had enough insight to "kill a horse." Since we didn't want any more of that to happen, I just asked her to go into trance and review her life in a new way. If she was going to be preoccupied with the past, she might at least do a little objective research on it.

She retreated into a nice trance and easily followed suggestions to imagine yourself in front of four doors with labels indicating "real," "far worse," "ideal," and "maze" pathways to the past. I asked her to open, go into, and quickly review the real past sufficiently to convince herself that there were probably no surprises there.

Then, by contrast, and per my instruction, she imagined herself opening and exploring the path to the worst possible past. I asked her to travel one step at a time. And with each step the scene changes. And with each step she became another year into the past . . . the worst possible past. See what is there. Feel what is felt living in that worst possible past. Take another step and experience the previous year. Then do it again. I spoke like that, and as I did she would feel another experience of the worst possible past.

She hadn't thought about the possibility of such a thing existing, of course, because she had been far too blinded with the injustices of her own real past to be sensitive to the hardships others have that might have even been worse than hers. So it was just a little difficult for her to follow those directions but she made a valiant effort and maybe she even had a learning.

In her case, I was far more interested in asking that she return to the starting point and open the door to the ideal past and just immerse herself in it. She had been wishing for the kind of experiences a person could have *there* all of her life, so why not just tumble right into the heart of it. You should be free to go anywhere you like in your imagination. Every child knows how, in a dream, you can discover a secret room that contains all of your heart's desires, represented as treasures, or something more literal like new bicycles or mysterious, never-seen-before toys. So, deeply within a comfortable trance, she opened that door and with a tentative eagerness proceeded deeper down that path.

I suggested that you can imagine it as a series of stepping stones that might represent one year at a time. Each time you take a step, go back one year. And with each year back you go, you can take all the time you like to pause and surround yourself with everything as ideal as you can possibly want. Feel it, touch it, see it, let yourself be touched by it.

She walked forward until, finally, reaching some tender year of girlhood, I reminded her that there is really no need to stay on the path. You can feel free, in the ideal past, to duck off the path, take a side trail, meet someone you want to meet, let yourself receive the kind of acceptance, nurturing, love, and warmth that you've always dreamed of and now find yourself surrounded by.

And every ideal past has an ideal parent or someone you can totally trust, maybe you see a grandfatherly figure sitting on the park bench, someone who radiates a kindness, compassion, interest, a benevolent twinkling of the eye. And you can really enjoy the kind of attention someone like that will be sure to give such a precious little girl as you—there in that ideal past present. You could probably just climb up into that lap and hear what you would have heard, ask the questions you might want to ask, and feel the tenderness and love that comes back to you. She sat there with tears streaming over her face, making rivers of excessive mascara. She came out of trance that day without much comment but the next week she came in and said, "You know, I met three decent men this week, and I think it had something to do with that old man on the park bench. But what I really need is a mother."

It was then that I thought about the movie *Harold and Maude*. Shara was thinking that she needed me to give her a mother somehow, but she was failing to realize that she had everything she needed to make her own mother, precisely because of her ability to feel that things had been so unjust. After all, if you know enough about what you needed to be angry about not getting it, you know enough to let your imagination put those desired qualities together into the ideal mother who will certainly be waiting for you on that park bench in the ideal past that you can journey to any time you like. But since she wanted my help, I directed her to develop that skill in another trance as a precursor to seeing a certain midnight movie. Maybe if she did a good enough job with her imagination, she wouldn't have to see the movie.

So Shara once again retreated quite rapidly into a comfortable trance and was soon on the path to the ideal past meeting the ideal mother whom she fashioned from her own desires. I reminded her that every ideal mother will have a variety of qualities, among which will be included a love so strong and so pure that she won't hesitate to expect the best from you and to be appropriately, lovingly, firm when she needs to help you learn and develop into the best you can be. And while she sat in trance, immersing herself in a mother's love, feeling the mother's strength, softness, tears, and laughter, I spoke to her about a few of the experiences that Harold and Maude had in that movie because maybe there were some other qualities she might add, qualities that Maude symbolized so uniquely. Now I don't know whether or not you've seen the movie. But you can understand something about the desperate context in which it took place and how completely Maude's love inspired and transformed a life.

Harold was a teenaged boy who was morbidly preoccupied with death. At least, that's what was said by the psychiatrist whom his mother had hired. She had been forced to consult with him because it looked as though Harold was never going to outgrow this obsession he had with faking suicides, and it was really getting so embarrassing for her. I mean, there she would be, impressing her friends at a nice tea party, when out on the lawn Harold would stage an elaborate and convincing production of lighting himself on fire, much to the horror of the surprised guests. He was, of course, unharmed and probably already planning his next spectacle.

One day, his mother had arranged a date with a very proper young lady whose company she thought Harold should begin keeping. Upon being introduced to the young woman, Harold convincingly pretended to commit "hara-kari," right there on the parlor floor. Or his mother would come home from her committee meetings and find Harold apparently dead from hanging, still dangling. She would sigh in an exasperated way and go about her business.

Harold also enjoyed driving a hearse, which he frequently drove when he attended funerals, not of anybody he knew, just funerals. It was all of these habits that had convinced the psychiatrist about the "morbid preoccupation with death" theory. But I think Harold was just desperate for some kind of experience of honest emotion.

You have to admit that those elaborate fake suicides should have elicited some kind of emotion from that superficial, social-climbing mother if anything would. But they didn't. She hardly blinked an eye. Maybe that's why he started going to the funerals. You can depend on finding some outpouring of honest, human emotion at a funeral. And, incidently, that's where he first met Maude. She also attended funerals recreationally, but for an entirely different reason than Harold.

Maude was 80-something and feeling pretty well satisfied and finished with her accomplishments for one lifetime. She was joyfully looking ahead to making the transition and joining her husband who had died some years before. But I guess when she saw Harold, she must have seen some kind of final project that needed attention, a life that needed to experience her unique kind of inspiration. So she took him under her wing and taught him a thing or two. For starters, she gave him an old banjo and insisted that he plunk at the strings, regardless of how little he knew about properly playing it because "Everyone has to be able to make some kind of music!" she said.

And then there was the day when walking along the city street, Maude saw the root-bound, smog-choked, nearly dead little tree that was struggling to live there on the sidewalk in the fumes and shadows of those tall buildings. Maude recognized it immediately as a tense situation that needed remedying and she elected herself for the job. In a matter of moments she had spotted an empty pickup truck, tossed a shovel into it, hefted the little tree, pot and all, with Harold's assistance, into the bed of the truck, and off they went. Maude did not exactly have a great deal of respect for conventional ways of doing things. I guess she had realized in her long lifetime that some things just need to be done with whatever means are available.

So they drove out of the city and into the surrounding countryside. Soon they came to a spot Maude deemed appropriate and they pulled off on the side of the road, unloaded the little tree and ceremoniously selected the site of its new home. There, Maude supervised the digging of a nice, roomy hole. Though it was only a movie, you could almost smell the richness of that moist, fertile earth that was made ready to receive the little tree. When the hole was just right, they busted that binding planter and carefully settled the tree into its new home, gently patting the earth in around it. Again, you could almost feel the relief that little tree must have been experiencing as it felt itself reaching its roots into honest, moist earth, feeling the sunshine kissing its leaves, protected from too much wind by the neighboring trees, and yet spaced far enough from them to have plenty of room to just *grow comfortably!*

And they had lots of other adventures together. Harold was walking with a noticeable bounce to his step, sort of a skip actually, and a smile was not uncommon on his face. They even had sex and it was as unusually memorable and transforming as all the other adventures had been. Harold became convinced that he wanted to marry Maude.

His mother, of course, was horrified and repulsed once she caught wind of the relationship, but that wasn't what put an end to it. Maude's birthday was coming up and unbeknownst to Harold, she had decided that her last project now was finished and she had planned her own death which she perceived as a gateway. So, while Harold worked to give her a surprise birthday party, complete with cakes, horns, hats, flowers, and all the things you would expect to celebrate with, Maude counted her sleeping pills and planned her goodbyes.

So the inevitable occurred. At the party, Harold discovered that Maude had taken her pills. She was dressed beautifully and had the eager demeanor of a schoolgirl excitedly preparing for her first date. Harold couldn't quite grasp the news at first, but once he did, he raged against it, rushing Maude over her objections to an emergency room to try and reverse her decision. But to no avail, Maude went through that gateway with a serene and happy smile on her old and beautiful face. Her only regret was leaving Harold but she knew something that Harold himself did not yet know.

As he left the hospital in an angry daze, he climbed into his hearse and drove recklessly to some cliffs near the city. As the viewer, you really wondered if maybe he wouldn't just drive right over those cliffs in his dejection and despair. But, no, he stopped short, got out, holding his banjo by the neck, and just stood there silently for a moment. Then, holding the banjo with both hands, he made a tiny little plink, then a plunk, took a step, and with another plink-plunk of those strings, actually hopped a little hop on his right foot before bringing down his left and doing the same.

Within a matter of moments, the tempo of the banjo music had gradually increased until there he was skipping about on the edge of that cliff, playing his banjo, albeit still badly. And he did it with a sense of joy that would have made Maude proud. And isn't that what you really owe someone you have loved, to live your life in a way that you let their love and joy live on in you?

And then I wanted her to finally open the fourth door that she knew was labeled "future." That was the one where the real learning occurred. But we had almost forgotten about that one. It's easy to forget about the pathways to the future. But, I said, "I want you to go with your back turned into the future. You have to discover your real future the way we all have to discover our future, looking at what you're going to accomplish for yourself. And as you find out what you accomplish with each step, you have continued chances to change whatever you did that got the result. Each time you observe and change, you improve the next set of results. And you will be remembered for the results *you* create. With each step you can determine how you modify your behavior when you take your next. And in that way you discover how you are using yourself. Leave a trail of accomplishments which show you that you are proud of yourself. That is all you can see in the future . . . you can only proceed with your back turned. Then emerge out to the door again." And the trance was over.

So, as a matter of fact, Shara decided that she would go to the midnight movie after all, and she didn't even complain about it. After sitting in her own ideal mother's lap in the ideal past during the time I spoke about Harold and Maude, she really wanted to continue the experiences and the learnings she had begun there. And she couldn't hardly wait to exit the past and the future, come out of trance, and look at a lot of things from a fresh perspective. And I'm sure she met some interesting people at that midnight movie and maybe she was able to look at them from that fresh perspective she was working on.

5. **Redecision goal:** *Find that part of self which decided not to have feelings and decide to do it differently.*

Metaphor

Dan is a man we worked with one time who wanted to get rid of the plastic wrap by which he felt himself separated from the rest of the world. He used some other interesting metaphors to describe his experience, like he was running out of gas, had a weight around his neck, wanted to live instead of just exist, and complained of a chronic tiredness and melancholy as long as he could remember. He felt miserable most all the time and tended to stay by himself when he would feel that way. I guess he hadn't heard that misery loves company. He even managed to be alone most of the time despite being married and having a young child in the house.

As you can imagine, his marriage was pitiful, if you would even call it a marriage. He said it was one of convenience but it didn't sound very convenient to us. He said he didn't love her at all, wouldn't make any advances and resisted any overtures she made. He didn't want to do his half because she might not do her half. He hadn't even told her the reason he had left town for three days when he visited us for therapy. He didn't figure the rotten marriage had anything to do with this chronic melancholy because he had felt that way even before he was married so no need to blame the marriage or exert any effort to improve it.

At first, he didn't think he had any feelings, but upon closer examination it turned out that he did feel angry sometimes, if he thought about it, and he could remember a lot of times in the past when he had felt angry. We asked him to get in touch with whatever anger he had, sort of as an experiment. If you were to think about something real pleasant and absorb yourself in that, and then identify the next thought about your experience, or the next thing you might picture, what would it be? We asked him. He thought about swimming in the ocean and then back to being age 18, 19, on vacation with a girlfriend, full of blisters and miserable. When we asked him to think of the worst thing he'd seen or heard and think the next thought that comes to mind, it wasn't significantly different. He was again back at 18 or 19 feeling different things.

So we asked him to see the events of the 18 or 19 age sequence and identify some of the feelings. We wondered if maybe he had made some conclusions. And at some point the conscious mind begins to wonder what you thought you might gain by concluding not to show your feelings, but that picture is not the only event for him which had that exact dynamic to it. And I wonder how long it will take you to think back to when as a younger teenager or child, in fact, you first could identify making that decision.

And it was a simple matter to remind him that the way a person goes back in time can be gradual or systematic, random or sudden. You can start with just a feeling, a visual image or an idea. And if it's meaningful, you can begin to recognize the meaning and the rest of the experience. Gradually you can even have amnesia for the fact that you had been a grown man, had lived in 1980, '84, '70. And the future can be something that dissociates from you and becomes forgotten. So you can just concentrate on the present. Usually the conscious mind doesn't need much explanation about why the voice of a hypnotist is still available. It could be your own voice, a teacher, acquaintance, friend.

Gradually you come to feel the experience and believe you're having it again, but this time make alterations in your understanding for your own future. Then we mentioned that soon he could tell us what he was thinking about, experiencing, that he could put it into words. You don't have to change the way you experience or feel.

Pretty soon he reported feeling blamed for a lot of things that weren't his fault, things from age four right on up. And at first he was only aware of that four-year-old boy feeling confused. That was understandable but we really wondered what else the boy was feeling, where he would feel the hurt, where he would feel the anger. And what did the four-year-old decide to do with his anger?

Now, at first, Dan said that he had cried out in his hurt and anger. But it was clear that at some age he had decided to abandon that course of action and keep it inside and keep up a wall and keep it going on and on. So we asked him to take a look at five and take a look at six. And the pained looks on Dan's face and the rapid gasping he began to do sure looked like he was finding a situation where he had gotten so mad he wasn't going to be able to hold it in the same way. And when you move into feelings from some time in your past, you are soon able to identify what was that situation? where are you? how old are you?

You can decide to talk about it. At first you might just communicate the intensity of the feelings breathing rapidly in through the nose and forceably out through the open mouth. That's what he did for quite a while before observing out loud that he felt all tingly, about 16, and like there was an electricity going through his body.

He described a situation when at age 16 his older sister had "egged him on" about something, teasing him to the point that he felt like hitting her, and did hit her in the arm. She fell down, went and told their dad. He came in, didn't listen.

Dan dissolved into heavy tears, covered his face, and cried even harder. It was obviously very painful and we asked him to tell that father what he was feeling. He stammered out that it wasn't his fault, and we told him to say it again, loud enough to make him hear you. But Dan just swallowed the feeling instead, and it was pretty clear that's where he had decided to clam up.

Breathing a deep breath and talking like a resigned adult, he explained that the father hadn't listened, didn't believe him when he said she egged him on. He was mad and shaking and said he felt like hitting Dan. Dan himself was still crying and shaking and identified the feeling he was still having as hurt.

And how does a person decide to stop trusting, stop sharing your hurt and asking for help. Was it just a thought you had? we asked him. But he didn't remember, he guessed it was just what you're supposed to do. He wasn't real sure whose rules this was according to. According to everybody, he supposed, you are just supposed to suck it in and handle it yourself, he said, resignedly. But in a situation like that you have to ask who are you going to make right? If this person grows up to be in his thirties, feeling rotten, then they weren't right. So why do them a favor? It seems like you're doing some violence on yourself while you're angry and hurt and then do them a favor by going along with their rules. Someone might suggest at a time like this that a person use their anger to decide not to do violence on themselves by holding the hurt in. That would be a good way to get even with everybody, to grow up and become the kind of person they were trying to keep you from becoming—a feeling person.

So we suggested that the thing to do is to go to a time before that incident and live through it with the firm cognition consciously: you are going to show your hurt, keep asking for help, even if they are unjust, even if it hurts you, even if you have to look for 21 years before you find any understanding.

And use your anger to reduce that conviction about holding anger within, and use your feelings to show you mean it and live through that scene blow by blow as minutely as you can slow time down. And take all the time you need, it can go slow. And show your hurt right through the whole incident, and own it and enjoy it. It's your hurt and you have a right to it. You're not free to experience joy to any greater degree than you're free to experience your hurt. You can't enjoy a satisfying meal except to the degree that you allow yourself to experience hunger. So own your hurt, feel it, have it, express it. Live the scene.

In your mind's eye, see it go, watch yourself crying. See it go with you finding a way to express your hurt to somebody who listens, develop a heavy train of thought that carries you to a conviction that your feelings belong to you and you're entitled to them. That's the way you were meant to operate. Own the part of you that is sensitive so that you can grow up to be you, a sensitive adult who can handle things. Let the four-year-old help you, who understands that you can get over something if you feel it fully. And let the grown-up part of you who is so macho and wants to cope help the sensitive man become a success.

And he just sat there crying more intensely, gasping, wiping, which is exactly the proper response. You just keep breathing through all the things people do, all a part of you. You can afford to feel all the unpleasantness. You can afford to empty out all the sludge and make room for the joy. Stay with it.

Don't let the rush and the recession of the rush take you into the here and now. Stay with your feelings "back then" because you have them now. You know when a rush comes and you think it's over, but the rush will come again.

And while he was doing that, we mentioned a few other things that a person needs to consider at a time like that. Most everybody has had a pet that dies. Most everybody loses something that's important to them. And not only is death going to visit you some day. It's going to visit your parents and your friends and the people you wish would have been your friends.

And it should be some kind of reminder to you that your only choice in between is to enjoy life and know how to say goodbye to things. It hurts to lose a dream; it hurts to lose your favorite pair of your shoes, your wallet; it hurts to lose a friend. The only reason that it's okay to lose those things is because it feels good to gain them and it all balances out in the end.

Everyone knows that. You spend a long time trying to keep it from going up and down and I don't think that suits you as a person. The only thing that remains for a lot of people is to be comfortable being awkward while they acquire new things they intend to do.

6. *Reliving and reassessing goal (using redecision):* Decide to say goodbye to a disappointing mother and gain permission to feel feelings.

Metaphor

And when you finally say goodbye to some image of your mother, you really do need to replace it with somebody, something. "Mother Ocean" is an excellent symbol for starters. And many people never really know what it is that attracts them so to the ocean. It can make you want to just camp out right beside it and feel its refreshing renewal, soothing acceptance, something like that.

Cara had done just that. She had lived intimately beside the ocean for almost 10 years, as soon as she had been independently able to leave home and select where she would live. She found herself irresistibly drawn to the edge zone of the ocean. She was fascinated by its ever-changing moods and also by its incredible constancy. When she married a man from another state, it was with great sadness that she left her oceanfront home. And because she moved a good distance away, she did not regularly see any of her family either.

Cara had been away from the ocean for some year and a half after her marriage when she returned for a visit. Her mother picked Cara and her husband up at the airport like a good mother who hasn't seen her daughter and drove them for two hours to the city where they would be staying. And in that two hours it was as though Cara saw and heard her mother for the first time clearly. It was as if she were two people, one who was hearing the mother and becoming aware of how superficially shallow she was. The other part of Cara was the little girl looking to that mother for support and guidance and nurturing and instruction.

The little girl part had been left to flounder and piece together her own understandings. And Cara was that little girl and she was the objective adult lady who could look at that mother and feel sorry for her, and at the same time feel irritated to pieces that her chattering just wouldn't shut up.

And then she looked at her husband who seemed to be feeling exactly the same way and also touched to the heart with a sense of compassion for the little girl part of his wife. And his caring for that little girl in a context where that mother was failing was so emotional for her. The little girl had gotten so used to fending for herself, she couldn't hardly believe it when she looked at him and saw that degree of compassion and understanding and love pouring from him. And it was like a moment of rebirthing, being born into one family and saying goodbye to another one.

And they drove as quickly as they possibly could and dropped the mother off at her hotel and with a great sense of relief just got as much distance and space between them and her as they possibly could and instinctively drove straight towards the ocean.

And Cara hadn't been around the ocean for a whole year and a half. And as they parked the car, even the smell of the ocean and the sound of the waves immediately brought tears to her eyes. It was as if there was a coming home to a real mother, a mother you could really depend on to be relevant, to be there for you. And they walked hand in hand closer and closer to the ocean until they were standing on top of the dune and finally caught the first glimpse of it just rolling in so dependably to the shore, so huge and deep.

And when you have a tender moment like that, understanding and separation mixed together, you're vulnerable and yet, paradoxically, strong. Depending on whether you're merging with the part that is tender and still having questions to answer, or you can merge with that part who can love in a way that was never available to the mother who taught you.

So you might imagine yourself being the little child who in finding that mother she can depend on, asks the questions from the little girl's point of view about what it's like to be a little girl and how it's all right to be a little girl and have all the feelings a little girl's entitled to feel. And hear the answers that she tells you.

And let that child part of you ask with all the innocence without any of the embarrassment or trappings of another era. Just ask, with all the innocence, all the innocent questions you withheld from asking. Why this feels good when I touch it? Why does my brother have a penis, Mom, what does he do with that, does that feel like this feels? Or as one little girl said when she saw her mother diapering her brand new baby brother, "Oh my God, Mamma, what has happened to him?" But it's just pure interest, pure perception unburdened by all those trappings of attitude that were inadvertently learned.

You can remember or watch the delight on the little girl's face, the way she lies waiting for a diaper change and she doesn't want the diaper back on yet, she just wants that wipe wipe please, wipe wipe, wipe wipe. Feels very good, doesn't it?

Memorize those feelings that little girl in you knew about so long ago, how powerful, how magical, how amazing. And when you reclaim those abilities and delights that were yours and have always been yours, that you store and save and let no one take away from you, it's possible to say goodbye quite comfortably to mothers who do the best they can do with their own struggles and with their learnings in their lives— you're only a part of it. As Kahlil Gibran said, "Your children come through you but they're not you; they're like arrows and you're the bow. And the more the bow does its job, the further and straighter the arrows fly."

7. *Reliving and reassessing goal (using redecision):* Decide to let go of inadequate parents and expectations of perfect parents.

Metaphor

Courage and compassion can take many forms, some of them quite unexpected. And I don't know why it is that a lot of responsibility for certain kinds of necessary developmental transitions in the family so often fall to the middle child, but it's a special vantage point squarely in the middle in the vortex of the family and the person there is able to see both sides and both ends. And if you are a middle child, you could consider yourself to be closer than anyone is to the heart of the matter.

And in that family I've mentioned before, the mother and father had celebrated their 50th anniversary with a divorce. They were unable to make adjustments to communicate their needs in the simplest ways and the relationship degenerated. That kind of situation is very sad because of all the love and caring that must have been part of those 50 years. But they couldn't make the adjustment.

The mother had suffered an organ loss which constituted a physiological tragedy. And she failed to recuperate in the ways the doctors had thought she would. Technically, the operation was a complete success. Initially her attitude about it was unbelievably positive. She was glad to have that colitis problem finally under control. She had that external bag but it didn't matter to her, she'd be able to live with that.

She sprang back into action as though she was some kind of superwoman and that superficial enthusiasm lasted about six months. Then the inevitable depression followed and the physiologically baffling situation began. She couldn't sleep and she was shaky and she was tired and she was weak and she was tentative and she was scared. And she was dependent on her children for advice, for the first time, and yet she wouldn't follow any of the advice.

Her oldest son set her up in an apartment within walking distance of everywhere and yet she wouldn't walk anywhere. What if she should fall down, what if she would faint out there—who would help her? And she'd call up the oldest daughter and say, "Could you please help, this is the worst I've ever felt," with that little shakiness in her voice. And it was a problem that stressed the entire family. Everyone was trying to figure out how to help that woman, make that woman recover inner strength, get back her positive sense of being able to do anything she wanted to do all her life prior to that bag. No one could understand that personality change or why she failed to recover.

And so finally one day the middle child drove to the city in which the woman lived, drove to her apartment, walked in, sat down to give the mother hugs. The mother was scarcely able to receive her daughter. She made an effort to "put on" a superficial brightness but was soon shaking and complaining of dizziness and preoccupation with her symptoms.

And the middle child just very lovingly, very matter-of-factly told her, "Mother, I've driven here today to tell you that it's really okay for you to die. You've done enough—you've loved us, you've taught us, you've given us everything that anyone could have possibly expected of you. You've given everything you knew how to give, you've worked, you've labored, you've given birth to each of us children, you've given us your love, you've given us your caring, protected us. And we all love you and you don't have to please us by getting well. You don't have to get well to take care of us any longer. And we forgive you for anything you didn't do. And it really would be all right to go ahead and die."

And, of course, at one level or another the mother objected saying, "That's just not something you decide to do. Of course I don't want to die, of course I want to get better." But the conscious mind can protest and protest about wanting to get better and at the unconscious level the message is real clear that she was moving in the other direction. And the middle child just wanted to give her the opportunity, to give her permission, to take a load off of her shoulders, thank her, and tell her goodbye in some measure. After all, it was as if she had already died, the whole family agreed on that. She wasn't herself anymore really. There was no reason to stick around thinking she had other tasks she had yet to accomplish.

Well, mission accomplished, the middle child left. She left that apartment as though she really was an adult for the first time. She was almost 40 years old. And it was an interesting way of being an adult because she was an adult and yet she was merely a child in a way that she couldn't quite explain. But it was a feeling that she was now being protected and watched after by a more adequate adult—and that her mother was not more adequate, the limits had been reached. Her mother was not omniscient—not the old one and not the one she had just said goodbye to.

And everyone knows that the more adequate the parent who is supervising the child, then the more the child can abandon herself delightfully to the responsibility of being a child, just to play and have every bit as much fun as you can. And you're free to have as much closeness and love as you can make. And the child of an inadequate parent relinquishes part of that ability to play because she senses she can't trust that parent to take care of her properly to supervise and help keep her in proper limits or else the parent tries to keep her too severely within rigid limits. And so that middle child set a precedence in the family when the word spread around the grapevine of brothers and sisters what she had said to the mother.

The middle daughter had another experience in the back of her mind, some years earlier when she had first taken the risk of expressing some things to the parents about who she really was and what she really believed that were quite radically different from the beliefs the parents had always tried to instil. Those times were about religious beliefs and preferences, nothing really earthshaking, different interpretations. She told them, with a conviction that honesty was more important than superficial lies in such an important relationship, that she didn't quite believe in their God in the same way that they did.

It was more that she believed in love and "after all, God is love. You've always taught me that," she said. She thought that would smooth things over. The parents absolutely couldn't accept that. They were angry, hurt, betrayed, frightened for their daughter's eternal salvation.

They couldn't begin to accept the honesty when she shared with them her sexual relationships with a man she was dating and didn't intend to marry. And she stopped the lying she had been doing all along to protect them all those years growing up.

And the father was so angry, he blamed the daughter, verbally attacked her, and tried his best to make her feel guilty. He told her how her mother probably would be willing to die as a result of having heard this—she had just about broken her mother's heart. And that was a chance she had taken way back then, that confrontation with the mother that might have resulted in her death, and yet that mother didn't die. She was able somehow to make room in her heart to love the daughter even though the daughter was different than her and honest about it.

Now, 20 years later she was giving her mother another opportunity to die. The word spread and people waited to see what would happen. And interestingly enough, the mother improved slightly. Not that she was rushing right out to swing on the park swings that were within easy walking distance of her apartment, but there was a subtle change.

The more lasting change was with the daughter who had become a woman that day in a new way after she said goodbye to her mother, relinquished her need for her mother to do any additional teaching or approving or protecting her. And once you move into a comfortable existential position like that, the sky's really the limit. And it is just like a blank piece of paper on which you can draw anything you want. What exactly do you want to draw? Perhaps the question comes through your conscious mind while your unconscious starts making some movements with color and texture. And you watch the picture take shape or you can do it according to a plan. You really can plan to play as carefully as you plan anything else that's important and vital. You can set out to make it enjoyable no matter how old you are.

10

Trance Phenomena Anecdotes

> *Don't part with your illusions. When they*
> *are gone you may still exist, but you*
> *have ceased to live.*
> —*Mark Twain*

This chapter focuses on short stories, or anecdotes, about various trance phenomena. As we have pointed out elsewhere (Lankton & Lankton, 1983), trance phenomena are common experiences which are not exclusive to trance. In fact, not only are they part of normal daily life as Milton Erickson repeatedly reminded us, but they are a part of most, if not all, nonhypnotic therapies (pp. 178–243). In clinical trance contexts, it is often desirable to apply these phenomena to situations in which they can be therapeutically used.

One such situation, for example, might be the pseudo-orientation-in-time experience for a client to conduct a vision of the future in the emanated-image stage of self-image thinking. Dissociation phenomena, and sometimes age regression experiences, are useful for conducting the elaborate dissociative reviews of the preceding chapter. And, of course, amnesia is not an uncommon part of therapy experiences involving emotionally threatening material. In each of these cases, retrieval of the desired trance phenomena is a step that precedes the actual therapy work.

Another area of hypnotherapy for which the use of trance phenomena is crucial involves the disruption or amelioration of a long-standing symptom. Success of such a therapeutic goal often depends upon helping clients relearn the manners of experiencing and behaving which existed before the symptom, prior to the consciousness of pain, and so on. Perhaps the most widely practiced application of trance phenomena for these circumstances involves their use for pain control.

For example, age regression is useful in diagnostic exploration as well as for revivification of pain-free experiential resources. Dissociation can be strategically applied to dissociating from pain and rendering the subjective experience of pain as lessened or nonexistent. Time distortion can be used to make the moments without pain very long and the times with lessened pain seem very short. Amnesia can be used to forget the shortened moments of lessened pain, and so on. In the case of each phenomenon, therapists will need to obtain verbal or other types of signal mechanisms which provide feedback regarding the client's experience of the phenomenon in order to therapeutically apply it within the trance.

The purpose for telling the anecdotes about a particular trance phenomenon is to help the client remember and stimulate, unconsciously, what they already know about an ability to have that experience. Suggestions and binds accompany, precede, or follow the anecdotes and further an association of the experience to a situation in which it is desired.

Often there is an organizing metaphoric "frame," as we have shown in some of the other protocols. Such a frame only provides a context for telling the anecdotes and accompanying suggestions about the trance phenomena. Since we often use trance phenomena when we are directing client experience related to a specific symptom, the metaphoric frame, in that case, usually involves an isomorphic or parallel structure to that aspect of the client's situation.

Continuing the above explanation in more detail, the first two examples demonstrate how various anecdotes are used to retrieve trance phenomena that will be applied to chronic pain problems. The third example involves anecdotes for age regression that serve a purpose for exploration and revivification of resources. In all three of these, the bulk of the induction has been omitted, but trance maintenance and arm levitation suggestions may remain. In those cases, these were often instrumental in creating a feedback mechanism for us regarding the client's subjective experience of trance maintenance and the development of dissociation or other phenomena.

1. **Trance phenomena goal:** *Use anecdotes for dissociation, time distortion, amnesia, age regression, and body distortion to be applied to chronic back pain, with an initial accompanying attitude protocol for a client who avoids feeling dependency needs.*

Metaphor context and anecdotes[37]

As you diminish your awareness of the stimuli outside of you, and more and more we apply the resources that you have to the pain, it's important that a woman like you know that your conscious mind can be quite an aid, or disability or liability. You've tried a number of things that your conscious mind thinks are important, but I bet that you really will have some doubt about your ability to fail at doing nothing, and I hope that you do. And I wouldn't be surprised if you do respond in a way that I would not predict.

While your conscious mind may be paying attention to, monitoring your responses, you might be glad to know that your unconscious is taking care of a lot of things, has regulated your breathing, has slowed it, is using lower lung breathing. Your muscles have relaxed, and the left side of your body has relaxed differently than the right side of your body.

Now I wonder which of your hands really needs to discover whether or not it will be the one to raise up to your face.

While you're wondering about that, I might just mention I hypnotized a woman in Jackson, Michigan, a long time ago who was our office manager. She had a pain in her hips. She wasn't going to let me use hypnosis to cure the pain, because she didn't believe in hypnosis. But she didn't know what happened behind the closed doors of my office. Being an office manager, she was very ambitious, very organized, very alert, very quick, very controlling.

She was seeing a chiropractor every day, and I suggested to her that it might be a nice idea for the holidays to let me do some hypnosis with her so she could save her money up for Christmas presents, New Year's parties, Hanukkah gifts. And I promised that if she felt badly for the chiropractor, her pain could come back and she could see him twice a day after the holiday season to make up for the loss of his income. She thought that was humorous, but she wasn't going to go

[37] The diagnosis of this client appears in detail in Lankton and Lankton, 1986, pp. 83–93.

very deeply into trance. Now I knew something about her. I knew that she was very curious the week before when a prostitute had been in my office. She wondered what was going on. She didn't attribute anything bad, but she wondered.

So I went about describing my relationship. Here was a woman who had different sexual values, and maybe I should call the office manager "Sally," in order to speak about her more easily. The prostitute had different values than Sally, she had a different life-style than Sally, she had a different orientation to men and women. She had a different sense of materialism than Sally.

I don't know if you've noticed the index finger of your left hand. Maybe that will be the ideomotor experience that spreads into your left palm and arm to begin the movement upward. And maybe the hand will move up towards your face, all the way to your face, halfway, maybe it will float out to the side, maybe it will get heavier and drop, maybe it will do something different that we can't even guess.

And I described all the things about the prostitute that I knew were going to make Sally's fantasy life even richer and make her even more curious, and more disgusted with that prostitute's life-style as it disagreed with her own. And when she was really full of disagreement and disidentification with that prostitute, I mentioned to her the final straw. That that prostitute was nothing like her, she would refuse to go into trance and let a man be in control of her experience. And with that, Sally promptly dropped into trance.

But you might need to hold onto something, keep control of something. You can hold onto the sound of my voice. You can hold onto the memory of how really you only hypnotize yourself. And you use anyone's words as a stimulus. Now your hand began to move, began to get cataleptic, began to get a tendency to rise, jerky movement, and then you might have noticed that your conscious mind wanted to get in there and think about it for a while. Analyze it. Go ahead and analyze everything that I do. Just as much as you can. Because at some point your conscious mind is going to go to sleep. And it might be in bed at night, and then your unconscious, having saved up the impulses to react in a useful way, can have free rein.

Maybe you'd like for your conscious mind to be confused about something. But I really doubt that you can be confused about the things I say, they're always so straightforward. Now, I'm going to have you sit there for a while, pay attention to that hand with your conscious mind, as it rises up towards your face.

You've already started thinking about a number of things. You probably couldn't just say what. You've only had enough time to become aware of some of your thoughts. Thought travels at the speed of electricity. All those brain cell responses. And now you know how your arm's going to move. And it's nice to know that your unconscious intends to do things in a way that fits for you as a person. I might suggest that your hand raise up to your face, but you're not bound to react in a way that works for my needs, but you are bound to react in a way that will meet your needs.

I agree. It's nice if you're left alone to do things your way. And I'd like to make a strong recommendation that while I'm talking to you, you might want to imagine, and just imagine, that the things I'm saying are flying overhead. You'll be free to eavesdrop on the things I say, use those suggestions that work for you. And just pretend and find out whether or not that's a useful way for you to learn.

I want to also recommend to you that you keep foremost in your mind the knowledge that's quite acute in my mind, that is, you've lived twice as long as I have almost, you've dealt with a good deal of changes in the world that I have yet to deal with. You've overcome without any help by me more pain than I ever intend to have. You've done it and kept a fine attitude, modeled for other people, a person who can really be respected. And I'm offering suggestions to you from the standpoint of that knowledge, and not from the standpoint that some hypnotists might suggest, that if you only did it their way, things would have been better by now. I think you really ought to do it your way. And I hope that I can confuse you enough that you have to work a little harder to find out what you know about your way.

The first thing that I'd like to remind you about is that in dreams at night, Dr. Erickson would work upon his pain with his protective dreams. Now I asked him about his protective dreams. You have some dissociation in your arm. You have to dissociate your arm, and its normal neurological muscular pattern of functioning, from the rest of your body in order for it to stay against your face comfortably, second after second. Perhaps you can begin to memorize that feeling of dissociation. I worked with an engineer named Stanley, and I knew he understood the multiplication table because of an engineering or science background. Everyone learns the multiplication tables sometimes. Your conscious mind, in remembering how you once labored to learn that multiplication table, may recall how it was a difficult job at first. Bits and pieces were all you could manage to hold onto.

And then finally, with the little pieces left up in the air, you began to fill in, and eventually you learned more and more until, finally, your conscious mind pays no attention at all.

You can multiply two numbers together, three numbers together, in fact if your conscious mind stays out of your way, you probably can multiply a two-digit number by a three-digit number. I know I can. And so your unconscious knows a great deal more about multiplication of your experience than your conscious mind could imagine. If you do remember some of that ability to multiply, you only remember the numerical indications. The task of multiplying can be applied to the feeling of dissociation in your arm. And the memorization that went into the multiplication table can as well.

Maybe you remember some other time you dissociated. Your conscious mind can pay attention, for your own aid, to the memory of the multiplication table and let your unconscious apply it to the dissociation, or your conscious mind could pay attention to the dissociation and let your unconscious remember the multiplication table. And apply it.

And while that's happening, I want to mention that you can move sensations in your body. I know that you're well aware that a smile can spread to the muscles in your face, ears, neck, and eyes. Hunger can overtake your stomach if you concentrate on it. A bladder pressure, begging you to urinate, can be diminished. Everyone has had a mosquito bite. I don't know if they have mosquitoes where you live, but they have insects that bite. And there comes a time, as a child, when no one's really going to be there if you moan about it, so you say you're just not going to pay any attention to that insect bite. And sure enough, you forget about it. And what child isn't amazed at how something will go away when you accidentally forget that you're ignoring it for a while.

In dreams at night, you forget a lot of things. I had a dream last night I doubt that can be remembered. I doubt that you failed to have a dream last night, yet it can't be remembered very well either. It's really remarkable how many things your body's taking care of by the use of trance phenomena. We have a child. That child is in deep trance a good deal of the time. Deeper than I can match. And I just wonder if he's already learned all of the alphabet, all of the words in my vocabulary, all of my nonverbal movements, all of the songs I've sung to him, and as we socialize and educate him, train his conscious mind to get in the way, he'll begin to have amnesia for all those learnings. And then we can take him to secondary school so they can help put little cracks in his conscious mind and drag through some of the amnesia-ed material, help him forget about his amnesia. I hope that people have helped you forget about your amnesia, so that you can really remember some of the things you knew as a child.

You used to pretend, you used to hide under a card table, I'll just bet. Maybe put a blanket or quilt over the card table and play house. You probably played house before the appointed age. Very safe. How nice to pretend. That blanket, maybe a pink blanket. Really no sound could get through. You might have heard plates clattering, and silverware jostling. And your conscious mind knew that mother was making dinner. But your unconscious knew that you could forget about it, ignore it. And you were there safe in your own little house.

You can learn to ignore stimuli in a lot of ways. Everyone knows that in order to go through college you have to learn to block out thoughts from your mind, so you can read a book. Ignore the shuffling in the library, ignore all those football players in the library so you can read a book. They made it difficult on me in the early sixties because they made me ignore miniskirts in the library. Hotpants. Now I'm very good at concentrating. I can appreciate the things that I ignored later.

What mother hasn't had the need to ignore a difficulty in order to attend to a child. What person, driving in the United States during rush hour, has failed to apply the ability to not notice that bladder pressure. You have a lot of things that you probably use that can help you, including the ability to ignore stimuli in your body somewhere.

I don't know if you remember about memorizing the dissociation in that arm. I'd like you to multiply its movement into your shoulder, into your neck. You can move it into your cheeks if you like. And you might need to go to the dentist sometime. And you'll want to know how. I had root canal surgery, by getting arm levitation, touching my fingers to my cheeks, and letting the dissociation roll off my fingertips into my jaw. You might let it roll down into your chest. Gradually into your shoulder muscles. Not too fast.

Now how do you ignore a stimulus in your body somewhere. In dreams at night, you often dream a stimulus in your body you don't even have. There must be an as-if mentality.

Now you can begin a visualization in a dream. And in the visualization you can see yourself, and you can see yourself doing anything. Your imagination is the limit. And now move that gradually into your breasts, into your sternum, and just let it continue to multiply. And in his protective dreams, Dr. Erickson would imagine himself doing a lot of things. You can imagine yourself swimming, falling asleep in a pile of leaves, taking a hayride, ice-fishing, sitting alone in a boat, letting the waves lap alongside of the boat. Anything you can imagine. You can imagine yourself flying over a cloud if you wanted to. I never did that.

Every child that I know has had dreams of flying out of their body. I don't know whether or not you can remember having had a dream like that. I don't know whether or not you can have one now. Maybe you can. Your dissociation spreading from your breast, your sternum, into your shoulders, around the back of your shoulders, down into your pelvis, might facilitate a memory of how.

Most children experience themselves moving out of their chest or out of the top of their head. And it's very much like those protective dreams of Dr. Erickson. Seeing an image of yourself, either back there on the bed or floating in the room somewhere.

Now I haven't mentioned time. Your unconscious responds rather quickly. Rather quickly your unconscious can respond to a stimulus. I mentioned that your eyes could close, and they closed. You needed to have them open and close again at your own speed. I mentioned that your hand could raise up to your face. It began to rise and then it fell, and then it raised up to the face. It's a real learning experience for everyone to realize that you've given more than one example of the way you're intending to learn something. I've mentioned time distortion. You might have thought about it. It would be a good idea for you to forget about it for the moment, so that when we come back to it you can really learn to have it last forever.

And speaking of coming back to it, the dissociation I have encouraged your awareness of, moving into your pelvis, can be moved into your buttocks or your upper hip. I don't know whether or not you'd like it to move into your back gradually, or suddenly, systematically, inter-mittently, or randomly. I bet you have some idea of what would be the best way to do that.

I just recalled working with a woman named Linda in Pensacola, Florida. She had back pain. Her back pain was psychodynamically regenerated again and again. There was no one there to give her support. A child who grew up too quickly became a doctor. To become a female doctor in Pensacola at the age that she did it, she certainly must have had some ambition to make her stand out from the crowd.

If you grow up too quickly, you can depend upon your body mis-understanding the use of your sympathetic nervous system. Some people are afraid to relax. Linda thought that the blood flow to her central apparatus—you know, your mucus membranes, esophagus, lungs, stomach, bladder, colon, alimentary sphincters, vagina—stimulation in that area was a signal, before she even could probably verbalize it, that she wasn't being strong enough. She might actually have the audacity to lie down and laugh or cry. And her parents would criticize her for being weak. "If you want something to cry about, I'll give it to you. Get up." And a child learns rather quickly that the parents are happier if you keep yourself strong, energize the sympathetic nervous system to pump adrenalin into the cardiovascular system, into the skin/muscle system. It is a good way to get arthritis. Into the skin/nervous system.

Some people have the opposite kind of problem. And in protective dreams it's a good idea to visualize yourself having the opposite kind of problem. Everyone knows you can forget your dreams when you wake up anyway. So in dreams at night, Dr. Erickson would imagine himself having an entirely different set of bodily reactions. And then step into the image and have those feelings. And he wouldn't remember them in the morning.

One time he came into the office and said, "I had a good deal of pain last night and I'm still having my protective dream." And I said, "I'm very glad to be here in your dreams with you."

And the opposite problem for Linda was the child who would cry at the drop of a hat, cry seeing a sad puppy, cry seeing Lassie, cry seeing a clown get too close too quickly. Get scared and turn to Mommie. Who would find herself in a fetal position. Who would beg for somebody to show her how to do something because she didn't know how. She would never have become a doctor had she had that mentality. And it's good that she didn't.

There's a lot of limits to the human being, but there's also a good deal of flexibility. You can get away with a lot and only pay for it with minimum problems in the body. And Linda paid a debt. No one was there to give her support. And her back became the locus of her difficulty. Needing someone to back you up, someone you can lean on. You might imagine a protective dream in which you can lean on the most appropriate healer you've ever met. And step into the dream and have the experiences. I asked Linda to use Dr. Erickson's method modified for her.

Now maybe you can verify your dissociation moving into your back. If you can notice that you have a stimulus somewhere in your body, then you can't be aware of all of your body at once. Then you must be able to not notice a stimulus in your body somewhere. I wonder if you failed to notice the feeling in your ankle. I imagine you did.

I know Stanley did not notice the feeling around his ears where his glasses touched his face. Most people need to forget that experience so that they're not distracted. And you can memorize the feeling of not noticing the stimulus over your ears, and move it other places in your body as well for your own support.

Now go ahead and let that feeling of dissociation mingle with the time distortion I spoke of seconds ago. You can be in a lecture that seems to go on for days. I hope this one does. Or you can be in a compromising situation that seems to last for seconds. And you wish it would last longer. What person in this room during courtship hasn't looked at their watch and found out that it was two in the morning and they got out of the movie at 11:30. Where did the time go? It must have more to do with time distortion in the mind than it does blood flow to the lips.

Let the feeling of dissociation be something that you use with the other trance phenomena. If your pain is constant, your dissociation can help it become intermittent. If your pain is intermittent, your dissociation can help it become diminished. And then let the moments of the pain become very short clockwise. Just like those moments when, on a date, time flew by. And you couldn't get enough time to make you realize time was up. And let those moments that you notice the pain being diminished or gone seem to last forever. And that will probably appeal to you, if you do it in the following way.

Knowing that you try out a response and inhibit it, and then move with it at your own speed, as you did with your arm and your eyes, try out the feeling of time distortion mixed with your dissociation, and then let the pain come back. And then redecide for yourself whether or not that was a useful way, and if it was, apply it so that the moments of pain are very short, and the moments without the pain can seem [*slowly*] two, three, four, five times longer, [*pause*] can seem to last forever.

Now, cholinergic fluid to your central apparatus will confuse the biochemistry. Linda's biochemistry learned to favor a sympathetic imbalance. Now that's really unfortunate. That's a good way to produce problems in the skin/nervous system, cardiovascular system, and musculo/skeletal system.

You're going to have to confuse your chemical balance. And the stimulus which is a signal for you unconsciously to stimulate adrenalin into the muscular system needs to be a stimulus for you to flood your central apparatus with cholinergic experience, sphincter relaxation. Maybe it will be a signal for you to think about those protective dreams.

Maybe when you're dreaming at night, it will be a signal for you to have them. Maybe during the daytime. And you ought to be able to operate with amnesia for the dreams, so that you can go about your normal daily business.

Now in dreams at night, you learn to forget a lot of things. You couldn't say how, and you can't really be sure you've forgotten about something unless you don't think about it again. Now that ought to be quite a challenge for you, how to remember to have amnesia without thinking about it. You haven't thought about your ankle again. How do you do that? Apply that same knowledge to those shortened moments of diminished pain, and then forget about the fact that you did so. And you have to pay attention to something else, maybe something that I said, something you've thought about.

Now you've got learnings, you've got experiences. You have a lot of ways of doing things in your own way, and trying other people's ways temporarily, modified to fit for yourself.

I suggested to Sally that her pain be gone for the duration of the holiday seasons, and I just happened to mention that one holiday is barely over before the next one begins. Thanksgiving's barely begun and Christmas is being advertised. Christmas is no more on the way when everyone's preparing for New Year's. You hardly get New Year's out of the way when you're ready for some president to have a birthday. Then there's Sweetest Day, and Valentine's Day, and then somebody has a birthday in there, maybe you have a birthday, and then everyone's preparing for spring vacation.

And even before that there's March first. And what child wouldn't want to march first? That's some kind of a holiday for a child. And March "forth" is another one if you think about it that way. And then you barely get ready for spring break, you're preparing for summer vacation, and whatever happened to the year? You're getting ready for Halloween, hayrides, romantic nights under the moonlight, and if you forgot to celebrate those, it's all right, because you're getting ready to celebrate Thanksgiving again.

So Sally's pain stayed gone throughout the entire year. Every day would be a holiday under those circumstances. And if your pain is going to be gone for the holidays, then you're really in quite a double bind there. It doesn't matter if your glass is half empty or half full. What matters is whether you like the taste of water. And you can think about that, your unconscious will know what I mean.

And I wonder how you're going to come out of trance. I'll just bet you'll come out of trance, and then discover that you'll have to go back into trance and come out your own way. And if so, that would be a good verification of our hypothesis. Let your unconscious continue the learnings that we began in the way that's right for you. If you need to keep an arm in trance when your mind comes out, it's an indicator to you that you can keep the learnings with you after the trance is over, and that would be fine. Maybe you'll do something in your own unique way.

2. *Trance phenomena goal:* Use anecdotes for dissociation, pseudo-orientation in time, body distortion, and negative hallucination to stop back pain and put aside introjected self-destructive thoughts of being unable to be physically well when the parent was not.

Metaphor context and anecdotes

I worked with a myasthenia gravis client one time. When she was in the hospital, under anesthesia, some absurd intern had the audacity to mention to her that she was going to have to "kill herself or learn to live with the pain." And every time she began to recover, she had suicidal ideation and thought maybe she ought to kill herself and it brought her to psychotherapy.

I put her in trance, I asked her wherever did you get such a silly notion as the fact that every time you get better, you're changing your behavior in a detrimental way? Don't you really realize when you begin to get better you ought to really reward yourself for your accomplishment? You're only 33 years old, and some day you're going to be 43, and 53. And you'll need to start listening to that body.

"But how did you gain such a silly notion?" And she said, "The intern. But I can't talk." And I said, "Why can't you talk?" She said, "The oxygen has been shut off!" And to make the story short, the strong emotional reaction of panic and the words of the intern had combined to create an awareness, an ego state, that contained that detrimental information, and it was recombining in her experience, out of her awareness, at the wrong time at the wrong place.

Now your hand's raised up halfway. I wonder if that means your unconscious is going to meet me halfway, and meet you halfway, and I know that your conscious mind is ambitious, and interested in solving the problem of the discomfort, and if you're willing to meet your unconscious halfway, your unconscious seems to be willing to meet halfway. And I think that's nice.

You should have no difficulty when you begin to move the feeling of dissociation from your arm up into your shoulder. The noise out there clinking like silverware clinking behind us is something you may have not thought about. It's not relevant to you. How many times have people heard silverware clanking as a child? Thanksgiving dinners, family get-togethers. And sometimes as children, you don't even care what the adults are doing, you're just doing your own children thing.

You might be practicing counting, counting the silverware falling. Practicing your one-to-tens. It can be so hard at first, children count to ten in their own way, it's very hard. You might count one, three, seven, nine, eleven, five, ten.

And just gradually I hope that you can appreciate or consciously help the feeling of dissociation in your right arm move over your elbow, or under your elbow, up into your forearm into your shoulder area. And just pay attention to the boundaries of the movement gradually. You might move it into the shoulder, or move it slightly back into the arm and then back into the shoulder.

And hearing the silverware dropping reminds me that you might be able to realize the experience of a child. Your conscious mind can remember the difficulty in counting, may even be interested in having that memory, but not nearly as quickly as your unconscious is able to begin the process of bringing the feelings that you had then. You don't need to have the emotional feelings that you had then, might not even remember them. They might have been far too difficult to articulate as a small child. Feeling satisfied, hearing your parents speaking in the other room, knowing that all was right with the world.

It's nice to be able to know that a child has amnesia for the future, and hasn't even had the future. There's no need for you to forget about a future that you can't even remember because it hasn't even happened. But you can memorize the feelings you have in your arm, in your shoulder. And you can memorize the feelings that you learned as a child in your body.

It's so interesting to know how many times babies can lift their feet up to their mouth. How many times we used to run around the block all day long. Sometimes we'd run around the yard several times, for no good reason at all, and we'd never understand why our parents wouldn't run around the yard for no good reason at all, because of that boundless energy. And your unconscious knows about that experience. Mine knows about it. Just as you know about that movement of the dissociation in your arm.

And I doubt that you really can move it as quickly as you want to. But I believe that you can appreciate the gradual movement that you can notice, however small that is. And move it down through your neck, since your hand has touched your glasses frame, maybe you can experience your hand moving some of that energy into your glasses frame, into your head. And that's just an imaginary way of speaking about something your unconscious can do.

But you wouldn't really have anything more than the use of your imagination to do it, maybe it's real. And that should be all right. And if so, then you can feel a certain experience where your glasses touch your nose and your ears. Maybe you can even remember how a person learns to not feel sensation around the glasses by the ears and the nose except under certain circumstances.

And I've been speaking to you about a number of trance phenomena, and I don't even need to speak to you about how the body learns to not notice the stimulus of the glasses touching slightly above the ear.

Now, of course, from time to time you do notice it. From time to time you notice different experiences, and gradually moving the dissociation down, near your diaphragm.

The myasthenia gravis client was so pleased to know that when I spoke about her diaphragm, I could complement her on her ease of breathing quite nicely. The doctors had scared her into thinking that she couldn't breathe nicely, because the oxygen had been turned off. "But you're breathing nicely now" was all I needed to say.

Gradually moving that dissociation in order, an orderly fashion, a child following an order, in order to accomplish something in a systematic way. Order food in a restaurant because you really want to eat what you have chosen from the menu. And you order to move that dissociation down your diaphragm, it's nice to realize your conscious mind has a different experience.

Your conscious mind notices the feeling in your body, because your unconscious is keeping your body working quite nicely without you. You could even imagine yourself sitting somewhere else in the room and looking back at yourself someplace. Your hand could be somewhere else in the room. And if your hand could be somewhere else in the room, then you must be somewhere else. Or you could be here and your hand could be elsewhere. Maybe you can see your hand elsewhere. And maybe if you can see your hand elsewhere, you can see your shoulder and your chest and your diaphragm and your stomach elsewhere, because dissociation can spread.

I know a lot of times we don't think that a feeling can spread in the body. We don't like to remember that poison ivy will spread on your body, we don't like to remember that a laugh will spread across your body. You don't like to remember sometimes that laughter will spread across your body, because we like to think that we're in control of our experience. So you can be in control by seeing your arm and shoulder and stomach in the room, or maybe they're right here near me in the chair while you're elsewhere in the room, and from that special and unique vantage point that might be possible for you, look back and find out how it appears to continually, gradually, orderly spread down into your pelvis, not to your genitals, but back into the area of affliction. And I doubt that it will move as quickly as you would like it.

But you can notice that as it moves, that feeling of not noticing your glasses against your ears came back. And you might not even have noticed that feeling of glasses against your ears, because it's an intermittent phenomenon, and an intermittent phenomenon just means that sometimes time can subjectively change your experience, if it's been a long, long, or a longer time since you've noticed that experience.

And maybe the rapid movement of your finger against your glasses, maybe it's been distracting. I wonder why your unconscious would create a distracting experience in your body. What good purpose could there be in having a seemingly unnecessary, possibly unpleasant agitation of muscle movement somewhere in the body. Your conscious mind probably couldn't begin to even think about the proper answer to that question, but it is reassuring to know that your unconscious works in your own behalf.

When I told the myasthenia gravis client that a woman with a toothache had come to my office, and just let that feeling of dissociation go from the area in your back, either more deeply into your back, or move back up into your hand to get replenished, and then come back up later. That the woman in my office with the toothache really didn't need to keep that toothache, once she knew that she was going to take proper care of it.

And then I helped her forget about the toothache by learning that you cannot notice the stimulus in your body somewhere. You know that your mind already can ignore the feeling of your glasses over your ears, and we all do that, even if we wear sunglasses on a sunny day. We think about the sunny day. Now, if you move the dissociation anywhere in your body, then I really wonder what good reason you'd have for not moving the feeling of not noticing.

Sometimes we have dreams at night that seem to last forever. Not noticing a stimulus somewhere around your ears, and beginning to move it, and multiplying one of the feelings that seems to last forever, moving it somewhere in the body where it could be a useful ally.

Is that experience of learning the multiplication table in, what was that, second grade, or third grade? You can't remember the grade as well as you can remember to multiply. It's an unconscious learning, just as the feeling around your ears is an unconscious feeling, and just like you cannot notice the multiplication table, you can multiply the feeling of not noticing.

And if you're somewhere else in the room watching your hand, your chest, your stomach, your back, having a feeling of dissociation, or whether you're having the feeling of dissociation not noticing your hand and your back and your stomach and your chest and your neck. Then you either can use the experience of not noticing around your ears to remember the multiplication table can be forgotten. And have that experience more fully.

Or, you can change places with the part of yourself that you notice elsewhere in the room, and multiply, using the multiplication table knowledge, that feeling of not noticing a stimulus somewhere. And once you learn the multiplication table, time seems to go so quickly when you multiply something. Your hand has moved away from your glasses. And your unconscious is not creating that distracting irritation in the way it had been. So I just wonder how that distracting irritation in the back has begun to change, and whether you can articulate it or just appreciate it, or whether you're waiting to find out more.

And multiplying that experience of not noticing, or remembering the ability to forget the multiplication table, allow that understanding to change location. Sometimes it gets hard to keep our peas from running into our corn, our mashed potatoes from running into our meat, and the gravy from running into the whole works. I hope that you've had that experience, or I hope that the feeling of dissociation begins to blend in with that sense of not noticing stimulation in your body. Or forgetting about something that had been as difficult and laborious as that multiplication table.

Now how do you back up a client with myasthenia gravis? How can the explanation of how tooth pain doesn't need to continue once you've taken adequate medical measures really help? Mostly it helped because I asked her in the trance to be certain that she reexamined her ability to breathe nicely, no need to have that same panic that had gone with the doctor's instruction.

And your hand is doing a nice job of fluttering. Waving goodbye. And we can say goodbye to a lot of things. We can say goodbye to people in the past, we can say goodbye to previous identifications. You probably used to think you were a cowboy. Maybe you don't even remember. You said goodbye. And maybe you thought you were an electrician. Or a fireman. And you said goodbye to that. And take on a grown-up role that suits you as a grown man. Maybe as a child you used to think you were your teddy bear and your mother and your father all blended together. I know many children do fail to discriminate how you're really different, different than your teddy bear, different than your mother. And waving goodbye to all those differences that you don't even need to think about, once you know that you're you.

And I said, "I want you to realize that attributions from your doctor were a coalition of strong emotional feeling and the only advice you had to cling on to. And now your emotional feeling is not that strong. So you can't possibly have the same integrity for that little bit of ego state that was formed. You could simply put the thought aside. And I asked her to lock it up in a little box. And I had to tell her how sometimes we lock up little teddy bears when we're children and we think that we've locked up a big lion, or a great big grizzly bear, only to find out later that it was only a little teddy bear that we locked up. It's nice to know that our childhood fears seem so small when we mature.

And speaking of being immature, I asked Dr. Erickson how he would cure back pain, using hypnosis to cure pain. All he said was "pseudo-orientation in time," which I didn't think was a very adequate answer. And I showed my intellectual resistance with that simple answer.

He said, "You simply go into the past where you didn't have that pain. Memorize those feelings and bring them back with you into the present." And that seemed like a pretty good idea, and obviously an answer to pseudo-orientation in time.

But I'll tell you what really confuses the conscious mind. He then said, "Or go into the future, where you're not going to have that pain anymore, and bring that good feeling back with you into the present." And that made me smile. And I didn't even know why. My unconscious was learning something that I intended to use and it didn't even dawn on me until later what a simple little trick he'd played on me.

A small child playing with silverware doesn't have any pain, doesn't have any worry. And you're entitled to know that experience exists in your unconscious, and you can use that experience whenever you intend to. You know how to count to 10, and you learn that. Now the question of letting the experience continue after trance, to increase and be useful. I don't know whether or not you really would like to let yourself be free of pain all of the time.

You can use the feeling of dissociation in your back to diminish the intensity of that experience of pain whenever you want to. And then the feeling of pain will be intermittent. And you can have the ability to slow down time so that the moments without the pain seem to last and last forever. And the moments of pain can be very short. And then during those short moments of diminished pain, you can apply the ability to forget about the multiplication table, or not notice the stimulus in your body anywhere you want.

And that way you can look forward, and how far should you look forward? I know my father, he's 72 years old, and when he's thinking about buying a car, he thought maybe he'd buy a Cadillac. And I said, "That's a good idea. You should buy a car that's going to last 20 or 30 years." And he laughed. And my mother asked me to help her with her neck pain the other day.

And she had difficulty relaxing that neck. And I said, "Just relax, you'll live longer," and she laughed. And how far into the future should you ask someone to think about living? A good deal. And you can think a good deal about living next year, because you want to pay taxes on this year's income. So wouldn't it be fun to worry about paying taxes on your income at age 89? You finally get even with the IRS. Because you wouldn't have to pay very many taxes on that income.

Now, your hand is just typing out a message on your thigh. You may have learned Morse code long ago. Dit dit dah dit. Dah dit dah. Dah dah dah dit, dit dah dit dit. And maybe your unconscious knows what that means. Maybe your conscious mind will even try to remember. And when you finally know what the message is, that's right. You can stop.

Well, I just want to know that there's some things that you're going to be left thinking about after the trance is over. And one of the things you can think about, that comes to mind, because I heard it last night before I fell asleep, is a Paul Simon song. He says, "Maybe I think too much." And in the song he says that one night his father came to him and held him to his chest. And he said, "There's really nothing more you can do—go on and get some rest." And he said, "Yea! Maybe I think too much."

And if you're going to think about something after the trance, you might as well think about that. And I wonder what way you're going to know that the feelings, the learnings, the buildings that have been learned, memorized, forgotten about, and begun are going to continue after trance. Maybe you'll know it because of the way you feel in the area that concerns you when you came to work on this.

Maybe you'll know it because of an idea that stays with you. Maybe you'll be more flamboyant, and your hand will stay in trance when you come out, just as a simple indication that the learnings that you have now were available to you after you came out of trance. Maybe you'll do it in some unique way that I couldn't even imagine. And the sounds behind us have changed. And the sounds through the wall have changed. I don't know if you realized when, but you can remember the sound of the air conditioner and traffic. These are just ways that a person has of reorienting the self into the room.

And bringing back that dissociated portion, so that you don't lose anything that you need to have about you. Or coming back into the chair where your body was, while I was speaking. And open your eyes and come on back.

3. **Trance phenomena goal:** *Use age regression anecdotes and suggestions for exploration and revivification of some pleasant childhood resources for subsequent therapy work.*

Metaphor

. . . And your conscious mind can be expecting, wondering, and let your unconscious mind go into the depth of trance you think you want. There really isn't much reason to . . . [long pause]

A friend of mine visited a woman in Santa Barbara, California. And they met on a mountaintop, outside the city, seven miles from the ocean. He had to drive up the mountain in the dark, following the instructions of turning left at the first dirt road and going three miles, turning right on the second dirt road, making a sharp left and going straight ahead until you fork to the right and climb up the hill, and coming down the mountain you had to bear left at the fork, and take the immediate right. Passing the next road on the left and taking the left and going three miles back on the dirt road to the main road.

It seemed like an odd instruction, but for some reason Mona wanted David to go halfway up the mountain and return. And he was to drive four miles further down the highway and to exit from the highway again to the left. And then the instructions were to "go up and up and up." That's it.

He was to begin to drive by going halfway up the mountain and by exiting on the first dirt road and going three miles, turning to the left and on the second road to the right, turning immediately and going straight and bearing to the right. And at some unknown point, he was to turn around and drive back down bearing to the left. Turning to the left and passing a road before turning to the right and going three miles on the dirt road back to the highway. A few miles further down the highway he was to turn left again and the only instruction was to "go up and up and up." He knew it was going to be interesting to be with Mona.

And when he finally got to the top of the mountain, there was her house. And the tree outside the house had hanging from it exercise rings that she liked to tumble on. As soon as daybreak came, Mona packed a small pack and they began hiking down the mountain on a dirt trail. She said, "It's only going to take 20 minutes."

And going down the mountain they passed on foot the road that he had circled. And further down the mountain stumbling in the dust, down small dirt roads, the road led to some houses off into the distance. And finally they came to the overturned tree, right beside a bright red tree, so bright red David thought the magic was already beginning.

Now every American child's heard about Alice in Wonderland, and how Alice went down a rabbit hole. David said, "You wouldn't believe the size of the hole that she went into, where the tree that had fallen on the edge of the cliff had an exposed root system." There was an opening about the size underneath your chair. And she disappeared right into that root system. He didn't even think his hips would fit into that hole, but they did.

And then, using your hands, you hold onto the branch with your right hand, lifting your butt up, put your butt down somewhere else, and lift up again with your hands against the overhanging branches which were actually the root system of the overturned tree. And somewhere from inside the large root system is the hole on the other side. Exiting and going down the hill, as your body becomes more accelerated, it feels lighter, and the opening of the root system that you held on to with your hands is the last time you held on to anything with that hand.

Deeper and deeper, off she went ahead of him in the distance. And you're just left, right there on the hillside, floating in the endless 20-minute experience. You may have your own idea about what David did then.

Now you've been sitting there in trance and your cheek muscles have flattened out and your right hand's found a way to raise off of your lap and float nicely in the air. It may go all the way to your face, it may go halfway to your face, it may stay right where it is floating nicely in the air. It may float in front of you. You may find that you have it right in front of your eyes, looking into the palm of your hand. Maybe it will go back down onto your thigh. Maybe it will do that after you come out of trance. Your conscious mind has something to wonder about.

I doubt if you're wondering about the pipeline that I haven't yet mentioned. It was almost hidden in the underbrush, but you could see that pipeline from somewhere to somewhere else. It doesn't really matter.

I wonder how many different ways can you recognize the unimportance of small events, the shoes you're wearing today, whether or not your shirt is red. Everybody has a lot of experiences in recognizing that the world can go on about you, it doesn't really affect you sometimes. And some people say, "It doesn't matter if I vote, what difference does it make?" You take time out just for you. And if the world goes on without you, it won't get very away. It doesn't really matter. Now you probably couldn't care less whether or not it was your right or left hand that raised to your face. You might not even be interested. Your conscious mind might wonder, and let your unconscious mind do what it wants. But who cares? The unconscious mind is going to do what it wants. It doesn't care.

Your conscious mind seems to be willing to observe and find out just as it did when you first went into trance. So, your conscious mind doesn't care. There are a lot of ways in which you cannot pay careful attention to things. You probably realize that. A person can make a lot of lists. And you don't even remember what you put on the list two days ago. Unless something is important, it's better for you to let your unconscious mind deal with it in appropriate ways. As a matter of fact, if something is very important, it's a good idea for you not to think about it very much consciously, and let your unconscious mind handle it in appropriate ways. So you can let your conscious mind not pay any attention to certain things of importance and let your unconscious mind handle the details. Or you can let your conscious mind notice the details that you're letting your unconscious mind handle and not think about.

You didn't have to be reminded that you weren't thinking about the location of your feet on the floor. You're relaxed in trance, you're sitting against the chair nicely. You may have not given any thought to some of the sounds in the room. Who cares about them actually? It would be nice to realize that they have nothing to do with your purpose.

And you might be interested in realizing that your unconscious knows a great deal about not noticing a lot of things, forgetting about them entirely. You don't need to not remember a lot of things, if you've already forgotten them. You know about Sunday mornings in April of 1983. And it's easy to forget about them just like it is Saturday afternoons. Some people said they forgot entirely what they did during the week before. I wonder if you can remember how. It's going to make it very easy to realize that Saturday afternoon wasn't worth remembering.

A lot of times things feel very good, very carefree. And you can remember that. But your conscious mind doesn't necessarily remember the Saturday afternoon. Could have been a Saturday afternoon in 1953. And you can remember carefree moments on Saturday afternoons.

Some people say they have carefree moments after they've completed the task of raking the leaves. And then it's okay to play in them. And then there are hills covered with snow. And you don't really remember which hill. Probably don't even care consciously. It's forgotten about. But your unconscious remembers a lot of things. It's a good idea to use those things.

I wonder what you'd think about if I talked about snowsledding down the hill behind my house. There were three hills in a row, separated by a road. And the road got so icy and snowy you could sled right across it. I'll tell you one thing, I got a lot of snow in my boots climbing up those hills. And it's always funny that brown corduroy pants collect little clots of snow around the top of your boots. And the little rope that's connected to the front of the sled gets so hardened and crusted with moisture that freezes.

Now I know that you are aware that most children experimented in the wintertime with their sleds. They usually forget about the time they touched their tongue to the metal, just as you can forget about a lot of things that aren't important at all. Sooner or later you have no business remembering experiences.

You can look forward or look back to the time when you don't remember when this session happened. Sometime in your life. And it's good to know that it's sometime in your life. But why should you remember whether or not something happened at 11 o'clock, or whether it was Thursday afternoon. You know it was in the 20th century. Er, or was that the 21st century? [*pause*]

A lot of people dream colors of blue. And you can have velvety textured backgrounds and velvety colored dreams. And you can think you're dreaming in color, but not the color blue. You think you're dreaming in colors of red, green. But as you begin to awaken from the dream, you only have those shades of blue.

And a lot of times it's the same with all of life's experiences. Blue velvet absorbs the light. You can't even tell if it's black. You have to look very closely. And if the entire room were wallpapered in dark blue velvet, I wonder how much easier it would make it to ignore all the stimulus in the room and forget about it entirely as if it were a dream.

Now sooner or later you are going to have some idea in your past that you'd like to recall. I don't know if you'd like to feel the snow on your face on a nice snowsledding trip down that hill. Maybe you'd like to feel holding a hammer in your hand. Sooner or later something of relevance from [*pause*] maybe biology class.

When I was in third grade, my airplane cards got left in my desk. I'd collected them quite a while and I can really try hard to remember what was on those airplane cards. I remember various features. Size, color, and that smell. It might be a good idea for you to pick some certain interesting memory that might come to your mind. Maybe it's trying to glue that cockpit into that classic airplane. And a lot of the thoughts that you have as you do that can become very absorbing in your current . . . time. Now your unconscious has a number of ideas regarding whether it would be useful for you to find some interesting moment, perhaps the age of eight or seven, maybe six.

And I don't know whether or not you will be able to revivify those experiences that happened just prior to the birthday at six. But you'll probably remember the day of the week, sooner or later. Probably realize it's possible to anticipate the lunch or the dinner that you're having that day. Maybe you'll remember what you expect to get for your birthday. Where you expect it to be hidden. Or maybe you'd prefer to bit by bit remember the experience before your eighth birthday instead. It really doesn't make any difference. You might want to remember the day before your seventh birthday.

And, of course, you're going to have a lot of thoughts of your own. Some of the thoughts you can share and some of them you won't share. Some of your mind is with me and some of your mind is with you.

But the more you have an opportunity to relive the experience of childhood, the more you ought to be reminded of the experiences of your conscious memories, the distant future. It's nice to know that you're going to have one.

And how many different ways can you know that sitting in this office as an adult is something you are going to do someday in your distant future. You don't need to think about it now. Because the more the conscious mind can be reassured about that, the more your unconscious has an opportunity to relive that earlier experience. In various ways you begin to recognize the belief that your experience is real.

At some time, I don't know just when, you really have those fleeting understandings of the reality of those thoughts and feelings, expectations about that birthday. You really ought to have an opportunity to keep some of it to yourself. But you can find things to talk about and you might find something to talk about to me.

Yes? It's all right to keep your experience while your words come. Tell me what you're aware of. Go on. Only the part you want others to know. The rest you keep.

[*Client*] "I have this, I see this, this cowboy suit. This cowboy suit has chaps, and there's a hat."

"When did you get it?"

"For my birthday."

"How far away is your birthday?"

"It feels like it's . . ."

"Today?"

"Yea. It's got a holster, and a gun." [*client laughs*]

"Is it leather?"

"Yea. Smells like a cowboy. It's beautiful."

"What color's the handle?"

"It's white. It's got a longhorn cow's head on it."

"Does it shoot?"

"Uh-huh. Shoots caps. There's a hat too."

"Have you opened all your presents?"

"That's all, just the cowboy suit. The chaps have fur."

"And how do you look with the chaps on?"

"Good."

"How do they feel? Do they stop your movement? Can you run?"

"Mm-hmm."

Let's go play in them. Memorize all those experiences. Give yourself permission to feel good, because the learnings we get in childhood are learnings that we use throughout our life. What else are you doing?

"Practicing drawing my gun."

And practicing drawing your gun you can feel so happy that . . . sometimes you can feel so happy you can't even tell other people how you feel. And being unable to tell other people how happy you feel doesn't stop you feeling that way, does it? That's true even if they won't listen, you can still feel happy, later in life. One time, when you're playing cowboys, you probably have a lot of time to daydream about the Indians, the horses.

Now I wonder if you ever realize how the Lone Ranger never stays around to take any thanks. Just leaves a silver bullet behind and that's enough. That must make him feel really good. And knowing that you're doing a good job builds your character, even if other people don't get around to telling you. And I just wonder if playing cowboy, you learn a lot about doing a good job and keeping it to yourself. Do you have silver bullets?

And I wonder if you realize that when you awaken from a dream you can remember glimpses of it, and they seem like black velvet on blue background.

You know your hand is halfway to your face. I wonder if your right hand will gradually or slowly begin to twist your wrist up comfortably, orienting towards your eyes, so that you can open your eyes just a little bit and look into the palm of your hand and see something that you'd like to remember. The fingers are moving just a little bit. I think your wrist is beginning to twist just a little bit. And you might not know what you expect to remember. That's right. Beginning to twist.

And as it does, it's bringing your palm into the vicinity that you could look into the palm of your hand. There's another quarter of an inch. Certainly exhibiting that cataleptic movement so typical of the trance subject. Nice unconscious response. The second hand of the clock moves around one-thirtieth of the way every two seconds. One sixtieth of the way every second. A hundred and eighty degrees different after only 30 seconds.

A small jerky movement. Now it moved another little notch. And I'd say your hand's about seven o'clock or seven-thirty. And another movement, it's more like eight o'clock, eight-fifteen. Another alteration, coming around to eight o'clock. I bet you hope it's not the hour hand we're watching. It must be your second hand. Your first hand's over here on your lap. And another alteration, another alteration. It's almost at nine o'clock. By the time it reaches ten o'clock, you should be able to open your eyes just a little bit.

[*A longer diagnostic and therapeutic age regressed exploration continued in the original transcript to further apply the content from the age regression phenomenon the client is experiencing. This portion is deleted here as it is not relevant to the goal of the chapter.*]

Finally, Mona announced that it was time to change directions and go back up the mountain. He heard that with mixed reactions. He wasn't sure he was ready to leave that comfortable and ever-so interesting nitch he had climbed down into, but there was that pipeline. It actually reached all the way down to a pool at the crevice of the mountains and somehow transported the fresh, pure water back up the mountain.

You might think about a pipeline to the unconscious that you could follow anytime, hand over hand, as far down as you care to go, or up.

He was also relieved, because there is something comfortable about the familiarity of the present time. And then he was amazed at how quickly they came back upon the exposed root system and the little hole through which he had slipped so long ago. And yet maybe it had only been moments before?

This time he took a moment lying there cradled in the heart of the root system to memorize the security, to be at one with the roots in which he was nestled so comfortably.

And then, only moments later, he was again blinded by the staggering beauty of that brilliantly red tree that had changed its hue only so slightly as the sun shone on it from a different angle.

"So, how did you like it and what did you learn?" Mona asked. He said he wasn't ready to answer her for a long time, and it's nice to know that you can take all the time you need to go backwards and forward in remembering an experience.

4. Trance phenomena goal: *Use body distortion for the modulation of emotional pain.*

Metaphor[38]

I had a client with a dental phobia. Because of early childhood traumas and learnings, he had not been to a dentist in [*age of client*] number of years. Because of lack of care, he had also developed a compound problem of being so ashamed of the state of his mouth that

---

[38] This metaphor was contributed by Gary Goodman, M.Ed., and Robert Schwarz, Ph.D.

he really had something to be embarrassed about. And that embarrassment really made it difficult to get the care that he needed. He was so embarrassed about his mouth that when he came to see me, he kept his hand in front of his mouth all the time. And that hand was an important protective mechanism. And you really ought to be able to protect your areas of pain and embarrassment and vulnerability in the best ways possible.

So I explained to him a simple procedure that every child has experienced when they played in the snow too long or held on to something very cold for a long time. This matter of glove anesthesia can really be of help to you, I said to him, in learning to regulate the level of pain that people can experience at various points in their life.

I asked him to imagine a memory where your hand became numb. There are many different experiences that a person has over the years of developing a feeling of numbness. There is the experience of novocaine, that feeling of thickness and tingling. Then, there is the strange experience of waking up comfortably, and discovering that your arm has gone totally asleep, because you rested on it in an unusual manner. You cannot move that arm. You cannot feel that arm. But you can feel that feeling of numbness in a variety of ways at different times. And you did not know it then, but it was an experience that would be useful to you later. And you were not unable to disregard that learning. It comes in the present when you least expect it.

Now, how does a person go about developing *sensory alteration?* Your unconscious mind can develop the abilities to be a part of and apart from simultaneously. Now an idea develops in the mind. First, you think about the possibility of that sensory alteration. And as the conscious mind thinks about that possibility of a sensory alteration, the unconscious mind begins to translate that possibility into an actuality. And how is it that an idea moves from the mind to become a part of and apart from the body?

Now Al first noticed the tingling developing in his finger tips which spread at a pace that was appropriate to his needs. And, of course, this is just a general example of how to apply learnings. Gradually, that tingling became a numbing kind of experience, the kind of numbing that you would really want to have to soothe a variety of kinds of discomfort. And everyone has their own ideas of a comfortable kind of numbness.

And being in a hypnotic state is similar to being in a dream state. In a dream you can go anywhere, do anything in the safety of your own developing experience, because your unconscious mind always protects you in your dreams. And you can dream during the night, and you can dream about your future, and you can wander safely in your daydreams now or tomorrow or anytime according to the developing needs of the present self in relation to the past and the future selves.

And I do not know exactly when he had those learnings in that dream. And in that dream, he found himself standing in front of a full-length mirror. He had the absorbing experience of watching himself sitting comfortably in the dentist chair, he noticed one of the hands begin to glow and gently vibrate. Simultaneously, he began to experience a sensory alteration in one of his hands. You can imagine that he was not surprised to feel that numbness in his hand, and it is a natural human experience to take a hand, especially your own hand, and to place it on that sensitive spot that needs healing. So Al watched that hand touch his jaw, and as that hand touched his cheek, that numbness spread into his jaw.

Simultaneously, he knew that those fears were being numbed as well. In a dream one can make novel connections. Al knew that he was going to be able to deal with that dentist from now on, and he also realized that what he just learned about soothing the physical could be applied to soothing all of those emotional sensitivities in an appropriate fashion.

He looked in the mirror again. The scene changed. He saw himself standing naked with different scenes from his life unfolding behind him. He saw different scars on his body, some of them from real injuries, but most of them were symbolic scars of the different emotional battles he had had to fight. He looked down to see his hand flowing. He watched in a detached manner as that hand reached up and started touching the different scars. One by one those areas also started to glow, and I'm not sure as to the sensations that went along with those changes.

But the unconscious mind can get used to that soothing feeling. And as each one of those symbolic scars started to melt away, Al could feel water developing in pools just in the corners of his eyes. And there are so many different kinds of tears: tears of pain, tears of sorrow, tears of hurt, tears of anger, tears of grief, tears of relief, tears of understanding, tears of strength, tears of forgiveness, tears of appreciation.

And the scene changed again. Al saw himself as he was, now with these new learnings, and standing along side of him was a younger version of himself. And I asked Al to retain all of the resources that you learned in this trance.

And each person's case is entirely different, and it would be nice to remind that adult self in that trance of the ability that belongs to everyone. And Al had relearned that you can take care of that physical pain in the present, that emotional pain in the past, in the present, and now he was going to learn how to apply those learnings in the future. Al was prepared to help that younger part of himself which had previously been so alone. And when you take care of a younger part of yourself, you need to take with you those new learnings.

And so he symbolically passed on to that part of himself a sense of belonging and the capacity to modulate painful experience to tolerable levels. And just what is a tolerable level? Every person has their own level of tolerance for different experiences. Of course, your level of tolerance is not the same as your level of perfect comfort. And it is a good thing that human beings can appreciate the importance of knowing the difference between perfection and tolerance.

Every child tolerates the inconvenience of falling down in exchange for learning how to walk, recognizing that you need to stumble before you are graceful. And, in fact, I suppose there is some similarity in the process of gradually strengthening the muscles of the legs and stomach and back that are necessary in learning how to walk and the process of gradually increasing the level of emotional intensity that is safe and productive.

In both situations it is impossible to notice the gradual changes until you can take the time to look back and appreciate your accomplishments. And as I asked Al to relive the incidents that had happened that were so important, his hand already was beginning to glow in anticipation of placing it on that younger part of himself at the appropriate times and certainly at the appropriate part of the body, especially one or two of them and observe how he would handle them using his adult self as a resource.

And I could see those small movements that were communications from the unconscious mind that Al was reliving those incidents. I do not know if they were occurring one at a time or in some simultaneous fashion, but I do know that the unconscious mind can transmit learnings at a pace that is within a person's limits of tolerance. And Al was touching that younger self and transferring just the right amount of numbness so that the pain would be there at tolerable levels.

And fear would be there at tolerable levels. And anxiety would be there at tolerable levels. And tears would be there at tolerable levels at the right time and place your hand there just where you need it to be. Because you need to know that all of those emotions can be useful when you can modulate their intensity.

And being there for yourself gives that child in you the strength to reexamine certain misconceptions of the young child with his own words. Make sure that you remind the little boy of something that you don't have to be told, but he needs to know. He did not know then that inherent in the capacity of every person is that ability to soothe those hurts. How could that young Al know that he would learn to develop a special type of glowing in the hand?

It is difficult to know how long it will take to solidify new learnings. It certainly was not necessary for me to give Al any posthypnotic suggestions about using these new learnings to deal with the dentist. But I did suggest to him, you employ your developing ability to explore these new possibilities in a series of dreams, over a series of weeks.

And rehearse your ability to modulate those feelings and experiences that, in the past, would have been so threatening to you. And I was not really sure how he would go about doing that. It may have been by seeing himself in that mirror again, either reviewing previous learning or applying the ability to use that glowing in your hand to meet current needs.

And he would be pleased to know that his unconscious mind was working overtime by that gentle recognition of a sensory alteration upon awakening.

11

Metaphors for Children

The child is father of the man.
—William Wordsworth

The potential possibilities of any child are the most intriguing and stimulating in all creation.
—Ray L. Wilbur

The best way to make children good is to make them happy.
—Oscar Wilde

In our final chapter we would like to be sensitive to the fact that stories are often thought to be the realm of the child. And, in so doing, we want to share some ideas and examples of these therapeutic protocols in children's stories. Each of us as therapists has had countless opportunities to tell stories to children who are in attendance in a therapy session. As a personal aside, each of us who is a parent has far more opportunity, even necessity, to tell stories to our children. We feel that many of the stories told to children—e.g., Mother Goose—are often of very little therapeutic value and sometimes are not even entertaining. There is, with the listening child, an inquiring mind. The unconscious mind of the child, as with the adult, is set to the purpose of learning to cope with and master the ecosystemic demands which face them.

And yet, when we look at the commercial stories available for children, the intended learnings are sometimes unclear. And even if the wicked witch is destroyed in the end, many times the experiences inadvertently retrieved on the way to this conclusion can be the traumatic stuff of which nightmares are made. At other times protagonists resort to the use of magic, which puts children in touch with few useful experiential resources, if any.

When we set out to tell a therapeutic story, of course, we are careful about our selection of experiences and the sequencing of those experiences. Generally, we apply the same criteria with children as we do with adults, that is, we ask ourselves which behaviors, attitudes, emotions, and so on need to be retrieved, illustrated, or developed. Then, we apply the same protocol guidelines in creating stories to address those goals. The imagery, context, or content that is selected and the age of the protagonists will be modified in accordance with who the client is. Several important features to keep in mind when the clients are children are summarized by Nick Seferlis, a school psychologist, who has often used this framework in telling therapeutic metaphors to the children in his school system:

1. Make sure to be age-appropriate or grade-appropriate with vocabulary selection.
2. Attention span is shorter with younger children and stories need to be shorter and contain less verbal drama and detail.
3. The child will show greater identification with children or people as opposed to inanimate objects. Therefore, the greater the base of reality in the story, as opposed to fantasy, the better. It seems that the child is able to identify quicker with real people as opposed to fantasized and made-up things.
4. Use story voices as dramatic devices. The use of rudimentary tonal emphasis, dropping tone or raising it to portray characters, is adequate for most children. Children become engrossed at the tone of the story, whereas adults often prefer that drama be regulated with syntactical (word selection) devices.
5. When children hear a story being told, they are more likely to respond with experiential participation if there is a slow delivery done with great emphasis.

We have told stories to children in situations involving groups of children and in family therapy, and we have told countless bedtime and other times stories to our own children. Sometimes the goal is therapy and sometimes the goal is pure enjoyment or entertainment.

A version of the first story in this section has been independently published as a children's book. In that context, it is illustrated and can be used by parents as an aid in helping children overcome fears without seeking professional help. As it is included here, it is offered as a guide or example to the professional of a type of story that can be told to children in therapy, with or without their parents.

1. Therapeutic goal (using self-image thinking protocol): Learn to overcome fears of noise, movement, people, animals, and crowds.

Metaphor: The Blammo—Surprise! Book[39]

This is the story of Poodgie, Paradora, and Knowsis and the *Blammo— Surprise! Book*. Poodgie, Paradora, and Knowsis are three wonderful and amazing children. They have many adventures together. They are about to become heroes today, at least heroes for their friend Terry. They are about to help Terry overcome a very big problem.

Well, actually, it was Knowsis who was really going to solve the problem and he was going to solve it with his *Blammo—Surprise! Book*, but he didn't know that at first. And Poodgie would also think that she had solved it. But what was the problem?

Well, we're getting a little bit ahead of the story because in the beginning no one even knew that there was a problem. This was especially true for Paradora, the big sister. She never ever knew that there were any problems. If there were any, she never noticed them. And she never talked about them if she should happen to notice one by accident. She was too busy saying, "Everything is wonderful, everything is lovely." She really meant it, too!

But Terry was dreading the trip they had all planned to go to the circus. Her friends intended to go on Saturday, and all week long she hoped that the school week would last longer than ever before. But, despite her wish that the day would never come, Saturday morning the sun grinned a big hello in her bedroom window.

Meanwhile, at his house, Knowsis was very excited about going to the circus, but he wondered what he was going to do before it was time to go. He got out his crayons and he started drawing in an empty book. When he got done he named it his *Blammo—Surprise! Book*, but he didn't show it to anybody. The only reason to mention it now is that Knowsis's *Blammo—Surprise! Book* was, mysteriously, going to turn out to be the very thing that Terry needed in order to enjoy the circus and solve a very big problem she had.

---

[39] Lankton, S. (1988). *The Blammo—Surprise! Book*. New York: Magination Press, Brunner/Mazel, Inc.

Everyone got in the car, finally, to go to the circus and they drove all the way across town to where the big tent was. Poodgie said she wanted to ride the elephants. She was too small last year to go to the circus. This year she really wanted to ride the elephant and smell the thick grey skin and feel it sway back and forth and hear its feet go clomp clomp around the ring. She asked Terry if she would come with her. But Terry said, "I don't think I will. It would probably be more fun for you to go alone."

While they were sitting in the bleachers at the circus, the clowns all ran out. Their faces were painted white with great big smiles and they had curly orange hair and baggy pants and big checkered shirts and suspenders. Poodgie and Paradora and Knowsis were giggling as the clowns' shoes flopped around. One clown turned and paddled another clown with a board, and one clown spilled a pitcher of water all over another clown. It was about this time that Poodgie looked over at Terry and said, "Isn't this fun?"

Terry just sat there. Terry was about as white as the clown. Poodgie said, "Aren't you having fun?" Terry said, "Oh, not very much." Poodgie thought she probably liked something better at the circus than the clowns. Paradora thought she was probably waiting for the acrobats and the lions. Knowsis noticed that Terry looked, in fact, a little bit scared and that she was holding on to the seat very tightly. He was enjoying the clowns, but he began thinking, "Pretty soon the clowns are going to be tripping over each other and riding around in little fire engines, and they're going to be knocking each other's hats off. I've seen all that before. I think I'll watch Terry a little more closely." You see, Knowsis always watched things carefully.

Terry, Knowsis noticed, just sat there with her knuckles turning white from gripping her seat. He guessed that she was afraid of the noise and clowns. He was about to say something when the whistle blew and the ringmaster threw his hat in the air. The lions came bounding out of their cages. "Wow," said Poodgie, "this is the part I like best!" "Look at those big teeth," said Paradora. Knowsis was caught up in the excitement, too. They watched as the lion tamer cracked his whip and made the lions jump through hoops of fire.

Pretty soon, Poodgie turned around to say to Terry, "Isn't this just the greatest circus of all?" Terry had her head down and she wasn't looking. "What's the matter?" asked Poodgie. "You're supposed to be having fun." Knowsis agreed with his little sister. He thought that everyone should be having fun when the lions were out. He said, "Terry, are you scared?" And Terry said, "Well, yes, a little bit."

Nobody knew what to do.

Just then the lions ran off the stage as fast as they had run on. And the tumblers came leaping across the circus ring.

Knowsis looked at Terry. Terry was still looking very uncomfortable. In fact, now she even had a little tear coming out of her eye. Knowsis said, "Why are you crying Terry?" She said, "I'm kind of afraid when the people start jumping around like that." The acrobats started climbing up the poles. Trapeze artists got on their swings, swinging back and forth and grabbing hold of each other. Terry was crying real hard now. "That's the part I hate the most. Those people are up so high and something terrible might happen."

"That's silly," said Poodgie. "They have a net. If they fell, they would fall right into the net." Knowsis said, "That's right. You're quite safe at the circus. There's no need to be scared." "I am, though," said Terry, "I'm *really* scared and I want to go home."

Poodgie said, "Oh, not before we ride the elephants. Come on Terry." She grabbed Terry's hand and ran off the bleachers with her to get a ticket for the elephant ride. "I don't want to ride the elephants," Terry said, "I just want to go home." But Poodgie said, "Oh, no, it will be so much fun riding on the elephant. It will sway back and forth and you'll be able to feel its thick grey skin. It will make a big noise with its trunk and you can even touch its ears!" "I don't want to do that," said Terry, "I want to go home. I'm very very scared, I never should have come at all." Then she pulled loose from Poodgie.

Knowsis had run behind and he had heard the whole conversation. While Paradora sat on the bleachers to enjoy the show, and Poodgie waited for the elephant ride, Knowsis took Terry by the hand. He said, "Terry, I want to show you something. It's my *Blammo—Surprise! Book.* I just made it today." "Okay," said Terry, because anything at all that would get her away from the circus was a good idea to her. Terry and Knowsis sat quietly outside the tent where nobody else was. Very officially and with great ceremony, Knowsis handed her his *Blammo—Surprise! Book.* "Now all you have to do," said Knowsis, "to use my *Blammo—Surprise! Book,*" and he said this in his most serious voice, "is to listen to what I'm going to say to you, to turn the pages when I tell you, and to read the pages when you turn them. Are you ready?" Terry said, "Yes." Terry was really good at reading books. In fact, she had often decided it was better to read books than to go places or do things that would scare her.

Now, Knowsis wasn't exactly sure what he was going to do with the *Blammo* book, but he knew that when he went to the circus, or for that matter, when he went anyplace, even if other people sometimes got scared, he didn't feel scared. He had figured out that the reason he didn't feel scared was because he was always busy feeling something else. He thought that his surprise book might help Terry feel something else. Here's how he decided to do it.

"First," he said to Terry, "you're going to have to think. Close your eyes and think of being really comfortable some place. You must have been really comfortable in a lot of places before." She agreed that she was really comfortable in a few places. She was comfortable when she visited her grandmother. She was comfortable when she took a bath. "Good, that's the idea," said Knowsis, "think of where you've been comfortable before. Then as soon as you are feeling comfortable, open the first page of the book and look at it while you're feeling really comfortable. Don't turn the page until you really feel a good, comfortable feeling." Then Knowsis waited.

Sure enough, in just a couple of minutes, Terry said, "I'm feeling pretty comfortable now." So she turned the page, and there, *blammo,* was a great big yellow sun with the word "blammo" on it.

"Don't turn any other pages yet," Knowsis said. "Before you do, think of all the things you would like to be feeling instead of scared." "Well," she said, "I would like to feel brave; I'd like to feel happy; I'd like to feel safe, and sometimes I'd like to feel silly. And sometimes I'd like to feel confident and, also, excited." "Good," he said. "Now, remember a time you felt very happy." Terry's face lit up when she remembered a time she felt really, really happy. Knowsis said, "Now, think about what was going on and who was there and how it felt to feel happy. When you feel really happy, turn the page."

Terry turned the page, with a big smile on her face, and, *blammo,* there was another big yellow sun with the word "blammo" on it. Terry laughed.

"Now," Knowsis said, "remember a time when you felt really brave. Remember a time and a place when you felt the brave kind of a feeling you would like to feel." When Terry's face changed from that smile to a look of being brave, Knowsis said, "Turn the page now while you feel that brave." Terry turned the page and, *blammo,* there was the sun looking back. And the smile from when she was happy came back to her face, also.

"Now," Knowsis said, "remember a time when you felt silly." That was easy for Terry, and she giggled. Knowsis said, "Turn the page right away now that you're silly." She turned the page and, *blammo,* there was another yellow sun with the word "blammo." On Terry's face was a giggle and a smile, and also a look of being brave.

"Now," Knowsis said, "remember a time when you felt really safe." Terry gave out a big relaxed sigh and a warm little smile. "When you feel safe, but not before, turn the page." Terry enjoyed that feeling of being safe and turned the page to see another sun—*blammo.* A little giggle and a little smile came to Terry's face, too, all mixing together with the feeling of being safe while looking at that blammo-sunshine.

"Now think of a time that you felt the other feelings you want to have. You've gotten happy and safe and brave and silly. How about the other feelings of confident or excited?" So Terry remembered a time when she had gotten all the right answers in a spelling bee. She couldn't decide whether it was a confident or an excited feeling or if she was having them both, but it sure was a good feeling. So she turned the page, and, *blammo,* there was another sun.

"Now," Knowsis said, "try to have all those feelings at the same time. Think of the earliest time you can think of ever being scared, but instead of being scared, look at the blammo-sunshine picture and feel all the feelings that you remember when you see that picture." So Terry turned the page and looked at the sun. A little smile and a look of being brave and that new feeling of confidence and excitement were all on Terry's face. Terry thought about the earliest time she could remember being scared, but thinking about that time didn't make her scared now because she was feeling all the good feelings even while thinking about that old time when she had been scared. "I'm not scared now," Terry said.

"Good," said Knowsis, "let's do that one more time." Terry thought and said "Okay, I'm going to think of another time I was scared and then turn the page just as I begin to remember feeling scared." She turned the page.

Blammo, there was the sunshine. She said, "I don't feel scared thinking about that one either."

"Good," said Knowsis. "Now think about being at the circus and turn the page just as you do." So Terry started thinking about being at the circus and just as that scary feeling started coming, she turned the page and, *Blammo,* saw the sunshine again. She giggled and a little smile came, and she said, "I'm still not afraid. That's amazing."

"Yes, but that's not the surprise," said Knowsis, "that's still coming." Now think about riding on the elephant. Terry confidently thought about riding on the elephant and turned the page and smiled and giggled and looked brave and happy.

"Now the surprise is really going to come," said Knowsis. "Think about how, in the future, you're not going to have that scary feeling anymore and look at the last page." By now Terry was sure that the last page was going to be another blammo-sunshine. She started thinking of a time in the future. She said, "Okay, now I'm thinking of a time in the future when I'm not going to be scared." She turned the page to find a mirror at the end of the book.

"Surprise!" said Knowsis. And there was Terry's face looking brave and happy and silly and safe and confident and excited. She saw that face in the mirror, her own face. And she said, "That's quite a surprise, Knowsis." "Yes, it is," he agreed, and added, "That's the *Blammo—Surprise! Book.*" "Thank you very much," she said, giving him a big hug.

"Come on, it's not too late to ride the elephant," Knowsis urged her. "Okay," said Terry, and she giggled thinking about the elephant. As she got up on that elephant to ride around the ring, Terry remembered the face that she saw reflected at the end of the *Blammo—Surprise! Book.* And that's the face that she wore all day long. And that's the face she wore most days after that.

And that's how Knowsis saved the day. But, of course, Poodgie thought that she had saved the day because it was her idea to buy tickets for the elephant ride. Poodgie thought, "Look how Terry stopped being afraid and had a lot of fun riding on the elephant. It's because of my good idea that Terry feels happy instead of scared."

The *Blammo—Surprise! Book* remained a special secret between Terry and Knowsis. But Knowsis knows that he and his book helped Terry to use thinking and imagination to stop feeling scared.

2. Therapeutic goal (using behavior and self-image protocols): *Learn self-control.*

Metaphor: "Timmy and the Magic Mirror"[40]

There's this kid at another school who has had a lot of trouble at recess. This boy Timmy would go out to the playground and he'd hit the other kids, saying they started it first, and ruin games that people were playing. Sometimes he'd grab a football and just start running, or there was the time he kept running through the girls' jump rope.

Timmy would lose a lot of his recesses. Sometimes the teacher would put him on the wall, other times he'd just be put in the classroom or

---

[40] This metaphor was contributed by Nicholas G. Seferlis, M.S.

the office until recess was over. But this is not the reason why this story is called "Timmy and the Magic Mirror."

I spoke to Timmy one day and asked him how he wound up missing so many of his recesses. Timmy told me that recess was for having fun. But some kids would call him a name or push him because they knew it would get him into trouble. Timmy told me he was not going to be a sissy and that it was important to be tough and strong. I told Timmy that of course it is important for him to be tough and strong. But do you think you're tough enough to try to last at recess for one minute *without any trouble*—no matter even if someone calls you a name, or pushes? Can you keep your hands to yourself?

Timmy told me that he would be able to do it—he said it was going to be easy. Still, this was not the reason this is called "Timmy and the Magic Mirror." But sure enough, Timmy went out the next day and nothing happened out on the playground. You know that one minute is not a very long time and Timmy did just fine.

When Timmy came in, I asked if he was tough enough to do five minutes of recess, keeping his hands to himself and not bothering any of the other children's games or playing. Five minutes can be a long time, but Timmy went out there on the playground and began playing catch with one of the other boys from his class. Then I told him that his five minutes were up.

I asked how he made out at recess, and he told me that he started playing catch and that the time really went by fast. Timmy told me he wanted to try a longer time the following day.

I told Timmy that a longer time might be a good idea. We decided that 10 minutes would be tried the next day. Well, when I looked out onto the playground, I saw Timmy playing touch football with a group of boys. They all were busy, planning each play and doing their best to get a goal.

During one of the breaks I saw Timmy waiting for the other team to get into position. All of a sudden a group of kids who were playing tag came by and one ran smack, dab into Timmy. I looked at Timmy and Timmy looked at the kid—and you probably guessed what I thought was going to happen. Timmy looked and then smiled. He had a smile on his face, breathing from the stomach, arm relaxed and in control. His head was held high and he returned to the football game.

After 10 minutes, I went out and got him. At first he asked if he could stay out just a little longer—I told him we could plan to have the whole recess tomorrow. When Timmy came in, we talked about today's recess and he said he was having a lot of fun and that he definitely wanted to stay out longer. Timmy told me that during the game a kid bumped into him and he thought it must have been an accident, since he knew what it was like to have fun and paying attention to only his game.

So we got set to have 15 minutes or a full recess the next day. We still wanted to see if he was strong and tough enough to last 15 minutes without any problems. On the big day, Timmy went out for recess and had a good time playing with the other kids. He played tag for a while and then was asked to play catch. All really went well until Timmy missed the ball and someone called him "fumbles."

He just looked at them, then pretended he didn't hear that. He kept playing and enjoying the fun a lot. Finally, at the end of recess, all the boys and girls lined up and Timmy took his place in line. All of a sudden a kid cut in front of Timmy and stepped on his toe, maybe even on purpose. You know what happened? Timmy stood straight up, breathed deep, and smiled. He had a smile on his face, breathing from the stomach, arm relaxed and in control. His head was held high.

Timmy came in and knew that he made it for a full 15 minutes. He walked with his head up and felt very proud. It was like the time he won the second-grade field race. You know that feeling of doing something special. Other teachers looked at Timmy. It was almost like the school had a new Timmy.

But this still doesn't explain about "Timmy and the Magic Mirror."

When he got to my office, I showed Timmy a mirror. I told him to take a good look at himself and remember what it's like feeling proud with a slight smile on his face, breathing regular and strong from his stomach. As we were talking there was the shuffling sound of a class going by, probably to the lunch room.

Timmy once again looked at the mirror and watched his face as he began to feel like what it was like to be able to control himself as he did on that playground. He thought about the different ways to handle situations, sometimes ignoring them, sometimes talking about them, or maybe some things he didn't even think of yet.

As he looked into the mirror, I asked him to see that feeling of pride and being able to control himself. You can see yourself with a smile on your face, breathing from the stomach, and in control. Your head is held high just like someone's pulling your hair straight up. And as he thought of that, I also asked him to think of all the other people who knew he had done a good job, like his teachers and me whom he could see behind him in the mirror. And there were the other kids who had played with him at recess.

Well, then the bell began to signal that it was time for the next lunch period to begin. But Timmy just kept right on looking into that mirror. He was seeing himself doing a good job and having fun, looking proud and in control the whole time. I told him that you can see yourself enjoying yourself at recess or on the playground doing what you enjoy.

As the sounds from the hallway grew louder as a class was going to the library, I asked Timmy to keep picturing himself doing a good job on the playground and keep that feeling of pride and control even while he watched and imagined someone call him a name. I don't know whether he just continued to enjoy what he was doing or pretended that he didn't hear it. But I reminded him how it is that you can be strong and in control even when people bump into you or step on your toe or even something we haven't thought up yet.

Timmy continued smiling with his head up, breathing from the stomach, feeling proud. He finally put down the mirror and said, "Hey, that's a magic mirror!"

3. **Existing attitude:** *I can't be successful if I'm quiet and shy.*
   Attitude goal: *Waiting and watching and moving slowly will get me there.*

Metaphor[41]

Maggie stood at the window watching the intermittent steady drizzle, typical of a late spring day in Maine. She had moved to Maine in late February from southern Louisiana. Anybody who is unfamiliar with Maine weather soon learns that nothing is as certain as fickle Maine weather. Staring out the window, she could almost see the leaves on the trees growing larger and greener, the grass growing plusher and the flowers with their droopy heads looking more vivid in color and more velvet to the touch.

There was something almost magical in looking out the window at the rainy drizzle. She thought fleetingly of the pretty porcelain box that now sat on top of her bureau. Ever since that special day when she received it, her life had somehow changed.

Maggie and Kari had moved to Maine that same week at the end of February and they both began school the first Monday in March—right at the official beginning of "mud season." Kari, who had moved

[41] This metaphor was contributed by Marianne Trottier, M.S.

many, many times in her life, but most recently came from Texas, was carefully trying to get around a hump of melting snow, when Maggie, who was very outgoing, friendly, and vivacious, went right over to help Kari and to introduce herself.

Everyone knows that it's not easy being a "new kid" and to have somebody speak to you and welcome you is a real relief. Soon Maggie and Kari were joined by other sixth-grade girls, all of whom were curious about the new girls and enchanted with their "southern accents." It wasn't long though before changes occurred. Although both girls were new and from the south, their relationship managed to grow separately together. You see, Maggie was expressive, talkative, outgoing, and vivacious. On the other hand, Kari was quiet, thoughtful, and observing. If other girls were congregating and chatting, Maggie would step right in and give her opinion. However, Kari would carefully observe and only politely enter the conversation.

All children know the feeling of wanting to belong and being included in friendships. Now Maggie just loved being the center of attention and would tell jokes and would gladly tell her secrets and everybody else's. She loved being in charge and telling others what to do. For some reason the other sixth-graders appeared to be enchanted with her and would listen intently to whatever she said. Wherever Maggie went she seemed to have a large following. During this time, Kari kept busy completing her studies, practicing gymnastics, and making a few good friends.

Maggie, in the meantime, utilized her sparkling personality and southern charm to become the biggest, most colossal flirt in the whole sixth grade. She flirted in the lunch line, in mud puddles, on the bus, in the classroom, in the rain, and while walking in the halls. She passed notes, told boys how cute they were, called them on the telephone, and was admired by all the other sixth-grade girls. They even began imitating her accent.

Now everybody has secret crushes, even Kari, but she foolishly didn't flirt, and nobody knew she liked anybody. Instead, she kept doing her work, listening, practicing gymnastics, and enjoying her few new friendships.

At first the other girls really worshipped Maggie for her outgoing flirtatious personality. However, before long some of the girls were being hurt because Maggie gave away their secrets, always wanted things her way, hogged the conversation, and worst of all flirted with their boyfriends. After all, it's not fair when one girl has all the boyfriends.

Soon, the other girls began giving Maggie the cold shoulder. They tried not to include her in their conversations. They wouldn't call her on the telephone or sit with her on the bus. You can imagine her feeling of rejection, but still it didn't stop Maggie. As bold as ever she would join the conversations, tell jokes, secrets, and even kept on flirting. She really enjoyed breaking up potential couples.

Kari watched Maggie from afar. They had never really been close friends, but Kari felt a certain bond towards Maggie. Not only were the other girls tired of Maggie's intrusiveness, bossiness, and southern charm, but the boys were fed up with her flirting. No matter how charming and enchanting she tried to be, the other children withdrew from her.

Kari, on the other hand, seemed to flourish and blossom. She had a growing number of friends who respected her friendship and enjoyed her warm sense of humor and thoughtfulness. With practice and determination she made the honor roll and the junior high gymnastics team, and was elected to the student council.

One rainy day when the children were having an indoor recess, Maggie stood alone at the window watching the pouring rain. All around her, children were playing games, using the computer, or just talking. However, Maggie was oblivious to her surroundings. You know how you can be so lost in thought that even if it's just for a second you may forget where you are. The rain was splattering in the road, glistening on the grass, and tapping at the window. The sky was gray, downcast, and gloomy. Maggie wallowed in this picture because she felt as sad and lonely as the outside looked.

Suddenly her thoughts were interrupted. Kari stood next to her. She was holding a beautifully decorated porcelain box. "Look inside," she said. When the cover was lifted, Maggie was surprised at what was inside. The jar was filled with water. Seeing Maggie's look of confusion, Kari said, "Nobody can reject you, you reject only yourself." Maggie didn't understand this, of course.

"This is a box of rain that I've collected from each state that I have lived in," Kari explained. "I used to watch the rain to remind me how sad and lonely I was at each new school, and I wallowed in my misery just like you are doing now. Finally, after we moved to Iowa, and I was sadly watching the rain, my mother reminded me how important the rain was. It brings new beginnings. That day I collected a few raindrops to remind me how gloomy I was feeling and how I never wanted to feel that way again.

"Nobody likes being the new kid in school, but I've learned a lot from this box of rain, and now I'm giving it to you. The rain I've collected in Oregon can remind you to watch and observe—whether you are observing the rain falling or the people around you. The rain I collected in Tennessee can remind you to listen to the raindrops as they fall, and listen to the people who are talking to you. Finally, the few raindrops I collected in Texas can remind you of a new beginning and remind you to love who you are and who you can become."

Maggie held the procelain box carefully in her hands as Kari smiled and walked away. Maggie was still a little startled and confused, but after watching a group of talkative classmates she walked over and listened to what they were saying.

4. *Existing attitude: When things are too hard, give up.*
   Attitude goal: When things seem too hard, keep on trying and they may "get hard" in a very beneficial way!

Metaphor[42]

There were once two little frogs who lived in a pond near a farm. One day they decided to explore their surroundings. They hopped to a nearby barn and hopped right into a fresh bucket of cream. The sides to the bucket were quite slippery and no matter how they tried, they just could not grasp the sides of the bucket to get out.

For a long time, both frogs kicked their front and back legs but it was no use. The task of getting out seemed impossible. You know how tired you get doing something that seems so difficult. There comes a time when you may want to just give up. That was exactly how one of the frogs felt. He knew it was silly to keep kicking and struggling, so he just stopped and slipped silently below the cream, never to struggle or be seen again.

But the other frog was either very persistent or very foolish and he kept kicking his little legs. He kicked and kicked and kicked and kicked and kicked and kicked and kicked and kicked, and no matter how tired he got, he just kept right on kicking. Suddenly, he felt something hard behind and around him and it was getting harder and harder with each kick.

[42] This metaphor was adapted by Marianne Trottier, M.S., in her practice as a school counselor. The story is of unknown origin.

He turned his head to look and was amazed to see that his kicking had caused the cream to turn to butter. He was able to lift himself up and hop out of the bucket and continue on his adventure. By the way, he loved butter!

5. *Existing attitude: I'm nobody unless I'm just like everyone else.*
   Attitude goal: I'm okay even if I'm different and not immediately accepted or recognized by everyone else.

Metaphor[43]

There was this boy, a third-grader, who had something very special about himself. Ralph would come to school, usually in clothes that weren't the latest, a pair of glasses with masking tape around one of the arms, and sometimes socks that didn't match. Boys and girls saw him and you know, they called him names like "weirdo, four eyes, slob," maybe even the worst—"biggest nerd in third."

Now you know as well as I do what happens when people keep calling you names. Ralph would get angry, and the more angry he got, the more kids picked on him and teased him. It was like a game. Kids would pick on Ralph just to see if they could get him mad. As you can imagine, Ralph didn't feel so good about himself.

One day a new kid came to school. His name was Josh. He came from far away and he talked a little bit different. Some of the kids even said he talked funny. He didn't dress the same either. And Josh had his problems also. Kids picked on him for his talking funny and for the way he dressed. For a new kid at school, Josh didn't seem to be able to make friends or fit in.

Kids teased him, imitating the way he talked. Out on the playground he had a hard time with the other kids teasing him and not letting him play in their games.

One day when the kids were busy picking on Josh, Ralph looked on. Ralph knew what it was like to be picked on and when they left, he decided to go over and talk to Josh. But he wondered if Josh would even want to talk to him and he certainly didn't need one more person picking on him.

Ralph looked over at Josh who was sitting there with his head hanging down, looking sad, and taking a deep breath occasionally.

---

[43] This metaphor was contributed by Nicholas G. Seferlis, M.S.

Ralph walked over slowly, still not sure how things would turn out. He just said, "Hi." Josh looked up at first, with his face still sad, but as his head turned up, his eyes met Ralph's through his glasses, and a slight smile came on to Josh's face as he said "hi" back.

Well, it seemed that these hellos led to a good friendship between the boys. At first they talked about being called names and how they didn't like it, how it didn't make them feel good. But they also discovered new things about one another.

Ralph discovered that Josh had a "matchbox" car collection. The boys would play with them and learn the names of each of the cars and anything special about them. Ralph learned that Josh came from Mississippi and that it didn't usually snow down there where he had lived. They became good friends and there were times that the other kids still picked on them but those times were less and less. Also, they decided that the other kids didn't know what they were missing by not having such a good friend.

6. *Existing attitude: I can't do things well, so I might as well act foolish and be the class cutup.*
Attitude goal: It can be fun to do things properly rather than clowning at them.

Metaphor: "The Little Class Clown"[44]

Chumpo was the little class clown of the clown class! He was a real little clown. He traveled with the circus and Chumpo didn't know how a pig was going to be changing his behavior. Every morning he attended clown class with the other circus clowns. Now all clowns love to make other people laugh and you may think that clowns are naturally funny, but did you know that clowns have a lot of lessons to learn? It's very important that clowns pay close attention to their clown teacher and that you follow directions.

Even putting on makeup is an important lesson if you're a clown. It takes hours of practice to get that real special face. And just how do you throw a pie so as not to hurt anybody? And how do clowns pile into a tiny little car and manage to all get out safely? Another important lesson was how to walk a tightrope. Many times when you learn how to walk a tightrope, you may fall. And you have to learn

---

[44] This metaphor was contributed by Marianne Trottier, M.S.

how to get back up. It takes proper balance and you need to walk a steady line and you always have to look where you're going. You may even wonder or you may have no idea how a small class clown could learn a lesson from a pig.

Now, unfortunately, Chumpo was a real goof-off. In class he talked out of turn and he didn't pay attention. He never practiced his lessons or did his homework. Now at first, the other clowns thought how cute and funny he was. They loved to watch his silly little dance and listen to his goofy little jokes. But little by little, the other clowns became discouraged with Chumpo.

He thought that it took too much work and too much practice to be a good clown. He used to push others out of the way so that he could be first and he loved to squirt those seltzer bottles, but he didn't squirt them carefully like real clowns are supposed to. He squirted them in any direction.

One time, he squirted Miss Fifi's purple wig right off her head. He laughed and laughed and thought it was so funny, but the other clowns thought he was just being fresh. And maybe you know what that's like when you think something is kind of fresh.

Now none of the other clowns knew at that moment how a pig was going to change their life too. Well, finally the day came of the grand opening performance. It was a magical time for all the people in the circus and all the audience too. Well, what do you think Chumpo did during that tiny car act? He began to tickle the other clowns while they were carefully piled in the car and they were all moving and poking and they couldn't help it because he was tickling them so hard. And you may even know what that's like when somebody's doing something that you don't like.

Well, later on, he tripped Lupo instead of Blippo and a pail of water went flying right into the audience. The customers certainly weren't very happy with that. Then, Chumpo jiggled the tightrope and he even hit the ringmaster with a pie. It was an accident but that ringmaster was really mad. And you may even understand what it's like when everybody seems to be mad at you. And you may not realize, as Chumpo didn't, that there really are no mistakes, only choices and their consequences.

Now Chumpo was faced with a lot of consequences. By now the other clowns were hurt and angry. The ringmaster felt that the clown act had been spoiled, and the customers were wet and upset. They didn't think things were very funny at all and some of them even wanted their money back. Chumpo's clown teacher felt that maybe

Chumpo needed some time out and decided that he couldn't be in the next show.

Instead, a replacement was hired and you wouldn't believe who Chumpo's replacement was, a cute little pig clown named Oinko. And if you listened carefully, you could even hear him say his name.

He wore a polka dot bow on his curly little tail. He wore a clown collar and a funny pointed hat with a pom-pom. He even wore a red clown nose over his snout.

And from the sidelines, Chumpo watched as Oinko jumped through hoops and walked the tightrope and even rode a bicycle. And he did it steadily and sturdily and with confidence. And the audience laughed and cheered with glee. And even the clowns clapped. Chumpo felt very left out and maybe you know what that's like, being left out and feeling like you don't belong.

Chumpo wondered how could a silly little pig manage to steal the show? And how could he perform so easily. Everybody just loved Oinko's performance and everybody wanted to see him. Night after night, Chumpo had to watch Oinko. Well, Oinko seemed to love to perform and he seemed to enjoy it so much. And every night Chumpo even had to listen as Oinko kept saying his name.

And what Chumpo didn't know was that two eyes were watching him watch Oinko. And Chumpo wondered, how was a pig able to do all his work and get it done and yet make people laugh and be so happy? One day, as Chumpo stood on the sidelines watching Oinko and feeling really rejected because he had been replaced by a pig, those two eyes that had been watching Chumpo came out of the sidelines, and to Chumpo's surprise, those eyes belonged to Oinko's trainer. He said, "I've been watching you, Chumpo, and I want you to know that pigs don't do this naturally. Pigs aren't born to be clowns. When I trained Oinko, I had him do things step by step. You do things step by step."

Upon hearing that, Chumpo thought that maybe he could enjoy performing in small steps. So at first he practiced juggling, one step at a time and one ball at a time. He never knew how much fun it could be because he had never bothered practicing juggling before. He always thought it was too much work. But he found out that he had a real talent for it. And little by little, day by day, he began to pay attention to his teacher and he realized how interesting and how funny his clown teacher could be. And before long, he was practicing and enjoying his work. And he realized it was more fun being a real clown, rather than a little class clown.

7. **Existing attitude:** *If I don't do something better than someone else, I am not special.*
   Attitude goal: *I can be special.*

Metaphor: "Just an Ordinary Joe"[45]

Joe was a boy I used to know at another school I was at, and Joe always wanted to be special. And he was in the second grade because that was the class I used to have. His best friend was named Randolph, and Randolph was big and strong and tall, and Joe really wished he was more like Randolph because when Randolph got up to bat, he could really slug that baseball and he could also throw a football real far, because he was so tall and he could see above all the other boys.

Maybe you've wondered at times about being taller or maybe even stronger and maybe you've thought of ways you would like to be. But Joe always wished he could be a little more like Randolph.

As he sat in his class, he thought maybe he would also like to be like Eric, who was smart and always seemed to know the answer. Every time the teacher asked a question, Eric would raise his hand and would always be right. And Joe would sit there and sometimes he knew the answer but other times he didn't want to volunteer and kind of hid, hoping the teacher wouldn't call on him. As you're sitting here, maybe you think about what that's like for you when the teacher asks a question.

And when he was out on the playground, he also noticed how fast Deborah could run. She was the fastest runner in class. And he thought how wonderful it would be if he could have a special talent or if he could do something that was really outstanding.

And Janny, she was very tiny and he wondered what it would be like to be so small and have everybody cater to you because you were so little and small.

But he was just a regular Joe, an ordinary Joe, and he wondered how could he be different or unique. And the teacher told him that everybody has a special talent, everybody is special in some way and you need to stop and think how you're special. That's what she said. But then he received his report card and he had average grades, just those regular grades, nothing super duper and nothing really terrible.

Well, the class was getting ready for spring concert. And as he was getting ready for spring concert, he noticed that Janny was put in front

---

[45] This metaphor was contributed by Marianne Trottier, M.S.

of the class and Mike, who had a big loud voice, was given a speaking part. And Randolph, who was so big and tall, was able to stand in the very back of the row and he was going to carry a flag because everybody would be able to see him. And Stacy and Jeff were going to sing a duet together because they had nice singing voices.

But ordinary Joe was just going to be part of the group. He wasn't given anything special to do. And as he was standing there, he noticed that Marcus had ears that stuck out just a little bit, and Marcus could actually wiggle those ears.

He thought, "Wouldn't it be great to have ears like that?" And he noticed as he was standing there in the group getting ready to practice that Phil had all these great freckles. He had so many that you couldn't really see his skin. It was all freckly. And he thought how wonderful it would be to have a face like that. Maybe you've thought of some ways that you would like to be special, just like ordinary Joe did. And then something happened.

He was reading a book that his uncle had given him a long time ago called *The Phantom Tollbooth* by Norton Jester. And as he was reading this story which is about a young boy named Mylo who receives a magical tollbooth as a gift. And as he drives through the tollbooth, he finds himself in the land beyond. And throughout his travels in this enchanted land, he is joined by Humbug and a watchdog named Toc. And in one of the chapters Mylo finds that he's lost. And as he wanders with Humbug and Toc, they come to a small house.

And on one of the doors to the small house, is a sign that reads "the giant." Mylo says, "Wow, a giant. I wonder if that giant can tell us if we're lost." So they knock on the door and a man opens the door but he's not a giant. He's sort of an ordinary-sized man. Mylo says: "Are you a giant?" And the man says, "Yes, I'm the smallest giant in the world." And Mylo said, "Are we lost?" The giant says, "Well, I think you ought to go to the next door and ask the midget."

So Mylo went to the next door and knocked on the door. A man came to that door who looked very much like the giant looked. It looked like the same man. They could be twins. Mylo asked, "Are you the midget?" And the man said, "Yes, I'm the tallest midget in the world." So Mylo said, "Are we lost?" The midget said he didn't know the answer to that question and suggested that Mylo ask the fat man at the next door. So they went to the next door of the same house and they knocked on the door. The same man answered the door.

Mylo asked, "Are you the fat man?" "Yes," answered the man, "I'm the thinnest fat man in the world." "Are we lost?" Mylo asked again.

"I don't know," said the fat man, "maybe you should go around back and ask the thin man." So he goes around to the next door of the same house and he knocks on the door marked "the thin man." Well, guess what, the same man answered the door. Mylo said, "Are you the thin man?" The man said, "Yes, I'm the fattest thin man in the world." Mylo said to him, "I think you're all the same man." The man said, "Well, I always thought of myself as an ordinary man, and I like to feel special. So I can be the fattest thin man or the thinnest fat man or the tallest midget or the shortest giant. It's all the way you imagine yourself to be."

As Joe read that story, he thought about it and somehow it stayed with him for quite a while. He remembered that story and on the night of the spring concert, when everyone was running around in costume and Jeff and Stacy were practicing for their duet and Debra was running around in her costume and Janny was getting prepared to be the tiniest one in the concert. As he walked through the hallway, he heard some sobbing, sort of like moans. And he stopped to take a peek and over in the darkest corner was Randolph, who he always wanted to be like. And he asked, "Randolph, what's wrong?"

You've probably been with friends who are crying and wondered how you could help and that's what happened to Joe. So Randolph was crying and he said, "I wish I wasn't as big as I am. I wish I could be like you, Joe. I wish I could be your size. Sometimes it's hard to be the biggest kid in class." Joe said, "Hey, Randolph, you can be the tallest short boy in class." And Randolph put a little smile on. Joe said, "Come on, you've got to get that flag." Randolph said, "Yea, okay." And they went down to the spring concert. And after that, Joe thought of himself not as an ordinary Joe, but as an extraordinary Joe, someone who could take a different look at himself and feel extraordinary.

8. *Affect goal: Sadness and grief*

Metaphor[46]

Dick wanted so badly to have that special Christmas gift. He made sure he did all the things in order to get it. He made sure that he wrote to Santa Claus. And he wanted it so bad that he made sure to

---

[46] This metaphor was contributed by Nicholas G. Seferlis, M.S.

tell Mom and Dad and made sure that they also told Santa Claus, and told his sister Jane.

And as you know, the days waiting for Christmas are very long. You know how long it takes when you're waiting for something special, especially something like Christmas. As he waited each day for that special toy, he imagined himself using it and how much fun he would have, you know, going and showing all of his friends and using it with them.

The closer it got to Christmas, the farther away it seemed. Finally, Christmas eve came and he knew it would not be that much longer. That night he could hardly get to sleep just thinking about that special new toy. Christmas morning, he got up from his bed and just ran to the tree. He started to unwrap the package he thought it would be in, but instead there was a new snowsuit.

He went to the next one that he thought might be it. This one looked a little bit heavier, and there it was—a brand new, wireless, remote-controlled car. He smiled and a little tear actually came to his eyes because he got what he wanted and he had wanted it so badly.

Dick was so busy testing out his new car that he almost forgot to open his other packages until Jane reminded him, "Hey, this one is for you!" But out of all the gifts, Dick loved that car the best. He would be able to go to the park and race it on the track sponsored by a local hobby shop.

Christmas day he just drove and drove. He was so excited he didn't even feel like coming to lunch when his mother called. Finally, he had to put the batteries in the charger so he could play with it at a later time and for a longer time. After lunch, he practiced going through the living room, through the kitchen, and back, and doing it with lots of speed and doing the turns very cleverly. That night when Dick went to bed, he put that remote control car right next to him on the bed so that nothing would happen to it. And every day of that Christmas vacation, he played and played with that remote-controlled car. As a matter of fact, there weren't really any times you would see Dick without that remote-controlled car zooming around him.

Finally, as it was coming to an end of the Christmas vacation, Dick was getting very excited about bringing his new car to school and sharing it with the others. The night before he went to school, he had his car all ready in a bag so he could go in and show everyone. He wanted to show them how much care he took of it and how well he could drive it. He had that bag with him and at recess he took it out.

They drove it on the playground by the fence. Some of his friends came over and asked if they could try it, but Dick said no because he wanted to take good care of it. And as Dick made that car speed up along the fence, there was real traffic on the other side in the street. Someone suggested they go by the opening in the fence because there would be more room and the car could turn around better.

As the car went by the opening of the fence, all of a sudden one of the kids came running by and kicked the car into the street, and under the tire of a passing car it went. Dick's eyes just opened wide, and before he could say anything, the sounds of the crushing of the plastic and the motor were heard.

Dick stood there with his mouth open, slightly turned down and his lips began to shake and quiver as he tried to hold back the tears that were swelling up. He could feel his chest tightening as he had to cry, and the other kids came over to see what was the matter. The teacher came over and saw that people were all right and went out to get the pieces of the remote-controlled car.

This was the saddest day of Dick's life, he thought, as the tears ran down his cheek. Everyone knows the sadness that comes immediately when you lose something. You don't think you can bear the ache that just seems to fill the chest and stomach. And there are the tears and the sobbing. Even a very young child will immediately begin that response when a balloon pops. And Dick, being a little older, was able to feel his pain and sadness even more thoroughly. At a time like that, nothing really helps, and his friends being sorry was no exception. Dick's face looked like it would never smile again and each breath just seemed to make more tears possible. You know what it is like to feel the wetness of a stream of tears and the empty ache of losing something you love. Everyone knows that feeling.

9. *Affect goal:* Mastery

Metaphor[47]

Jane came home from school and showed her parents what she had gotten on her spelling paper. Mom and Dad said, "Wow, Jane, you need to study these spelling words!" Jane said, "I tried, but no matter how hard I try I just can't seem to get it." As the parents looked at

---

[47] This metaphor was contributed by Nicholas G. Seferlis, M.S.

the low grade, Dick had heard what was going on. Dick said, "Hey, spelling has always been one of my better subjects, Jane. Let me help you with your spelling words and we'll see how we can do." That week, Jane had gotten her spelling list and brought it home for her brother to help her.

Dick said, "These words are very, very easy. You shouldn't have any problem spelling these: dog, cat, run, be, and sit."

Jane said, "Maybe I shouldn't have any problems spelling them but I do. No matter how hard I study, when I sit there and the teacher calls out those spelling words to me, I just can't seem to get them right on the paper."

Well, Dick sat with Jane, and after a while he said, "Let me show you something special, something that has always worked for me. As a matter of fact, it almost seems like magic. This is the secret way I do my spelling."

Jane looked at him, wondering what kind of secret, magic way Dick had to show her how to do her spelling. And as she sat there, Dick said, "Let's see, 'dog'—d-o-g, 'dog.' Jane, I want you to do this—look up in the air and pretend there is a magic screen, like a movie or TV screen and I just want you to pretend you're writing on it with magic chalk, write the word 'dog'—d-o-g. I want you to then close your eyes and tell me if you can see the word 'dog' on the screen."

Well, Jane looked up and pretended that she saw that magic screen and wrote the word 'd-o-g,' closed her eyes, and found that she could see it. And Dick went right on to the next word. He said, "Look up at your magic screen again and write 'cat'—c-a-t. Close your eyes and just see it up on your magic screen." Jane did that again, pictured the magic screen, wrote on it "c-a-t," closed her eyes, and was able to see it. Dick told her to do the same thing for the word "run" on her own. She followed his instructions, and all of a sudden her brother Dick said, *"Stop."*

"I want you to see if you can spell the word 'dog' for me," he said. "Hmmm. . . ." This had always caused Jane a problem when she didn't have the words in front of her. But she was able to look up, and you know what, she was able to see "d-o-g" and she told her brother. Dick said, "Great! Try 'cat' now." And sure enough, Jane was able to look up and see "c-a-t."

Then she tried "run" again and the same thing happened. Dick said, "Okay, Jane, you have two more words, 'be' and 'sit,' so I'm going to give you a few minutes and let you do those two on your own, and then I'm going to come in and test you on these five words." He went off to the kitchen to get himself some milk and cookies.

Dick came back in a little while and asked, "How do you think you're doing, Jane?" Jane said, "Well, it seems to be a fun way and I think I'm doing okay!" He asked if she was all set for her practice quiz and Jane said she was.

Sure enough, he asked her all of the words, starting off with the ones she had just studied. She would look up, see the word on her magic screen, and then spell the letters. She did the same thing for "be," "sit," "run," "cat," "dog." Dick congratulated her and reminded her that she also needed to be able to write the words, not just spell them out loud. So he got a piece of paper and a pencil for Jane and they went through the spelling list one more time. She got every single word right!

So, that was okay for there at the house, but would it work at school too, Jane wondered. Dick said sure it would because all you have to do is look up and you can look up at school. You can even close your eyes if you have to. Jane agreed. Well, on the night before the spelling test, Jane had studied all her words in the secret way Dick had shown her. She was going in to see how well she could do on her spelling test that next day. The teacher said, "Okay class, it's time to get ready for spelling." Jane sat there with her pencil in hand, paper on the desk, as the teacher began to go through the list, word by word. Jane was able to look up, see how to spell those words, and then put them right down on paper. Sure enough, that day Jane had a 100 on her spelling paper. She looked down at that grade and felt very proud! She wore a great big smile of satisfaction, of accomplishing that spelling goal using the secret method Dick had taught her. She felt so good that she just couldn't wait to get home and show her Mom and Dad and Dick what a great job she had done in spelling.

All the rest of that day, Jane seemed to stand up a little bit taller, breathe just a little bit deeper, and she kept that proud feeling of success right in her chest and it kind of seemed to spread all over her. She felt good about being herself and at recess it was even like she could run and jump faster and farther! You know what it is like when you have a good feeling, when you've done something you can be proud of, and you don't even have to know how you keep the good feeling to enjoy it. And even if you forget about enjoying it, you can still breathe deeper and hold your shoulders higher and keep that big smile on your face.

10. *Affect goal:* Courage

Metaphor[48]

Dick and his friend, Bill, were playing in the yard, building a fort with some boards and sticks they found. Dick suggested that they should put the boards straight up but Bill thought they would be better on their sides. So they made two high sides and two low sides, which was kind of the best of both their ideas.

While they were trying to get the boards to stand up, Dick noticed that Bill kept rubbing his pants. He didn't think of it as anything but he kept noticing that Bill was doing it more and more. Dick went to get some more nails. I guess you know how important it is for nails to hold together a couple of pieces of wood. Finally, Dick came back and they kept on working, just banging those boards until they were soon able to get two sides, a high side and a low side, to stand up all by themselves.

And as they were standing there looking at their half-fort, once again, Dick noticed Bill rubbing himself. So Dick decided to say, "Hey Bill, what are you doing?" Bill turned red, took a deep breath. He was very, very embarrassed. He whispered, "Can you keep a secret?" Dick nodded yes. Bill said, "Are you sure?" and he made Dick promise to keep that secret. You probably couldn't imagine what Bill told Dick.

He talked about his uncle and how they used to wrestle and then he added that "sometimes my uncle touches me, it doesn't feel good and I don't like how he touches me." Dick said, "Hey, that isn't right, we have to go tell somebody." Bill said, "Hold it, you promised to keep it a secret!" Dick said, "But you've got to tell somebody because he may not stop doing it."

Dick had seen a film at school about what to do when someone touches you or tries to hurt you and he tried to explain to Bill how important it was that he go and tell somebody. Bill said that he had tried but people wouldn't believe him. He had tried to tell his parents what his uncle was doing and they just wouldn't believe him. And his uncle had told him that if he ever told anybody, the uncle would get in big trouble and it would be all Bill's fault. Dick suggested that maybe he should tell somebody at school. Bill said he would be way too embarrassed. But Dick knew that it was important to keep telling until somebody listened.

---

[48] This metaphor was contributed by Nicholas G. Seferlis, M.S.

Bill didn't like what his uncle was doing. He knew that he had to tell someone in order for it to stop. Both boys decided to stop building the fort for the day and both headed home in their own directions. At school the next day Bill decided that he needed to tell someone. He thought about all the things that Dick had told him. The question was whom should he tell at school—Mr. Phillips, the janitor? No, that didn't seem quite right. He could tell his teacher, but that didn't seem quite the right place to go either. It would have been all right, but then he decided to go to the counselor's office.

Bill took a deep breath. He could feel his heart pounding in his chest because he knew he was going to be doing something very scary and it was something where he didn't know how things were going to turn out. And he walked into the counselor's office and asked to speak to her for just a moment about something very, very important. When she looked at him, she could see that he was certainly ready to talk about something.

He looked a little frightened, but more than that, she noticed how he somehow looked quite brave and determined. He just stood there with his jaw very firm, taking deep breaths, looking straight ahead, and standing up quite straight. He told her the whole thing and as he talked, he could tell that she was listening and believing him. He still didn't know how it was going to all turn out, but he wasn't so scared and he could feel his heart pounding in a way that reminded him how strong he was and how brave he was to be talking about this secret. The more questions the counselor asked, the more he knew he could answer each one and that somehow they would figure out how to make his parents help him too. And his face reflected in the windows of the door showed his cheeks were a little red, his shoulders back, his chest up. He was standing on the floor balanced on both feet. His jaw was set, and he looked straight ahead. He was ready to talk.

*11. **Affect goal:** Love, friendship, and joy*

Metaphor: "Two Golden Princesses"[49]

It was the first day of school for Jenny and Kristen and they didn't know it, but they were at a turning point in their life, a time when new things are going to happen. Well, you know what it's like on that

---

[49] This metaphor was contributed by Marianne Trottier, M.S.

very first day of school, and maybe you can remember what it was like for you on that first day, hearing the sounds of being in the classroom and seeing all of the things that were decorated, and seeing all different kinds of children, children that you never saw before.

And what was that like on that very first day, holding those crayons in your hand and drawing on that big piece of paper? And maybe your teacher even put that it was your first drawing in school on that paper that went home that day. Well, that's what it was like for Jenny and Kristen. They felt a little unsure, but wasn't it lucky for them that they were assigned as partners?

And when they lined up, they had to line up in partners. And Jenny was Kristen's partner and Kristen was Jenny's and right away they became best friends. And how wonderful it was to have a very good friend, somebody you can swing on the swings with and wait for at bus recess, just waiting for that special friend to come off the bus.

Well, Jenny and Kristen had a wonderful time that first year. They loved to balance on the seesaw. And sometimes they would go up and down. And it was during that first year that people began to call them "the two golden princesses." They both had long, golden hair, and at first glance it seemed that they even looked alike. They were about the same height and the closer they came, the more they even liked to dress alike in the same style, not necessarily the exact same clothes, but the same style.

And during that very special first year, they had their first sleepover. And you can imagine how exciting that was, the first time you sleep over at your best friend's house. And making all those decisions about what you will bring, should you bring that special stuffed animal that you love to have with you? Well, it was certainly fun for Jenny and Kristen, even though deep down, Kristen really missed her brother, but she would never admit that.

Well, time went by and before long, it was the next year. And there was the discovery of a rock group. All little children just seem to love music. And that's what it was like with Jenny and Kristen as somehow they found that rock group, Bon Jovi, and they both thought that John Bon Jovi was just so cute. They even began to spend time on the telephone and as the time went by, they even spent more time on that telephone, even after they had spent the whole day together, they could still find so much to talk about.

Maybe you know what that's like with your best friend, sharing secrets and just feeling that wonderful glow when you're with that very special person. They even had a special hideout where they played with their toys and talked about all kinds of things, telling secrets and sharing so much.

Those two golden princesses, like everyone called them, always wanted to be together, even though they occasionally played with Julie and Aubry and Robert and Jeffrey. They would always manage to be together and there was this wonderful time when they were both invited to Jimmy's birthday party which was held at McDonald's.

They actually were feeling a little bit nervous about walking into McDonald's, but because they had each other, it wasn't quite as scary. They had a wonderful time, of course, and through the years they helped each other with homework, continued talking on the phone, listening to songs, sometimes talking their moms and dads into taking them to the skating rink. And they had their regular sleepovers. You know that really happy time you share with a friend and how important it is to develop that friendship. They even enjoyed the arguments that they had because later they would always manage to make up, those two golden princesses. And even though they didn't really look alike, people would get them confused: "Which one is Jenny and exactly which one is Kristen?"

And the feeling of friendship is something that you memorize without even thinking about it. It is a joy that you know with the way you move and breathe and laugh and look forward to being with that friend. And Jenny and Kristen didn't even realize how that feeling was something they would keep with them forever, long after their lives went in different directions. Because it's a learning that you store up in the back of your mind or maybe you keep it in your heart. And just look at the face of one and you would see the same thing that was on the face of the other: a smile from cheek to cheek, rosy, round cheeks, smile lines on the right and left of their eyes, twinkling eyes, and even a little head tilt to the side and one eyebrow raised up higher than the other. Each face made the other look that much more that same beautiful and happy way. And no one would have known that would happen on the first day of school.

12. *Affect goal: Sadness and grief*

Metaphor[50]

Have you ever heard the saying, "Birds of a feather flock together"? Well, at the beginning of fourth grade, something began to happen, and at first it wasn't really that noticeable, but somehow Kristen and Jenny seemed to have different interests. At first, neither one of them

[50] This metaphor was contributed by Marianne Trottier, M.S.

would admit that. That summer, Kristen had received a soccer ball and she began to bring it to school. Well, of course, lots of other children wanted to play soccer and Kristen would go off with them and play soccer.

Jenny never really liked to play sports that much and she would play on the sidelines. She wanted to be with Kristen but she didn't really want to play soccer. She just wanted to do the things that they had always done, play on the swings, go on the see-saw, or just talk, find their special secret hiding place. Well sure, Kristen would still call and they would sit together at lunch, and they still both liked Bon Jovi, but something was missing.

At first, Jenny didn't want to believe that anything was wrong, but deep in her heart, she felt that things were not quite right. And she noticed that other kids wanted to sit with Kristen, and Kristen seemed to enjoy and want to be with those other kids. Jenny thought, if only it could just be the two of us again, the two golden princesses, that's the way it should be.

The more Jenny wanted to be with Kristen, the more she realized they were drifting farther apart. Maybe you can recall a time when you had a special friend and you had that same feeling that you cared a lot more than they did. Well, it wasn't long before they started to have arguments and they were the kind of arguments that are hard to make up after. They called names and talked behind each other's back.

In Jenny's mind, she kept thinking that there just must be a way to be best friends again. And she was angry. It didn't seem quite fair. She and Kristen had been friends since kindergarten. How could they break up and drift farther apart? She denied this was happening, but she realized that somehow they just seemed to be separating. Of course, she felt hurt and frustrated.

It's hard when you want to be with somebody and they don't want to be with you as much. Kristen was all of a sudden popular. Jenny thought she would do anything to be Kristen's friend again. She felt so left out. And there were those times when she would feel real sad and a little tear would form in her eye. Sometimes her eyes would just well up with tears and she would walk to the hideout and sit there by herself and remember the times she and Kristen had been there laughing and joking and talking about Derryk and John Bon Jovi, listening to a song on their "walkman."

And those days just seemed to be gone. She remembered trading "garbage pail kids" even though she wasn't supposed to have them, playing with their favorite toys, and how sad she felt as she watched

Kristen and the others playing at a distance. And she would be there alone. Now there were fewer and fewer phone calls and before long there weren't any phone calls. And what do you do when you feel that you've lost your best friend.

All of a sudden, Jenny realized that time was going on and she was at another turning point. But one of the things she had to experience before the turn was over was a big feeling of sadness. She felt so empty and so alone. Crying came naturally but didn't seem to help. Even when she wasn't crying, she would just take deep breaths and sigh loudly, with her face very long and forlorn. Sometimes she would climb up into her favorite tree and just feel that feeling inside and wonder if she would ever be happy again. But you learn something about each feeling that you have and she sure had an opportunity to learn a lot about her sadness those several weeks in that turning point. And this time her face had an open-mouthed frown, her cheeks were flattened, her eyes were red, she swallowed hard, she looked down a lot. Her hair fell into her eyes. They were not birds of a feather anymore.

Bibliography

Bettelheim, B. (1977). *The Uses of Enchantment: The Meaning and Importance of Fairy Tales.* New York: Vintage Books.

Erickson, M. H., & Rossi, E. L. (1980a). The varieties of double bind. In E. L. Rossi (Ed.), *The collected papers of Milton H. Erickson on hypnosis: Vol. 1. The nature of hypnosis and suggestion* (pp. 412–429). New York: Irvington.

Erickson, M. H., & Rossi, E. L. (1980b). Two level communication and the Micro-dynamics of trance and suggestion. In E. L. Rossi (Ed.), *The collected papers of Milton H. Erickson on hypnosis: Vol. 1. The nature of hypnosis and suggestion* (pp. 430–451). New York: Irvington.

Erickson, M.H., & Rossi, E. L. (1980c). The indirect forms of suggestion. In E. L. Rossi (Ed.), *The collected papers of Milton H. Erickson on hypnosis: Vol. 1. The nature of hypnosis and suggestion* (pp. 452–477). New York: Irvington.

Erickson, M. H., & Rossi, E. L. (1980d). The interspersal hypnotic technique for symptom correction and pain control. In E. L. Rossi (Ed.), *The collected papers of Milton H. Erickson on hypnosis: Vol. 4. Innovative hypnotherapy* (pp. 262–280). New York: Irvington.

Gordon, D. (1978). *Therapeutic metaphors: Helping others through the looking glass.* Cupertino, CA: Meta Publications.

Goulding, M., & Goulding, R. (1979). *Changing lives through redecision therapy.* New York: Brunner/Mazel.

Lankton, S. (1980). *Practical magic: A translation of basic neuro-linguistic programming into clinical psychotherapy.* Cupertino, CA: Meta Publications.

Lankton, S. (Ed.). (1985). *Ericksonian monographs, number 1: Elements and dimensions of an Ericksonian approach.* New York: Brunner/Mazel.

Lankton, S. (Ed.). (1987). *Ericksonian monographs, number 2: Central themes and underlying principles.* New York: Brunner/Mazel.

Lankton, S. (Ed.). (1988). *Ericksonian monographs, number 3: Special populations.* New York: Brunner/Mazel.

Lankton, S., & Lankton, C. (1983). *The answer within: A clinical framework of Ericksonian hypnotherapy.* New York: Brunner/Mazel.

Lankton, S., & Lankton, C. (1986). *Enchantment and intervention in family therapy: Training in Ericksonian approaches.* New York: Brunner/Mazel.

Lankton, S., & Zeig, J. (Eds.). (1988). *Developing Ericksonian psychotherapy: State of the art. The proceedings of the third international congress on Ericksonian psychotherapy.* New York: Brunner/Mazel.

Matthews, B., Kirsch, I., & Allen, G. (1984). Posthypnotic conflict and psychopathology—Controlling for the effects of posthypnotic suggestion: A brief communication. *The International Journal of Clinical and Experimental Hypnosis, XXXII*(4), 362–365.

Matthews, B., Bennett, H., Bean, W., & Gallagher, M. (1985). Indirect versus direct hypnotic suggestions—An initial investigation: A brief communication. *The International Journal of Clinical and Experimental Hypnosis, XXXIII*(3), 219–223.